*Daily Devotions
for a Deeper Christian Life*

His

Victorious

Indwelling

Nick Harrison
Editor

GRAND RAPIDS, MICHIGAN 49530

WWW.ZONDERVAN.COM

His Victorious Indwelling
Copyright © 1998 by Nick Harrison

Requests for information should be addressed to:

ZONDERVAN™

GRAND RAPIDS, MICHIGAN 49530

Library of Congress Cataloging-in-Publication Data

His victorious indwelling : daily devotions for a deeper Christian life /
Nick Harrison, editor.
    p. cm.
  Includes bibliographical references and index.
  ISBN: 0-310-21849-7
  1. Devotional calendars. I. Harrison, Nick.
BV4810.H57 1998
242'.2—dc21   98-23522
                                                   CIP

Interior design by Jody DeNeef

Printed in the United States of America

HB 11.30.2023

Contents

To Christians everywhere
seeking a deeper walk with God.

Acknowledgments

*M*any people have been influential in the birth of this book and I'd like to acknowledge them:

Miles Stanford, whose small book, *The Principle of Position,* first awakened in me the desire for a deeper life, and who, now in his eighties, still labors to bring this life-changing message to believers. It was Mr. Stanford whose research for his devotional book, *None But the Hungry Heart,* provided many of the secondary entries in *His Victorious Indwelling.*

The several people who opened their collection of books to me: Eldan Kaukonen, Richard Robletto, Tim McConnaughy, and Mike and Judy Phillips.

To my wife, Beverly, and daughters Rachel, Rebecca, and Bethany, and my friend Brad Richardson, all for their help in the project; Zondervan Publishing House for their support and belief in the book; and finally, the many wonderful men and women of God who wrote and spoke so meaningfully on this subject and whose teachings made possible *His Victorious Indwelling.*

Introduction

$\mathcal{M}$ore than a hundred years ago, Presbyterian minister Dr. Adolph Saphir observed, "If we review the history of the church, we notice how many important truths, clearly revealed in Scripture, have been allowed to lie dormant for centuries, unknown and unappreciated except by a few isolated Christians, until it pleased God to enlighten the church by chosen witnesses. Then He bestowed on His children the knowledge of hidden and forgotten treasures. For how long a period, even after the Reformation, were the doctrines of the Holy Ghost, His work in conversion, and His indwelling in the believer, almost unknown!"

How long indeed. Even today many Christians are wholly unaware of the spiritual resources they possess in Christ. Nor do most believers in Christ daily experience an awareness of the indwelling presence of the Holy Spirit in their lives.

And yet at what time in history has the Christian church and her teachings been so widely disseminated? Our church services are broadcast daily on television and radio; Christian literature is abundantly available in both Christian and secular bookstores, and evangelistic rallies routinely fill stadiums with eager listeners.

Yet for all this exposure, the perception of many is that the depth of our Christian life and witness is perhaps a mile wide, but an inch deep. We believe Christian principles and doctrines, but how different are our homes, our neighborhoods, and especially our individual lives from those of our unbelieving neighbors?

Perhaps Dr. Saphir's comments on the dormancy of the Scriptural truth of the Holy Spirit's indwelling the believer have some bearing here. For all our talk about the Holy Spirit, do we know Him as our indwelling life? Can we say with Paul that it's "no longer I, but Christ liveth in me"?

I believe many Christians are genuinely hungry for a deeper walk with their God. Some, in frustration, turn to aberrant teachings about the Holy Spirit, expecting Him to somehow cause their behavior to change in some dramatic and flashy manner under the guidance of a dynamic pulpit personality.

Yet God chooses to work on us from the inside out. He wants to live His life through us, by the agency of His Spirit, so that our lives reflect the presence of Christ to those around us. There will indeed be dramatic change in the Christian who purposes to know God and His victorious indwelling—but it will be largely through the process of learning to abide in Christ, rather than an instantaneous divine "touch" from God.

Down through the centuries, as Dr. Saphir noted, there have been "chosen witnesses" who understood the importance of this divine truth of Christ's indwelling and taught it with great vigor. Over the course of the next year, these "chosen witnesses" will once again speak to us about God's indwelling the believer and other related teachings associated with the "deeper life."

Some of these men and women, unknown to most Christians, came out of the Brethren movement of the 19th century, when John Darby, Edward Dennett, George Wigram, J. B. Stoney, and other men of God began to understand the importance of this neglected truth of the indwelling Holy Spirit. Because of their intense devotion to this neglected principle of the Christian life, the reader will find, on the following pages, numerous entries from these early Brethren writers—many of whose writings are still in print and widely recommended for those who desire further reading in the "deeper life."

Late in the 19th century, conferences were held in the Keswick region of Great Britain, largely devoted to this re-emerging truth. Those "Keswick" conferences continued well into the last half of the twentieth century and produced many fine teachers of God's

Word on this subject—several of whom are represented on the following pages.

Other isolated believers down through the history of the Church have well understood "His victorious indwelling" and sought to teach it where they could. Some, such as Madame Jeanne Marie Bouvier Guyon, were imprisoned for their teaching.

George Fox of the Quakers knew the importance of an intimate walk with God. St. Bernard of Clairvaux also understood, as did Dutch Reformed pastor Andrew Murray. In our own century, Watchman Nee, the great Chinese Christian teacher was adamant about the importance of living what he simply called the "normal Christian life."

Missionary to China Hudson Taylor's term was the "exchanged life," wherein the believer's life of defeat is "exchanged" for the victorious life of Christ. Others have referred to it as the "Christ-life." Hannah Whitall Smith referred to it as "the Christian's secret of a happy life," which became the title of her classic book, still in print more than a century after it was first published. The teachings themselves have sometimes been called the "Keswick" teachings or the "identification truths of Scripture."

Whatever name we choose to call it, let it be, not just teaching, but true of us in experience. The unbelieving world awaits the witness of a generation of Christians who will show forth the Christ in whom they believe.

One final note: Although the emphasis of *His Victorious Indwelling* is Christ's presence in the believer, not all of the readings express this theme overtly. In some cases, I've chosen to include worthy thoughts by these godly writers that, while still in the spirit of His victorious indwelling, address tangential issues of interest to the believer seeking the deeper life.

It's my prayer that this next year will bring each reader into a deeper experience of "His victorious indwelling."

*. . . do not worry about tomorrow, for tomorrow will worry about itself.
Each day has enough trouble of its own.*

MATTHEW 6:34

I compare the troubles which we have to undergo in the course
of a year to a great bundle of sticks, far too large for us to lift. But
God does not require us to carry the whole at once. He merciful-
ly unties the bundle, and gives us first one stick, which we are to
carry today, and then another, which we are to carry tomorrow and
so on. This we might easily manage, if we would only take the burden appointed for each day—instead we choose to increase our
troubles by carrying yesterday's stick over again today, and adding
tomorrow's burden to the load, before we are required to carry it.

JOHN NEWTON

*L*et the year be given to God in its every moment! The year is
made up of minutes. Let these be watched as dedicated to God! It is
in the sanctification of the small that hallowing of the large is secure.

G. CAMPBELL MORGAN

*L*et us face this New Year, with all its hidden possibilities, with
quiet, brave hearts, resolved to fulfill our duty as those ought who
have a past to remember and a future to hope for. It may be the last
on earth for some of us. It will probably contain great sorrows for
some of us, and great joys for others. It will be comparatively
uneventful for others. It may bring great outward changes for us, or
it may leave us much as it found us. But, at all events, God will be
in it, and work for Him should be in it.

May it be, that when its final hours have slidden away into the
gray past, they continue to witness to us of His love, even as, while
they were wrapped in the mists of the future, they prevailed on us
to hope in Him!

ALEXANDER MACLAREN

The night is nearly over; the day is almost here. So let us put aside the deeds of darkness and put on the armor of light. Let us behave decently, as in the daytime, not in orgies and drunkenness, not in sexual immorality and debauchery, not in dissension and jealousy. Rather, clothe yourselves with the Lord Jesus Christ, and do not think about how to gratify the desires of the sinful nature.

ROMANS 13:12–14

*I*n the early morning, as soon as you awake, remember that you are in the very presence of God, who has been watching beside you through the long dark hours; look up to His face, and thank Him.

Consecrate to Him those first few moments before you leave your bed. Look towards the coming day, through the golden haze of light that streams from the angel of His presence.

You cannot forecast very largely what your difficulties are likely to be, the quarters from which you may be attacked, the burdens that may need carrying. Take care not to view any of these apart from God. Be sure that He will be between you and them, as the ship is between the traveler and the ocean, be it fair or stormy.

As you dress yourself for the day, remember that God supplies you with vesture clean and white, with the meekness and gentleness of Christ, with the garments of salvation, the robes of righteousness, and the jewels of Christian virtue.

Do not look at these things apart from Him; but remember that they are attributes and graces of His own nature with which to array yourself. And above all put on the armor of light; remembering that God is light.

You are to put on Christ, who is God manifest in the flesh, and you are to descend from your room into the arena of daily battle as one who is endued with the beauty of His character. This concentration of thought upon God, during the act of dressing, will prepare the soul for those acts of adoration, thanksgiving, and intercession, which arise to God as the fragrant incense of the Temple.

F. B. MEYER

*T*he greatest of all blessings and the most ennobling of all privileges is to be indeed a Christian.

SAMUEL TAYLOR COLERIDGE

January 3

But speaking the truth in love, may [you] grow up into him in all things, which is the head, even Christ.

EPHESIANS 4:15, KJV

*T*he life of the Christian is the Christ life. So far as *our* will and responsibility are concerned there must be *personal* feeding on Christ, and in order to do this we must live in the atmosphere of the Spirit exclusively. As there must be no neglect in partaking the bread of heaven, so also must there be no descent to the malarial valleys. Life must be lived in the mountain heights in unceasing relation to the Spirit, who is the one and only Interpreter of Christ.

Some years ago I met in England a dear friend and, looking at him, was filled with sorrow as I saw that he was in the grasp of an insidious disease which with deadly uncertainty saps away the life. After a long interval, when I was in Colorado I saw him again, and hardly knew him. The rare air of the mountains had given him back his old strength, and had made impossible the spread of his disease. He told me, however, that while feeling perfectly well, it was necessary for him to stay upon those mountain heights, or the old trouble would return.

Let us keep ever in the mountain air. If we descend into the old valleys, the paralysis of the past will come again. We must live in the atmosphere of the Spirit, high on the mountains of vision, and there the appetite for the bread of heaven will be strong, and, feeding upon Christ, we will "grow up into Him all things."

G. CAMPBELL MORGAN

To live on Christ's love is a king's life.

SAMUEL RUTHERFORD

January 4

But when the Comforter is come, whom I will send unto you from the Father, even the Spirit of truth, which proceedeth from the Father, he shall testify of me.

JOHN 15:26, KJV

Wherever you have to go, whatever you may have to do, however isolated your life may be, the Holy Spirit is with you and in you to make you aware of the presence of Christ. Christ reveals Himself to you thus; and every time of awareness, every time of recollectedness, is the direct result of the operation of the Holy Spirit in your mind bringing you to think about, recollect, and to respond to the presence of your Lord.

Whatever you have to do in the shop, or office, or factory, or home, on the street, or as you travel, as you in these varied senses and occupations recall Jesus Christ, it is the Holy Spirit who is enabling you to do it.

In the special circumstances of your life, you may be cut off from Christian fellowship. But you can face all such loneliness in the calm confidence that the Spirit of God is always within you to remind you of the presence of Christ.

Christian fellowship is a glad and happy thing, but it is not the chief thing in a Christian's life. The chief thing is to have Christ Himself. And that gracious presence is ministered to you through the indwelling Holy Spirit, the Comforter.

Thus in every time of temptation or difficulty the Holy Spirit is ready to reveal Christ as the answer to all your problems and the Savior from all temptations.

J. RUSSELL HOWDEN

*E*veryone of us who has been called of God finds, more or less, that he is isolated unto Him that called him, just as Christ was apart to God.

G. V. WIGRAM

*M*uch as I love the brethren, my happiness has always been from God, not from them.

JOHN DARBY

January 5

When Simon Peter saw this, he fell at Jesus' knees and said, "Go away from me, Lord; I am a sinful man!"

LUKE 5:8

*D*ry wells send us to the fountain.

SAMUEL RUTHERFORD

*B*ehold, Lord, an empty vessel that needs to be filled. My Lord, fill it. I am weak in faith, strengthen me. My love is cold; warm me and make me fervent in love toward my neighbor. I do not have a strong and firm faith. At times I doubt and am unable to trust thee altogether. O Lord, help me. Strengthen my faith and trust in thee.

In thee I have sealed the treasures of all I own. I am poor; thou art rich and didst come to be merciful to the poor. I am a sinner; thou art upright. With me there is an abundance of sin; in thee is the fullness of righteousness. Therefore, I will remain with thee of whom I can receive but to whom I may not give. Amen.

MARTIN LUTHER

> God, harden me against myself,
> The coward with pathetic voice
> Who craves for ease and rest and joy.
> Myself, arch-traitor to myself,
> My hollowest friend,
> My deadliest foe,
> My clog, whatever road I go.

AMY CARMICHAEL

January 6

To do your will, O my God, is my desire, your law is within my heart.
PSALM 40:8

There are many Christians to whom it appears impossible to think of accepting all the will of God or of their being one with it. They look upon God's will and see a thousand commands and numberless providential orderings ...

They imagine that they would need to be a thousandfold holier and stronger in grace, before being able to do or bear all of God's will. They don't understand that the difficulty comes from their misunderstanding of God's will. They look at it as at variance with their natural will and feel that natural will will never delight in God's will.

They forget that the Christian has a renewed will. This new will delights in the will of God, because it is born of it. This new will sees the beauty and the glory of God's will, and is in harmony with it.

If they are indeed God's children, the very first impulse of the spirit of a child is surely to do the will of the Father in heaven. And they have but to yield themselves heartily and wholly to this spirit of sonship, and they need not fear to accept God's will as theirs.

ANDREW MURRAY

*W*ill to do God's will for your life instead of your own. Do not launch out upon the sea of life headed for a port of your own choosing, guided by a map of your own making, driven by the power of your own selfish pleasures or ambitions.

Come to God. Yield your life to Him by one act of trustful, irrevocable surrender ... So shall you come steadily to know and see God's will for your life ... Without a shadow of doubt, we will begin to know God's will as soon as we begin to choose His will for our lives, instead of our own.

JAMES MCCONKEY

January 7

Not by works of righteousness which we have done, but according to his mercy he saved us, by the washing of regeneration, and renewing of the Holy Ghost.

TITUS 3:5, KJV

A full Christ is for an empty sinner, and an empty sinner for a full Christ. They are morally fitted to each other; and the more I experience the emptiness, the more I shall enjoy the fullness. So long as I am full of trust in MY morality, MY benevolence, MY amiability, MY religiousness, MY righteousness, I have no room for Christ.

All these things must be thrown overboard, before a full Christ can be apprehended. It cannot be partly self and partly Christ. It must be either one or the other; and one reason why so many are tossed up and down in dark uncertainty is because they are still cleaving to some little bit of self. It may be a very little bit. They may not, perhaps, be trusting in any works of righteousness that they have done; but still there is something of self retained and trusted in. It may be the very smallest possible atom of the creature—its state, its feelings, its mode of appropriating, its experiences, something or other of the creature kept in which Christ keeps out. In short, it must be so, for if a full Christ were received, a full peace would be enjoyed; and if a full peace be not enjoyed, it is only because a full Christ has not been received.

C. H. MACKINTOSH

*I*f you feel, " I can do this or that service," you are not the vessel God can use.

EDWARD DENNETT

*G*od's power is just fitted for the Christian's weakness; and the Christian's weakness is just fitted for God's power, so we suit each other.

"FOOD FOR THE DESERT"

January 8

That which is born of the flesh is flesh; and that which is born of the Spirit is Spirit.

JOHN 3:6, KJV

*T*oo often we believers have a serious misconception—imagining that while salvation comes to us freely, victory depends on ourselves. We know we cannot add any merit or work of ours to obtain salvation. We must simply come to the cross and accept the Lord

Jesus as our Savior. This is the gospel! We realize we cannot be saved by works, yet we reason that for sanctification we must do good works after we are saved. This is to say that though you cannot be saved by works, you need to depend on works for victory.

Let me tell you that just as you are not *saved* by works, so you do not *overcome* by works. God has declared that you are unable to do good. Christ has died for you on the cross, and He is now living for you within. That which is of the flesh is flesh, and God rejects all that came from it. Nevertheless, we usually surmise that while salvation is dependent upon the substitutionary death of Christ on the cross, we should think of doing good, should do good, and expect to do good for victory in our lives. Let us realize, though, that we can do *no* good. Victory is freely given us by God!

WATCHMAN NEE

*V*ictory is the believer's right—as truly his as the air he breathes. However, he must understand the conditions. He must see himself enthroned with Christ. He must see himself according to God's own Holy Word, as crucified with the Lord Jesus, dead, buried, raised, and made to sit in heavenly places with his Lord and Savior Jesus Christ.

Without this, he will go down in defeat in spite of all his strivings and his prayers. With this position he is more than conqueror through Him who loved him and gave Himself for him.

F. J. HUEGEL

January 9

Just as you used to offer the parts of your body in slavery to impurity and to ever-increasing wickedness, so now offer them in slavery to righteousness leading to holiness.

ROMANS 6:19

*I*t is *ourselves* that God wants. No gift of money, time, service, or talents will meet the yearning of His heart for ourselves. For God is love, and Love would above all things have the heart. Thus surrender is a transaction between Redeemer and redeemed, and whatsoever falls short of the sacred gift of a yielded heart falls short of all.

Even the heart of the poorest and most degraded shrinks from money when it needs love. How much more so with the Lover of our souls. Silver and gold, time and talents, ministry and service, are acceptable to God as an *accompaniment* of surrender, but never as an *evasion* of it.

There are those who will give wealth, time and effort, but who in their secret hearts have never yet yielded themselves to God. When in the silence and secrecy of their own communion with God, this issue rises before them, they tremble and grow pale, and shrink back from this definite transaction with God. And yet if God is to be all to us, we must yield all to Him.

Never can that confidential relationship between the Redeemer and His redeemed, which is the highest blessedness of the believer's life, be established until we give ourselves to Him who gave Himself for us. Without this yielding of ourselves to Him we have not, in a profound sense of the word, received Him as *Lord*, even though we know him as Savior.

James McConkey

*I*s there any point of dispute between your Lord and yourself? One little thing which you cannot surrender? Yet God is always in the right, and He will not change. It is *your* heart which must surrender. Then, His peace will be yours. He has made the offering which atones for all your sins, but now you must yield up your will to Him.

Shall it be now?

T. C. Horton

"My ears had heard of you but now my eyes have seen you."
JOB 42:5

*D*o let us realize, dear friends, that there is a great difference between knowing God by hearing and knowing Him by seeing. Job confessed that his knowledge of God in the past had come by hearing; which is to say, that it had been indirect and informational in character and had therefore not been intimate, personal, and experiential enough. It had been more a mental than a spiritual knowledge. Such a knowledge is entirely inadequate, since it puffs up a person instead of bringing him low. Knowing God only by hearing makes one into a somebody, but knowing Him by seeing reduces one to a nobody; to dust and ashes. And this was truly Job's experience. Through the Lord's painful dealing, he has at last seen God. Through the Lord's affliction he has come into a very close and personal encounter with Him.

It is good that in afflictions we meet God. It is He who solves our problems, yet not by explanation but by appearance. Our problems are solved when we see Him. For when we see God, we are not so much concerned with our problems as we are concerned with *ourselves* being the problem; so that we abhor our very selves and repent in dust and ashes. In giving up ourselves we receive more of God, just as John the Baptist expressed it when he confided, I must decrease but He must increase. As we become nothing, God becomes everything.

STEPHEN KAUNG

*H*e is enough for us though the path be ten thousand times more sad and difficult.

GEORGE V. WIGRAM

Anyone who loves his father or mother more than me is not worthy of me; anyone who loves his son or daughter more than me is not worthy of me; and anyone who does not take his cross and follow me is not worthy of me. Whoever finds his life will lose it, and whoever loses his life for my sake will find it.

MATTHEW 10:37–39

*W*e who follow the Crucified are not here to make a pleasant thing of life; we are called to suffering for the sake of a suffering, sinful world. The Lord forgive us our shameful evasion and hesitations. His brow was crowned with thorns; do we then seek rosebuds for our crowning?

His hands were pierced with nails, are our hands ringed with jewels? His feet were bare and bound; do our feet walk delicately? What do we know of travail? Of tears that scald before they fall? Of heartbreak? Of being scorned?

God forgive us our love of ease. God forgive us that so often we turn our faces from a life that is even remotely like His. Forgive us that we all but worship comfort, the delight of the presence of loved ones, possessions, treasures on earth.

Far, far from our prayers too often is any thought of prayer which will lead us to give one whom we love to follow our Lord to Gethsemane, to Calvary—perhaps because we have never been there ourselves.

AMY CARMICHAEL

I will place no value on anything I have or may possess except in relation to the Kingdom of Christ.

DAVID LIVINGSTONE

Resist the devil, and he will flee from you.

JAMES 4:7B

*T*he grace of God filling the heart with Christ, alone enables us to give up self, and its idols. The more filled we are with Him, and His grace and truth, the more readily and thoroughly we can yield up all that His eye condemns.

For it is only as we are led by the God of all grace that we can really go *down*, really be *nothing*, or really admit *all* his rebukes, and the hollowness of *all* not given by His grace. Christ enters, and all that cannot live in his company goes out.

Slowly it may be—unwilling to yield possession—but the inflowing of *blessing* through the knowledge and power of *Christ*, must cleanse the heart, while filling it.

This is indeed a *process*, not a thing done at *once, once for all*. There is conflict. There are sad advantages often gained by the enemy. But just as Christ enters and abides—dwelling in the heart by faith—so are the many suggestions of the enemy driven outside, and kept outside.

Yea, so full may the blessing be, that the enemy may be driven *away from the gate*. The devil flees from us, because he not only has no place *within*, but because he is *resisted* in the power of Christ, and for Christ's sake. Then there is peace and joy *around* as well as within. Let our weakness humble us and cast us upon God; but let it not induce unbelief, and so set us against God.

"CRUMBS FOR THE LORD'S LITTLE ONES"

I find that it was easier to get Israel *out* of Egypt than to get them into Canaan. Each step in advance evokes more opposition than the previous step—but then God is more and more to us as we advance, and this means everything to the committed heart.

J. B. STONEY

It is easier to keep the enemy out than it is to expel him after he has gained entrance.

AUTHOR UNKNOWN

January 13

Remember Lot's wife. Whosoever shall seek to save his life shall lose it.
LUKE 17:32

Had Lot's wife not left Sodom? Indeed she had. But her flesh still fed on Sodom's sweets, and so her heart had not left it, had not lost it.

To God, Sodom was only fit to be turned into a cinder; to Lot's wife it was still worth saving. She still sought to save her "life" from the falling fire—not her bodily life—for she was already outside the city; but the things of her desire, the things of the world that remained in Sodom.

She so loved that life and longed for it that she looked back and *lost it all*—her life in Sodom and indeed, her bodily life; her all. There she stood, a pillar of salt, an external warning to those who long after the flesh.

My friend, the Lord is coming. What is your life? Is it lived in the Spirit? Oh the power of the Cross to sever every relationship that would bind us to the flesh! We are debtors only to the Holy Spirit. Give the Cross full place in your life; abandon yourself recklessly to the Crucified, for over His crucified life the flesh has not one speck of power. Let the Cross seize you and sever you from that enthrallment with the flesh.

It's been said that "Every strong conviction ends by taking possession of us; it overcomes and absorbs us, and tears us ruthlessly from everything else."

Has the Cross so seized upon your life?

If it has, you can live for self nevermore. Rather, you will cry out with a determined saint of yore, "Oh my God, hear the cries of one on whom Thou has had mercy, and prepare my heart to receive whatever Christ has purchased for me. Allow me not to rest short of it."

L. E. MAXWELL

𝒯he most miserable person on the face of the earth is the Christian who is trying to enjoy both worlds.

EDWARD DENNETT

𝒥 am most joyously content that Christ would break all my idols to bits. It renews my love for Christ to see that he is jealous of my love, and will have it all to Himself.

SAMUEL RUTHERFORD

January 14

Wait for the Lord; be strong and take heart and wait for the Lord.
PSALM 27:14

𝒯he natural mind is ever prone to *reason*, when we ought to *believe*; and to be at *work*, when we ought to be *quiet*; to go our own way, when we ought steadily to walk on in God's ways, however trying to our human nature.

When first converted, I could have said, "What harm can there be to take some of the money, which has been put aside for the Orphanage Building Fund? God will [eventually bless my work for the orphans], and then I can replace it."

I know that many Christians would reason thus. But how does it work, when we thus presume upon God, by going our own way? We bring, in many instances, guilt on our conscience; but if not, we certainly weaken faith, instead of increasing it; and each time we try to work a deliverance of our own, we find it more and more difficult to trust in God, till at last we give way entirely to our natural fallen reason, and unbelief prevails.

How different, if one waits for God's own time, and looks alone to Him for help and deliverance! When at last help comes, after many seasons of prayer it may be, and after much exercise of faith and patience it may be, how sweet it is, and what present recompense does the soul at once receive for trusting in God, and waiting patiently for His deliverance!

Dear Christian reader, if you have never walked in this path of obedience before, do so now, and you will then know experientially the sweetness of joy!

GEORGE MUELLER

*W*e ought to be patient, for He is the doer of everything—and when we are not patient we really are finding fault with Him and His doing.

GEORGE V. WIGRAM

*H*e is a great giver, and if He hides His hand from giving today, tomorrow He often gives two-fold.

GEORGE V. WIGRAM

January 15

Above the Horse Gate, the priests made repairs, each in front of his own house. Next to them, Zadok son of Immer made repairs opposite his house. Next to him, Shemaiah son of Shecaniah, the guard at the East Gate, made repairs. Next to him, Hananiah son of Shelemiah, and Hanun, the sixth son of Zalaph, repaired another section. Next to them, Meshullam son of Berekiah made repairs opposite his living quarters.

NEHEMIAH 3:28–30

$\mathcal{I}$t is important to remember that all who are Christians have one life. In the sight of heaven there is only one life that matters before God—the life of the Lord Jesus, indwelling each of us by His Spirit.

This is an amazing fellowship. Because we share that one life, we share one great purpose and one great work: it is the building of lives into the Kingdom of God, and in such a task one hundred percent cooperation between Christian people is absolutely vital. The greatest menace to revival is the Christian who refuses to work with other people because his views differ on certain matters of Biblical interpretation which are nonessential in relation to evangelism.

It is interesting to note that Nehemiah set each group to work on that part of the wall which was nearest to where the group member lived. [I believe] our first obligation for Christ is always our own neighborhood. Wouldn't the bells of heaven ring today if every believer would say before God, "Lord, I will make my own immediate locality my mission field. I will see to it that every family is regularly supplied with gospel literature and urged to attend church"?

You see, my friends, in Christian work, organizing and agonizing should go together. Alas, too often organizing has crowded out agonizing. There is too much working before men and too little waiting before God. There is more and more motion and less and less unction. We wrestle with problems in endless committees and conferences, but we seldom wrestle on our knees against our real enemy, Satan.

Many a committee, of course, has a fine program, but how many have a real spiritual burden?

Oh, may God give each of us that burden in order that there may be one hundred per cent cooperation in this work! We have no room here for the independent Christian; we are engaged in one supreme task, that of reaching this world for God, and it will take all of us.

ALAN REDPATH

There is one thing I have noticed as I have traveled in different countries; I never have known the Spirit of God to work where the Lord's people are divided. Unity is one thing that we must have for the Holy Spirit of God to work in our midst.

DWIGHT L. MOODY

See how these Christians love one another.

TERTULLIAN

January 16

. . . ye in me, and I in you.
JOHN 14:20B, KJV

The spiritual history of every Christian could be written in two phrases, "Ye in me" and "I in you."

In God's reckoning Christ and the Christian become one in such a way that Christ is both in the heavenlies and upon earth and the Christian is both on earth and in the heavenlies. Christ in the heavenlies is the invisible part of the Christian. The Christian on earth is the visible part of Christ. This is a staggering thought. Its plain import is that you and I are to bring Christ down from heaven to earth that men may see who He is and what He can do in a human life. It is to have Christ's life lived out in us in such fullness that by seeing Him in us, people are drawn to Him in faith and love.

RUTH PAXSON

God has but one way of revealing Himself. It is "Christ in you." He has no other way of showing Himself to men except as Christ lives in us; not by the Shekinah glory in the temple built with hands of men, but in lives redeemed and freed and cleansed as they walk about in this dark world with Christ living in them.

L. L. LETGERS

*C*hrist has taken our nature into Heaven to represent us; and has left us on earth with His nature, to represent Him.

JOHN NEWTON

January 17

Beloved, if our heart condemn us not, then we have confidence before God.

1 JOHN 3:21, KJV

For the accuser of our brothers, who accuses them before our God day and night, has been hurled down. They overcame him by the blood of the Lamb and by the word of their testimony . . .

REVELATION 12:10B–11

*I*t is only when our heart condemns us not that we have boldness toward God. The adversary knows this, and so is the "accuser of our brothers" seeking to bring the believer into condemnation before God.

Decision on the part of the believer is necessary here, and a knowledge of the power of the blood of the Lamb. Let the believer remember that the Lord Christ is a faithful witness, and will faithfully tell his possessed ones the moment they are out of accord with His will.

He is always definite in His dealings with His children, and the soul in the fellowship with Him quickly knows when He speaks with the still small voice of conscience; then it must at once obey, and claim the cleansing of the precious blood.

The condemnation of the evil one is usually vague, and should be met by the believer claiming the constant cleansing of the blood; whilst doubtful things must be dealt with by a committal to the Lord, and trust that He will remove what comes from the accuser, and deepen and renew all that comes from Himself. The breastplate of righteousness will then be kept upon the heart to protect it from the enemy.

JESSIE PENN-LEWIS

*S*ometimes, when after a sin committed, I have looked for sore chastisement from the hand of God, instead, the very next that I have had from him has been the discovery of His grace.

JOHN BUNYAN

January 18

I am the vine; you are the branches. If a man remains in me and I in him he will bear much fruit; apart from me you can do nothing.
JOHN 15:5

*W*hat is fruit?

Fruit is the over-plus of the tree's life, over and above what it uses up on itself, for self-existence.

Fruit has the flavor of the tree, is separable from the tree, can be given away, is such as to be a blessing to others.

Jesus showed us we are so united to Him, as branches to Vine, that His life flows into and through us, manifesting itself as fruit. That is, we are so to appropriate and live His life as not to use it up on ourselves; not, as is often said, in "trying to live a Christian life."

What self-centeredness! Rather, to let Christ so realize His own life in us that His very quality of life, with all its power to bless, is manifest through our transformed, yielded, self-effaced personalities.

Should there be no such fruit, we defeat the very purpose of our being "in Christ," but as we abide, draw upon Him, the inexhaustible Source, and yield ourselves to His *in-flowing*, there results an *out*-flowing of His life in "fruit."

As we learn better to abide, the fruit becomes "more fruit." But Christ is satisfied only when the "more" becomes the abounding "much fruit."

NORMAN B. HARRISON

*T*here is nothing static in spiritual experience—every real Christian is a growing Christian. The purpose of fruit-bearing is to glorify Christ. The branch doesn't bear fruit to glorify itself, it bears much fruit to glorify the vine. But only the "much fruit" glorifies the Father. Anything short of that, although it may bring Him joy and may please Him, fails to glorify the Father fully.

RUTH PAXSON

*F*ruit is not produced by making fruit an object, nor by thinking of fruit; it is the outcome of having the Lord Jesus as one's object, of thinking of Him. He is the one True Vine who precedes and produces fruit.

HANNAH WHITALL SMITH

January 19

That I may know him, and the power of his resurrection, and the fellowship of his sufferings, being made conformable unto his death.
PHILIPPIANS 3:10, KJV

*M*ore Christians go on the rocks, defeated, over the nasty little thing we call "hurt feelings" than over the so-called great crises which test the very fiber of the soul.

I have been slighted. I have not been given the place I feel I merit or, I have been treated inconsiderately, unjustly. My opinions and feelings have not been consulted. Self has been wounded.

As a result I have begun to sink. I am being defeated, not by a monster, but by a mere fly. And yet it is no less defeat. A "scum" covers my spirit formerly free and rejoicing. I have sunk down into the so-called "vessel of the soul." I have become soulish.

The stream of eternal life from the throne and from the Lamb has ceased to flow in and out of my being. My step has become heavy, and my face now carries an unhappy, darkened look. I am plainly defeated. Wounded pride did it. I looked at my self and took my eyes off Jesus my Lord.

How different all would have been if my answer had been the sublime answer of death! I would immediately have said, "They crucified my Lord—this is nothing. It is my chance to go a little deeper into the fellowship of my Savior's sufferings, being made conformable unto His death. The result will be a fuller participation of His resurrection.

"Thank you, Lord, for these things that have hurt. Bless those who have hurt me. I forgive as Thou didst forgive. I am deeply grateful for this reminder of my nothingness. I am willing to be nothing that Thou mightest be all. Amen!"

Now when our answer is the answer of the Cross, nothing can hurt us. We immediately turn everything into a blessing. We go up by going down. We triumph through death. We feed on the holy Cross and live. The kick backward was really a kick forward. The hurt feeling is immediately seen in light of the Savior's death which the Holy Spirit has freshly applied, and the stream of eternal life from the throne flows richer and fuller than ever. Our concern is that Christ be glorified, the rest does not matter.

F. J. HUEGEL

*Th*ere is never much use in contending with restless and disaffected people—better far leave them in the Lord's hands, for in reality, their controversy is with Him.

"FOOD FOR THE DESERT"

I will not drive them out from before thee in one year; lest the land become desolate, and the beast of the field multiply against thee. Little by little I will drive them out from before thee, until thou be increased.
EXODUS 23:29–30, KJV

So often in the battle we go to the Lord, and pray and plead, and appeal for victory, for ascendancy, for mastery over the forces of evil and death, and our thought is that in some way God is going to come in with a mighty exercise of power and put us into a place of spiritual maturity as in an act. We must have this mentality corrected.

What the Lord does is to enlarge us to possess. He takes us through some exercise, some experience, takes us by some way which means our spiritual expansion, an increase of spirituality so we occupy the larger place spontaneously because of our growth.

T. AUSTIN-SPARKS

Many Christians keep themselves in a perpetual foment by hoping they will get into a situation where they can enjoy a better (and easier) Christian life. They feel enclosed in a net of circumstances from which they cannot escape. They are so wearied and baffled and beaten by the continuous pressure about them that they wish and itch for things to be different, quite sure that if they were only different Christ would be more real. It has not dawned on them that at the heart of these very circumstances they are to find the Lord Jesus, find His grace sufficient, find the life more abundant.

L. E. MAXWELL

January 21

The Spirit itself beareth witness with our Spirit, that we are the children of God.

ROMANS 8:16, KJV

There is all the difference in the world between having the Spirit, and not having Him. It comes out in the prayers of God's people. You can tell where a Christian is spiritually, better by his prayers, than by his general speech.

I have heard some of the children of God pray, as if they were poor beggars. Suppose a beggar comes to your house. You hear his knock. By its very character you learn who it is, and say, "That is a beggar!" You know it is a beggar. He gets a crust, or a copper, and goes his way.

Half-an-hour goes by when the bell rings violently, then a loud knock, and if there be any delay in opening, perhaps even a kick at the door follows. "Ah!" you say, "that is my boy come home from school." The boy knows he is perfectly welcome, and he is in haste to get in, where love waits to receive him. I believe that many of the children of God do not know what it is to be thoroughly at home, in the presence of the Lord, with this sense, "I am a child, as near to the heart of God, as Christ is; I am welcome there, and He loves to hear my voice. The atonement is accepted for me, and the Holy Spirit is dwelling in me, to lead me into, and keep me happily occupied with, the love that has brought me near to itself."

The Holy Spirit has come to bear witness with our spirit of all that Christ is to us and to put the saint in the enjoyment now of what belongs to him for eternity. Well, you say, I shall be very happy in heaven in eternity! Why are you not now happy on earth?

If somebody left you a fortune in the bank, would you say, I will make the first withdrawal when I die? I do not think that you would. You would rather say, I would like to draw upon it immediately.

"ANOTHER COMFORTER"

*F*aith doesn't show what a Christian you are, but shows what a God you have. The more we get from God, the bigger beggars we are, and the grander Father He is. That is, he puts us in a position where we must take a great deal from His resources and He is disappointed when we fail to do so.

A. B. SIMPSON

January 22

Do not let your hearts be troubled. Trust in God; trust also in me. In my Father's house there are many rooms; if it were not so, I would have told you. I am going there to prepare a place for you. And if I go and prepare a place for you, I will come back and take you to be with me that you also may be where I am.

JOHN 14:1–3

*T*here are souls being added to the Church every day, and often in numbers greater than in any previous age. For each of these added souls new preparation for growth may be, and indeed would seem clearly to be, required.

The tastes, the energies, the bent of mind, the interests of people are varied ... yet Heaven will provide a glory adapted to each of the millions whom grace saves.

See what a work the Lord foreshadowed when He said those simple words, "I am going there to prepare a place for you." What sort of a place are you aiming at? Yes, you would rather be a doorkeeper there than to dwell in the tents of wickedness. But this is not now the question. Would you prefer to be a doorkeeper to being an ambassador? Would you prefer to serve self, and pleasure, and wealth on earth, and be of little or no use hereafter; or will you choose to live for Christ heart and soul, forgetting things past and pressing on toward the mark, keen and strong. Which?

Christ is preparing your place. He is, to that end, watching your course on earth. The sons of Zebedee demanded to sit on the right and left of the King Himself. Do not follow the other disciples in their anger at this request. It is well to aim high. It is contemptible to seek merely to "get saved." But remember our Lord's reply to the disciples, "Can ye drink of My cup, and be baptized with My baptism?" Ah, that is it! We are carving out our own destiny every moment. The Judgment Seat of Christ will settle all. There will be no respect of persons there. But the faithful servant will take a higher place and portion, and the slothful and worldly will be saved, that is all.

"Soul Food"

*G*o up beforehand and see the place He is preparing for you. Look through all your Father's rooms in heaven. In your Father's house are many dwelling places. Prudent buyers take a look at land before they purchase it. And though Christ has made the sale for us already, yet we still may see, by faith, the house to which we will go, indeed we may see it often as we wish.

Samuel Rutherford

January 23

Bless the Lord, O my soul! And all that is within me, bless His holy name. Bless the Lord, O my soul, and forget not all his benefits.
Psalm 103:1–2, KJV

*D*oesn't all nature urge us to praise Him? If we remain silent, we should be the exceptions in the universe. Doesn't the thunder praise Him as it rolls like drums in the advancing army of God? Don't the mountains praise Him when the forest trees at the summit wave in adoration? Doesn't the lightning write His name in letters of fire upon the midnight darkness? Hasn't the whole earth a voice, and shall we, can we, remain silent?

CHARLES SPURGEON

Of all spiritual activities, the one which most honors God is that of blessing Him. More is involved in that than just thanksgiving. To bless the Lord is certainly to speak His praise with words, but it is also to take up an attitude toward Him.

The word translated "bless" is somehow related to a word meaning "to kneel," so that the person who blesses the Lord is doing more than opening his mouth—he is bowing his knees to God. Blessing God gives Him the honor due to Him because the lips are opened to praise Him and the knees are bent to worship and adore Him.

When Elijah went up Carmel to give God the praise for the great victory of the fire, the king could go off to feast but the prophet only wished to worship. We do not read of any words which he spoke, but we are told that he put his face between his knees. That is more than some of us are able to do, for one reason or another, but he did it.

Those who are still young and supple should try it. They should sit down on their heels and put their head between their knees, and they will then appreciate just how low before God Elijah came. It was not just that he wished to say, "Thank you, Lord," but he wanted in the deepest sense to bless the Lord. There is nothing that gives God the honor that is due to Him more than that we should bless the Lord. This is more than just thanksgiving; it also contains that all too rare activity, the adoring of God, the appreciation of His true greatness, the worshipping of Him not only for what He has done, but for who He is.

J. ALEC MOTZER

And Elijah went up to the top of Carmel; and he cast himself down upon the earth, and put his face between his knees.

2 KINGS 18:42B, KJV

January 24

I made haste, and delayed not to keep thy commandments.
PSALM 119:60, KJV

$\mathcal{D}$on't be in a hurry to run ahead of God.

When the Israelites were crossing the Jordan they were told to leave a great space between themselves and the guiding ark, that they might know how to go, because "they had not passed that way heretofore." Impatiently hurrying at God's heels is apt to lead us astray. Let Him get well in front, that you may be quite sure which way He wants you to go, before you go. And if you are not sure which way He wants you to go, be sure that He does not at that moment want you to go anywhere.

We need to hold the present with a slack hand, so as to be ready to fold our tents and take to the road if God wills. We must not presume continuance, nor strike our roots so deep that it needs a hurricane to remove us.

To those who set their gaze on Christ, no present from which He wishes them to move can be so good for them as the new conditions into which He would have them pass.

It's hard to leave the spot, though it be in the desert, where we have so long encamped that it has come to look like home. We may look with regret on the circle of black ashes on the sand where our little fire glinted cheerily, and our feet may ache and our hearts ache more as we begin our tramp once again, but we must set ourselves to meet the God-appointed change cheerfully, in the confidence that nothing will be left behind which it is not good to lose, nor anything met which does not bring a blessing, however its first aspect may be—harsh or sad.

We need, too, to cultivate the habit of prompt obedience. "I made haste and delayed not to keep Thy commandments" is the only safe motto. Slow obedience is often the germ of incipient disobedience ... It's easiest to do our duty when we are first sure of it. It then comes with an impelling power which carries us over obstacles on the crest of a wave, while hesitation and delay leave us stranded in shallow water. If we would follow the pillar, we must follow it at once.

A heart that waits and watches for God's direction, that uses common sense as well as faith to unravel small and great perplexities, and is willing to sit loose to the present, however pleasant, in order not to miss indications which say, "Arise! this is not your rest"—fulfills the conditions on which, if we keep them, we may be sure that He will guide us by the right way, and bring us at last to the city of habitation.

ALEXANDER MACLAREN

If we wait upon God, there is no danger. If we rush on, He must let us see the consequences of it.

JOHN DARBY

January 25

For God will bring every deed into judgment, including every hidden thing, whether it is good or evil.

ECCLESIASTES 12:14

The whole of our past lives, the significance of every act, its motive as well as its object, will be made clear to us—clear as to the source of all, whether our activities sprang from the energy of the flesh or were produced by the Spirit of God, and how much of mixture there had been in what seemed to be our most devoted service.

All this will be manifested to us at that time in the patient grace of our blessed Lord; to us individually, not necessarily to others in public.

The effect will be that we shall magnify as never before the grace of our God, and we will be content to acknowledge, as the Apostle Paul has said, that it was not we, but the grace of God which was with us that gave both the opportunity and the ability to do anything in His service.

It will, on the other hand, be the delight of Christ, in that day, to attribute every good work done, good according to His perfect estimate, to His beloved people.

Should anyone ask, how it will be possible to endure the exposures which must necessarily be made, however tenderly, in the perfect light of that day, let us remember that when we are before the judgment seat of Christ, we are already conformed to His image. We shall, therefore, be in full communion with His own mind, and so, our hearts will offer a hearty "Amen" to every condemnation which He shall pass on any work of the flesh which we had done.

Even more, we shall rejoice before Him because our presence there will but intensify our appreciation for His grace and enlarge our thoughts of His eternal love which He has revealed to us through His beloved Son.

EDWARD DENNETT

If He uses me, it is a great honor. If He lays me aside because self was elated, it is a great mercy. He is saying, as it were, "Be satisfied with Myself, be content to know *I love thee.*"

Are you content with His love? The secret of all service is the due appreciation of the Master's grace.

JOHN DARBY

> *Blessed is the people that know the joyful sound: they shall walk,*
> *O LORD, in the light of thy countenance.*
> PSALM 89:15, KJV

The joyful sound!

Souls that are called by the sound of the gospel—how joyful does it render them! The trumpets of the Gospel do to the soul as the harps of David did to Saul—they drive away the evil spirit of sorrow, sadness, and despair.

The trumpets of the Gospel call us to appointments with God, wherein we glorify Him with the sacrifices of praise and righteousness. They bring the joyful sound of the promises of God's most gracious covenant with us—they call us to claim His great and precious promises—oh, the joyful sound of them!

Rejoice, Christian! God the Father is your Friend; God the Son is your guarantee for good; God the Spirit is your Guide and Comforter—be of good cheer, your sins are forgiven!

Consider also: The angels are your guardians, you are a temple of God. God will make all things work together for your good. These are the spiritual blessings reserved for the believer. Joyful sound! How reviving! How ravishing!

The blessings which the Word of God leads us to are matchless treasures. What a joyful trumpet sound it must be that leads us to them!

A people that have the Gospel, and know the joyful sound enjoy the rich favor of God. And the places which enjoy the Scriptures and have the Church state, with the faith of the Gospel, are highly favored of the Lord.

COTTON MATHER

If you have no joy in your religion, there's a leak in your Christianity somewhere.

BILLY SUNDAY

*J*oy! Joy! Tears! Tears!"

January 27

Since you are my rock and my fortress, for the sake of your name lead and guide me.

PSALM 31:3

*T*here's a tender awe in knowing that there's Someone at your side guiding your every step, restraining here, leading on there. He knows the way better than the ablest Swiss guide knows the mountain trail. He has love's concern that all shall go well with you.

When you come to the fork in the road with yet a third path splitting off from the others, there's a peace in just holding steady and quiet while you put your hand out and say, "Jesus, Master, guide here."

And then to hear a Voice so soft that only in great quiet is it heard, softer than the faintest breath on your cheek, or the slightest touch at your arm, telling the way with peace unspeakable.

If perhaps the chosen road then leads to crowds and the praise of men, you will be knowing that it was His leading that brought you there, not your own wisdom or talent. He will have some great purpose for these crowds, and maybe some purpose through these crowds farther on.

You will also be very careful not to disappoint or thwart His plans. And, you will be very careful that the dust the crowd is raising may not dim your vision of His face.

S. D. GORDON

*T*he grace of God is a very great thing. It is mighty to save, to keep, to use, and to make us a blessing. When we respond to the grace of

God, we find ourselves in something very great—something that could never be compensated for anything or everything else that we might have.

T. AUSTIN-SPARKS

It is not great talents God blesses so much as great likeness to the Lord Jesus. A holy ministry is an awful weapon in the hands of God.

ROBERT MURRAY MCCHEYNE

January 28

He that believeth on me, the works that I do shall he do also, and greater works than these, because I go to the Father.
JOHN 14:12, KJV

Christ draws the believer to Himself—into Himself—into closest communion of life and work. He identified us with Him. As He is, so are we in the world. He is the light of the world, and He assigns to us the same position. Like Him, we are witnesses, priests, and kings. As the Father sent Christ, so He sends us.

He wants to raise us into the most intimate union of life and power. When the disciples wondered that at Christ's word, the fig tree withered, the Savior said: "Have faith in God!"

If in union with Christ we have faith as a grain of mustard seed, we shall be able to remove mountains, and nothing shall be impossible to us.

The Spirit is given to us as the Spirit of Sonship. We are not merely in the position of children, but we are in truth and reality the children of God. Our adoption is an actual investment with Sonship. There can be in the nature of things, no parallel to this in the earthly sphere. Christ is the only begotten of the Father, and we in Him are truly sons of God, for we are born of God and one with Christ . . .

Think of it believer—that the Spirit of communion and delight in the Father, that was in Christ, is in you also, and that you know the Father is always with you and that He loves you with an infinite love.

Take hold of Christ, therefore, and trusting Him as Savior, rise with Him above all fears, above all of the earthly creation into the heavenly region of Sonship, and say "Abba" in the full assurance of faith. And then go back to earth and man, to work and suffering, in the Spirit of liberty which only the Son of God can give, and which only Sons and Daughters possess.

To do the will of God, if in the time of suffering, will be no hardship or bondage, but will be, as it was to Christ, "meat"—the strength and refreshment of your life, until in Heaven you possess that perfect and true liberty, when God's will is your will, and when all that is within you praises His holy name.

ADOLPH SAPHIR

$\mathscr{I}$t is a marvelous grace that we should be conformed to the image of God's Son. I think it is very sad that the highest thought which God has about us, and that which His heart is set on, is that which is least known by Christians; for I know no truth that is so little realized as union with Christ.

J. B. STONEY

$\mathscr{T}$he Lord Jesus is the Christian's very life, and the Holy Spirit dwells within our spirit to manifest Him, to work out all that is in Him and to reproduce Him in us. We must remember that there is something in the sight of God that is higher than work. There is Christ-likeness. That is our Father's purpose, and it is His work.

ANDREW MURRAY

Dearly beloved, I beseech you as strangers and pilgrims, abstain from fleshly lusts which war against the soul.

1 PETER 2:11, KJV

*W*hy are you a stranger?

Because you are away from home.

Why are you a pilgrim?

Because you are journeying to a spot which you want to reach. You are a stranger because your hopes, your joys, and the One you love best are all in heaven, and that is what makes heaven the home of your heart.

Born from heaven, you belong to heaven. Your Father is in heaven, your Savior is in heaven, your springs of supply are in heaven; your hopes, your joys, are all in heaven; in short, you are like an exotic plant down here, a stranger to this clime. You are a pilgrim, too, and a pilgrim never thinks his pilgrimage over till he reaches the spot towards which his course is bent.

W. T. P. WOLSTON

*W*e belong to another sphere altogether. We have died and our life is "hidden with Christ in God." We are like a tree that has its roots in heaven, and its branches down here. No doubt our branches are blown and ripped by the atmosphere here, but nothing can touch the roots up there. Planted inside, they flourish outside.

J. B. STONEY

*T*o abide in heaven in the Lord Jesus is my place. My faith is exercised here, and the suffering here may be prolonged and continued; but I abide *there*, and while abiding I engage myself with everything connected with my Father, and with reference to the place He has set me in.

In that blessed region where He has placed me, and where He alone can keep me, and where I am simply dependent upon Him, it is His interests alone which engage me, and thus it is that I minister to the brethren.

JOHN DARBY

January 30

Whereby are given unto us exceeding great and precious promises, that through these ye might be partakers of the divine nature . . .
2 PETER 1:4, KJV

*W*e cannot too highly value and appreciate heart-hunger for the Word. It is the Spirit of Truth. We may have been born again without knowing much of the Bible, but we certainly are not going to grow to any extent apart from a careful and persistent study of the Word of God. Yes, the maturing believer is a Spirit-dependent student of the Scriptures, "whereby are given unto us exceeding great and precious promises; that by these ye might be partakers of the divine nature."

Christian progress is not a question of attaining to some abstract standard, or of pressing through to some far-off goal. It is wholly a question of seeing God's standard in God's Word. You advance spiritually by finding out what you really are (in Christ), not by trying to become what you hope to be. That goal you will never reach, however earnestly you may strive.

It is when you see you are dead unto sin that you die to it (daily); it is when you see you are risen that you arise; it is when you see you are a 'new creature' in Him that you (progressively) grow. Seeing the accomplished fact in the Word determines the pathway to the realizing of that fact. The end is reached by seeing, not by desiring or working. The only possibility of spiritual progress lies in our discovering the truth as God sees it; the truth concerning Christ, the truth concerning ourselves in Christ.

Watchman Nee

*B*elieve God's Word and power more than you believe your own feelings and experiences. Your Rock is Christ and it isn't that Rock that ebbs and flows—but your sea.

Samuel Rutherford

January 31

He will swallow up death in victory; and the LORD God will wipe away tears from off all faces; and the rebuke of his people shall he take away from off all the earth: for the LORD hath spoken it. And it shall be said in that day, Lo, this is our God; we have waited for him, and he will save us: this is the LORD; we have waited for him, we will be glad and rejoice in his salvation.

Isaiah 25:8–9, KJV

*T*o every soul there must come a time when he too can say, "Lo, this is our God; we have waited for him, we will be glad and rejoice in his salvation." Through all the experiences of life this is what we are waiting for, and all our training and discipline is to lead us to this.

I say waiting, not due to any delay on God's part but because of the delay on our own part. God is always seeking to make Himself our joy, but until we have been detached from all earthly joys and are ready to find our joy in Him alone, we must still wait for Him. We think that the delay is altogether on His part, but the real truth is that all the waiting that is necessary is for Him to wait for us.

To go to Him is nothing mysterious. It simply means to turn our minds to Him, to rest our hearts on Him, and to turn away from all other resting places. It means that we must not look at, think about, and trouble over our circumstances, our surroundings, our perplexities, or our experiences. We must look at and think about the Lord; we must ask ourselves not, "How do I feel about this?" but, "How does the Lord feel?" We must not ask, "How shall I manage it?" but, "How will He manage it?"

HANNAH WHITALL SMITH

*G*od, in His infinite grace, always takes the initiative in bringing us into a fuller experience of our inheritance in Christ. So the Lord Jesus stands outside the door of every unyielded room in your life seeking entrance. If He enters, the door must be opened from the inside.

RUTH PAXSON

. . . I tell you, there is rejoicing in the presence of the angels of God over one sinner who repents.

LUKE 15:10

*W*e cannot convey the Living Water to another heart without being watered ourselves on the way. There is no joy more exquisite than the joy of leading a soul to Christ. It is like the mother's strange, instinctive rapture over her newborn baby.

The other day a precious friend passed through the gates of Heaven a few moments after her baby was born, but in the hour of her agony her very first word was, "How is my baby?" It was the first thrill of that strange delight which is the very touch of the love which the Holy Spirit will give us for the souls He permits us to win for Christ. It is indeed a spiritual motherhood, and it has all the joy and all the pain of a mother's love.

Beloved, do you know the ecstasy of feeling the new life of an immortal spirit sweeping through your very veins, as, kneeling by the side of one just born to die no more, you place it, as a newborn babe in the bosom of your Savior?

You may know this joy, and every Christian ought to know it a hundredfold. It is the joy of angels, setting all the harps of heaven ringing, and surely it were strange if it were not the higher joy of ransomed saints.

A. B. SIMPSON

*W*e are left here to display Christ; if we are not doing this, we are of no use to the world.

EDWARD DENNETT

> *. . . . One thing I do: Forgetting what is behind and straining toward*
> *what is ahead, I press on toward the goal to win the prize for which*
> *God has called me heavenward in Christ Jesus.*
>
> PHILIPPIANS 3:13–14

*I*t is never wise to live in the past. There are, indeed, some uses of our past which are helpful, which bring blessing. We should remember our past lost condition to keep us humble and faithful. We should remember past mercies, that we may have confidence in new needs or trials in the future. We should remember past comforts, that there may be stars in our sky when night comes again.

But while there are these true uses of memory, we should guard against living in the past. We should draw our life's inspirations not from memory, but from hope; not from what is gone, but from what is yet to come. Forgetting the things which are behind, we should reach forward unto those things which are before.

J. R. MILLER

*T*here is a sense in which we do well to remember the past misdoings of our lives—that we may be humbled and warned; that we may not expose ourselves to temptations which have shown themselves too strong for us; that we may be led to a more careful self-watch and more entire dependence upon God. But we ought not to dwell upon our past sins as though they were ever present to the eye of God, and incapacitated us for high and holy service.

What would Peter have done on the Day of Pentecost if he had persisted in pensively dwelling on the scenes of the denial, and had not dared to believe that all was forgiven and forgotten? What would have been the effect on the [Apostle Paul], if he had allowed the memory of his share in the harrying of the saints to overcast his spirit when summoned to found churches, write epistles, and traverse continents?

When once we confess it, our sin is immediately and forever put away. God will never mention it again. It need not be a barrier on our service; it should not hinder us from aspiring to and enjoying the most intimate fellowship which is within the reach of mortals. Forget the past sins and failures of your life in the sense of brooding over them with perpetual lamentation.

F. B. MEYER

It is a positive barrier to blessing to trust to experience in the past.

E. P. C.

February 3

Whoever serves me must follow me; and where I am, my servant also will be. My Father will honor the one who serves me.
JOHN 12:26

Precious words! May they be engraved on our hearts, forever. Then shall we be steady in our course, and effective in our service. We shall not be distracted or unhinged by the thoughts and opinions of men.

It may happen that we shall get very few to understand us or sympathize with us—few to approve or appreciate our work. It matters not. The Master knows all about it. Let us only be sure of what He has told us to do, and do it. If a master tells one of his servants, distinctly, to go and do a certain thing, or occupy a certain post, it is his business to go and do that thing, or occupy that post, no matter what his fellow-servants may think. They may tell him that he ought to be somewhere else, or to do something else; but a proper servant will heed them not; he knows his master's mind, and has to do his master's work.

C. H. MACKINTOSH

While women weep as they do now—
I'll fight!
While little children go hungry as they do now—
I'll fight!
While men go to prison, in and out, in and out—
I'll fight!
While there is a drunkard left—
while there is a poor lost girl upon the streets—
where there remains on dark soul without the light of God—
I'll fight!
I'll fight to the very end!

General William Booth, Salvation Army

February 4

For God so loved the world, that he gave His only begotten Son, that whosoever believeth in Him should not perish, but have everlasting life.
John 3:16, KJV

*J*ust as an infant's hand can grasp the acorn which holds the giant oak within it, so the youngest child who can lisp "the Nicodemus sermon" of John 3:16 may with truth be said to know the gospel. And yet in every word of it there is a depth and mystery of meaning which God alone can fathom.

Tell me what it means to *perish*, and enable me to grasp the thought of a life that is eternal. Measure for me the abyss of man's wickedness and guilt during all the ages of his black and hateful history, that I may realize in some degree what that world is which God has loved. Then, pausing for a moment in wonder at the thought that such a world could be loved at all, hasten on to speak of love that gave the Son. And when you have enabled me to know this love, which cannot be known, for it passes knowledge, press on still and tell me of the sacrifice by which it has measured and proved itself—His Son, His Only-begotten Son.

Make me to know, in the fullness of knowledge, Him who declared that the Father alone could know Him. And when you have achieved all this, I turn again to the words of Christ, and I read that it was GOD who so loved the world, and I crave to know Who and What God is.

I can rise to the thought of love, perhaps even to an evil world, and the conception of love giving up an only son is not beyond me; but when I come to know that it was GOD who loved, that GOD was the giver, and GOD's Son the gift, I stand as a wondering worshipper in the presence of the Infinite, and confess that such knowledge is too high for me.

SIR ROBERT ANDERSON

*T*he world appears very little to a soul that contemplates the greatness of God. My business is to remain in the presence of God.

BROTHER LAWRENCE

*Y*our thoughts of God are too human.

MARTIN LUTHER

February 5

. . . always abounding in the work of the Lord.
1 CORINTHIANS 15:58, KJV

A wasted life is the result of unredeemed time. Careless work habits, impulsive giving, fitful planning, irregular reading, ill-assorted hours, perfunctory or unpunctual execution of business, hurry and bustle, loitering and unreadiness—these, and such like, are the things which take out the whole pith and power from life, which hinder holiness, and which eat like a canker into our moral being, which make success and progress an impossibility, either in things temporal or spiritual.

There needs not to be routine, but there must be regularity; there ought not to be mechanical stiffness, but there must be order; there may not be haste, but there must be no trifling with our own time or that of others.

If the thing is worth doing at all, it is worth doing well; and, in little things as well as great, we must show that we are in earnest. There must be no idling, but a girding up of the loins; a running the race with patience; the warring of a good warfare; steadfastness and perseverance, "always abounding in the work of the Lord."

The flowers are constant in their growing, the stars are constant in their courses; the rivers are constant in their flowing; they lose no time; so must our life be, not one of fits, or starts, or random impulses: not one of levity or inconstancy, or fickle scheming, but steady and resolute; the life of men who know their earthly mission, and have their eye upon the heavenly goal.

HORATIUS BONAR

*I*n my daily calling, make me diligent in business, fervent in spirit, serving the Lord. May I do my work, not for the wages I may get, nor to secure a promotion—but so as to please You, O Lord. May it be the one object of my daily striving to do all to the glory of God—not with eye-service, as pleasing men; but in singleness of heart, fearing the Lord; doing the will of God, as it is indicated in the circumstances of my life, and looking for my reward from your hand, O Divine Master!

F. B. MEYER

*L*et us build for the years we shall not see.

SIR HENRY JOHN NEWBOLT

Therefore, since we have been justified through faith, we have peace with God through our Lord Jesus Christ, through whom we have gained access by faith into this grace in which we now stand. And we rejoice in the hope of the glory of God.

ROMANS 5:1–2

*E*very Christian is justified by faith and has peace with God—therefore he rejoices in hope of the glory of God. It simply cannot be otherwise. It is true of you, too. Since Christ has justified you for time and eternity, since He has established peace between you and God for time and eternity, then He will also give you the glory of God when in due time He presents you with all His own, having neither spot, nor wrinkle, nor any such thing. You may look forward to this day with joyful expectation.

All of us have sinned and come short of the glory of God, but all who by the grace of God have been justified by faith are now convinced that when we see our Lord we shall be like Him. This is our hope.

We use the word "hope" in its biblical sense. Elsewhere hopes can be uncertain, but the biblical meaning involves absolute certainty, covering what God has promised will surely be for us at the appearing of our Lord Jesus Christ.

Just as no Christian has more peace with God than others, no one has more hope of the glory of God than others, for all is due to Christ alone. This is how Paul knows that the Romans also, though personally unknown to him, all rejoice in hope of the glory of God. And so do we!

PAOL MADSEN

*A*ll which happens in the whole world happens through hope. No farmer would sow a grain of corn, if he hadn't the hope that it would spring up and bring forth the ear. How much more are we helped on by hope in the way to eternal life.

MARTIN LUTHER

February 7

Hallelujah! Praise Jehovah from the heavens;
  praise him in the heights.
Praise ye him, all his angels;
  praise ye him, all his hosts.
Praise him, sun and moon;
  praise him, all ye stars of light.
Praise him, ye heavens of heavens,
  and ye waters that are above the heavens.
Let them praise the name of Jehovah,
  for he it is that commanded, and they were created:
And he established them for ever and ever;
  he made (for them) a statute which shall not pass.
Praise Jehovah from the earth,
  ye sea-monsters, and all deeps;
Fire and hail, snow and vapour,
  stormy wind fulfilling his word;
Mountains and all hills, fruit-trees and all cedars;
Beasts and all cattle, creeping things and winged fowl;
Kings of the earth and all peoples,
  princes and all judges of the earth;
Both young men and maidens, old men with youths,
Let them praise the name of Jehovah:
  for his name alone is exalted;
  his majesty is above the earth and the heavens.

And he hath lifted up the horn of his people,
  the praise of all his saints,
  (even) of the children of Israel,
  a people near unto him. Hallelujah!
<small>PSALM 148, DARBY</small>

There are four "Hallelujah Psalms" closing the Book of Psalms. They begin and end with "Hallelujah!"

I say, brother, sister, do you ever give the Lord a real, good, hearty, and reverent Hallelujah? Or are you afraid to hear your own voice saying it? And so you think it instead, or it comes out under your breath!

Oh, you say, "the Psalms are all Jewish and literal, and we are Christians and worship God by the Spirit, and it is quiet, and reverent, and not a thing for outward show." Oh, that's it, is it? But how about the prayers and the blessings in Psalms?

Don't you use their very language in some of your prayers when your soul has been in great distress like David? Do you never take Him at His word and "open your mouth wide" because He said He would fill it if you did so? Or did you never "call upon Him in the day of trouble" and find Him true to His word and "deliver you"?

Oh, fie, my brother! You creep in to get your share in the blessing—you know you do! And you creep in oftener still to tell Him your troubles and ask Him for help, you know you do! In fact you visit the Psalms, and use the Psalms oftener than any of the other books of the Bible, because they just express your feelings—you know you do!

Then why not chime in and give a real, hearty, Hallelujah? Don't be afraid lest the angels should hear you; they'll do it themselves by and by "with a loud voice" (Rev. 5), and glad of the chance, too! It would do you a lot of good to praise the Lord a little more than you do at present. Just you try it!

<small>WILLIAM EASTON</small>

The secret of victory is not praying, but praising; not asking but thanking. All eternity will not be long enough to finish praising and thanking our Lord Jesus Christ for the simple, glorious fact that His grace *is* sufficient for us.

CHARLES G. TRUMBULL

February 8

Even if I should choose to boast, I would not be a fool, because I would be speaking the truth. But I refrain, so no one will think more of me than is warranted by what I do or say. To keep me from becoming conceited because of these surpassingly great revelations, there was given me a thorn in my flesh, a messenger of Satan, to torment me. Three times I pleaded with the Lord to take it away from me. But he said to me, "My grace is sufficient for you, for my power is made perfect in weakness." Therefore I will boast all the more gladly about my weaknesses, so that Christ's power may rest on me. That is why, for Christ's sake, I delight in weaknesses, in insults, in hardships, in persecutions, in difficulties. For when I am weak, then I am strong.

2 CORINTHIANS 12:6–10

The one who would walk in victory must also take heed not to glory in, or boast of his experiences. Often he may not even *tell them* without opening the door to the evil one. The Apostle Paul felt it necessary to draw a veil over this aspect of his inner life. "I forbear to speak," he said, "that I may not cause any man to think of me more highly than when he sees my deeds, or hears my teaching."

Paul knew how men were disposed to "glory in men" and account them wonderful, as the Lycaonians did Barnabas and himself when they saw the miracle of healing done in the crippled man in answer to their simple words. "We are men of like nature with you," the Apostles cried, as with horror they sought to prevent them giving them the worship due to God alone.

In the life of Paul we also see the means used by the Lord to counterbalance the danger of "abundance of revelations"—for Paul is given a "thorn in the flesh," a "messenger of Satan" to buffet him, so that he should not be exalted overmuch. The Lord's plan fulfilled its purpose, for the Apostle is kept broken and humbled, saying, "I delight in weaknesses, in insults, in hardships, in persecutions, in difficulties. For when I am weak, then I am strong."

We need to walk carefully with God at this stage of the spiritual life, and hide very deeply in the Cross, not coveting wonderful experiences, but rather an ever-deepening conformity to the death of Jesus, that the life of Jesus may be manifested to all around.

Let us realize too that our faith is more precious to God than gold, and be content to walk by faith not sight. We need to remember also that "visions and revelations" are not given to the soul for its own comfort or enjoyment, but for some definite purpose in the counsels of God, or in a special and critical time of need, as with the Apostle Paul when he was stoned in Lystra called to Macedonia; or needed clear guidance to remain in Athens. But normally, as the believer matures, the "eyes of his heart"—the *spiritual power of sight* possessed by the inner man of the new creation—must be more and more filled with light. Thus the spiritual vision becomes acute, and able to see the things of the spiritual world, not so much by "revelations" as by the simple power of *seeing*, a faculty of the Christian which is called by Paul "discernment."

At all stages of experience let the one who would walk in safety in the Spirit-sphere, test all visions and revelations, by direct appeal to the Spirit to apply the power of the death of Christ, which disperses all that may come from the adversary fashioned as an angel of light. Then quickly any counterfeit will fade away, and the believer will press on victoriously over all wiles of the devil.

JESSIE PENN-LEWIS

If you remain in me and my words remain in you, ask whatever you wish, and it will be given you.

JOHN 15:7

*I*n creation God acts sovereignly and alone. But in the unfolding of His redemptive purposes, He wills it otherwise. He chooses to unite with Himself human instruments and share with them the excitement of creativity. The incarnation was part of the working out of this plan.

In sending His Son to become man, God revealed in a new way His purpose to limit Himself to working in and through a relationship with man. The vital, indispensable part of this working relationship is prayer. God communicated His will to the Son in the intensive exercise of prayer that occupied so many of our Lord's nights in desert places.

Then on earth, working according to His Father's will, the Human Instrument acted in the performance of signs and wonders, counting on the power he had requested in prayer because His will was one with the Father's.

This brings us to the basic divine principle in prayer—that God unites His people with Himself in whatever He wants to do, first leading them to pray and then giving the thing for which He burdened them to pray. God's will is to send rain on Ahab's drought-stricken land. He will not act alone. He unites Elijah with Him in His purposes by communicating to him His intention; then when Elijah prays, God acts. Elijah could bring a drought on Israel in the first place, not just because he prayed the rain out of the sky, but because he could first say, "As the Lord God of Israel liveth, before whom I stand." He was not initiating some self-conceived idea, but was acting with God for the performance of God's will ... for just such a situation as prevailed in his days.

The same principle is taught by the Lord Jesus in His Upper Room discourse under the symbolism of the vine and the branches. Abiding in Him is the condition He established for our asking and His acting. What had been set up as the working arrangement between Himself and His Father is perpetuated in the New Covenant-based relationship between Himself and His Church. It was to be standard operational procedure.

ARTHUR MATTHEWS

*P*rayer is an impossible task without the Holy Spirit.

SAMUEL CHADWICK

*W*hen God intends great mercy for His people, He first sets them praying.

MATTHEW HENRY

February 10

"Now give me this hill country that the Lord promised me that day. You yourself heard then that the Anakites were there and their cities were large and fortified, but, the Lord helping me, I will drive them out just as he said."

Then Joshua blessed Caleb son of Jephunneh and gave him Hebron as his inheritance. So Hebron has belonged to Caleb son of Jephunneh the Kenizzite ever since, because he followed the Lord, the God of Israel, wholeheartedly.

JOSHUA 14:12–14

*M*any people are all the time thinking of their failures, and by so doing they pave the way for further failure. Defeat is certain if we are constantly contemplating defeat. If we keep thinking there is no

way through, that thought blocks the way through. We are coura-
geous only as we keep God's promises in view. Alas that so many of
God's people lack the virile faith that characterized Caleb and con-
centrate their thoughts on the intensity of their sufferings and the
insurmountable nature of their difficulties! But those who do not
fear "the sons of Anak"—the giants that inhabit the land of
promise—are "well able to overcome." Caleb was so unafraid of the
Anakim that he actually requested Joshua to appoint as his portion
in the land of promise the mountain in which they had their
stronghold (Joshua 14:12–15). He was not dismayed by the fact that
they were "men of great stature," nor by the fact that their cities
were "great and fenced," so he overcame them without any strain.

The whole question in relation to overcoming is: Are you trusting in yourself, or are you trusting in the Lord? If you are relying
on yourself then of course you have to consider whether the
Anakim are strong or weak, and whether their cities are well fortified or not; but if your reliance is on God, then the question of
human resources does not even arise. If you are trusting in God
there is no ground for fear since victory is assured to all who put
their trust in Him.

There is another noteworthy matter in connection with Caleb.
He exhorted the whole congregation of the children of Israel, saying: "Rebel not against the Lord, neither fear ye the people of the
land; for they are bread for us." He sought to show the children of
Israel that in the land itself there were resources upon which they
could draw in order to possess it. "The people of the land ... are
bread for us," he declared. What is bread? Bread is something you
eat. Bread is something that brings increased strength. The inhabitants of the land were admittedly "men of great stature," but Caleb
promised that they were food for God's people. He not only honored God's promises, he despised the difficulties that stood in the
way of their realization. And every true believer, like Caleb, honors

God and lightly esteems all obstacles. But this leaves no room for pride, for only they who humble themselves before God are able to take their stand on His side.

Every time you meet a difficulty, every time you find yourself in an impossible situation, ask yourself this question: Am I going to starve here, or am I going to eat the food that is set before me? If you are relying on the Lord for victory and let His overcoming life be manifested in you, you will find fresh nourishment and increased vitality in accepting as "bread" those Anakim that are contesting your progress. Do bear in mind that people who do not eat well cannot grow into maturity. Many people take the Word of God as their meat and the doing of His will as their meat, but they reject the Anakim as unpalatable food. The more we eat such food the stronger we shall become. Caleb is a grand illustration of this. Because he accepted the Anakim as "bread" he was still full of vitality at the age of eighty-five: So many Anakim had been assimilated by him over the years that he had developed a constitution which showed no trace of age.

So it is in the spiritual realm. Some brothers and sisters have met few difficulties, but they are spiritually feeble. The explanation is, they have not consumed enough Anakim. On the other hand there are those who have met and overcome difficulty after difficulty, temptation after temptation; and they are full of vigor. The reason is, they have fed well on Anakim. Every difficulty and every temptation Satan puts in our way is food for us. This is a divinely appointed means of spiritual progress. The sight of any great trouble strikes terror into the heart of those who do not believe God, but those who trust Him say: "Praise God, here is some more food!" All our trials, without exception, are bread for us, and as we accept one trial after the other, we are more and more richly nourished and the result is a continuous increase of strength.

WATCHMAN NEE

*E*xtraordinary afflictions are not always the punishment of extraordinary sins, but sometimes the trial of extraordinary graces. Sanctified afflictions are spiritual promotions.

MATTHEW HENRY

*W*hich would you rather have, a smooth path, or a path so rough that the Lord is compelled to show His face to you every step of the way?

GEORGE V. WIGRAM

February 11

O the depth of the riches both of the wisdom and knowledge of God! How unsearchable are his judgments, and his ways past finding out.
ROMANS 11:33

*I*f you ask me how I know that the Lord is present, since His ways are past finding out, my answer is that the Word is living and active, and as soon as ever He entered me, He aroused my sleeping soul, and stirred and softened and pricked my heart, that had been sick and as hard as stone.

He began to pluck up and destroy, to build and plant, to water the dry places and shed light upon the dark, to open what was shut, to warm the chill, to make the crooked straight and the rough places plain; so that my soul has blessed the Lord and all that is within me has praised His holy Name.

Thus has the Bridegroom entered into me; my senses told me nothing of His coming, I knew that He was present only by the movement of my heart. I perceived His power, because it put my sins to flight and exercises a strong control on all my impulses. I am moved to wonder at His wisdom too, uncovering my secret faults and teaching me to see their sinfulness; and I have experienced His gentleness and kindness in such measure as to astonish me.

In the renewal and remaking of the spirit of my mind—that is, my inmost being—I have beheld the beauty of His glory and have been filled with awe as I gazed at His manifold greatness.

BERNARD OF CLAIRVAUX

*G*od is such an infinite blessing that every sense of His glorious presence gives gladness to the heart. Every step toward Him, is likewise, a measure of happiness.

SUSANNA WESLEY

February 12

You adulterous people, don't you know that friendship with the world is hatred toward God? Anyone who chooses to be a friend of the world becomes an enemy of God.

JAMES 4:4

*S*uch a thing as the Holy Spirit taking up His abode and dwelling in a human being never took place in the history of mankind till our Lord Jesus Christ rose from the dead.

The Holy Spirit had entered into men, took hold of them, came upon them, moved them and greatly used them, but He never made the body His permanent dwelling place.

But He does this great thing today.

Today He enters the body of the believer, owning it as a blood-bought body, and makes it His temple, the most wonderful, the most sacred, temple on earth, the most sacred thing this side of Heaven.

It is this indwelling of the Holy Spirit that rails us off as believers from the world, from all material beings, from angels and spirits, from all other creatures in the universe of God.

Just as Aaron and his sons were separated from the camp and separated themselves from it, we are to own ourselves in this age as a separated people and shut ourselves up by faith with Christ in His Holy Place.

The true Church, the living and spiritual Church, can find no place, no comfort, nor fellowship with a world system that repudiates her Lord; no matter what schemes of morals or righteousness the world may advertise, the Church can have no partnership therein; she is not called to cleanse Sodom, but to come out of it, not to empty old wells but to dig new ones, and under no circumstances to identify herself with reformation, but to demand regeneration.

I. M. HALDEMAN

A Christian in the world is like a man who has had a long intimacy with one, whom he eventually discovers was the murderer of a kind father. The intimacy, after this, will surely be broken.

JOHN NEWTON

February 13

For me, to live is Christ and to die is gain.
PHILIPPIANS 1:21

A Christian is one who has become spiritually alive from the dead. The presence of spiritual life within him is the one fundamental thing that distinguishes him from the unregenerate world about him.

This spiritual life is not native to us, nor can it be *developed* out of anything we have or are by nature. It must be *given* to us. So God has given us eternal life, "and this life is in His Son," through whose possession of us when we believed on him we were born from above; "not of blood, nor of the will of the flesh, nor of the will of man, but of God"; by which we have become a "new creation" in Christ, being thereby made "partakers of the divine nature."

The life of a Christian, therefore, is the life of Christ within us through the Holy Spirit. It is not a life similar to his, it is *his life*. This is shown by the fact that what we receive in the new birth is not only "everlasting life," but also "eternal life," which is far more than "everlasting life." For while everlasting life has no end, yet it may have a beginning; but eternal life has neither beginning nor end.

Now the Triune God is the only one in the universe who has eternal life. The only way He can give us eternal life, therefore, is to possess us with his own life, through Christ, by the Holy Spirit. This is one thing Paul meant when he said, "To me to live *is Christ.*" This is a mystery that is too high for us. We can none of us understand it; but we can believe it.

J. E. CONANT

*H*appiness is neither within us only, or outside of us. Rather, it is the union of ourselves with God.

BLAISE PASCAL

February 14

According as he hath chosen us in him before the foundation of the world . . .
EPHESIANS 1:4A, KJV

*T*here is great comfort in the doctrine of election. It tells me that my history is a very old one. It did not begin when I believed. My faith in Christ was an event or fact far down in the course of my history.

The story itself, written (wondrous to tell it!) by a divine hand, began before the world was formed, and covenant counsels concerning me constituted the first great fact. My foundation is *there*, be my faith weak or strong.

Others brightly outshine me, and rapidly outrun me. I will rejoice in that, and neither envy their fruitfulness, nor be alarmed because of my comparative leanness. My origin is as divine, and venerable, and holy as theirs, and my foundation as immovable. Much more luxuriant branches may spread themselves at my side, but we have all one root.

"Crumbs for the Little Ones"

People may quarrel with the sovereignty of God, but I love it, because I know enough about my natural bent and will to be sure that if left to myself I should have gone straight to perdition. Some believers talk about free will when they are on their feet, but all are firm believers in God's sovereignty when they get on their knees.

C. A. Coates

February 15

It is the spirit that quickeneth; the flesh profiteth nothing: the words that I speak unto you, they are spirit, and they are life.
John 6:63, kjv

Very few persons realize the effect of thought upon the condition of the soul; that it is in fact its food, the substance from which it evolves its strength and health and beauty, or upon which it may become weak and unhealthy and deformed.

The things we think about are the things we feed upon. If we think low and corrupt thoughts, we bring diseases upon our body by eating corrupt and improper food. The man who thinks about self feeds on self just in proportion to the amount of thought he gives to self. He may at last become puffed up with self and suffer from the dreadful disease of self-conceit and self-importance.

On the other hand, if we think of Christ, we feed on Christ. We eat His flesh and blood by filling our souls with believing thoughts of Him.

The Jews asked, "How can this man give us his flesh to eat?" And a great many people ask the same today.

The answer becomes apparent to those who fill their souls with believing thoughts of Christ. They will find practically that they do feed upon Him, to the joy and delight of their hearts.

Jesus confirms this when He says, "It is the spirit that quickeneth; the flesh profiteth nothing: the words that I speak unto you, they are spirit, and they are life." He meant them to understand that to feed on Him was to receive and believe His words, that it was not His literal flesh they were to eat, but the words that He spake unto them, the truths that He taught them.

HANNAH WHITALL SMITH

*F*eed on Christ, and then go and live your life, and it is Christ in you that lives your life, that helps the poor, that tells only the truth, that fights the battle and that wins the crown.

PHILLIPS BROOKS

February 16

Cast all your anxiety on him because he cares for you.
1 PETER 5:7

*H*ave you one anxious thought you do not bring to Jesus? Have you one care you consider too light, too small, to lay before Him? It is then too small to give you one moment's concern. Either cast your care (great or small) upon Him that careth for you, or cast it away from you altogether: if it be unfit for His sympathy, it is unworthy of you.

If we examine the troubles of God's children, we shall find that too many of them arise from unbelieving fears concerning the future; let me but remember that Christ, at the right hand of God, counts *all my* troubles *His own*; and then banish all my fears concerning tomorrow!

ROBERT C. CHAPMAN

*O*ne finds constantly that ninety percent of our trials and sorrows are made up of anticipated or imaginary evils, which only exist in our disordered, unbelieving minds.

"FOOD FOR THE DESERT"

*Y*ou would not be easily startled by events if you saw all that you have in Christ to enable you to meet everything calmly.

GEORGE V. WIGRAM

*Y*ou ought to begin your day with this confidence, that you have enough in Christ to meet every difficulty that may befall you.

J. B. STONEY

February 17

And it came to pass, when he had made an end of speaking unto Saul, that the soul of Jonathan was knit with the soul of David: and Jonathan loved him as his own soul . . . Then Jonathan and David made a covenant, because he loved him as his own soul. And Jonathan stripped himself of the robe that was upon him, and gave it to David, and his garments, even to his sword, and to his bow, and to his girdle.

1 SAMUEL 18:1–4, KJV

*W*hat an exquisite picture we have here! A picture of love stripping itself to clothe its object. There is a vast difference between Saul and his son, Jonathan. Saul took David home with him in order to magnify himself by keeping such an important hero near him and in his house.

But Jonathan stripped himself to clothe David. This was love in one of its charming activities. Jonathan, in common with the many thousands of Israel, had watched, with breathless interest, the scene in the valley of Elah. He had seen David go forth, single-handed, to meet the terrible foe, Goliath, whose height, demeanor, and words had struck terror into the hearts of the people. He had seen that haughty giant laid low by the hand of faith. He participated with all in the splendid victory.

But there was more than this. It was not merely the victory but the victor that filled the heart of Jonathan—not merely the work done, but the one who had done it. Jonathan was not satisfied with saying, "Thank God, the giant is dead, and we are delivered, and may return to our homes and enjoy ourselves."

Ah! no; he felt his heart drawn and knit to the person of the conqueror. It was not that he valued the victory less, but he valued the victor more, and hence he found his joy in stripping himself of his robes and his armor in order to put them upon the object of his affection.

Christian, there is a lesson here for us; and not only a lesson but a rebuke. How prone are we to be occupied with redemption rather than the Redeemer—with salvation rather than with the Savior!

No doubt we should rejoice in our salvation; but should we rest here? Should we not, like Jonathan, seek to strip ourselves in order to magnify the Person of Him who went down into the dust of death for us? Assuredly we should, and all the more because He does not exact aught of us. David did not ask Jonathan for his robe or his sword. Had he done so, it would have robbed the scene of all its charms. But no; it was a purely voluntary act. Jonathan forgot himself and thought only of David.

Thus it should be with us and the true David. Love delights to strip itself for its object.

Oh! for more of this spirit of humility! May our hearts be drawn out and knit, more and more, to Christ, in this day of hollow profession, and empty, religious formality! May we be so filled with the Holy Spirit, that with purpose of heart we may cleave unto our Lord and Savior Jesus Christ!

C. H. MACKINTOSH

*T*here is great need for David's mighty men in this day—*men devoted to David.* The nation gains from their services, but they are thinking only of David.

J. B. STONEY

February 18

Knowing therefore the terror of the Lord, we persuade men . . .
2 CORINTHIANS 5:11A, KJV

*H*as the *fear of Christ*, the One, Who sits in glory at the right hand of God, its due sway over our consciences? I am not speaking of legal or slavish fear but of a reverential fear, which is produced by *authority*, when recognized, felt, and willingly *bowed* to.

A soldier, when in the presence of those higher in authority, feels very different from what he does, when among his equals. And the higher the rank or lawful authority of the one in the superior place, the greater would be the sense of reverential fear on the part of his subordinate before his presence.

Any soldier, however submissive, if he be a good soldier, his behavior may be before his superiors, if only a degree or two above him in rank, will feel and behave very differently, when standing before his commander-in-chief. And in the presence of the highest authority, of a mighty King or Emperor, will not that feeling of reverential fear, produced by such a presence, pervade every one before him, from the commander-in-chief or his Prime Minister down to the lowest servant? ... We have understood so little, what it means, in the power of faith and of an ungrieved Spirit, to be really in His Presence, where we discover our nothingness, yes, and our own *good-for-nothingness* too.

We have been too much in the presence of each other, or of the world and daily circumstances, permitting all kinds of things, such as the church, ministry, plus much else to step in between Christ and our souls, instead of keeping Christ between us and circumstances.

Thus it is that the "fear of Christ," which is produced by being in His Presence, is so feebly known amongst and within us. It is all right and well, talking of the constraining love of Christ, but let us not forget that His great apostle Paul knew also what "the terror of the Lord" means.

Not, I repeat, as if that terror made him tremble in slavish fear, but it had impressed his conscience with its awful solemnity *for others*, so that he was able to "*persuade*" men—to appeal to their consciences first with the power of a preacher whose own heart had been solemnized by the thought of the terror of the Lord. And *then* feeling in his heart the constraining power of the *love* of Christ, he was enabled to "*beseech* poor sinners and enemies to be reconciled to God."

His own conscience was clear. He was perfect and at ease in the Presence of God, but his heart was solemnly impressed with what "the terror of the Lord" meant for His rejectors. So, in the power of that solemn impression he reached out to every unbeliever he could, and appealed to their consciences, all the while remembering the "small voice" of God's grace in his ministry of reconciliation, and applying the balm of the gospel to brokenhearted and troubled ones.

J. A. VON POSECK

The fear of God kills all other fears.

HUGH BLACK

February 19

For you died, and your life is now hidden with Christ in God.
COLOSSIANS 3:3

The redeemed one who has been shown the truth of Christ's complete victory over Satan, and of his own complete identification with his victorious Lord, knows that he is in a place of safety.

He rests upon the fact that his life is *hid with Christ in God*; therefore the wicked one touches him not. He has but one thing to do—reckon upon the fact of his identification with his Ascended Lord sitting in the calmness of assured victory.

MARY MCDONOUGH

It is because our life is hid with Christ in God that it is beyond the reach of Satan. The Enemy cannot touch our life in its source, for the Father is its Source and he cannot touch Him. He cannot touch our life in its channel, for the risen Lord Jesus is its channel, and he cannot touch Him. He cannot touch our life in its power, for the Holy Spirit is its power, and he cannot touch the Spirit. He cannot touch our life in its duration, for eternity is its duration, and he cannot touch eternity. The child of God is eternally safe.

J. E. CONANT

February 20

... if any man build upon this foundation gold, silver, precious stones, wood, hay, stubble; Every man's work shall be made manifest: for the day shall declare it. . . .

1 Corinthians 3:12–13a, kjv

The only power God recognizes in His church is the power of His Spirit whereas the only power actually recognized today by the majority of evangelicals is the power of man. God does His work by the operation of the Spirit, while Christian leaders attempt to do theirs by the power of trained and devoted intellect. Bright personality has taken the place of divine anointing.

Everything that men do in their own strength and by means of their own abilities is done for time alone; the quality of eternity is not in it. Only what is done through the Eternal Spirit will abide eternally; all else is wood, hay, stubble.

A. W. Tozer

Only one life, 'twill soon be past, only what's done for Christ will last.

And when I'm dying, how happy I'll be, if the lamp of my life has been burned out for Thee.

Author Unknown

February 21

...To them God has chosen to make known among the Gentiles the glorious riches of this mystery, which is Christ in you, the hope of glory.

Colossians 1:27

When the Holy Spirit comes into our hearts He brings Christ in the completeness of His finished work on the cross, and then proceeds progressively to conform us to Christ.

Do you realize that the Christ in you is not an imperfect Christ? When the Lord Jesus wrought His Calvary work He not only dealt with the matter of forgiveness but He went right on to the perfection of redemption, finally reaching the throne as the great Overcomer.

In Him, the Person, the whole ground of spiritual experience is covered and completed. There is no experience that can ever come to you or me which makes impossible the reaching of God's end, for Christ has already met and overcome it.

So we are not to struggle in vain attempts after perfection, but to cooperate with the Holy Spirit as He seeks to make good in us the power of Christ's finished work on the cross. It is Christ in you who is the hope of glory. Anything less or anything else will bring no hope of glory but rather despair.

T. Austin-Sparks

*T*he perfection of the Christian life is to lose sight of oneself completely and to make everything of Christ.

The sign of a good state of soul is enjoyment of the presence of Christ.

Edward Dennett

February 22

But God forbid that I should glory, save in the cross our Lord Jesus Christ, by whom the world is crucified unto me, and I unto the world.
Galatians 6:14, kjv

*T*he cross is the secret of power. The cross is what we can glory in. It sets us aside, breaks us to pieces, writes upon us the sentence of death, in order that the power of Christ, through the Holy Spirit, may rest upon us. The one who has learned death, who has the sentence of death in himself, is the one who will have power . . .

You are to make a complete surrender of your will, strength, time, talents—all that you are and have to be put upon the altar. But *who* makes this surrender, and what is the altar? If *you* make the surrender, it is self surrendering self, a most subtle form of self-righteousness. But when we see it is the cross of our Lord—that cross by which I am, I was crucified, in His death; that "I am crucified with Christ"—when we see this, we find that it is not a question of surrender for me, but of the cross which has set me aside, that Christ may be all. Anything short of the cross only fosters pride, and pride in its worst form.

SAMUEL RIDOUT

The Cross is like the fruit of the walnut tree. The outer rind is bitter, but the kernel is refreshing and strengthening. From the outside the Cross has neither beauty nor goodness; its essence is only revealed to those who bear it. They find a kernel of spiritual sweetness and inward peace.

SADU SUNDAR SINGH

February 23

Don't you know that you yourselves are God's temple and that God's Spirit lives in you? If anyone destroys God's temple, God will destroy him; for God's temple is sacred, and you are that temple.

1 CORINTHIANS 3:16

You will remember that in the Upper Room, in that last talk of the Lord to His disciples, He spoke very much about the Holy Spirit. One thing He said was, "He is with you, and shall be in you."

Was He not in them then? Apparently not. The Spirit was active and operating in the Old Testament dispensation. He came *upon* the people of God, and upon some specially for special service, but He did not *indwell* and *abide*. What is characteristic of this Christian age as distinguished from that age is the fact that now He not only comes *upon* the people of God, but dwells *within* them.

This is a matter which does not depend upon Christian accomplishment and character. Notice that the passage occurs in the letter to the Church at Corinth. We know what state that Church was in, from what is said to it in these two letters; the type of life was low, the witness was poor, and the members were chargeable with moral and theological error. The apostle does not say, "Don't you know that you *should* be indwelt by the Holy Spirit, and if only you would dedicate yourselves to God, He would come and indwell you?" On the contrary, he makes the fact of their being indwelt the ground and reason for a nobler type of Christian life.

They boasted of their knowledge, and the apostle says, "With all your knowing, do you not know this, that you are a temple of God, and that the Spirit of God dwells in you?"

Of course, this is a profound mystery. We cannot say how a person can dwell in a person. But all the great truths are profound mysteries. We must receive them by faith, and as we do so we shall have some experience of what is declared. The Spirit of God indwells us, that is to say, He is not sojourning with us, but abiding in us.

W. Graham Scroggie

February 24

Do you not know that in a race all the runners run, but only one gets the prize? Run in such a way as to get the prize. Everyone who competes in the games goes into strict training. They do it to get a crown that will not last; but we do it to get a crown that will last forever. Therefore I do not run like a man running aimlessly; I do not fight like a man beating the air. No, I beat my body and make it my slave so that after I have preached to others, I myself will not be disqualified for the prize.

1 CORINTHIANS 9:24–27

*T*here is a race set before us. Every human life may be viewed as a race, even as every human life may be compared with a fight.

There is, however, a good fight of faith, and there is a bad fight against and without faith. So there is the race which the world sets before us, which our own ambition chooses, and which we run in our own unrenewed energy—and there is the race set before us of God, on which we enter when we give our hearts to Jesus, and hear from His lips the words of majesty and love—"Follow Me."

The one race appeals to us in our natural state: animated by merely human, if not sinful motives, and pursuing earthly methods, we may reach the goal—a crown of fading leaves; but in the God-appointed race, all is of God—heavenly, spiritual, and eternal. The prize of the high calling in Christ Jesus is the crown, immortal and unfading, the inheritance of light and blessedness, the throne of Jesus Himself, who will associate with Himself the disciples, who have overcome and finished their course.

The method and laws of the race are the words of Jesus abiding in the heart, the mind of Christ implanted by the Holy Ghost. The strength and energy of the race is the influence, faith-renewing, which the Lord sends unto all that wait upon Him. The race is set before us of God, and God renews our strength to run the race.

ADOLPH SAPHIR

Also before the throne there was what looked like a sea of glass, clear as crystal. In the center, around the throne, were four living creatures, and they were covered with eyes, in front and in back. The first living creature was like a lion, the second was like an ox, the third had a face like a man, the fourth was like a flying eagle. Each of the four living creatures had six wings and was covered with eyes all around, even under his wings. Day and night they never stop saying: "Holy, holy, holy is the Lord God Almighty, who was, and is, and is to come." Whenever the living creatures give glory, honor and thanks to him who sits on the throne and who lives for ever and ever, the twenty-four elders fall down before him who sits on the throne, and worship him who lives for ever and ever. They lay their crowns before the throne and say: "You are worthy, our Lord and God, to receive glory and honor and power, for you created all things, and by your will they were created and have their being."

REVELATION 4:6–11

*C*onsidering that God is the only perfect Being, that He is infinitely glorious and good, the greatest good that can possibly come to man is that he may know Him.

As we come to know God better through His Word, and through the Holy Spirit's work within us, we realize that He gives us an inward sense of His blessedness, a realization of His glories and beauties of His Being and attributes. Those who are privileged to know Him thus are changed more and more into His image.

Now worship is just an outward expression of this inward knowledge and appreciation of Him. When the heavenly beings cry, "Holy, holy, holy, LORD God Almighty," they are filled with an inward appreciation of His holiness. It would not be acceptable to God for them to cry out an acknowledgment of His holiness if they knew nothing of it.

Through outward expression of the inward blessing of the knowledge of God, we are able to become channels of these infinite blessings. We cannot hold much at a time, but we can overflow; "My cup runneth over." When we realize that worshipping God is not just going through a form of bowing down to Him, but a blessed experience of the new nature, through the help of God's Holy Spirit, we come to know something of God's greatness and infinite worth as we actually experience the Holy Spirit's leadings. What marvelous things are in store for us in glory when we shall be better able to rejoice in the more perfect knowledge of Him!

Le Baron W. Kinney

*A*ll that makes heaven a home to Christ will make it a home to me. O come, Lord Jesus!

John Darby

February 26

Yet I hold this against you: You have forsaken your first love. Remember the height from which you have fallen! Repent and do the things you did at first. If you do not repent, I will come to you and remove your lampstand from its place.

Revelation 2:4–5

A saintly African Christian told a congregation once that, as he was climbing the hill to the meeting, he heard steps behind him. He turned and saw a man carrying a very heavy load up the hill on his back. He was full of sympathy for him and spoke to him. Then he noticed that His hands were scarred, and he realized that it was Jesus.

He said to Him, "Lord, are you carrying the world's sins up the hill?"

"No," said the Lord Jesus, "Not the *world's* sins, just yours!" As that African simply told the vision God had just given him, the people's hearts and his heart were broken as they saw their sins at the Cross. Our hearts need to be broken too, and only when they are shall we be willing for the confessions, the apologies, the reconciliations and the restitutions, that are involved in a true repentance of sin. Then, when we have been willing to humble ourselves, as the Lord humbled Himself, the Dove will return to us.

ROY HESSION

Oh, to be but emptier, lowlier,
Mean, unnoticed and unknown,
And to God a vessel holier,
Filled with Christ, and Christ alone;
Naught of earth to cloud the glory,
Naught of self the light to dim,
Telling forth the wondrous story,
Emptied—to be filled with Him.

P. G.

February 27

. . . the worshippers once purged should have had no conscience of sins.
HEBREWS 10:2, KJV

There is no such thing now as a worshipper once purged, having any more conscience of sins. God does not impute sin to the believer, He never makes a claim on me for a sin again.

Again I say, He has no claim against me regarding sin. If He had a claim on me, there must be an atonement.

Do you mean He passes sin over? No—that which does the sin will pay for the sin, if you do not judge it. Mark my words! You will find in your history that this is true—the thing that does the sins will pay for the sin, will suffer for the sin, unless you judge it.

Paul said, "Deliver ... to Satan for the destruction of the flesh"—that was not atonement for him—"Deliver ... to Satan for the destruction of the flesh, that the spirit might be saved in the day of the Lord Jesus." I say, beloved friends, if you have really judged your sin, you have put it as far from you as God has put it from Himself. He put it away on the cross, there is no other place for you; that is really what liberty is.

J. B. STONEY

*A*ll believers, then, are accepted—perfectly and forever accepted in the Beloved. God sees them in Christ, and as Christ, He thinks of them as the He thinks of Him; loves them as He loves Him. They are ever before Him, in perfect acceptance in the blessed Son of His love, nor can anything, or anyone, ever interfere with this, their high and glorious position, which rest on the eternal stability of the grace of God, the accomplished work of His Son, and attested by the Holy Spirit sent down from heaven.

C. H. MACKINTOSH

February 28

Wherein ye greatly rejoice, though now for a season, if needs be, ye are in heaviness through manifold temptations.

1 PETER 1:6, KJV

*T*he Lord makes no mistakes. So, whatever comes to us, then, let our hearts just turn to the Father, with this thought, "There is a 'needs be'."

Moreover, these trials are not always chastisement, they are His training of His children. There is such a thing as *education*, not instruction merely. He wants to draw out, to develop, to make manifest that which is the result of His own grace working in our souls, that which is the fruit of the Spirit, "love, joy, peace, long-suffering," and He takes His own way to produce these lovely fruits.

You and I may often not see the "needs be" for this or that trial, but what does our Father say? There is a needs be: and as it is only for "*a season*" and is not to last for ever, this sustains the heart.

It is a great thing for our souls always to seek to find the bright side of every trial, and to have beaming, radiant faces all the while we are in deep trouble!

Look at Paul and Silas at Philippi. What could be more dismal? Thrust into the inner prison, and their feet made fast in the stocks, what do we find them doing?—praying and singing praises to God. They were exercising their holy, royal priesthoods in that prison.

When they sang praises they were holy priests; when they said to the terrified jailer, "Do thyself no harm, for we are all here," they were royal priests. It is a charming picture! They are as full of joy as they can be, and they get that jailer converted! That was the wonderful result of their bleeding, wounded backs—that previously godless and apparently unreachable soul was saved!

Tribulation will come in various ways, but we must make up our minds to accept it while here, "Knowing that tribulation worketh patience; and patience experience; and experience hope; and hope maketh not ashamed; because the love of God is shed abroad in our hearts, by the Holy Ghost which is given unto us" (Rom. 5:3–5).

But the pathway of trial has a very bright end. "That the trial of your faith, being much more precious than of gold that perisheth, though it be tried with fire, might be found unto praise and honor and glory at the appearing of Jesus Christ" (v. 7). Faith's sphere is on earth, and God tries it. He never gives faith that He does not prove it; and this brings forth the fruit that will appear in eternity, when everything is made manifest, at the appearing of Jesus Christ.

W. T. P. WOLSTON

*R*eceive every inward and outward trouble, every disappointment, pain, uneasiness, temptation, darkness and desolation with *both hands* as a true opportunity and blessed occasion of dying to self, and entering into fuller fellowship with thy self-denying and suffering Savior. Look at no inward or outward trouble in any other way. *Reject* every other thought about it, then every kind of trial and distress will be the blessed day of thy prosperity.

WILLIAM LAW

*F*aith must pass through the furnace—it will not do to *say* that we trust in the Lord, we must *prove* that we do, and that when everything is against us.

C. H. MACKINTOSH

February 29

Now on his way to Jerusalem, Jesus traveled along the border between Samaria and Galilee. As he was going into a village, ten men who had leprosy met him. They stood at a distance and called out in a loud voice, "Jesus, Master, have pity on us!"

When he saw them, he said, "Go, show yourselves to the priests." And as they went, they were cleansed.

One of them, when he saw he was healed, came back, praising God in a loud voice. He threw himself at Jesus' feet and thanked him—and he was a Samaritan.

Jesus asked, "Were not all ten cleansed? Where are the other nine? Was no one found to return and give praise to God except this foreigner?" Then he said to him, "Rise and go; your faith has made you well."

LUKE 17:11–19

$\mathcal{I}$t is recorded in Exodus 12 that while the Israelites were enjoying protection from the sword of judgment by the blood of the lamb outside upon their doors, that they were feasting upon the flesh of the roasted lamb inside.

Who can estimate the fullness of the twofold blessing that was theirs in the paschal lamb? Its blood sheltered their firstborn from the stroke of death, and its tender flesh was rich food for a redeemed people. While rejoicing in salvation by its blood, by eating its flesh they received strength to march from a land of slavery and woe.

Dear fellow-Christian, by the Blood of our Passover we have been saved from our sins and from eternal judgment, and for unending glory. Blessed be His peerless name forever, that while our salvation was His work, it is our holy and precious privilege to be daily feeding upon Him who accomplished that work! Israel ate of a dead lamb, but ours is a Living Christ at God's right hand.

Sad indeed is the condition of that soul who has received forgiveness of sins, exemption from judgment, the promise of glory, and countless blessings from His loving hands, and yet is not devoted to, nor occupied with Him, not concerned about the things that pertain to His glory.

We see that He felt deeply the lack of gratitude on the part of nine lepers whom He had cleansed, but appreciated the thanksgiving of the tenth—though he was a "foreigner."

C. C. CROWSTON

$\mathcal{S}$atisfied with God, rejoicing in Christ, full of the Holy Spirit, the weakest believer may well be wondered at by men of the earth who feel an incessant craving for they know not what.

GEORGE V. WIGRAM

The LORD will guide you always;
  he will satisfy your needs in a sun-scorched land
  and will strengthen your frame.
You will be like a well-watered garden,
  like a spring whose waters never fail.

ISAIAH 58:11

$\mathcal{W}$e do not doubt that God can speak to men now by means of a dream or a vision of the night; but we consider that the true and proper way for a child of God to be guided, is by the word and by the Spirit of God. It is very unsafe ground indeed to be merely guided by dreams or by the impressions of a man's mind. We vastly prefer the solid imperishable word of God.

It is greatly to be feared that very many mistake their own inclinations for the movings of the Spirit of God—a terrible mistake! It needs much brokenness, self-emptiness, and singleness of eye to discern and follow the precious leadings of the Holy Ghost.

As a general rule, we should say that where the glory of Christ is the exclusive object of any act to which we feel led, we may conclude that it is the Spirit that moves us. The Lord is so gracious that we can fully count upon Him to guide, and keep, and use us, where the heart is simple.

C. H. MACKINTOSH

$\mathcal{T}$here is a way to distinguish between the Father's leading and Satan's "angel of light" leadings. The Father's promptings never nag, or worry, or harass. Satan's do just that. If one has a seeming "leading" to do something that in itself is good, yet with the impulse there is a sense of nagging disquiet, and being driven in a certain direction, that is the Enemy's trademark; and his false leading is to be immediately recognized and rejected. The Holy Spirit's leadings come with a sense of peace and quiet, even if they point in a really difficult direction which only the grace of the Father can enable one to follow.

CHARLES G. TRUMBULL

March 2

And we, who with unveiled faces all reflect the Lord's glory, are being transformed into his likeness with ever-increasing glory, which comes from the Lord, who is the Spirit.

2 CORINTHIANS 3:18

The majority of active members in our sound churches today are primarily doers; their chief concern is to work for the Lord. But, service being the emphasis of their life, they are for the most part motivated by self.

We must all learn, sooner or later, that the result of every form of self-effort is nothing but a barren waste, a spiritual Death Valley. Our growth is bound to falter and dry up when service is predominant in the life, especially in the formative years.

Conversely, when *growth in Christ* is given first place, service will never suffer. Furthermore, our life work will be accomplished in His time and way—and that without physical, mental, or spiritual breakdown.

The tragedy of the church is that the service-centered believer has little or no concern for spiritual growth, other than enough development and training for what he considers to be fruitful service. Naturally altruistic, he is appalled at the thought of placing growth ahead of outreach. The activist rarely seems to become aware of the sin of self, of the necessity of the Cross in his life, or of God's purpose for him to be conformed to the image of Christ.

There are many believers who feel that the chief problem in our congregations is the existence of an overwhelming number of pew parasites. But, on the other hand, the vast army of busy-bee workers in our midst constitutes a comparable problem. Both doing nothing, and doing too much, are a hindrance to God's purpose. His will for the Christian is expressed in the word *being*, which in turn will result in effective *doing*.

MILES STANFORD

*T*he more you honor God by keeping man in the background, the more blessing you will have in the work.

EDWARD DENNETT

*A*h! It is hard to believe that God is doing your business in this world. It is much easier to do Christ's work that to believe He has done ours.

J. G. BELLETT

March 3

About the eleventh hour he went out and found still others standing around. He asked them, "Why have you been standing here all day long doing nothing?" "Because no one has hired us," they answered. He said to them, "You also go and work in my vineyard."
MATTHEW 20:6–7

*G*od does not want us to stand idle but to work. [This verse] tells us that God has His determined field of labor—the vineyard. Perhaps you will say you are very busy and have no leisure. But *where* on earth are you so busy? If you are not working in the vineyard, what difference is that from "standing idle"? If you are not living in the will of God, you are in God's sight as one standing idle, no matter how much other work you have been doing.

Or possibly you are busily engaged in so-called spiritual work, yet God may still say to you: "Why do you stand idle? Works done outside of *this* vineyard are not Mine." Though you may be very busy, in God's eye you are idle nonetheless. Only works done *in the vineyard* are recognized by Him. Such works originate in God and are for God. If your work is done outside His will, all the days you have spent on it are reckoned by Him as making you as one who is standing idle . . .

"All day" points to a lifetime. How about you? Are you standing all the day idle? Or are you working in the vineyard? Do not misunderstand me as suggesting that you should resign from your work and preach. What is most essential is that whatever we do we must be clear we are standing in the will of God. Working in the vineyard means working in the will of God. And in the vineyard of His will are all sorts of labors: some laborers are digging the ground, some are sowing the seed, and some are making repairs. No matter what work is being done, it will be acceptable if it is done for the good of the vineyard. And hence we need not be so exclusive as to consider only certain walks or works done by certain people as being God's works. No, as long as the days are spent *in the vineyard*, they will be remembered.

WATCHMAN NEE

I am large about redeeming time, because therein the sum of a holy, obedient life is included.

RICHARD BAXTER

. . . Jesus said unto her, neither do I condemn thee: go, and sin no more.
JOHN 8:11B

One day a Nigerian preacher was expounding the sixth of Romans to his congregation. The first verse was his text, "What then: shall we continue in sin that grace may abound?" His audience was composed almost entirely of folk who had never worn shoes in their lives. Even the children run with fleet step over the rock fields and paths. It is a country of many thorns, and it goes without saying that every foot has been pierced some time or other.

One of the great desires of every man is to possess a type of steel prod that is sold in the markets and that is very useful for dislodging any thorn or splinter that has pierced the foot. The evangelist spoke of a man who longed to possess the steel, who saved his money and finally purchased the implement.

The preacher asked his audience, "Did he then cry out, 'Now I can run in thorny paths with impunity. It makes the more difference, for I now have a prod with which I may remove the thorns that may pierce my feet?'"

And the preacher concluded, "What then? shall we continue to walk freely upon thorns in order than we may use a steel to remove those that pierce us? God forbid!" For the thorn-wound may become infected, and may leave a scar, and may leave us lame in our walk. God forbid!

The love of Christ constraineth us. The love that painted forgiveness on the walls of our chastisement constraineth us. The same voice says to us to-day, "Neither do I condemn thee. Go in peace, and sin no more."

DONALD GREY BARNHOUSE

$\mathscr{I}$t is true, the Gospel demands our *all*; but I fear that, in the general claim on *all*, we have shortened the claim on *everything*. We are not under law. True; but that is not to make our obedience less complete, or our giving less bountiful. Rather, is it not, that after all claims of the law are settled, the new nature finds its joy in doing more than the law requires? Let us abound in the work of the Lord more and more.

GEORGE MUELLER

March 5

For if we have been planted together in the likeness of his death, we shall be also in the likeness of his resurrection.

ROMANS 6:5, KJV

$\mathscr{W}$e mistake our experiences when we attempt, as mere copyists, to reproduce our Master's life within us! We put joy where the divine order would dictate sorrow, and nurse our sorrow when the Lord would have us rejoice in Him.

We reach after the unseasonable fruits of victory, when it is more needful as yet that we should endure the discipline of defeat so that divine strength may be made perfect in our weakness.

Our leaf withers in yellow melancholy, when He would have it green and flourishing. What we would do, we continually do not, because we lack a true and steadfast hold on strength.

Blessed is he, who, instead of seeking to attain the likeness of Christ as something only without Him, realizes that he has been planted in that likeness.

A. J. GORDON

$\mathcal{T}$he truth is not Christ, but Christ is the truth. You can have the truth without having Christ, but if you have Christ, you must have the truth and all the influences that flow out from the truth because He is THE TRUTH.

EDWARD DENNETT

$\mathcal{C}$hristian experience is simply the experience of Christ. A deeper Christian experience is a deeper experience of Christ; and the fullest possible Christian experience is simply the fullest possible experience of Christ. It is He, and there is no substitute for Him.

COLIN C. KERR

$\mathcal{M}$arch 6

When tempted, no one should say, "God is tempting me." For God cannot be tempted by evil, nor does he tempt anyone; but each one is tempted when, by his own evil desire, he is dragged away and enticed. Then, after desire has conceived, it gives birth to sin, when it is full-grown, gives birth to death.

JAMES 1:13–15

$\mathcal{T}$emptation touches us where we need to be touched, for its origin is our own stimulated desire. Temptation, therefore, establishes us in sanctification; it presses us into Christ. It exercises us in conscious abiding; it compels us, by trial and error, to find our helplessness with no hope outside of Christ living in us.

We shall continue to be tempted where we are most vulnerable, that is God's right way with us, until at last it dawns on us that appetites do not change, human responses do not change, temptations do not change; there will never be a hope of relief or release, not after forty years any more than after one year, except in the

Absolute Other within, who is the Positive that negates the negative, the Light that swallows the darkness. That fact will stabilize us in the only way of deliverance, the daily walk of faith.

NORMAN GRUBB

*S*inners are not saved until they trust the Savior, and saints are not delivered until they trust the Deliverer. God has made both possible through the Cross of His Son.

LEWIS SPERRY CHAFER

*I*f the Lord Jesus is not positively before the soul, it is enough— the enemy's work is done!

F. W. GRANT

March 7

Commit to the LORD whatever you do, and your plans will succeed.
PROVERBS 16:3

*S*eek entirely to depend on God for everything. Put yourself and your work into His hands. When thinking of any new undertaking, ask, "Is this agreeable to the mind of God? Is it for His glory?"

If it is not for His glory, it is not for your good, and you must have nothing to do with it. Mind that! Having settled that a certain course is for the glory of God, begin it in His name, and continue it to the end.

Undertake it in prayer and faith, and never give up! Pray, pray, pray! Do not regard iniquity in your heart. If you do, the Lord will not hear you. Keep that before you always. Then trust in God. Depend only on God. Wait on Him. Believe on Him. Expect great things from Him. Faint not if the blessing tarries. Pray, pray, pray!

And, above all, rely only upon the merits of our ever-adorable Lord and Savior, that, according to His infinite merits, and not your own, the prayers you offer and the work you do, will be accepted.

GEORGE MUELLER

March 8

While they were stoning him, Stephen prayed, "Lord Jesus, receive my spirit." Then he fell on his knees and cried out, "Lord, do not hold this sin against them." When he had said this, he fell asleep. And Saul was there, giving approval to his death.

ACTS 7:59–8:1A

The believer should always look upon Satan as a defeated foe. He has already been overcome by the Captain of our host. Any power which he exercises today is only a permitted power that God may get greater glory to Himself through the victory gained by His child before a doubting world, and also that the Christian's life in Christ may be deepened and strengthened.

Satan was permitted through his human tools to stone Stephen to death but through Stephen's gloriously triumphant martyrdom God won the crown jewel from Satan's diadem, Saul of Tarsus. Satan was allowed through human instruments to put to death the Lord of glory but in doing it he sent himself to the bottomless pit.

That wicked one has no claim whatever upon one who is born of God and he has no power to harm or hurt him. The believer who is hid with Christ in God and who is one with his ascended Lord has the right to claim the perfect protection which that position provides and to reckon himself as a conqueror in Christ Jesus.

RUTH PAXSON

$\mathcal{W}$e must tread upon the lion and adder. We must take the place of victory. We must put our feet upon the necks of our adversaries. We must treat our spiritual enemies as conquered foes and we must do it in the very beginning, while they are young, before they get the mastery.

A. B. SIMPSON

Thou shalt tread upon the lion and the adder: the young lion and the dragon shalt thou trample under feet.

PSALM 91:13, KJV

March 9

"I do believe; help me overcome my unbelief!"
MARK 9:24B

The Proper Attitude of the Christian Under Grace

1. To believe, and to consent to be loved while unworthy, is the great secret.
2. To refuse to make resolutions and vows, for that is to trust in the flesh.
3. To expect to be blessed, though realizing more and more lack of worth.
4. To testify of God's goodness at all times.
5. To be certain of God's future favor; yet to be ever more tender in conscience toward Him.
6. To rely on God's chastening hand as a mark of his kindness.
7. A Christian under grace has no burdens regarding himself; but many about others.

WILLIAM R. NEWELL

$\mathcal{A}$s grace is first from God, so it is continually from Him, as much as light is all day long from the sun, as well as at first dawn or at sunrising.

JONATHAN EDWARDS

March 10

"*Be still, and know that I am God . . .*"
PSALM 46:10, KJV

$\mathcal{I}$n order to know God, inward stillness is absolutely necessary. I remember when I first learned this. A time of great emergency had arisen in my life when every part of my being seemed to throb with anxiety and when the necessity for immediate and vigorous action seemed overpowering. And yet circumstances were such that I could do nothing and the person who could, would not stir.

For a while it seemed as if I would fly to pieces with the inward turmoil when suddenly the still small voice whispered in the depths of my soul, "Be still, and know that I am God." The word was with power, and I hearkened.

I composed my body to perfect stillness, I constrained my troubled spirit into quietness, and I looked up and waited. And then I did *know* that it was God, God even in the very emergency and in my helplessness to meet it; and I rested in Him. He was exalted "among the heathen" and in my heart. It was an experience that I would not have missed for worlds. And I may add also that out of this stillness seemed to arise a power to deal with the emergency that very soon brought it to a successful issue.

I learned then the lesson that my strength was to sit still.

I believe it is often helpful to compel the body to be still as an aid to the quieting of the spirit. Where this cannot be, let me entreat you to begin from this time onward to sit still in your hearts, sure that the *Lord* will not be in rest until He has finished the matter, whatever it may be, that concerns you.

HANNAH WHITALL SMITH

O beauty of ancient days, ancient but ever new! Too late I sought Thee, too late I found Thee. I sought Thee at a distance, and did not know that Thou wast near. I sought thee abroad in thy works, and behold, Thou wast within me.

AUGUSTINE

. . . the kingdom of God is within you.

LUKE 17:21B, KJV

March 11

There remains, then, a Sabbath-rest for the people of God; for anyone who enters God's rest also rests from his own work, just as God did from his.
HEBREWS 4:9–10

*I*t is this resting from their own work which many Christians cannot understand. They think of it as a state of passive and selfish enjoyment, of still contemplation which leads to the neglect of the duties of life, and undermines the watchfulness and warfare to which Scripture calls.

Yet, this is an entire misunderstanding of God's call to rest. As the Almighty, God is the only source of power. In nature He works all. In grace He waits to work all too, if man will but consent and allow. Truly to rest in God is to yield oneself up to the highest activity. We work, because He worketh in us to will and to do.

As Paul says of himself, "I labor, striving according to His working who worketh in me with might" which literally means "agonizing according to His energy who energizes in me with might." Entering the rest of God is the ceasing from self-effort, and the yielding up oneself in the full surrender of faith to God's working.

How many Christians are there who need nothing so much as rightly to apprehend this word. Their life is one of earnest effort and ceaseless struggling. They do long to do God's will, and to live to His glory. Continued failure and bitter disappointment is their too frequent experience. Very often as the result they give themselves up to a feeling of hopelessness: it never will be otherwise. Theirs is truly the wilderness life—they have not entered into God's rest.

Would that God might open their eyes, and show them Jesus as our Joshua, who has entered into God's presence, who sits upon the throne as High Priest, bringing us in living union with Himself into that place of rest and of love, and, by His Spirit within us, making that life of heaven a reality and an experience.

ANDREW MURRAY

A great many people have the faith that seeks, but they have not a faith that rests. The Lord Jesus is here, rest in Him, let the burden go. "Lord, I trust you now. I abide in you now. Lord, as I think about my home problems, my business pressures, my personal difficulties in every sphere of life, I bring them all, and give them all to You." Believe that He keeps you. I am sure this rest of faith is the center of all activity.

EVAN HOPKINS

> But many who are first will be last, and many who are last will
> be first.
>
> MATTHEW 19:30

*A*lways take for yourself the lowest place, and you shall be award-
ed the highest; for the highest cannot stand without the lowest. The
Christians stand highest in God's eyes who are lowest in their own;
and the more glorious they are, the more humble is their spirit.

Filled with truth and heavenly glory, they have no desire for
vain glory. Grounded and established in God, they cannot be proud.
They ascribe all goodness to God; they seek no glory from one
another, but the glory which comes from God alone. They desire
above all things, and strive always, that God be praised in themselves
and in all His children.

Be thankful for the smallest blessing, and you will receive
greater. Value the least gifts no less than the greatest, and simple
graces as special favors. If you remember the character of the Giver,
no gift will seem small or meaningless, for nothing can be valueless
that is given by the most high God.

THOMAS À KEMPIS

Give me the lowest place; not that I dare
Ask for that lowest place, but Thou hast died
That I might live and share
Thy glory by Thy side.
Give me the lowest place; or if for me
That lowest place too high, make one more low,
Where I may sit and see
My God and love Thee so.

CHRISTINA ROSSETTI

*W*e need God's power to be little.

JOHN DARBY

> *To will is present with me; but how to perform that which is good I find not. For the good that I would I do not: but the evil which I would not, that I do.*
>
> ROMANS 7:18–19, KJV

*I*f souls would be honest, many would confess that this has been their condition for years—a condition which brings no glory to God and no happiness to themselves.

What is the cause? Simply the mistake of thinking that all depends upon their own efforts instead of accepting the truth that they are utterly without strength, and that, therefore, everything depends upon God.

You have fought with your foes again and again with undaunted courage, but you have never gained the victory. Pause, for a moment, and ask this simple question, What am I to learn by this sorrowful experiment? . . . It is that the enemy is too strong for you, and that you cannot cope with his power . . .

If you continue upon the present line of *effort* it is only to court defeat in the future as in the past. Your case is, as far as your own strength is concerned, hopeless.

If, on the other hand, you come to the end of your own strength, it will bring rest to your soul, because you will understand that your help, strength and succor come from Christ and not from yourselves.

Oh, the unspeakable blessedness of such a discovery! Ceasing henceforward to struggle, you will know what it is to rest in Another, and to take up the song of David, "The Lord is my light and my salvation."

EDWARD DENNETT

I would rather climb to the moon by a rope of sand than try to achieve heaven by works.

GEORGE WHITEFIELD

To make a saint out of a human being, it must indeed be by grace. Whoever doubts this does not know what a saint is—nor a human being.

BLAISE PASCAL

March 14

Thou shalt hide them in the secret of thy presence . . .
PSALM 31:20, KJV

All our best experiences come when we are alone with God. There are sorrows which we can endure in no other place. Grief is of many kinds, but all grief that is really terrible and heart-crushing sends us into speechless solitude to weep it out upon the heart of God.

There are temptations which can be overcome only when alone with Him. The fight with the adversary is a solitary combat after all. And there are deep joys that can come into us only when alone with God, the joy of feeling Christ's personal love, the joy of finding His strength made perfect in our weakness, the joy of bringing our empty vessels to the Divine fullness of His grace, waiting till he fills them, and seeing them overflow.

For quickening faith, intensifying love, and renewing strength, there is no place like "the secret of His Presence." Strange and sad that we do not seek it more!

For the strength will not come to us without our going deep to find it. A few hasty and lazy prayers will never bring it into us.

We need *deep* communion with Christ if we are to get it at all. There is no part of a tree so *invisible* as its roots: but none more essential to its growth and fruitfulness: and just as the visible condition of the tree is an unfailing index of what the unseen roots are doing, our visible lives will soon tell whether or not our invisible roots are going deep: for dryness below ground soon means deadness above ground.

G. H. Knight

*G*od has made me a lonely person. . . . I was always a solitary soul, thinking more for, than with people: but it is good to be more alone—most good, if it be more alone with Christ. What a place that is!

John Darby

A little bird I am,
Shut from the fields of air;
And in my cage I sit and sing
To Him who placed me there;
Well pleased a prisoner to be,
Because, my God, it pleases Thee.

Jeanne Guyon

March 15

. . . And she named the child Ichabod, saying "The glory is departed . . ."
1 Samuel 4:21a, KJV

*C*hristian workers in the present day are perplexed how to act when they find themselves involved in a machinery of work which has unwittingly grown around them—or in a "machinery" which they no longer find they have strength to sustain, and they know not why.

Let such believers ask whether the machinery needed for that specific piece of work has already fulfilled its purpose, and whether its continued presence is not an indication that the Spirit of God is no longer supplying power for a service, from which He wills to withdraw His instrument.

A spiritual worker—one dependent upon the Holy Spirit for the carrying out of any service—will not find the blessing of the Spirit in the midst of "machinery" which has already fulfilled its purpose, and if the worker clings to the outward organized work after the Spirit of God ceases to need it, or utilize it, he will find himself compelled to draw upon his own resources instead of the power of the Holy Spirit.

If such a one discovers that he has become entangled in machinery, he may have great conflict in finding his way out into the stream of the Spirit flowing in another direction. Workers should, therefore, keenly watch where the unction of the Spirit is with their service, so that they may co-work only with Him, and discovering His leading follow in the stream of His power wheresoever it may be flowing.

Workers need to recognize that when the machinery of any good work SUPPRESSES the spirit life, instead of being a means for expressing it; or obstructs that life so that the worker loses the domination and overflow of the Spirit in personal life and victory, then the "machinery" of the work has become a hindrance, and must either be given up, or reduced to its right place of subservience to the life in the spirit, or, in some cases, it may be the worker needs to be adjusted in his relationship to it.

The history of the Church is full of examples of those who have been caught in the entanglement of "organization" to the injury of their own spiritual life, or service.

For example, a worker receives the Baptism of the Spirit. God pours out blessings on souls. Meetings are crowded. God mightily works. "Machinery" then becomes necessary to "conserve the results of blessing," and before long the Spirit-filled worker is compelled to carry on this or that work because he is committed to do so. He becomes *circumstantially* bound, and is no longer free to follow the leading of the Spirit of God.

The Divine tide of life then slowly recedes, and finally the worker goes on, content—or not, as the case may be—with the outward and visible form of the work in his hands. This is the story of thousands of Spirit baptized servants of God who began work in the Spirit, but failed to understand how to continue that work in the Spirit to the end.

It is also the duty of the workers in charge of any organized work to see that the spiritual life of their helpers is not sacrificed to the "work," by having so much to do in the *organizational* part of the Lord's service that their spiritual life has no opportunity of development, or expression; nor should a chief worker nurture his own spiritual life at the cost of another's "drudgery," any more than employers of labor should enrich themselves at the cost of overworked employees.

Those who *do the work in the background should have the same opportunity for spiritual advancement* as those who work in the front.

The supreme need of every spiritual worker is that he should discern the "stream" of the Spirit, and follow that stream. "Machinery" which is no longer lubricated by God—or is "out of the stream" of the Spirit—gives a spiritual worker a sense of stagnation, whilst outside of it he may find a stream. Some will discover this sooner than others through keen spiritual discernment.

The supreme question today is *where* is the "stream" of the Spirit, and *whither* is it flowing? The Holy Spirit is moving toward Rapture. He is preparing to leave the world and to ascend, and they who will go with Him find the unction only upon the heavenward call.

Workers often are not able to discern between the enemy's obstructions preventing them from carrying out work, and God checking them from going on in any specific direction. If they think it is the opposition of the devil when it is the Spirit of God saying "stop," in their wrong interpretation and effort to "go forward in spite of Satanic hindrances," they will descend from working after the Spirit, into drawing upon their own mental and physical resources, and so lose the stream—or unction—of the co-working Spirit of God.

They will then go on against the will of God, and into a false fight, and a conflict which has no victory. Workers in the face of spiritual obstruction, needing to discern whether this is of God, or of the enemy, should watch the effect of the attitude they take on *their own spirit.* For instance going forward with God in prayer and service in the face of demon-obstruction will bring liberation of spirit while going forward *without God* brings *compression of spirit*— a sense of heaviness and deadness of spirit, a loss of "spring" and liberty of spirit.

All workers in view of the Lord's coming should eagerly ask God to enable them to *finish* their own work, and in preparation for rapture take up every *attitude* which the Spirit of God can work out for them. They should pray against (1) all *spurious* work—work which God has not given them to do; (2) all work which they should have left alone long ago; (3) all work which is of the flesh and not the spirit; (4) all work which suppresses the spirit, or draws the worker *out* of the spirit; (5) all waste work, and work which may be *good* yet keeping the worker from some higher service. Only as workers *pray* themselves free of all work God has not given them to do, will they find out what is their own work, and be released to finish it, so as to have a fully completed service when He comes.

Evan Roberts

If God has accepted my service, then I am immortal until my work is done.

David Livingstone

I am crucified with Christ: nevertheless I live; yet not I, but Christ liveth in me . . .

GALATIANS 2:20A, KJV

The true Christian life, which begins with a supernatural transition, consists and continues in a supernatural *transfusion*.

The very life and nature of Christ are transfused into the innermost being of the Christian believer by the Holy Spirit. Thus our Saviour's word is fulfilled: "Because I live, ye shall live also" (John 14:19). Paul not only says, "I live, yet not I"; he goes on to say, "but *Christ liveth in me.*" There is not only transition; there is transfusion. This is the most precious and sacred secret of the Christian life. . . . The man of the world neither understands it nor even suspects it. Yet oh, how real it is to our Lord's own!

Now just because of this supernatural transfusion, the New Testament ideal for our Christian life is that there shall be within us a continual displacement of the old self-life, and an ever-clearer enthronement of the new Christ-life. All of us, by nature, are egocentric, self-centered; but we are meant to become Christocentric, or Christ-centered. Christ is to be the new life within our life; the new mind within our mind; the new will within our will; the new love within our love; the new Person within our personality.

We cannot always be on the mountaintop of transfiguration, seeing heavenly visions and hearing heavenly voices. We cannot always be experiencing spiritual raptures and sensory ecstasies. A high frequency of these is neither necessary nor desirable in our present state; nor could our nervous system sustain too much of it.

Often we must be down on the long-stretching plains of everyday hum-drum realities; and sometimes we must needs be down in some grim valley, drawing the sword in fierce battle against Apollyon himself.

Yet whether up on the mountain top, or down on the monotonous plain, or deep in some valley of trial, I am convinced of this, that we Christian believers need never lose an uninterrupted consciousness of our indwelling Saviour. Surely this is implied in the words, "Christ liveth in me." To be Christocentric is to be all the while Christ-conscious.

The whole of our consciousness is meant to be interpenetrated with the consciousness of *His* indwelling life and mind and will and love, even as the air in Summer is transfused with sunshine.

J. SIDLOW BAXTER

*J*esus Christ is the center of all, and the goal to which all tends.

BLAISE PASCAL

March 17

For where two or three are gathered together in my name, there am I in the midst of them.

MATTHEW 18:20, KJV

*T*he Church is the glory, crown, joy, and fullness of Christ; over it He is especially LORD; in it He delights to dwell, as in His "own house"; and when any of the living stones that compose this spiritual temple meet together in His name, there He especially resides "in the midst of them."

But as we may individually walk so as to grieve Him, and thereby lose the sense of His presence in our souls, we may also collectively so dishonor Him, by neglecting His word, and turning aside from reliance on His Spirit, as to render our church meetings powerless and dead; the living presence of Christ may not be experienced, and fellowship with Him may altogether be lost.

We may be assured of this, that if we desire to have the consciousness of the Lord's presence with us when we meet together, we must each cultivate communion with Him in our own hearts and homes; we shall find the best way to ensure a happy meeting with the saints will be to be happy with the Lord Himself in private.

When, therefore, we find our services cold and spiritless, let us ask ourselves if our own hearts have not been previously wandering away from the Lord; for if the majority of us bring cold and worldly hearts, our collective meeting will partake of the deadness of those who mainly compose it.

"CRUMBS FOR THE LORD'S LITTLE ONES"

March 18

In a large house there are articles not only of gold and silver, but also of wood and clay; some are for noble purposes and some for ignoble. If a man cleanses himself from the latter, he will be an instrument for noble purposes, made holy, useful to the Master and prepared to do any good work.

2 TIMOTHY 2:20–21

*W*hen we say that Christ's life has come into us to displace ours, what do we mean? We do not mean that this life of the Lord Jesus has come in to displace our personality. When I speak of our fallen life, I do not mean the human personality as such. I mean the poison which permeates our personality, the poison of sin which has degraded and defiled and distorted our humanity.

It is not that this new life of the Lord Jesus comes in to take the place of our personality, to take the place of our faculties created by God, but it comes in to take the place of the sinful life which is operating in our personality and employing our faculties. The vessel is the same, but the contents are different—the same vessel, the same person, the same faculties, but the contents different. No longer this sinful element, but the very holy nature of the Lord Jesus Christ filling, interpenetrating, permeating.

NORMAN DOUTY

*H*ave you ever watched a blacksmith? Did you notice how as he held the iron in the fire, it became more and more glowing the longer it lay in the forge, until at last it looked quite like fire? The iron was in the fire, and the fire was in the iron, but the iron was not on fire, nor the fire the iron. When the iron began to glow, the blacksmith could bend it into any shape he desired, but it still remained iron. Even so, we still retain our personality when we allow ourselves to be penetrated by Christ.

SADU SUNDAR SINGH

March 19

The earth is the LORD's, and everything in it, the world and all who live in it . . .
PSALM 24:1

*T*he true Christian, in strict propriety of speech, has no home here: he is, and must be, a stranger and a pilgrim upon the earth: his citizenship, treasure, and real home are in a better world; and every step he takes, whether to the east or to the west, is a step nearer to his Father's house.

On the other hand, when in the path of duty, he is always at home; for the whole earth is the Lord's: and, as we see the same sun in England or Italy, in Europe or Asia, so, wherever he is, equally sets the Lord always before him, and finds himself equally near the Throne of Grace at all times and in all places. God is everywhere; and, by faith in the Great Mediator, he dwells in God, and God in him.

JOHN NEWTON

*I*f a man have Christ in his heart, heaven before his eyes, and only as much of temporal blessing as is just needful to carry him safely through life, then pain and sorrow have little to shoot at. . . . To be in union with Him Who is the Shepherd of Israel, to walk very near Him Who is both sun and shield, comprehends all a poor sinner requires to make him happy between this and heaven.

WILLIAM BURNS

*L*ive near to God, and so all things will appear to you little in comparison with eternal realities.

ROBERT M. MCCHEYNE

March 20

He shall see the travail of his soul, and shall be satisfied: by his knowledge shall my righteous servant justify many; for he shall bear iniquities.
ISAIAH 53:11, KJV

*B*lessed be the God and Father of our Lord Jesus Christ." We are blessed in God, but do we realize how blessed God is in us? We scarcely understand the surface meaning of such words, to say nothing of their hidden depths. A blessed people with a blessed God! Not one of us is going to be disappointed. A thousandth part has not been told. We shall be satisfied; and shall Christ be dissatisfied concerning us? "He shall see of the travail of His soul, and shall be satisfied." These are wonderful things to read and speak of.

Let us open our hearts to let in the love that all these blessings imply. More wonderful is it to think of the Hand that gives them to poor, condemned sinners. Let the most tried child of God realize how blessed he is, and how blessed God is in him, and sorrow will turn to joy.

He Who is "the Counsellor" is also "the Mighty God," the Son that is "*given*" unto us (Isaiah 9:6). Oh, could we only thus realize the gift of God, and make use of the gift by faith, we should never be in uncertainty when called to act, and never be powerless in execution!

HENRY GROVES

The saints are God's jewels, highly esteemed by and dear to Him; they are a royal diadem in His hand.

MATTHEW HENRY

The Christian ought to be the most dignified person in the world. We do not think half enough of ourselves as we are before God.

EDWARD DENNETT

March 21

Redeeming the time, because the days are evil.
EPHESIANS 5:16, KJV

All Christians greatly need certain free time to be given to recollection. Try to steal some such hours, knowing that such little parings of time will be your best treasures. Try to save your mornings—defend them like a besieged city! Make vigorous defenses against all intruders, clear out the trenches, and then shut yourself up with God! Even the afternoon is too long a period to let go by without taking spiritual breath.

Recollection is a great cure against such evils as pride, a critical spirit, the wanderings of your imagination, impatience with others, love of pleasure, and all such faults. It is an excellent remedy, but it needs frequent repetition, much like an expensive watch, which needs constant winding.

Another suggestion: reread the books which moved you; they will do so again, and with greater profit than the first time. Also, be patient with yourself, avoiding both self-deception and discouragement. This is often hard to do—people either look complacently on themselves and their good intentions, or they despair utterly.

Expect nothing of yourself, but all things of God. Knowledge of our own hopeless, incorrigible weakness, coupled with an unreserved confidence in God's Power is the true foundation of all spiritual life.

If you have not much time at your own disposal—make good use of every moment you have. It does not take long hours to love God, to renew the consciousness of His Presence, to lift up the heart to Him or worship Him, to offer Him all we do or bear. This is the true Kingdom of God within us, which nothing can disturb.

FRANÇOIS FÉNELON

*W*e are just as spiritual when resting, playing, sleeping, ill or incapacitated, if it is His will for us, as when we are directly serving God. We can maintain an undercurrent of knowing that we are in complete accord with God and pleasing to Him whatever we are doing.

LEWIS SPERRY CHAFER

. . . as God hath said, I will dwell in them and walk in them; and I will be their God, and they shall be my people.

2 CORINTHIANS 6:16

*G*od's aim and purpose in the Gospel is not to make good people, a mere matter of conduct; but rather a people "peculiar" to Him—so peculiar to Himself that He can come and live in them and be Himself the regulator of their lives. This is really wonderful!

Stated boldly, stripped of superficialities, the Christian life is a reincarnation of Christ. He who walked the earth nineteen hundred years ago walks again in us: "I will dwell in them, and walk in them." He who once found flesh and blood expression for Himself in one body now claims a similar expression in any body—yours and mine—the bodies of all who will believe and receive the benefits of the Gospel.

The life thus depicted is too wonderful for words. It is staggering in its possibilities. To think of anyone missing it! "But," says some doubting Thomas, "it's wonderful, if it works, if one could live it."

Let us acknowledge that if it fails to work, the failure is ours, not His. As in the case of an automobile with the engine running at full speed and the wheels standing still—plenty of power but no transmission—we have failed to transmit and transmute His power into our daily living.

NORMAN B. HARRISON

*O*ur very helplessness is our resource. We find that God Himself must come in because we can do nothing.

JOHN DARBY

. . . I seek not mine own will, but the will of the Father which hath sent me.

JOHN 5:30, KJV

*I*n seeking the will of God, there must be no bias of our own will toward one course or the other in the matter on which guidance is sought. Our will should be like the compass needle, turning toward the Lord as the needle turns to the north, whichever way the compass is held.

The very least "desire" toward one way or another in a debatable course, prevents us from obtaining the mind of the Lord. The believer seeking guidance should therefore wait before the Lord for His light to reveal the attitude of the will before Him, with an attitude of surrender on the point where any bias is discovered.

There is a stage of maturity in the Spirit-filled life, where the will is so truly one with God, that it has no desire outside of His will, but this means that deep Gethsemane experiences, and fellowship with Christ in His sufferings, have been passed through, until the soul is one with Christ in God. Let the believer take special heed to his point of a surrendered will, for many have often sought their own will thinking it to be the will of God.

JESSIE PENN-LEWIS

*T*he Christian is always solemnly bound to submit himself to the revealed mind of God. To plead circumstances as an excuse for doing wrong, or for neglecting any truth of God, is simply flying in the face of divine authority, and making God the author of our disobedience.

"FOOD FOR THE DESERT"

*T*he hand of God never deals but in concert with His heart of infinite love towards us.

JOHN DARBY

For which of you, intending to build a tower, sitteth not down and counteth the cost, whether he have sufficient to finish it.

LUKE 14:28, KJV

*W*hy are we so deficient in divine power? Simply because we do not like the way it begins. Its beginning is to hate one's own life, and this is an awful start. But there is no "tower" built without it. You must refuse human material, or you cannot build to true structure.

Power enabled Elisha to take hold of his own clothes and tear them into two pieces. Power begins with self-abnegation. This explains the reason why there is so little power. Very often one lingers over his losses like an exile, but he must rise out of it; he must bury his dead out of his sight; it is a great day when that comes to pass, and then he can be useful to others.

J. B. STONEY

*I*t must not be forgotten that power does not act independently of our spiritual condition. The Holy Spirit dwells within, so that our bodies are His temples. If we are careless, unwatchful, if we seek our pleasure in the world, rather than in Christ, let us not for one moment suppose that He will condescend to use us as vessels of His power. . . . But on the other hand, if the eye be single, and a single eye sees nothing but Christ, if He is the object of our lives, the Holy Spirit then ungrieved will sustain us in every situation in which we are placed, and bring us victoriously out of the very conflict through which we may pass.

Let us not rest until we know practically something of being channels for the manifestation of divine power in this world.

EDWARD DENNETT

*W*hy do you want power? For the rare enjoyment of ecstatic moods? For some hidden selfish purpose like Simon of Samaria? So that you may move men? These motives are all selfish. Better stop before you begin. But if your uppermost and undermost desire is to glorify Jesus and let Him do in you and with you whatever He chooses, then He will flood the channels of your life with a new stream of power.

S. D. GORDON

March 25

That if you confess with your mouth, "Jesus is Lord," and believe with your heart that God raised him from the dead, you will be saved. For it is with your heart that you believe and are justified, and it is with your mouth that you confess and are saved. As the Scripture says, "Everyone who trusts in him will never be put to shame."

ROMANS 10:9–11

A confessor of Jesus as Lord is freed from the influences which govern men in the world—influences which are really the enemy's power over men's souls—and he comes under the protective power of the One whom he confesses. Hence it is that with the mouth confession is made to salvation.

If a Christian finds himself falling under the power of the world it is well for him to be exercised about his "mouth." Let him remember that God has put a "word" in his mouth, and that word is the confession of Jesus as Lord. As he allows that "word" to come out of his mouth, he will find that it means reproach and rejection here, but that it carries with it the power of God's salvation.

When Jesus is confessed as Lord it means that He has become Lord to us. There is something behind the confession to support it. Souls are sometimes pressed to confess what has not yet become true to their faith, but this is very injurious, and only tends to put them in a false position. How could I confess boldly and clearly Jesus as Lord if He were not Lord to me?

The blessed reality that Jesus is Lord is known in the heart; then it is confessed definitely and publicly here; and salvation is found thereby.

There is immense power in the spiritual confession of Jesus as Lord; it arrests the conscience of the one to whom He is confessed, for *he* knows in the depths of his soul that Jesus ought to be Lord to him also. There is the power of a divine salvation with the confessor of Jesus as Lord.

C. A. COATES

*T*here are only two channels of testimony—the lip and the life, and the lip should be but the expression of what has been first produced in the life. What we should all desire is intense reality, to be possessed and controlled by the truth we profess to hold, and thus to shun the use of phrases and sentences which we have never eaten, digested, and found true in our souls.

EDWARD DENNETT

March 26

He hath not beheld iniquity in Jacob; neither hath he seen perverseness in Israel. . .

NUMBERS 23:21, KJV

*O*ur salvation is of God, of the Father, who chose us before the beginning of time; and of the eternal Son, who, in the deep counsel of the ever-blessed Trinity, undertook to redeem us and to bring us unto glory; and of the Spirit, who in the same eternal love was appointed to enlighten, quicken, and renew the elect unto the blessedness of the everlasting inheritance.

This eternal, absolute, free, and unchanging love is revealed and given to us in the Lord Jesus, who by one offering has perfected for ever all who believe in His name. By His death He has separated us from our guilt and death, and brought us unto God.

He has sanctified Himself for us, and us to Him. Believers have been sanctified and presented unblamable before the Father in the person of the Lord Jesus. The Father's good pleasure or delight rests now on the people for whom Jesus died.

Thus God is always beholding us in Christ, and with eternal love. He beholds neither iniquity in Jacob, nor doth He see perverseness in Israel; although we stand before Him in the brightness of the all-revealing light, He sees us clothed with white garments, and cleansed in the blood of Jesus Christ His Son.

And although we are constantly failing and falling, yet doth He behold our faith as never failing, and ourselves as firm as Mount Zion, which cannot be moved, but standeth fast for ever. With never-changing fervency and tenderness of love God beholds us chosen, redeemed, sanctified in Christ Jesus.

Perfection is now given to all who believe. God Himself is our salvation. Jehovah Himself is our righteousness. Christ's inheritance is our inheritance. The source is eternal love, self-moved, infinite, ocean without shore; the channel is free abounding grace, the gift is eternal life, even life by the Holy Ghost in oneness with Jesus; the foundation is the obedience of Christ, eternal in its origin, infinite in its value, and unspeakably God-pleasing in its character.

How willing are we to forsake our own thoughts, to give up our own righteousness, to forget our works and feelings, and to stand still, in awe and joyous adoration beholding Jehovah bringing near His salvation and His righteousness! "Of God are we in Christ Jesus, whom God hath made for us wisdom, and righteousness, and sanctification, and redemption: that, according as it is written, He that glorieth, let him glory in the Lord."

ADOLPH SAPHIR

A Christian is one who when he thinks of the past thinks of the grace of which he has partaken. When he thinks of the future, he thinks of the sharing in the glory that is to be revealed. The whole of our life is bounded by these.

J. C. MANN

March 27

The man with the two talents also came. "Master," he said, "you entrusted me with two talents; see, I have gained two more." His master replied, "Well done, good and faithful servant! You have been faithful with a few things; I will put you in charge of many things. Come and share your master's happiness!"

MATTHEW 25:22–23

*I*t is for us to choose whether, molding our lives after His will and pattern, we shall hereafter be made like Him in completeness. It is for us to choose whether, seeing Him here, we shall, when the brightness of His coming draws near, be flooded with gladness, or whether we shall call upon the rocks and the hills to cover us from the face of Him that sitteth on the throne.

Time is the mother of Eternity. Today molds tomorrow; and, when all the todays and tomorrows have become yesterdays, they will have determined our destiny, because they will have settled our characters. Let us keep Christ's commandments, and we shall be invested with dignity and illuminated with glory and intrusted with work far beyond anything that we can conceive here, though in their furthest reach and most dazzling brightness these are but the continuation and the perfecting of the feeble beginnings of earthly conflict and service.

ALEXANDER MACLAREN

$\mathcal{W}$e have no time to sport away the hours; all must be in earnest in a world like ours.

HORATIUS BONAR

March 28

Thou wilt keep him in perfect peace, whose mind is stayed on thee; because he hath trusteth in thee.
ISAIAH 26:3, KJV

$\mathcal{D}$ear Friend,

This is the word of the Lord God to thee:

Live in the wisdom of the life of God. And be still and silent from thy own wisdom, wit, craft, or policy that would arise in thee, stand single to the Lord, without any end to thyself. Then God will bless thee and prosper thee in his ways; thou wilt feel his blessing in thy generation.

And with thy mind stayed upon the Lord, thou wilt be kept in perfect peace, without any intent to thyself, to the glory of God. And there wilt thou feel no want, nor never a failing, nor forsaking, but the presence of the Lord God of life with thee. For now the state of this present age is, that the Lord is bringing his people into the life the Scriptures were given forth from, in which life people shall come to have unity with God, with Scriptures and one with another, for the establishing righteousness, truth, and peace, in which is the kingdom of God.

GEORGE FOX

$\mathcal{T}$his is the secret of all blessing—giving the Lord the supreme place. Thinking first of what is due to Him, and losing sight of all else until this is rendered.

EDWARD DENNETT

But the fruit of the Spirit is love, joy, peace, patience, kindness, good-ness, faithfulness, gentleness and self-control. Against such things there is no law.

GALATIANS 5:22–23

$\mathcal{I}$s not this the life that we all long for, the Christlike life? But this life is not natural to us and is not attainable by us by any effort of what we are in ourselves. The life that is natural to us is set forth in the preceding verses: "Now the works of the flesh are manifest, which are these, fornication, uncleanness, lasciviousness, idolatry, sorcery, enmities, strife, jealousies, wraths, factions, divisions, here-sies, envyings, drunkenness, revellings and such like" (Gal. 5:21).

All these works of the flesh will not manifest themselves in each individual; some will manifest themselves in one, others in others, but they have one common source—the flesh, and if we live in the flesh, this is the kind of a life that we will live. It is the life that is natural to us.

But when the indwelling Spirit is given control in the one He inhabits, when we are brought to realize the utter badness of the flesh and give up in hopeless despair of ever attaining to anything in its power, when, in other words, we come to the end of our-selves, and just give over the whole work of making us what we ought to be to the indwelling Holy Spirit, then and only then, does this fruit of the spirit become the fruit of our lives.

Do you wish these graces in your character and life? Do you really wish them? Then renounce self utterly and all its strivings after holiness, give up any thought that you can ever attain to any-thing really morally beautiful in your own strength and let the Holy Spirit, who already dwells in you, if you are a child of God, take full control and bear His own glorious fruit in your daily life.

R. A. TORREY

Ye have not chosen me, but I have chosen you . . .
JOHN 15:16, KJV

Let no one be troubled by this matter of election. It is a family secret. I would not preach election to the world. Election goes before all. I come to the door of a certain place, where peace and plenty reign, and joy and happiness fill the hearts of all the dwellers therein. On the door I find written, "Whosoever will may enter in." That is the Gospel: I enter, and on the other side of the door I find written, "Whosoever gets in here will never get out!" That is my security, the fruit of election.

There is nothing to trouble a soul in election, but contrariwise, much to comfort. God has chosen you, if a believer in Christ, before the foundation of the world. The things which are in heaven God is going to keep for you, and He is going to keep you for them.

W. T. P. WOLSTON

I believe the doctrine of election because I am quite sure that if God had not chosen me, I would never have chosen Him; and I am sure He chose me before I was born, or else he never would have chosen me afterwards.

CHARLES SPURGEON

Human history is not the grip of fate, but in the hands of Him Who was pierced for us on Calvary.

W. G. S.

It was now about the sixth hour, and darkness came over the whole land until the ninth hour, for the sun stopped shining. And the curtain of the temple was torn in two. Jesus called out with a loud voice, "Father, into your hands I commit my spirit." When he had said this, he breathed his last. The centurion, seeing what had happened, praised God and said, "Surely this was a righteous man." When all the people who had gathered to witness this sight saw what took place, they beat their breasts and went away. But all those who knew him, including the women who had followed him from Galilee, stood at a distance, watching these things.

LUKE 23:44–49

One summer day there strolled into the little church a young nobleman. Loitering along the aisle his attention was arrested by the painting, into which the Spirit of God had breathed His own love through the fashioning hands of the artist. As he saw the love depicted in every lineament of that divine face; as he saw the pierced hands, and bleeding brow, the wounded side; as he slowly scanned the couplet under the art,

"All this I did for thee,
What hast thou done for Me?"

A new revelation of the claim of Jesus Christ upon every life upon which His grace had been outpoured flashed upon him. Hour after hour passed as he sat intently gazing upon the face of the Suffering One.

As the day wore on, and the lingering rays of sunlight shot aslant aisle and pew, they fell upon the bowed form of the young noble, Count Zinzendorf, weeping and sobbing out his devotion to the Christ whose love had not only saved his soul, but conquered his heart.

Out from that little church he went forth to do a mighty life work, which has circled the earth with the missions of that Moravian people, who seem to have realized and incarnated the love of Christ for a lost world, as no other denomination of God's Church militant has yet done.

Believer, have *you* had this vision of the suffering Christ, not only as Savior, but as the wooer and the winner of your own heart's best love? Has His passion for you kindled in your heart a responsive, burning love for Him? Has His love unto death not only brought you glad salvation, but stirred you to willing surrender? Accepting His redemption do you also joyously acknowledge His ownership? Is He a crowned King *in* your life, as well as a Lamb bleeding *for* your life? Do you recognize the claims of His love, as well as the privilege of it? Or, exulting in its sacrifice are you yet mute to its appeals?

JAMES McCONKEY

Following Christ

Jesus, day by day
Lead us on life's way;
Nought of dangers will we reckon,
Simply haste where Thou dost beckon,
Lead us by the hand
To our Fatherland!
Hard should seem our lot,
Let us waver not;
Never murmur at our crosses
In dark days of grief and losses;
'Tis through trial here
We must reach thy sphere.
When the heart must know
Pain for others' woe,

When beneath its own 'tis sinking,
Give us patience, hope unshrinking,
Fix our eyes, O Friend,
On our journey's end!
Thus our path shall be
Daily traced by Thee;
Draw thou nearer when 'tis rougher,
Help us most when most we suffer,
And when all is o'er
Open to us thy door!

COUNT NICHOLAUS VON ZINZENDORF

But thanks be to God! He gives us victory through our Lord Jesus Christ.
1 CORINTHIANS 15:57

A pickpocket once strolled into a rescue mission and was converted. He saw in Christ pardon for his sins and power against them. Rejoicing in a new life he went on his way planning for the future. "In my unregenerate days," said he to himself, "I used to pick quite twenty pockets a day. But now I am a Christian man, and I know that to pick pockets is a sin. So I must give it up—gradually, of course. Tomorrow I'll make a start and for the rest of this month I shall pick only ten pockets a day: next month by striving and struggling against this sin, I'll cut down to five a day—for I'm a Christian man now. By the end of the year by constant endeavor (and the help of God) I hope to give up picking pockets altogether."

Do you believe that story? The writer does not. But have we not all been guilty of this very thing in our dealings with bad temper, pride, irritability, jealousy, unloved? We expect a pickpocket, or a drunkard, or a gambler to give up his sin once and for all—the very moment of his conversion. We tell him—and tell him truly—that Christ is able to give him complete and instant victory. Is God unable to give us a similar victory over what we deem to be lesser sins? He is able to make us "more than conquerors."

Victory over sin is a gift of God and not a growth. Paul recognized this. He did not say, "Thanks be to God, which giveth us a gradual victory," but "giveth us the victory through Jesus Christ our Lord."

There is no such thing as a gradual victory over sin—although we may think there is. God's gifts are perfect. The fact is, He gives us Jesus Christ Himself to dwell in our hearts by faith. And Jesus Christ keeps us.

Can we trust Christ to do it?

AN UNKNOWN CHRISTIAN

If God has ever given you a victory over one sin, He can give you victory over all sin. He who has kept you from sin for a moment, can with equal ease keep you from the same sin for a day or a month.

RUTH PAXSON

April 2

So whether you eat or drink or whatever you do, do it all for the glory of God.

1 CORINTHIANS 10:31

Having surrendered the whole life to the mastery of the Lord, having given up the pride of the flesh, all luxuries and self-gratification, there is the peril of asceticism. Perhaps fine clothes, or jewelry, or overindulgence in food were among the things that had to go when we surrendered wholly to the Lord. As we find our new joy in Him, not in these things, we may be driven beyond the will of God into an asceticism that dishonors Him.

More than one wholly surrendered Christian has mistakenly become indifferent and careless about personal attire or appearance, and has actually become repellent to others because of this mistake. Or, having been delivered from the sin of luxury in jewelry, we may be driven beyond the will of God into supposing that every bit of gold or silver we have should now be given away or sold and the proceeds given directly to the Lord's service. Christian women have actually sold their wedding rings under this form of sadly mistaken asceticism. The spirit is commendable, but neither the guidance nor the results are necessarily of God.

We are to maintain a golden mean between the extremes of asceticism and luxury. We are to take care of our personal appearance, our cleanliness, our clothing, so as to be attractive to our fellow men; it is a positive duty to be attractive Christians, both in dress and appearance, that others may be won to us in order that we may win them to our Lord. We are to do all things to the glory of God.

Another common form of asceticism among Christians is to assume the mistaken idea that when we have a choice between something that is hard and something that is easy, the hard thing is always God's will. His will may be just the opposite. There is not necessarily any virtue in difficulty, and there isn't necessarily any sin in ease. The only question is, What is God's will for us in each matter that comes before us?

CHARLES G. TRUMBULL

*T*his is true perfection: not to avoid a wicked life because like slaves we fear punishment; nor to do good because we hope for rewards, as if cashing in on the virtuous life by some business-like agreement. On the contrary, we disregard all those things for which we hope and which have been promised us, instead we regard losing God's friendship as the only dreadful thing—and we consider being God's friend as the only true thing worthy of honor and our desire. This, I say again, is the perfection of life.

GREGORY OF NYSSA

April 3 ═══════════════════════════════════════

. . . the strength of sin is the law.

1 CORINTHIANS 15:56B

*Y*ou can have Christian law just as much as you can have Mosaic law; you can be in bondage in Christianity just as much as men were in Judaism. Christianity can be made into an imposed system just as much as Mosaic law was, and there are many Christians today who live under the fear of the "Thou shalt" and the "Thou shalt not" of a legalistic conception of the Christian life.

You can take the Bible as God's standard for your life and try to fulfill it and yet be burdened with a sense of constant failure. It is God's standard, and it is a very exhaustive one which leaves no part of the practical life untouched, but those who make the effort to try to live up to it only end in disillusion.

No, it is not just a matter of a Book, but of a Person, the Person who did live up to that standard, absolutely fulfilling every least demand and with the most perfect success, so satisfying God to the full. By His death He has delivered us from the bondage of legal demands. This same person now lives in us by His Holy Spirit, seeking to work out that perfect will of God not on the basis of some binding instructions from without but as a living force within. We have the law written in our hearts.

To be in Christ is a matter of life and not of legalism.

T. AUSTIN-SPARKS

*S*ome good Christians who, in sad error, would impose the law as a rule of life for the believer mean very well by it—for they strive to be righteous—but the whole principle is false. The law, instead of being a rule of life, is necessarily a rule of death to one who has a sin nature. Far from being a delivering power, it can only condemn. Far from being a means of holiness, it is, in fact, according to Paul, "the strength of sin."

WILLIAM KELLY

April 4

Abstain from all appearance of evil.
1 THESSALONIANS 5:22, KJV

*W*hatever the form, no child of God should allow himself to be for one moment attached to what is evil. The Holy Spirit is a power in you to emancipate you from things which overcame you before your conversion. If evil takes shape in your mind, and you see it to be wrong, instantly abstain from it, avoid all appearance of it. And by that you maintain not only actual progress in the divine life, but also a holy abiding frame which is in the sight of God more than any occasional act, for God looks behind our acts, which are so comparatively transient and unimportant, to that which is the habit.

"SOUL FOOD"

$\mathscr{I}$t is not wickedness to be harassed by bad thoughts if you resist them. It is Satan's effort to get you to adopt them, and thus you are compromised. You will find, if you keep near the Lord, that you are more established after resisting such an attack than before; and the only way to combat Satan's attacks is by the Word of God. If Satan can lead you to become indifferent to these attacks, then great damage will result. But if, on the other hand, they urge you to be more dependent on the Lord Himself and on His Word, they will eventually cease, and you will no longer be prey for the enemy in this regard.

J. B. STONEY

April 5

LORD, *Thou wilt ordain peace for us; for thou hast wrought all our works in us.*
ISAIAH 26:12, KJV

$\mathscr{T}$hat every child of God has a specific work which involves both gifts and calling is clearly indicated in Scripture. We need only remind ourselves of the man in Matthew 25:14–15 who upon a leave of absence for a while handed over to his servants the reins of government and distributed talents so that they would be equipped—*"to every man according to his individual ability."* Mark has a similar account in which a certain man "left his house and gave authority to his servants and *to every man his work."*

In these two parables we have it stated by implication that to every man talents are given and to every man is given a work which is specifically his. Peter tells us (1 Peter 4:10) that "every man has received a gift." There is no definite article in the original, a circumstance which has the effect of strengthening the implications of universality. We are simply being assured that every one of the Lord's children (for this letter is specifically addressed to the Lord's children) does have a gift.

It is impossible to conceive of God's plan, thought out in eternity and guaranteed at such a cost, failing to ensure not only an appropriate work for each of those who are to engage in it, but also appropriate qualifications. And as a reflection of the wisdom of God, the perfecting of each individual involved in the plan is to be secured by fitting his capacity to do the work he has to do. When any man or woman consciously works at full capacity in the sense of using his abilities with maximum effectiveness, that individual is likely to derive the greatest possible personal satisfaction, and will be maturing most effectively. This is God's way. And it is almost certainly true, as Augustine said, that the child of God is physically immortal until his appointed work is done. Indeed, this may be the intent of Paul's observation regarding David when he said, "After he had served his own generation, he fell asleep" (Acts 13:36).

It is Paul who was inspired to make it very clear that the position which any child of God occupies within the Body of Christ is in no sense accidental; it is a divinely appointed position effectively realized by the Holy Spirit. Paul spent a whole chapter on the matter (1 Cor. 12:12–31), [affirming this principle] with the words, "Now hath God set the members *every one of them* in the Body, as it hath pleased Him" (v. 18).

So there we have in effect the gifts and the calling which are both of God, and which "are without repentance" (Rom. 11:29), without anything tentative about them, without any possibility of His changing His mind about them. The gifts are secured to us by providential overruling of our genetic heritage whereby we are equipped constitutionally to fulfill some specific role to which we are elected—for Election is not only to salvation. I believe that Peter is speaking of Election in this sense when he says (2 Peter 1:10): "Wherefore, brethren, give diligence to make your calling an election sure," and then it follows naturally, as Peter goes on to say, that "if ye do these things, ye shall never fail." For how could we possibly fail if we are fulfilling the role which God has called us to fill, and using the talents with which He has endowed us?

The calling, the circumstances in which our lot is cast, are providentially of His overruling. Should these circumstances become difficult and we be under the impression that we could do better elsewhere, nevertheless, we should not be too ready to move away. The casting of our lot is truly in God's hands. "As God hath distributed *to every man*, as the Lord hath called *every one*, so let him walk.... Let every man abide in the same calling wherein he is called" (1 Cor. 7:17, 20).

What a comfort to know that our lot is cast by the Lord, our gifts are of his appointing, and our life work planned way back there in eternity! If we could only rest assured of this in times of delay, or defeat, or uncertainty. Such assurance does not lead to inaction; it leads to freedom of action with the right kind of confidence. Any kind of confidence other than based securely upon the sovereignty of the grace of God is misplaced. Isaiah said (26:12): "Lord, Thou wilt ordain peace for us; for Thou hast wrought all our works in us." Amen!

ARTHUR CUSTANCE

It is plain enough that every believer is called of God to something definite. The real difficulty is to ascertain the specialty, and this

I do not think can be discovered but in nearness to the Lord, and when you are interested in His interests. We first learn that He is interested in us, and then we gradually become interested in His interests. It is then you apprehend your mission in life.

J. B. STONEY

April 6

Humble yourselves therefore, under God's mighty hand, that he may lift you up in due time.

1 PETER 5:6

The blessed Lord Jesus took the very lowest place; but God has given Him the very highest. He made Himself nothing; but God has made Him everything. He said, "I am a worm and no man"; but God has set Him as Head over all. He went into the very dust of death; but God has placed Him on the throne of the Majesty in the heavens.

What does all this teach us? It teaches us that *the way to go up is to go down.* This is a grand lesson, and one which we very much need to learn. It would effectually deliver us from envy and jealousy, from strife and vain glory, from self-importance and self-occupation. God will assuredly exalt those who, in the spirit and mind of Christ, take the low place; and, on the other hand, He will, as assuredly, abase those who seek to be somebody.

Oh! to be nothing! This is true liberty—true happiness—true moral elevation. And then what intense power of attraction in one who makes nothing of himself! And, on the other hand, how repulsive is a pushing, forward, elbowing, self-exalting spirit! How utterly unworthy of one bearing the name of Him who made Himself of no reputation! May we set it down as a fixed truth that ambition cannot possibly live in the presence of One who emptied Himself? No doubt. An ambitious Christian is a flagrant contradiction.

C. H. MACKINTOSH

*L*et every day be a day of humility; condescend to all the weaknesses and infirmities of your fellow creatures, cover their frailties, love their excellencies, encourage their virtues, relieve their wants, rejoice in their prosperities, compassionate their distress, receive their friendship, overlook their unkindness, forgive their malice, be a servant of servants, and condescend to do the lowliest offices of the lowest of mankind.

WILLIAM LAW

April 7

You yourselves are our letter, written on our hearts, known and read by everybody. You show that you are a letter from Christ, the result of our ministry, written not with ink but with the Spirit of the living God, not on tablets of stone but on tablets of human hearts.

2 CORINTHIANS 3:2–3

*T*he Christian life can only be explained in terms of Jesus Christ, and if your life as a Christian can still be explained in terms of *you*—*your* personality, *your* will-power, *your* gift, *your* talent, *your* money, *your* courage, *your* scholarship, *your* dedication, *your* sacrifice, or *your* anything—then although you may *have* the Christian life, you are not yet living it!

If the way you live your life as a Christian can be explained in terms of *you*, what have you to offer to the man who lives next door? The way he lives his life can be explained in terms of *him*, and so far as he is concerned, you happen to be "religious"—but he is not! Christianity may be *your* hobby, but it is not *his*, and there is nothing about the way you practice it which strikes him as at all remarkable. There is nothing about you which leaves him guessing, and nothing commendable of which he does not feel himself equally capable without the inconvenience of becoming a Christian.

It is only when your quality of life *baffles* the neighbors that you are likely to *impress* them. It has got to become patently obvious to others that the kind of life you are living is not only highly commendable, but that it is beyond all human explanation. That it is beyond the consequences of man's capacity to imitate, and however little they may understand this, clearly the consequence only of God's capacity to reproduce Himself in you.

In a nutshell, this means that your fellow-men must become convinced that the Lord Jesus Christ of whom you speak, is essentially Himself the ingredient of the Life you live.

MAJOR IAN THOMAS

*W*e can present Christ to the hearts of men in our lives as well as by our words. We may not be able to explain a single passage of scripture, but we can *live Christ*. You may teach a Sunday school, or visit among the poor, and that is all right and good, but there is something far better—live *Christ*, present *Christ*.

EDWARD DENNETT

> Live Christ!—and though the way may be
> In this world's sight adversity,
> He who doth heed thy every need
> Shall give thy soul prosperity.
> Live Christ!—and though the road may be
> The narrow street of poverty,
> He had not where to lay His head,
> Yet lived in largest liberty.

Live Christ!—and though thy life may be
In much a valedictory,
The heavy cross brings seeming loss,
But wins the crown of victory.
Live Christ!—and all thy life shall be
A High Way of Delivery—
A Royal Road of goodly deeds,
Gold paved with sweetest charity.
Live Christ!—and all thy life shall be
A sweet, uplifting ministry,
A sowing of the fair white seeds
That fruit through all eternity.

JOHN OXENHAM

April 8

"Woe to me!" I cried. "I am ruined! For I am a man of unclean lips,
and I live among a people of unclean lips, and my eyes have seen the
King, the LORD Almighty."

ISAIAH 6:5

When the revelation of God came to Isaiah it dealt with his lips.
If the tongue is under God's control He will keep us silent about
other people; silent over injuries, and sometimes silent over our
experiences. The life of Christ was a very silent one.

If we are to dwell unbrokenly under the power of God, we shall
have to learn, not a strained unnatural silence, but that quiet hiding
in God which makes us so still that whatever goes wrong, we are
kept quite calm; and unkind words do not spring to our lips. It is
one of the signs of a deep walk with God, that we have no need to
speak to others of our experience, our injuries, or our works. It

shows, too, how God has us under control, when we can be used greatly, and yet never be the one to say it—that we can be injured and misunderstood, and yet never speak of it to anyone else.

JESSIE PENN-LEWIS

*J*f God sets a Christian in a certain position, and gives him a certain work to do, and his fellows think proper to quarrel with him simply on the score of his doing that work, and filling that position, then their quarrel is really with God, who knows how to settle it, and will do it in His own way. The assurance of this gives holy calmness and moral elevation to the Lord's servant, in moments when envious and turbulent spirits rise up against him.

"FOOD FOR THE DESERT"

April 9

"Deep calleth unto deep . . ."
PSALM 42:7, KJV

*B*y His grace God has accomplished something through us, but do remember that what He accomplished is not matter for advertisement or propaganda. If we expose the work of God we shall find that the touch of death will come upon it immediately . . .

Our secret history with the Lord must be preserved, apart from that which He requires us to disclose. Only if He moves within us to reveal anything dare we reveal it. If He wants us to share some experience with a brother, we dare not withhold it, for that would be violating a law of the Body of Christ. Fellowship is a law of corporate life, so when the life rises within one member to flow out toward another, it must not be suppressed. We must be positive, not negative, and must always minister life to others. If we are engrossed the live-long day with ours own experiences, and talk of them from morning to night, we expose ourselves to assault from the enemy. I trust we shall learn what the Body of Christ is, and what interflow of life among the members is; but I trust we shall also learn the need of safeguarding that which is specifically our as members of the Body.

As your secret life deepens you will discover that "deep calleth unto deep." When you can bring forth values from the depths of your inner life, you will find that other lives will be deeply affected. Without any mighty outward movement—just a quiet response to the moving of life within—you will reach out to another life, and that other life will be helped, and into his life will come the awareness that in a depth deeper than consciousness he has met depth: deep has answered deep. If your life has no depth, your superficial work will only affect other lives superficially. We repeat yet again—only "deep calleth unto deep."

WATCHMAN NEE

*T*he higher acknowledgement of Christ, the more spiritual energy in going through this world and overcoming it. If one believer is more spiritual than another, it is because he understands the person of Christ better.

JOHN DARBY

April 10

And [Moses] took the book of the covenant and read in the audience of the people: and they said, "All that the LORD hath said we will do, and be obedient."

EXODUS 24:7

*L*ust is natural inclination run wild, overlapping all restraint, and asserting its own imperious will. When we are yet in the darkness of nature, unillumined by the grace of God, these lusts fashion us. Beneath their touch we are molded or *fashioned*, as clay by the potter's hand. Ignorant of the abominableness of sin, of its disastrous results, of its insidious growth, we yield to it until it becomes our tyrant and our ruin. Oh, the horror of awakening, should we see the depths of this terrible precipice descending sheer beneath us to hell!

When we no longer fashion ourselves according to the former lusts, but according to the will of God—that is *obedience.*

It is impossible to exaggerate the importance of this truth. Obedience is not holiness; holiness is the possession of the soul by God. But holiness always leads to obedience. And each time we obey, we receive into our natures a little more of the Divine nature. "If ye shall indeed obey my voice, ye shall be a holy nation unto Me." Do, then, whatever it is right to do. Forsake all which begins and ends with self. Be not satisfied with prayer and desire, but DO. And thus there will come over your face and life more likeness to the Father of your spirits; and you will be holy.

How few Christian people seem to realize that obedience in trifles, in all things to the will and law of Jesus, is the indispensable condition of life and joy and power. The obedient soul is the holy soul, penetrated and filled by the presence of God, and all aglow with light and love.

Dear Christian, resolve from this moment to live up to the margin of your light. Let this be your motto: "All that the Lord hath said will we do, and be obedient."

F. B. MEYER

Jesus answered and said unto him, "What I do thou knowest not now; but thou shalt know hereafter."

JOHN 13:7, KJV

*D*uring the early pioneer years of our missionary work in China, when laying the foundation of the Changte Church, my own weak faith was often rebuked when I saw the results of the simple child-like faith of our Chinese Christians. Some of the answers to prayer were of such an extraordinary character that, when told in the homeland, even ministers expressed doubts as to their genuineness. But, praise God, I know they are true. Here are two concrete examples:

Li-ming, a warmhearted, earnest evangelist, owned land some miles north of Chang Te Fu. On one occasion, when visiting the place, he found the neighbors all busy placing around their fields little sticks with tiny flags. They believed this would keep the locusts from eating their grain. All urged Li-ming to do the same, and to worship the locust god, or his grain would be destroyed. Li-ming replied: "I worship the one only true God, and I will pray Him to keep my grain, that you may know that He only is God."

The locusts came and ate on all sides of Li-ming's grain, but did not touch his. When my husband heard this story he determined to get further proof, so he visited the place for himself, and inquired of Li-ming's heathen neighbors what they knew of the matter. One and all testified that, when the locusts came, their grain was eaten and Li-ming's was not.

The Lord Jesus once said, after a conflict with unbelief and hypocrisy: "I thank thee, O Father, Lord of heaven and earth, because thou hast hid these things from the wise and prudent, and hast revealed them unto babes."

The second example concerns our little daughter Gracie who became ill with a terribly fatal disease, so common in malarious districts—an enlarged spleen. The doctors pronounced her condition quite hopeless. Once day a Chinese Christian woman came in with her little child, of about the same age as our Gracie, and very ill with the same disease. The poor mother was in great distress, for the doctor had told her also that there was no hope. She thought that if we would plead with the doctor he could save her child. At last my husband pointed to our little Gracie, saying: "Surely, if the doctors cannot save our child, neither can he save yours; your only hope and ours is in the Lord Himself."

The mother was a poor, hard-working, ignorant woman, but she had the simple faith of a little child. Some few weeks later she called again, and told me the following story:

"When your husband told me my only hope was in the Lord, I believed him. When I reached home I called my husband, and together we committed our child into the Lord's hands. I felt perfectly sure the child would get well, so I did not take more care of him than of a well child. In about two weeks he seemed so perfectly well that I took him to the doctor again, and the doctor said that he could discover nothing the matter with him."

That Chinese child is now a grownup, healthy man. And *our child died.* Yet we had prayed for her as few, perhaps, have prayed for any child. Why, then, was she not spared? I do not know. But I do know that there was in my life, at that time, the sin of bitterness toward another, and an unwillingness to forgive a wrong. This was quite sufficient to hinder any prayer, and did hinder for years, until it was set right.

Does this case of unanswered prayer shake my faith in God's willingness and power to answer prayer? No, no! My own child might just as reasonably decide never again to come to me with a request because I have, in my superior wisdom, denied a petition.

Is it not true, in our human relationships with our children, that we see best to grant at one time what we withhold at another? "What I do thou knowest not now, but thou shalt know hereafter."

And one of the most precious experiences of God's loving mercy came to me in connection with our little Gracie's death. We had been warned that the end would probably come in convulsions; two of our dear children had been so taken. Only a mother who has gone through such an experience can fully understand the horror of the possibility that such might come again at any time.

One evening I was watching beside our little one, Miss P— being with me, when suddenly the child said very decidedly: "Call Papa; I want to see Papa." I hesitated to rouse her father, as it was his time to rest; so I tried to put her off with some excuse; but again she repeated her request, and so I called her father, asking him to walk up and down with her until I returned.

Going into the next room I cried in an agony to the Lord not to let Gracie suffer; but, if it was indeed His will to take the child, then to do so without her suffering. As I prayed, a wonderful peace came over me, and the promise came so clearly it was as if spoken: "Before they call I will answer; and while they are yet speaking I will hear."

Rising, I was met at the door by Miss P— who said, "Gracie is with Jesus." While I was on my knees our beloved child, after resting a few moments in her father's arms, had looked into his face with one of her loveliest smiles, and then quietly closed her eyes and had ceased to breathe. No struggle, no pain, but a "falling asleep."

ROSALIND GOFORTH

They are not lost to you, those that are laid up in Christ's treasury in heaven. At the resurrection you shall meet with them. They are there, sent before you, but not sent away. Your Lord loves you and is generous to take and give, borrow and lend.

SAMUEL RUTHERFORD

The thief cometh not, but for to steal, and to kill, and to destroy. I am come that they might have life, and that they might have it more abundantly.

JOHN 10:10, KJV

*A*ll spiritual privileges are conditional. The condition of the "life abundant" lies in becoming a partaker of the mind of Him who died unto sin, to be armed with that mind. This is not an isolated experience, a single act, it is a *mind*—that is, a spiritual condition to be ever maintained, and becoming more and more deepened.

We do not have to strain our energies in order to live, or increase our strength. The living Christ within us will put forth His own power and manifest His own life; there shall be no lack of vitality. But what we are required to do is voluntarily to submit to die; and this, not by direct efforts upon ourselves, but by a participation of the mind of Him who died unto sin once, and now lives unto God.

EVAN HOPKINS

*I*t is just a matter of taking a position that is already yours. The enemy has filled the mind of many believers with the delusion that they are poor, and in their poverty they must work and grind and toil in order to buy the blessings which are already theirs in Christ. It is time to see that all you need, you have in Christ. There is no need of yours which is not fully met in Him. And you are in Him. You only need to take the position which is already yours. Abide!

D. TRYON

*C*ommunion with the Lord Jesus requires our coming to Him in the Word. Meditating upon His person and His work requires the prayerful study of His Word. Many fail to abide in Him because they habitually fast instead of feast.

J. H. T.

April 13

. . .count yourselves dead to sin but alive to God in Christ Jesus.

ROMANS 6:11

The charm of sin is gone the moment it is perpetrated.

JOHN BELLETT

Do not accept the suggestion of the tempter that you are power-less to break away from evil habits. Remember, it is not a question of your own power, but when you honestly repent of the wrong-doing and turn to the Lord for divine help to overcome your beset-ting sin, He will undertake for you. As you reckon yourself to be dead indeed unto sin, but alive unto God through Jesus Christ our Lord, the Holy Spirit will work in you and through you. He will cause you to triumph over tendencies toward evil and enable you to live victoriously to the glory of the God who has saved you.

HENRY A. IRONSIDE

There is no necessity to have even a *single* evil thought.

JOHN DARBY

April 14

Now to him who is able to do immeasurably more than all we ask or imagine, according to his power that is at work within us, to him be glory in the church and in Christ Jesus throughout all generations, for ever and ever! Amen.

EPHESIANS 3:20–21

The resurrection life of Christ, in the power of the Spirit of God, is the "power at work within us." When that power is checked from entering into our daily life we come to a standstill—the Church of God comes to a standstill. All the power of all the saints upon earth cannot push it forward. We may resort to all sorts of expedients—"methods of work" and what not—but the snail-like progress of things shows how unavailing it all is. But now the Spirit of God, if we may use such imagery, as the engineer, applies the lever—the cross of Christ—and the throttle is removed. What is that throttle? It is *self* in all its forms; not naughty self merely, but religious self as well. The cross has brought in the sentence of death upon *me*, and when the blessed Spirit of God applies that, all His own energy and power passes into our everyday life, and we shall speed along as on the wings of the wind—"mount up with wings as eagles, run and not be weary, walk and not faint." Was any new power obtained? No, but "the power at work within us" was permitted to work out as well.

You may apply the illustration to questions of detail as well, no doubt. The Spirit of God may be laying upon your conscience some specific obstruction, some self-will, disobedience, association, sin. By all means, yield to what He says. But after all, the cross is the lever, and self—all self—is the obstruction that stands in the way of a divine energy that dwells in every child of God.

Does it not make you weep to think of all the hindered power in the Church of Christ? Sad it would be if we had no power—if we had to call it down from heaven. But to be indwelt by the Spirit of God—omnipotent power—and yet to be idle and helpless!

Oh, beloved brethren! Let us awake; let us make sharp knives—yea, let us know the fellowship of Christ's sufferings, that thus also we may learn the power of His resurrection. May our God awaken us, for the responsibility is ours; we must enter into these divine facts for our own souls. Soon, soon would shouts of victory and rejoicing sound throughout the army of the Lord.

SAMUEL RIDOUT

For the Son of man is as a man taking a far journey, who left his
house, and gave authority to his servants, and to every man his work,
and commanded the porter to watch. Watch ye therefore: for ye know
not when the master of the house cometh, at even, or at midnight, or at
the cock-crowing, or in the morning; lest, coming suddenly, he find you
sleeping. And what I say unto you, I say unto all, Watch.

MARK 13:33–37, KJV

*T*wo important points are to be observed. While *watching* is the
attitude of the servant, *working* is his characteristic. How sweet to
notice that the Lord has given "to every man his work." There is
room for all, place for all, and work for all, that love Him. No two
have the same work, nor can another really do that which is allot-
ted to each. Therefore to know one's work, and then to stick to it,
is of prime importance.

Were we each to get really hold of this divinely important principle, how it would foster the work of the Lord! What a cure would
it be for the little petty jealousies that, alas! often spring up amongst
the Lord's servants, and hinder His work. It is a happy moment in
the soul's history when it can say: "I have my little bit of work from
the Lord to do; I can do no one else's little bit, and no one can do
mine." Coupled with the diligence and responsibility of service, how
sweetly is here intertwined the call on the affections to "watch."

Blessed Master, help us all to *watch unremittingly* for Thy coming; and, till Thou comest back to *work unweariedly* in thy harvest
field!

W. T. P. WOLSTON

*L*et us be on the watch for opportunities of usefulness.

Let us go about the world with our ears and our eyes open,
ready to avail ourselves of every occasion for doing good. Let us not

be content till we are useful, but make this the main desire and ambition of our lives.

CHARLES SPURGEON

Rise! for the day is passing,
And you lie dreaming on;
The others have buckled their armour,
And forth to the fight have gone.
A place in the ranks awaits you,
Each man has some part to play;
The Past and the Future are nothing,
In the face of the stern Today.
Rise from your dreams of the future,
Of gaining some hard-fought field,
Of storming some airy fortress,
Of bidding some giant yield;
Your future has deeds of glory,
Of honor (God grant it may!),
But your arm will never be stronger,
Or the need so great as Today.

ADELAIDE ANNE PROCTOR

April 16

.... To him who overcomes, I will give some of the hidden manna.
REVELATION 2:17A

*J*esus said that He was the "Bread of Life." He also said: "I am the true bread which came down from heaven." The world still looks on, and of Christ and the Word of God they are saying, "What is it?" The true believer is he that can use the word in the Chaldean sense and say, concerning the Word of God: "It is a portion," and concerning Christ Himself, "He is a portion."

What kind of portion was the manna to this army of pilgrims? It was a

Sufficient Portion. There was enough for all and no lack.

Suitable Portion. It suited every palate, young and old alike, also the weak and the strong. The Jews say, "It tasted to every man as he pleased."

Satisfying Portion. No man ever went hungry. "The young lions do lack, and suffer hunger; but they that seek the Lord shall not want any good thing."

Strengthening Portion. It made strong men of them. They were able to journey in a desert, to work, and to fight.

Sustaining Portion. On it they lived for forty years. It must have been very nutritious.

Sure Portion. It never failed.

Cannot all this be said of Christ Jesus our Lord? He suits all classes, all nationalities, all ages, yea, all men everywhere. He certainly satisfies those who trust Him. "All that I want is in Jesus, he satisfies, joy He supplies. Life would be worthless without Him. All things in Jesus I find." He also strengthens His followers for life and service. He will sustain us all through life's journey and will never fail. Joshua tells us that there was an overlap in the supply of manna. "And the manna ceased on the morrow after they had eaten of the old corn of the land" (Josh. 5:12). Christ is not only our supply in life but He will take us through until we get right into the heavenly land to feast upon "hidden manna."

C. W. SLEMMING

*T*he Israelites were to gather the manna every man according to his eating (Exodus 16:16). The appetite, then, governed the amount collected. How strikingly true this is of the believer! *We have as much of Christ as our desire—no more, and no less.* If our desires are large, if we will open our mouth wide, he will fill it ... On the other hand, if we are but feebly conscious of our need, only a little of Christ will be supplied.

EDWARD DENNETT

April 17

Greater love has no one than this, that he lay down his life for his friends.

JOHN 15:13

*T*he greatest honor a great king or noble lord can do a poor servant is to treat him as a friend, especially if, in public and private alike, it is seen to be both genuine and spontaneous. The poor man will think something like this, "What greater honor or pleasure could my noble lord confer on me than to show a simple man like me such marvelous friendliness? Indeed, it gives me much more pleasure than would the greatest gifts if they were bestowed condescendingly." This physical illustration was showed so vividly that it demonstrated the man's heartfelt delight and almost delirious joy at such great friendliness.

It is the same with our Lord Jesus and ourselves. Surely there can be no greater joy than that he, the most supreme, mighty, noble, and worthy of all, should also be the most lowly, humble, friendly, and considerate. In very truth this marvelous joy will be ours when we see him. His will for us is that we should seek for and trust him, rejoice and delight in him, while he in turn strengthens and comforts us until such time as we realize it all in very fact. The fullest joy we can have springs from the marvelous consideration and friendliness shown us by our Father and our Maker, through our Lord Jesus Christ, our Brother and our Savior.

JULIAN OF NORWICH

The Christian should never complain of his hard fortune while he knows that Christ is his friend.

AUTHOR UNKNOWN

. . .a friend of publicans and sinners. . .

MATTHEW 11:19, KJV

April 18

My beloved is mine, and I am his. . .
SONG OF SOLOMON 2:16

What an infinite pleasure it is to lose ourselves in Him, and being swallowed up in the overcoming sense of his goodness, to offer ourselves a living sacrifice always ascending unto him in flames of love. Never does a soul know what solid joy and substantial pleasure is, till once, being weary of itself, it renounce all propriety, give itself up unto the Author of its being, and feel itself become a hallowed and devoted thing, and can say, from an inward sense and feeling: "My beloved is mine." I account all his interest mine own, "and I am his." I am content to be anything for him, and care not for myself, but that I may serve him.

A person molded into this temper would find pleasure in all the dispensations of Providence: temporal enjoyments would have another relish, when he should taste the divine goodness in them, and consider them as tokens of love sent by his dearest Lord and Maker; and chastisements, though they be not joyous but grievous, would hereby lose their sting, the rod as well as the staff would comfort him—he would snatch a kiss from the hand that was smiting him, and gather sweetness from that severity—nay, he would rejoice that through God did not the will of such a worthless and foolish creature as himself, yet he did his own will, and accomplished his won designs, which are definitely more holy and wise.

HENRY SCOUGAL

There is no limit to God's favor toward those in Christ.

WILLIAM NEWELL

April 19

So, my brothers, you also died to the law through the body of Christ, that you might belong to another, to him who was raised from the dead, in order that we might bear fruit to God. For when we were controlled by the sinful nature, the sinful passions aroused but the law were at work in our bodies, so that we bore fruit for death. But now, by dying to what once bound us, we have been released from the law so that we serve in the new way of the Spirit, are not in the old way of the written code.

ROMANS 7:4–6

*B*elievers in Jesus! Oh, beware of touching the law of Moses; surely it is the ministration of condemnation and death. Harbor no other thought than that of justification by CHRIST ALONE. Let Christ crucified and risen be the sole spring of your joy and peace. Never think of the law of Moses, but as having been perfectly fulfilled, magnified, and made honorable, and all its curse unsparingly borne by Christ on your behalf. Look at it nailed to the cross of Jesus, taken out of the way, and all its enmity so perfectly abolished, that it can be boldly said to the feeblest believer in Christ, "sin shall not have dominion over you, for ye are not under the law but under grace."

"CRUMBS FOR THE LORD'S LITTLE ONES"

*N*ot only does the Lord Jesus live in us, but He becomes the motivating Object of our life as Christians. The law is no longer our motive or rule of life. It is entirely displaced by a Person, and that Person is "the Son of God, who loved me and gave Himself for me." Henceforth, the soul has a new center and source—it is no longer self-centered, but Christ-centered.

C. A. COATES

*G*ood and holy and perfect as the law of God is, it is entirely powerless either to justify or sanctify. It cannot in any way make the old nature better; neither is it the rule of the new nature. The old man is not subject to it, and the new man does not need it. The new creation has another object before it, and another power that acts upon it, in order to produce what is lovely and acceptable to God— Christ the object, realized by the power of the Holy Spirit.

WILLIAM KELLY

April 20

Study to show thyself approved unto God, a workman that needeth not to be ashamed, rightly dividing the word of truth.
2 TIMOTHY 2:15, KJV

*O*ur mental capacity will never know their full wealth of power and spiritual effectiveness until they become simply the vessels of His quickening life, and these brains of ours are laid at His feet simply as the censers which are to hold His holy fire.

He will think in us, remember in us, judge in us, impart definiteness and clearness to our conceptions of truth, give us the tongue of fire, the illustration that both illuminates and melts, the accent and tone of persuasiveness and sympathy, the power of quick expression and utterance, and all the equipment necessary to make us "workmen that need not to be ashamed, rightly dividing the word of truth." Not of course without diligent and faithful attention to His wise and holy teaching, as He leads us in His work to see at once our own shortcomings and His full purpose for us.

We must be taught of God, and teaching is sometimes very gradual, and even slow; but "He will guide us into all truth," and "perfect that which concerneth" our education and preparation for His work and will; and the mind that the Holy Spirit quickens and uses shall accomplish results for God which all the brilliancy of human genius and the scholarship of human learning can never approach.

A. B. SIMPSON

*L*earning is very real work, and there is no maturing without it, and I do not believe that anyone matures brilliantly who does not learn sufferingly. Easily got—easily gone, is never so true as in the highest things.

J. B. STONEY

*D*o good with what you have, or it will do you no good.

WILLIAM PENN

April 21

Thou will show me the path of life: in thy presence is fullness of joy; at thy right hand there are pleasures for evermore.

PSALM 16:11, KJV

*I*f we want a joy that no man can take from us, we must find it in something no man can disturb. No element of joy that is subject to human fluctuations can be in the least depended on. The only lasting joy is to be found in the everlasting God. In God alone apart from all else: apart from His gifts, apart from His blessings, apart from all that can by any possibility change. He alone is unchangeable. He is always the same good, loving, tender God, and we can rejoice in Him whether we are able to rejoice in His gifts and His promises or not. We rejoice in a baby just because it is, not because of anything it has done or can do for us. To rejoice in God means something infinitely deeper and wider.

In His presence is fullness of joy, and fullness of joy is nowhere else. Just as the simple presence of the mother makes the child's joy, so does the simple fact of God's presence with us make our joy. The mother may not make a single promise to the child or explain any of her plans or purposes, but *she is*, and that is enough for the child. The child rejoices in the mother herself, not in her promises. And to the child there is behind all that changes and can change the one unchangeable joy of the mother's existence. While the mother lives, the child will be cared for, and the child instinctively, if not intelligently, rejoices in knowing this.

And to the children of God as well there is behind all that changes and can change the once unchangeable joy that God is. And while He is, His children will be cared for, and they ought to know it and rejoice in it as instinctively and far more intelligently than the child of human parents. For what else can God do, being what He is? Neglect, indifference, forgetfulness, ignorance are all impossible to Him. He knows everything. He cares about everything. He can manage everything. And He loves us!

HANNAH WHITALL SMITH

And they that went in, went in male and female of all flesh, as God
had commanded him: and the LORD shut him in.

GENESIS 7:16, KJV

*J*ust as with Noah, how completely has God shut us in a place of
better blessing, by a covenant in His own blood! There can then be
no more offering for sin—because there has been remission of all
the believer's sins and iniquities; but the blessing does not stop here;
the knowledge of the remission sets a man apart to and for God—
saying to him, as it were, "You need look for nothing more either
to cleanse you or to make you meet. I, the Blood, am all you want
as to the question of acceptance: By me you are perfected for ever;
go, go away from thinking about self; go, go and *serve* God; for you
are set apart to Him—yea, perfected for Him. Let Him be your
study, your delight, your end in everything you do, or think, or say."

GEORGE V. WIGRAM

*J*t is a wonderful thing to be so satisfied with the Lord Jesus' company, that we can be tranquil about everything. I remember when I
used to think that I should be happy beyond conception if I were
able to say, "I will fear no evil. My heart is fixed, trusting in the
Lord." In order to reach this, you must find Him enough, without
anything else. You can never prove the worth of anyone, until you
are absolutely dependent on Him.

J. B. STONEY

*W*hat we love, we shall grow to resemble.

BERNARD OF CLAIRVAUX

We give thanks to you O God, we give thanks, for your Name is near.
PSALM 75:1

God is very near to each one of us. Though we see Him not, yet is He nearer than the very air we breathe; for our very being and living and moving is in Him. He is very near unto us, and all our thoughts and desires are open before Him, who is the searcher of our hearts.

Yet, although such is the exceeding nearness of God to us, we are at an exceeding great distance from God. Who can measure the distance of the prodigal in the far country from the father's house? But we can describe that distance by one syllable, short though terrible—*sin.*

Now He by whom alone sin can be forgiven and removed is nowhere else but on the throne of God—on his right hand. With Him is forgiveness of sin. In heaven is my righteousness; in the throne of God, and nowhere else, my hope, my comfort, and my trust. He who has found and saved me, lost and guilty sheep; He who by His death has redeemed me, has taken me on His shoulder. He is no longer here. As He died unto sin once, I seek Him no longer among the dead. He is ascended. Rejoicing has He gone home, and called His friends together to rejoice over the sheep now with Him in the land of peace. Hence there is no other place for me but heaven itself. *Everywhere else I see only sin and condemnation.*

Where can I pray or approach God without a Mediator, without the blood, without the High Priest? But the blood of Jesus, the Mediator of the new covenant, the interceding High Priest Jesus, *is in heaven itself.* Then I also must pray and worship there. I have no other hiding place but *Christ in heaven.*

You who have come to Jesus, who have looked unto Him and were healed, you stand now on the other side of the cross, within the veil, in the holy of holies. You have obtained mercy. God forgave all your sins, and clothed you with Christ.

In this state into which God has brought you there can henceforth be no change. Your knowledge and enjoyment of it may vary and grow, your faithfulness and service fluctuate, your experience may rise and fall; but you are always children of God, forgiven, beloved, compassed about with divine mercy, and embraced in the very love which the father has to Jesus.

ADOLPH SAPHIR

*N*o sin the believer brings to God, when it comes to being weighed, is not greatly outweighed by the blood of Christ.

G. V. WIGRAM

April 24

But seek first his kingdom and his righteousness, and all these things will be given to you as well.

MATTHEW 6:33

*F*or the first two or three years after my conversion, I used to ask for specific things. Now I ask for God.

Supposing there is a tree full of fruits—you will have to go and buy or beg the fruits from the owner of the tree. Every day you would have to go for one or two fruits. But if you can make the tree your own property, then all the fruits will be your own.

In the same way, if God is your own, then all things in Heaven and on earth will be your own, because He is your Father and is everything to you; otherwise you will have to go and ask like a beggar for certain things. When they are used up, you will have to ask again. So ask not for gifts but for the Giver of Gifts; not for life but for the Giver of Life—then life and the things needed for life will be added unto you.

SADU SUNDAR SINGH

Once it was blessing,
Now it is the Lord;
Once it was the feeling,
Now it is His Word;
Once His gift I wanted,
Now the Giver own;
Once I sought for healing,
Now Himself alone.

W. M. Turnbull

April 25

Verily Thou art a God that hidest thyself, O God of Israel, the Savior.
Isaiah 45:15, kjv

Men and women! What are you living for? What is your life yielding you? If you are not finding God in all parts of your life— what a fatal mistake you are making! And what a magnificent reward you are forever missing!

But, when all is said, it is not to be wondered at that so few of us seek, and *seek out,* God. For His greatness passes all comprehension, and imagination, and searching out of men and angels. His holiness also makes Him a "consuming fire" to such sinners as we are.

And then, His awful spirituality, omnipresence, and inwardness— we would go mad, if we once saw Him as He is, and at the same time saw ourselves as we are. We must grow like God before we can both see Him and live. And thus it is that it is only His very choices and chiefest saints who do seek Him out to the end, either in His Son, or in the Scriptures, or in their own hearts, or in Providence, or in nature, or in unceasing prayer.

It is only one here, and another there, who ever identify with the cry of Job, "Oh, that I knew where I might find Him." And with Isaiah, "Verily Thou art a God that hidest thyself." And with Paul, "Dwelling in light which no man can approach unto: Whom no man hath seen, or can see."

But, just in the depth and adoration of their cry; and just as their sight and sense is of the greatness and the glory of God—just in that kind, and just in that degree, will their reward be, when He shall reveal Himself at last as their very reward.

ALEXANDER WHYTE

There is many a Christian who has not reached Christ, and there is the weakness. There is a larger blessing than forgiveness—that is, *Himself*. Nothing will satisfy Christ but revealing His heart to you, and you will never grow until you know Him. It is impossible to grow unless you are under the power of His love.

EDWARD DENNETT

April 26

. . .be filled with the Spirit.

EPHESIANS 5:18B

The promise of the Spirit is not for great or exceptional Christians, but for any Christian who yields himself to God. Paul addressed everyday Christian believers at Ephesus: husband, wife, parent, child, master, slave. He encouraged all to live lives full of the divine Holy Spirit, full from within.

What this command to be filled with the Spirit meant in Ephesus, it means in England, it means to the one who is writing

these words in his study at Cambridge, and to his brother in Christ
who reads them, wherever and whenever God has bid him dwell.

HENDLEY MOULE

I *must* be filled. It is absolutely *necessary.*
I *may* be filled. God has made it blessedly *possible.*
I *want* to be filled. It is eminently *desirable.*
I *will* be filled. It is so blessedly *certain.*

ANDREW MURRAY

April 27

*. . . and our fellowship is with the Father and with his Son, Jesus
Christ.*
1 JOHN 1:3B

*I*t has come these days with new light and power that the first
thing we have to see to as we draw near to God day by day is that
our fellowship is with the Father, and with His Son Jesus Christ. If
we listen in the stillness till our hearts begin to respond to what he
is thinking and feeling about the matter in question, whether it
concerns ourselves or others, we can, from that moment, begin
praying downwards from the Throne, instead of praying upwards
from ourselves.

L. TROTTER

*Y*ou must abide in Christ in heaven before you can descend with
heavenly ability to act for Him down here. The great secret of all
blessing is to come *from* the Lord. Most Christians go *to* Him.

A. J.

April 28

If a blind man leads a blind man, both will fall into a pit.

MATTHEW 15:14

*I*t is a fatal mistake to suppose that, in order to pluck people out of the fire, we must go into the fire ourselves. This would never do. The best way to deliver people from an evil position is to be thoroughly out of that position myself.

How can I best pull a man out of quicksand? Surely not by going into the quicksand, but by standing on firm ground and from thence lending him a helping hand. I cannot pull a man out of anything unless I am out myself. If we want to help the people of God who are mixed up with the surrounding ruin, the first thing for ourselves is to be in thorough and decided separation; and the next thing is to have our hearts brimful and flowing over with tender and fervent love to all who bear the precious name of Jesus.

C. H. MACKINTOSH

*M*y counsel is, that you come out and leave the multitude, and let Christ have your company. Let them have this present world, who love it. Christ is a more worthy and noble choice. Blessed are those who receive Him.

SAMUEL RUTHERFORD

April 29

We live by faith, not by sight.

2 CORINTHIANS 5:7

*T*here are but two ruling principles of action—sight and faith. Sight is the principle which guides the natural senses, but faith is the principle which guides the enlightened soul. Sight is worldly wisdom, but faith is heavenly wisdom. Sight's horizons are the mountain-tops, but faith has an ever-receding and ever-widening skyline.

These principles of action are mutually exclusive because they are absolutely contradictory. Sight's objects are the material and the visible, but faith's objects are the spiritual and the unseen. Sight declares that only present things have existence, but faith gives present existence to future things. The life of every one of us is governed by one or other of these principles, but no one can be governed by the both at the same time. They can no more agree with one another than do fire and water; they can no more co-exist than can light and darkness. The world's principle of action is sight, but the Christian principle of action is faith. The Christian's great days are the days when faith dominates, and our sad and bad days are the days when sight rules. We know that well enough, and memories will rush in upon us as we speak about these things, and we may well say:

Oh! To go back across the years long vanished,
To have the words unsaid, the deeds undone,
The errors cancelled and the deep shadows banished.
In the glad sense of a new life begun.

We think of wasted days and sad failures because we were guided by the principle of sight, instead of by faith. This conflict remains as long as we are in our present estate. There never will come a time, while we are in this world, when we shall be beyond the reach of this principle of sight; but it should become weaker and weaker as the principle of faith becomes stronger and stronger.

In Ernest Raymond's *Life of St. Francis of Assisi*, he gives a chapter to two brothers in the Franciscan Order, Elias and Francis. Elias sought position, power, place and popularity. Brother Francis had no wish for any of these things, but liked to be among the birds, to listen to them and to talk to them; to be amongst and preach to the poor, himself poor, for he had abandoned everything. How are these two men thought of today? Has anybody here heard of Brother Elias? But Francis of Assisi! Many a long journey has been taken to see his memorial. We have all heard of him and read of him—why? One chose to be guided by sight, an the other by faith; and so while one failed, the other succeeded.

W. GRAHAM SCROGGIE

April 30

Then Peter and the other apostles answered and said, "We ought to obey God rather than men."
ACTS 5:29, KJV

*H*as the Spirit borne witness that you are to do a certain work for God? As you heed that impression and pray over it, does it become deeper and more indelible on your heart? As you yield toward the carrying out of that impression does there come a deep and settled peace to your soul? If so, it is doubtless the leading of the Holy Spirit.

Have you yielded your life completely to the Holy Spirit? As you know your own heart, have you utterly yielded yourself to God? Has there been a time in your life when you came to the place where it became your fixed intention to surrender everything to the will and working of the Spirit? One missionary has put it, "Such a surrender is not easy, nor as complete as we oftentimes suppose." Yet, is it right to expect God to lead you to the field of *His* choice if you have already determined in your own heart where *you* want to go? If you really want His guidance, you have to be ready to put yourself in His hands and gladly follow His directions, *wherever they may lead*. Does selfish ambition enter into your plans, the desire for recognition and praise from other Christians? It is better, and infinitely more satisfying to please God than men.

G. Christian Weiss

It is said that a certain society in South Africa once wrote to missionary David Livingstone, "Have you found a good road to where you are? If not we want to know how to send other men to join you."

Livingstone replied, "I don't know what you mean by asking about other men joining me when none have come as yet, and if you have men who will only come if they know there's a good road, well, I don't want them. I want men who will come even if there is *no* road!"

"World Conquest"

For when we were yet without strength, in due time, Christ died for the ungodly. For scarcely for a righteous man will one die; yet peradventure for a good man some would even dare to die. But God commendeth his love toward us, in that, while we were yet sinners, Christ died for us. Much more then, being now justified by his blood, we shall be saved from wrath through him. For when we were enemies, we were reconciled to God by the death of his Son, much more, being reconciled we shall be saved by his life.

ROMANS 5:6–10, KJV

*I*s there any who, in false humility, would doubt the love of God and Christ, *because* of what he is in himself? Let such a one read this passage, and see how the Lord gathers those who are without strength—the ungodly, the enemies, sinners, as those to whom He would demonstrate in the death of Jesus, the love He *commends* to such—to us.

Wondrous, the love discovered in God towards us; but more wondrous still, how amid all the discouragements to it in us, it should yet not only not be able to shut itself up, but seek to *commend* itself to us.

To how many an object does a man feel pity, aye and love too, to whom he will never attempt to communicate it, for to do so he would prove a desire of fellowship, and the recognition of power of response in the object loved; and surely our God's seeking to commend His love to us does tell His desire of fellowship, while, where it is made known, it gives the power, through grace, of response, and we, reconciled by the death of His Son, love Him because He first loved us.

GEORGE V. WIGRAM

*A*nyone can devise a plan by which good people may go to Heaven. Only God can devise a plan whereby sinners, who are His enemies, can go to Heaven.

LEWIS SPERRY CHAFER

*G*race is not looking for good men whom it may approve, for it is not grace but mere justice to approve goodness. But it is looking for condemned, guilty, speechless and helpless men whom it may save, sanctify and glorify.

C. I. SCOFIELD

May 2

You do not have because you do not ask God . . .
JAMES 4:2B

*T*rue praying involves serious attention and time, which flesh and blood do not relish. Few people have such strong fiber that they will make a costly outlay when inferior work will pass just as well in the marketplace.

To be little *with* God is to be little *for* God. It takes much time for the fullness of God to flow into the spirit. Short devotions cut the pipe of God's full flow. We live shabbily because we pray meagerly. This is not a day of prayer. Few men pray. In these days of hurry and bustle men will not take time to pray. Prayer is out-of-date, almost a lost art.

Where are the Christlike leaders who can teach modern saints how to pray and put them at it? Do we know that we are raising up a prayerless set of saints? Only praying leaders can have praying followers. We greatly need somebody who can set the saints to this business of praying!

E. M. BOUNDS

There are beautiful birds in the air, and twinkling stars in the heavens, but if you desire pearls you must plunge down into the depths of the ocean to find them. There are many beautiful things in the world around us, but pearls can only be discovered in the depths of the sea. If we wish to possess spiritual pearls we must plunge into the depths, that is, we must pray, we must sink down into the secret depths of contemplation and prayer. Then we shall perceive precious pearls.

SADU SUNDAR SINGH

Believe me, you can only plead with God as you know Christ. He alone is the channel by which God can bless. . . . The power of intercession is a great thing to the servant of God.

GEORGE V. WIGRAM

May 3

Commit thy way unto the LORD; Trust also in him; and he shall bring it to pass.

PSALM 37:5, KJV

Victorious living is the heritage of every believer. It is supernatural. It is the life that Christ came to give. The same Lord who lived in his sinless humanity on earth over 1900 years ago now dwells in the heart of everyone who has received him as Savior.

Are you thanking the Father that Jesus Christ came and clothed himself with your humanity the moment you believed in him? Are you counting on the fact that because you put your trust in Christ, he, in you, is equal to every situation and every circumstance as it arises?

Just as you stood back from your guilt and said, "Thank you for my redemption"—which you never deserved—are you now meeting every circumstance, every temptation by saying, "Thank you, Lord Jesus, for your all-sufficiency"?

God says your whole life is to be wholly abandoned to him. How simple it is to put God in charge to live his life in and through you, so he can bring to pass that which is his perfect will for you. Then you will live positively and productively. Then he will *bring it to pass*.

ETHEL JONES WILCOX

The believer who knows how to abandon himself to the Lord will soon become perfect.

JEANNE GUYON

May 4

Forever, O LORD, thy word is settled in heaven.
PSALM 119:89, KJV

The Christian is not blind or oblivious to the power arrayed against him. He sees it, he knows it, he is fully aware of its vastness and greatness; but he looks up to God. He takes in the fact that God is almighty, and greater than all the powers that can be arrayed against Him, and he trusts Him.

Is it modern Philistines who seek to rob us of what God has given us in Christ? We turn to God's word which is forever settled in Heaven. Nothing can change it, and we hold it fast in spite of all the wiles or power of the enemy to compel us to give it up.

Our heavenly reward is the object of the enemy's attack; and he would seek to get us to give it up and get us down to the level of the world—so worldly that we become practically servants to the Philistines and useless for God. How true it is, that the more worldly a Christian is, the more useless for God he is.

And so must it be with us today. Do we expect God to work for us in any special way, or use us to the deliverance and blessing of those around us?

Be sure there are sharp rocks on either side to hinder us—difficulties which must be surmounted—hindrances which must be overcome, and Satan knows how to pile them up and make them sharp and cutting.

It is over these we must pass before the victory can be gained, and we can only get past them on our hands and knees as it were—low down before God, in the place of dependence, and in the path of obedience. In the recognition and confession of our own nothingness, helplessness, and unworthiness, and His Almightiness so that all the glory may be His.

It is when we have reached that place and state we give Him room to work, and then He lays hold of us and uses us for blessing to others. Brothers and sisters, we must be praying Christians.

WILLIAM EASTON

The moment we enter upon the enjoyment of any blessing, Satan will seek to rob us of it.

AUTHOR UNKNOWN

If thine eye be single, thy whole body shall be full of light." If it is so with you, there is sure to be light in the path—light not for ten years from now but this one step that is before you, and then for the next.

JOHN DARBY

If any of you lacks wisdom, he should ask God, who gives generously to all without finding fault, and it will be given to him. But when he asks, he must believe and not doubt, because he who doubts is like a wave of the sea, blown and tossed by the wind. That man should not think he will receive anything from the Lord; he is a double-minded man, unstable in all he does.

JAMES 1:5–8

*B*e slow to take new steps in the Lord's service, or in your business, or in your families. Weigh everything well; weigh all in the light of the Holy Scriptures, and in the fear of God.

Seek to have no will of your own, in order to ascertain the mind of God, regarding any steps you propose to take, so that you can honestly say, you are willing to do the will of God, if He will only please to instruct you.

But when you have found out what the will of God is, seek for His help, and seek it earnestly, perseveringly, patiently, believingly, and expectingly: and you will surely, in His own time and way, obtain it.

GEORGE MUELLER

*A*n open door in service is from the Lord and not from man. We may therefore, be independent of man altogether, and we shall be if we keep our eyes wholly upon the Lord, remembering He always sets an open door before us if we keep His word and do not deny His name.

EDWARD DENNETT

But the path of the just is as the shining light, that shineth more and more unto the perfect day.

PSALM 4:18, KJV

*G*od will give Himself to you, and in the very heart of your decaying nature will plant the seed of an immortal being which shall, like His own, shake off fatigue from the limbs, and never tend to dissolution or an end.

The life of nature dies by living; the life of grace, which may belong to us all, lives by living, and lives evermore thereby. And so that life is continuous and progressive, with no tendency to decay, nor term to its being.

Each of you, looking forward to the certain ebbing away of creatural power, to the certain changes that may pass upon you, may say, "I know that I shall have to leave behind me my present youthful strength, my unworn freshness, my buoyancy, my confidence, my wonder, my hope; but I shall carry my Christ; and in Him I shall possess the secret of an immortal youth."

The oldest angels are the youngest. The longer men live in fellowship with Christ the stronger do they grow. And though our lives, whether we be Christians or no, are necessarily subject to the common laws of mortality; we may carry all that is worth preserving of the earliest stages into the latest; and when gray hairs are upon us, and we are living next door to our graves, we may still have the enthusiasm, the energy, and above all, the boundless hopefulness that made the gladness and the spring of our long-buried youth.

Again, you may have strength to run—that is to say, there is power waiting for you for all the great crises of your lives which call for special, though it may be brief, exertion. Such crises will come to each of you, in sorrow, work, difficulty, hard conflicts.

Moments will be sprung upon you without warning, in which you will feel that years hang on the issue of an instant. Great tasks will be clashed down before you unexpectedly which will demand the gathering together of all your power. And there is only one way to be ready for such times as these, and that is to live waiting on the Lord, near Christ, with Him in your hearts, and then nothing will come that will be too big for you.

However rough the road, and however severe the struggle, and however swift the pace, you will be able to keep it up. Though it may be with panting lungs and a throbbing heart, and dim eyes and quivering muscles, yet if you wait on the Lord you will run and not be weary. You will be masters of the crises.

ALEXANDER MACLAREN

*T*here is a God above *all* adverse circumstances and undesirable influences. And our path for power is in letting patience have its perfect work. . . . Trust Him. He has the power to work where we least expect it.

JOHN DARBY

May 7

. . . blessed are they that have not seen, and yet believed.
JOHN 20:29B

*H*uman hearts are amazingly alike. As I talk with people in America, England, Switzerland, Germany, and Holland, I frequently find the same need, the same ignorance of what we can be in Jesus Christ, if only we accept the Bible in a simple, childlike way as the Word of God, the Word that teaches us the foolishness of God that is wiser than the wisdom of men, the love of God that passes all understanding.

When we read the Bible we should never use as our guide the wisdom of men or the standards of our own reason.

I was once a passenger aboard a ship that was being guided by radar. The fog was so dense we couldn't see even the water about us. But the radar screen showed a streak of light, indicating the presence of another ship far ahead. The radar penetrated the fog and picked up its image. So, also, is faith the radar that sees reality through the clouds.

The reality of the victory of Christ can be seen only by faith, which is our radar. Our faith perceives what is actual and real; our senses perceive only that which is limited to three dimensions and comprehended by our intellect. Faith sees more.

CORRIE TEN BOOM

*I*t must be ever remembered that guidance is a matter of faith, not sight.

EDWARD DENNETT

May 8

Again Jesus said, "Peace be with you! As the Father has sent me, I am sending you." And with that he breathed on them and said, "Receive the Holy Spirit."

JOHN 20:21–22

I believe the "show business" which is incorporated into so much Christian work today is causing the church to drift far from the conception of our Lord concerning discipleship.

It seems to be instilled in us that we have to do something exceptional for God as a sort of token, as an example of courage and of sacrifice at which everybody will gaze, openmouthed, and say, "What a wonderful man!"

You do not need the grace of God for that. Human nature and human pride will take us through many a crisis in life, and make us do what seems to be the big thing in leaving our home and offering ourselves for Christian service.

"My, what a man," says the world. That requires no grace; it appeals to the flesh. But I want to say to you from the depths of my heart that it needs all the grace of God to go through drudgery and poverty, to live an ignored existence as a saint, unnoticed by anybody. For if this commission is behind us in Christian work, remember, always we are sent out to be exceptional in ordinary things, among sometimes mean people, in frequently sordid surroundings. Only the man sent by the King of kings could take that, and only the man with a true burden will ever accept it.

After three years of intimate fellowship with Jesus Christ, all the disciples forsook Him and fled. They came to the end of themselves and their self-sufficiency, and they realized that if ever they were to be any different, it must be by receiving a different spirit altogether, and Jesus breathed upon them and said, " . . . as my Father hath sent me, even so send I you . . . Receive ye the Holy Ghost." Have you been sent to the work that you are doing for God today? If you haven't, the sooner you quit, the better.

ALAN REDPATH

A just appreciation of a crucified Christ is the living spring of all that is acceptable to God, whether in the life and conduct of an individual Christian, or in all that goes on in our church services.

Genuine attachment to Christ and occupation with Him must characterize us personally and congregationally, else our life and history will prove of little worth in the judgment of heaven, however it may be in the judgment of earth.

We know of nothing which imparts such moral power to the individual walk and character as intense devotion to Christ. It is not merely being a man of great faith, a man of prayer, a deeply taught student of Scripture or a scholar, a gifted preacher, or a powerful writer.

No, it is being a lover of Christ.

C. H. MACKINTOSH

May 9

. . . we also should walk in newness of life.
ROMANS 6:4, KJV

*I*t is not a *life* merely to which we are called, but a *walk* (a "walking about," as the Greek implies); not a sitting alone; not a private enjoying of religion, but a *walk*; a walk in which we are visible on all sides; a walk which fixes many eyes upon us; a walk in which we are "made a spectacle" to heaven and earth, and hell.

It is no motionless resting or retirement from our fellows, but a moving about in the midst of them, a coming into contact with friends and foes, a going to and fro upon the high-ways and by-ways of earth. As was the master, so must the servant be. On his way to the cross, he looked round and said, "Follow me" (John 12:26); on his way to the throne, after he had passed the cross, he said the same (John 21:22). To the cross, then, and to the crown alike, we are to follow him. It is one way to both.

He then that would be holy must be like Christ; and he that would be like Christ must be "filled with the Spirit"; he that would have in him the mind of Christ must have the same "anointing" as he had, the same indwelling and inworking Spirit; the Spirit of "adoption," of life, faith, truth, liberty, strength, and holy joy.

It is through this mighty quickener that we are quickened; it is through "sanctification of the Spirit" that we are sanctified. It is as our *guest* that he does his work; not working without dwelling, nor dwelling without working; not exerting a mere influence, like that of music on the ruffled soul, but coming into us and abiding with us; so that being "filled with his company" as well as pervaded by his power, we are thoroughly transformed; not merely plying us with arguments, not affecting us with moral suasion, but impressing us with the irresistible touch of his divine hand, and penetrating us with his own vital energy; nay, impregnating us with his own purity and life, in spite of resistance and unteachableness and unbelief on our part, all the days of our life.

He that would be like Christ, moreover, must *study* him. We cannot make ourselves holy by merely *trying* to be so, any more than we can make ourselves believe and love by simple energy of endeavor. No force can effect this.

Men *try* to be holy, and they fail. They cannot by direct effort work themselves into holiness. They must gaze upon a holy object; and so be changed into its likeness "from glory to glory."

They must have a holy being for their bosom friend. Companionship with Jesus, like that of John, can alone make us to resemble either the disciple or the Master.

HORATIUS BONAR

*L*ook at the Lord Jesus firmly and fixedly, never letting your gaze wander elsewhere; and whatever temporal objects come between you and your Lord, look right through them, as through a mist, and fix your eyes and heart upon Him and Him alone. Whatever condition you find yourself in, do not let either earth or heaven hide Him.

JOHN HARRIS

There is neither Jew nor Greek, slave nor free, male nor female, for you are all one in Christ Jesus.

GALATIANS 3:28

*T*he more the believer *grasps the fact of the completed work of his death with Christ as accomplished*, the more effectually does the Holy Spirit work in him to bring that completed work into actual being; conditionally, of course, upon his consenting unflinchingly to separation from all the works of the flesh; and conditionally also upon his active co-operation with the Holy Spirit in refusing to let sin reign in his mortal body.

The Cross is the birthplace of a new creation for every one who turns to Christ as his Savior, but it is also in a wider sense the birthplace of the NEW MAN consisting of Christ and His members. Each member who becomes a new creation in his own life, is but one of many units who, tempered together, form a Body with Christ as Head. All partaking of one life, made to drink of one Spirit, it is "fitly framed and knit together through every joint of the supply, according to the working in due measure of each several part, maketh the increase of the body . . . in love."

Through the Cross all the *divisions* of the fallen creation are done away. Distinctions of nationality or sect no longer divide, but are part of the outward order of things of earth, which are surface and temporary. For "the new man" created by God, is being renewed in the believer in a sphere in Christ, "where there cannot be Greek and Jew, circumcision and uncircumcision, Barbarian, Scythian, bondman, freeman, but Christ is all and in all . . ." and also where there "*can* be no male or female: for all are one man in Christ Jesus." It means, blessed be God, that no external and temporary distinction can enter that sphere in Christ where CHRIST IS ALL, *and in all . . .*

Where the believer has really and experientially apprehended his death in the death of Christ, and learned his place in the Body of Christ; that we are members one of another, as well as of Christ, the inward spiritual union of life in Christ is kept unbroken. With Calvary as the center and basis of unity, no other member of Christ, can ever be looked upon as an "opponent," whilst we witness to truth which that fellow member of Christ may not yet apprehend.

When all the members of Christ can see in that death on the Tree their own death, not only to sin, but *to all that pertains to the religion of the "old man,"* they will find a practical and real oneness with all who are one with their Risen and Ascended Head.

JESSIE PENN-LEWIS

*O*nly let us seek to aim after this: that we see Christ in each other, and not the old nature; the life of the risen Jesus in each other. If we seek to discern Christ in each other, how we shall be drawn to each other!

GEORGE MUELLER

May 11

. . . oil to make his face to shine . . .
PSALM 104:15, KJV

*T*he Holy Spirit has adjusted His mode of living to actually inhabit, indwell our lives. We must, in turn, adjust our living, in its every thought, aspiration and action, to the fact that He is there, in us, a part of us.

Since our physical senses cannot apprehend Him, we must exercise our spiritual faculties in the art of knowing Him. We must practice His presence. We must make it the business of our lives to live in the momentary consciousness of His abiding presence.

How shall we practice His presence? The means of grace are really His appointed provision to the end. As we turn to His Word, we must trust the Spirit in us to answer to the Spirit in the Word. Thus, as we read, our spirits are quickened into conscious realization of His Spirit indwelling us. As the love letter serves to satisfy the heart by enabling us to feed upon the object of our love, so is His Word to the heart that hungers after Him.

Prayer is essentially the practice of His presence. True prayer is talking to God. It is claiming audience with God. Resolute in the purpose not to neglect prayer, nor yet to use it merely to get something from God, we need to seize upon it with renewed avidity, as the opportunity to commune with Him, to school our spirits in responding to His Spirit, to practice His presence.

Particularly we must practice His presence in our daily round. Life must become the *out*living of His *in*living. Many are familiar with the story of Brother Lawrence, a monk of the seventeenth century. His life was characterized by the perpetual sense of God's presence. All his thoughts and aspirations were tempered by the fact of God in his life. Assigned to menial kitchen duties, he found Him as consciously real and near as when engaged in his daily devotions.

It is from such daily practice of His presence that the radiant life is realized. In the diary of Henry Martyn, the sainted missionary of India, is found this entry: "My principal enjoyment is the enjoyment of God's presence." Did the fact disclose itself in any way to others? The natives of Cawnpore used to say of him: "God is shining in that man's face."

In our modern life it is possible, even necessary, to seize upon some portion of the day—the worker setting out for business, the mother starting breakfast, the student for school.

Let this daily act serve as a signal for lifting the heart into conscious communion with Him, to claim His presence and partnership in the particular task or at some anticipated point of need. Simple in itself, the practice will return large spiritual dividends.

NORMAN B. HARRISON

Begin the day with God!
He is thy Sun and Day!
His the radiance of thy dawn;
To Him address thy day.
Sing thy first song to God!
Not to thy fellow men;
Not to the creatures of His hand,
But to the glorious One.
Take thy first walk with God!
Him go forth with Thee;
By stream, or sea, or mountain path,
Seek still His company.
Thy first transaction be
With God Himself above;
So shall thy business prosper well,
All thy day be love.

Horatius Bonar

May 12

I give them eternal life and they shall never perish; no one can snatch them out of my hand.

John 10:28

The way to heaven is as free as the way to hell. In hell there is an accuser, but in heaven there is no one to condemn. The only being in the universe of God who has a right to judge the sinner is now exalted to be a Savior. Amid the wonders and terrors of that throne, He is a Savior, and He is sitting there in grace.

The Savior shall yet become the Judge, but judgment waits on grace. Sin has reigned, and death can boast its victories, but shall grace not have its triumphs too?

As surely as the sin of man brought death, the grace of God shall bring eternal life to every sinner who believes. *One* sin brought death, but grace masters *all* sin. If sin abounded, grace abounds far more. Grace is conqueror. GRACE REIGNS.

Not at the expense of righteousness, but in virtue of it. Righteousness requires the sinner's death, and yet grace has intervened to give him life. Righteousness itself has set grace upon the throne in order that the sinner may have life: "That as sin hath reigned unto death, even so might grace reign, through Jesus Christ our Lord."

Such is the triumph of the cross. It has made it possible for God to bless us in perfect harmony with everything He is, and everything He has ever declared Himself to be, and in spite of all that we are, and of all that He has ever said we ought to be.

SIR ROBERT ANDERSON

*I*t is not God who sends the sinner to hell, it is his own sins. God allows everyone to come to heaven; indeed He invites everyone most earnestly to come in. But sinners themselves feel that it is a torture to stay there; that is why they do not desire it. God does not make their entrance into heaven either difficult or impossible, no, it is their own inner attitude which makes it impossible for them to have any joy in eternal life.

SADU SUNDAR SINGH

May 13

But he that glorieth, let him glory in the Lord.

2 CORINTHIANS 10:17, KJV

*O*n this planet Earth, since the cross, and not before, God is pleased to make His people to be His habitation. He came down in the person of Christ, but Christ abode alone as far as the dwelling-place of God was concerned.

"Destroy this temple," Jesus said. He was the only true temple. But when He died and rose, what then? Redemption was accomplished; and now God could descend holily, righteously, suitably to His own character, and could dwell in His people.

It is not because the New Testament saints are more worthy in themselves than those of old. He that knows himself and redemption knows that such an idea is a fallacy and a falsehood; he knows that human nature is good for nothing as before God; he knows that, in His presence, there is no question of flesh, or what flesh can glory in, "but he that glorieth, let him glory in the Lord."

But this is not all; not only is there a Lord to glory in, but now we have actual redemption in Christ through His blood. How does God estimate the precious blood of His Son? What does He feel about those on whom that blood is put by faith—those who are washed in it? Does He not as it were say, " I can come now and take my place in their midst?" This is indeed one of the precious characteristics of the church.

WILLIAM KELLY

So many Christians are disturbed, so many are restless, because they are not living in the knowledge that they are under the care of the Lord; and then there is no power to walk. Why have you so little power in walk or service? It is because you are not yet clear that the Lord is caring for you, that He is in all watchfulness over you, that He has let down the strong pinions of His protecting care till they sweep the ground around you, and if you are wise, you will creep up close under His wings, into the very down.

J. B. STONEY

I will be as the dew to Israel . . .

HOSEA 14:5

*H*ave you noticed that this old earth receives a fresh baptism of life daily? Every night the life-giving dew falls. The moisture rises during the day from ocean, and lake, and river, undergoes a chemical change in God's laboratory and returns nightly in dew to refresh the earth.

It brings to all nature new life, with rare beauty, and fills the air with the exquisite fragrance drawn from flowers and plants. Its power to purify and revitalize is peculiar and remarkable. It falls only in the night when the world is at rest. It can come only on clear calm nights. Both cloud and wind disturb and prevent its working. It comes quietly and works noiselessly. But the changes effected are radical and immeasurable. Literally it gives to the earth a nightly baptism of new life. That is God's plan for the earth. And that, too, let me say to you, is His plan for our day-by-day life.

It hushes one's heart with a gentle awe to go out early in the morning after a clear night when air and flower and leaf are fragrant with an indescribable freshness, and listen to God's voice saying, "I will be as the dew unto Israel." That sentence is the climax of the book where it occurs. God is trying through Hosea to woo his people away from their evil leaders up to Himself again. To a people who knew well the vitalizing power of the deep dews of an Oriental night, and their own dependence upon them, He says with pleading voice, "I will be to you as the dew."

S. D. GORDON

*And make straight paths for your feet, lest that which is lame be turned
out of the way; but let it rather be healed.*

HEBREWS 12:13, KJV

*H*ave you ever watched a farmer plowing a field? In order to
make straight furrows, he must fix his eyes on a tree or a post in the
fence or some object at the far side of the field. He then will guide
his plow unwaveringly toward the object. If he begins to look
behind him to see whether he has made a straight furrow, the plow
begins to jerk from side to side. As a result, the furrow he is making becomes a zigzag.

If we want to make straight paths for our feet, we must do what
Paul did and forget those things which are behind, and reach forth
unto those things which are before, pressing toward the mark for
the prize of the high calling of God in Christ Jesus.

To forget the things that are behind is an essential part of pressing forward toward the prize of our high calling. This prize can
never be reached unless we forget the past. When we do, we put an
end to all our self-examination because if we do not look back over
our past misdoings, we will find little food for self-reflection.

HANNAH WHITALL SMITH

*W*hy should I wince at the pull of the plow of my Lord, that
makes deep furrows on my soul? I know that He is no idle farmer,
but rather, He purposes a crop.

SAMUEL RUTHERFORD

Ah! give me, Lord, the single eye,
Which aims at nought but Thee;
I fain would live, and yet not I—
But Jesus live in me.

AUGUSTUS TOPLADY

And some [seed] fell on rocky ground where it had not much earth; and straightway it sprang up because it had no deepness of earth: and when the sun was risen, it was scorched; and because it had no root, it withered away.

MARK 4: 5–6, KJV

*W*hat is root? It is growth beneath the soil. What are leaves? Growth above the soil. Root is hidden life; leaves are manifest life. The trouble with many Christians is that, while there is much apparent life, there is very little secret life.

You have been a Christian for a number of years, have you not? Then let me ask: How much of your life is hidden from view? How much is unknown to others? You stress outward works. Yes, good works are important; but apart from that manifest expression of your life, how much of your life remains hidden? If all your spiritual life is exposed, than all your growth is upward, and because there is no downward growth you lack root.

In our Christian life it is necessary that we learn the meaning of the Body of Christ; we must learn to live corporately. On the other hand, we must learn that the life given to each member of His Body by the Lord is distinctly individual; and that measure given to you personally by Him needs to be guarded, otherwise it will lose its specific character and will be of no particular use to Him. If that which has been specially committed to you is exposed it will wither.

The discourse of the Lord Jesus on the Mounts was most remarkable. On the one hand He said: "Ye are the light of the world. A city set on a hill cannot be hid . . . Let your light shine before men, that they may see your good works and glorify your Father which is in heaven" (Matthew 5.14–16). On the other hand He said: "Take heed that ye do not your righteousness before men, to be seen of them . . . But when thou doest alms, let not thy left hand know what thy right hand doeth: that thine alms may be in secret . . . When thou prayest, enter into thine inner chamber, and having shut thy door, pray to thy Father which is in secret" (Matthew 6.1–6).

On the one hand, if you are a Christian you must come right out into the open and make a public profession; on the other hand, there are Christian virtues which you should preserve from the public gaze. The Christian who parades all his virtues has no depth, and because he lacks root he will not be able to stand in the day of trial and temptation. Let us who have been the Lord's children these many years ask Him to show us to what extent our experiences have become exposed to view, and let us ask Him also to work a work in these lives of ours that will ensure our becoming deeply rooted in Him.

WATCHMAN NEE

. . . the root of the righteous yieldeth fruit.

PROVERBS 12:12, KJV

May 17

There is one body and one Spirit—just as you were called to one hope when you were called—one Lord, one faith, one baptism, one God and Father of all, who is over all and through all and in all.

EPHESIANS 4:4–6

*D*o not expect any blessing *out* of Him; but in, by, and through Him look for all blessing. Let Him be your life and do not wish to live a moment longer, unless quickened by Him. Find Him as your Wisdom, Righteousness, Sanctification, Redemption, your Riches, Strength, and Glory!

Apply to yourself all that your Savior is, or has done. Do you wish for all the graces of God's Spirit? You will find them in His anointing. Do you wish for power against spiritual enemies? You will find it is His sovereignty. Is it redemption you seek? You will find it in His passion. Is it absolution you need? You will find it is His perfect innocence. Freedom from the curse? Find it as His Cross. Satisfaction? See it in His sacrifice. Cleansing from sin? Find it in His blood. Mortification? It is yours in His grave. Newness of Life? Find it in His resurrection. The right to heaven? It is insured for you by His intercession. Do you seek salvation? It is yours because He is seated at the right hand of the Majesty on high. Do you desire all? Then find it in Him Who is "One Lord, one God, and Father of all, Who is above all, through all, and in all."

As your faith this gives you an interest in Christ your Head, so let love unite you to His body, the Church, both on earth and in heaven. Keep close, unbroken fellowship with your brethren. Do not divide from either in judgment or affection. Remember that there is not one of God's saints on earth who has not a claim upon you, and freely communicate all your graces, and useful gifts, by example, admonition, exhortation, consolation, prayer, and charity, for the good of the church.

When you look up to heaven, think of the blessed society of saints already there, triumphing and reigning in the wonder of eternal glory. Praise God for them, tread in their footsteps, and set your ambition upon the crown of glory and immortality, which is already shining on their heads, with whom you are one in Christ Jesus.

BISHOP JOSEPH HALL

Through the Lord Jesus, every true believer is united to God in Heaven by a life-link. We are not praying down here on earth to One who is a long way off in Heaven. We are one with Him there and He is one with us here!

The devil is all the time trying to create a sense of distance between us and the Lord—but there is no distance between if we abide in Christ, for no one can be closer to the Father than the Son, and we are in Him!

T. L. M.

May 18

For he will be like a refiner's fire . . .
MALACHI 3:2B

*H*ow does the Holy Spirit purify? He purifies by separation. That is how the refiner purifies his metal. In Malachi 3, the refiner is sitting before the crucible in which is the precious silver.

How does the refiner know that his metal is ready for him to use? Well, he sits there; he tempers the fire and then as the hard silver is made liquid and the fire operates, and the dross gradually comes to the surface, he keeps on separating the dross from the silver; skims the surface as the dross is forced out of the metal through the action of the fire. He skims the surface, removes the dross, and when ultimately he sees his face reflected in the molten metal, he knows that it is ready.

The Holy Spirit sits alongside the crucible of your life and mine, and as the fire, He keeps separating the dross from the metal, and He will keep on the with holy work until He can see the face of the Lord He loves to magnify and glorify. Fire purifies.

Take the illustration of the great plague in London. In 1665 they walked through the streets and cried, "Bring out your dead; bring out your dead." And through the plague multitudes died. The plague of 1665 was followed by the great fire of 1666, and as the result of that great fire, something happened. The whole city was purged of the dread disease. But something else happened. The fire not only destroyed germs bringing death to myriads, but it penetrated the soil. It warned the soil and after a while, unknown flowers sprang up from long, deeply buried seeds. The warming of the soil made possible the wonderful fertility of the seeds. That is the great work of the Holy Ghost.

There are some who have within them the long-buried seeds of Divine truth, and then the Holy Ghost operates, and as the Spirit of Fire He destroys the plague of sin. Then He penetrates and warms the soil causing the life to bear fruit to the glory of God.

HERBERT LOCKYER

*W*hat fire is this that warms my soul? What light is this that so brightens my soul? O fire that burns forever, and never dies, kindle me! O light which shines eternally, and never darkens, illumine me! O that I had my heat from you, most Holy fire! How sweetly do you burn!

AUGUSTINE

May 19

If we confess our sins, he is faithful and just to forgive us our sins, and to cleanse us from all unrighteousness.

1 JOHN 1:9, KJV

*W*hen the believer sins, fellowship is interrupted and joy is lost until he comes to the Father in self-judgment, confessing his sins. Then the believer knows that he is forgiven, for God's Word declares him so in 1 John.

Always remember that there is nothing as strong as the link of relationship and nothing so tender as the link of communion. All the power on earth cannot sever the relationship, but an impure motive or a word spoken out of turn will break the fellowship.

When you find that you have lost the joy of your salvation, humble yourself before God, find out what has caused you to lose your joy, and confess that sin to God your Father. However, you should never confuse your safety with your joy.

We may illustrate this truth thusly: The moon was full and shining with more than ordinary silvery brightness. A man was gazing intently at a deep, still pond, where he saw the moon reflected. He remarked to a friend, "How beautiful the moon is tonight! Did you ever see it so bright and full?"

Suddenly the friend tossed a small pebble into the pond. Then the man exclaimed, "Hey, something has happened! The moon is broken into pieces!"

"Don't be silly," his friend remarked. "Look up, man! The moon hasn't changed a bit. It's the condition of the pond that reflects it that has changed."

Apply this simple illustration. Your heart is the pond. When there is no evil, God reveals to you the glories and wonders of Christ for your comfort and joy. But the moment a wrong motive comes to you or an idle word escapes yours lips unjudged, the Holy Spirit begins to disturb the pond, your heart. Then your happy experiences are smashed to pieces, and you are restless and disturbed until you come to God and confess your sin. Only then can you be restored to the calm, sweet joy of fellowship with God.

GEORGE CUTTING

Christian, how you think lightly of sin. Take heed, lest you fall, little by little. Sin, a little thing? Is it not a poison? Who knows its deadliness? Sin, a little thing? Do not the little foxes spoil the grapes? Do not little strokes fell mighty oaks? Will not continual droppings wear away stones? Sin, a little thing? It girded the

Redeemer's head with thorns and pierced His heart! It made Him suffer anguish, bitterness and woe.

Could you weigh the least sin in the scales of eternity, you would flee from it as from a poisonous snake and abhor the least appearance of evil. Look upon all sin as that which crucified the Savior, and you will see it to be exceeding sinful.

As for our own faults, it would take a large slate to hold the account of them; but thank God we know where to take them, and how to get the better of them.

CHARLES SPURGEON

May 20

" . . . As I was with Moses, so I will be with you; I will never leave you nor forsake you."
JOSHUA 1:5B

I thought that holiness, practical holiness, was to be gradually attained by a diligent use of the means of grace. There was nothing I so much desired as holiness, nothing I so much needed; but far from in any measure attaining it, the more I strove after it, the more it eluded my grasp, until hope itself almost died out, and I began to think that—perhaps to make heaven the sweeter—God would not give it down here. I do not think that I was striving to attain it in my own strength. I knew I was powerless. I told the Lord so, and asked Him to give me help and strength. Sometimes I almost believed that He would keep and uphold me; but on looking back in the evening—alas! there was but sin and failure to confess and mourn before God . . . All the time I felt assured that there was in Christ all I needed, but the practical question was—how to get it *out*. He was rich truly, but I was poor; He was strong, but I weak. I knew full well that there was in the root, the stem, abundant fatness, but how to get it into my puny little branch was the question. As gradually light dawned, I saw that faith was the only requisite—was the hand to lay hold on His fullness and make it mine. But I had not this faith.

I strove for faith, but it would not come; I tried to exercise it, but in vain. Seeing more and more the wondrous supply of grace laid up in Jesus, the fullness of our precious Savior, my guilt and helplessness seemed to increase. Sins committed appeared but as trifles compared with the sin of unbelief which was their cause, which could not or would not take God at His word, but rather made Him a liar! Unbelief was I felt *the* damning sin of the world; yet I indulged in it. I prayed for faith, but it came not. What was I to do?

When my agony of soul was at its height, a sentence in a letter from [my dear friend] McCarthy was used to remove the scales from my eyes, and the Spirit of God revealed to me the truth of our *oneness with Jesus* as I had never known it before. McCarthy, who had been much exercised by the same sense of failure but saw the light before I did, wrote (I quote from memory):

"But how to get faith strengthened? Not by striving after faith, but by resting on the Faithful One."

As I read, I saw it all! "If we believe not, he abideth faithful." I looked to Jesus and saw (and when I saw, oh, how joy flowed!) that He had said, "*I* will never leave thee."

"Ah, *there* is rest!" I thought. "I have striven in vain to rest in Him. I'll strive no more. For has not *He* promised to abide with *me*—never to leave me, never to forsake me?" And, dearie, *He never will!*

HUDSON TAYLOR

*O*ne day in the city of New York—oh! what a day—I cannot describe it, I seldom refer to it—it is almost too sacred an experience to name. I can only say God revealed Himself to me, and I had such an experience of His love that I had to ask Him to stay His hand. I went to preaching again. The sermons were no different. I did not present any new ideas, yet hundreds were converted. I would not be placed back where I was before that blessed experience if you were to give me all Glasgow.

DWIGHT L. MOODY

I became a believer in the Lord Jesus in November, 1825, nearly seventy years ago. The first four years after my conversion were spent in spiritual weakness; but in July, 1829, now sixty-six years ago, I came to a place of entire and full surrender of heart. I gave myself fully to the Lord. Honors, pleasure, money, my physical powers, my mental powers, all were laid down at the feet of Jesus, and I became a great lover of God. I found my all in God, and have continued to do so, in all my temporal and spiritual trials, for these past sixty-six years. My faith does not pertain to only temporal blessings, but to everything, because I stand constantly on God's Word. It has been my knowledge of God and His Word that has thus sustained me.

GEORGE MUELLER

There are Christians who are always reflecting on the past, because they are not rejoicing in the present—Christians who are only too ready to tell you of George Mueller and Hudson Taylor, but do not attempt to add instances of prayer experience of their own. But when did Hudson Taylor live? When did George Mueller die? With his death, did the Almighty depart?

COLIN C. KERR

May 21

But if we judged ourselves, we would not come under judgement. When we are judged by the Lord, we are being disciplined so that we will not be condemned with the world.

1 CORINTHIANS 11:31–32

If self-discipline does not go on in private, it must go on in some other way; thus it is that Christians often become rods to each other, and thus the work of bruising and humbling is so largely manifest in the Church openly.

The stones of Solomon's temples were *hewn*, and *squared*, and *prepared*, and *made ready*, before they were brought to the house, "so that there was neither hammer, nor axe, nor tool of iron heard in the house while it was building."

If discipline were to go on secretly with us, there would be less need of public humiliation and judging; the latter is attended with deep sorrow and shame, the former with joy and peace.

"CRUMBS FOR THE LORD'S LITTLE ONES"

May 22

I have given you authority to trample on snakes and scorpions, and to overcome all the power of the enemy; nothing will harm you.

LUKE 10:19

Through the death and resurrection of Jesus Christ, as twin events, certain definite issues in the conflict between God and Satan were met and eternally settled. The victory over Satan was fully and finally won which robbed him of the last vestige of claim to sovereignty over the earth or the race. He is henceforth a usurper and a thief.

Jesus Christ gained back all that had been lost and now the earth and all that is therein are His not only by the right of creation but by right of conquest.

To the believer in Jesus Christ it means that the sovereignty of Satan over his life is ended and the sovereignty of God begins; that he leaves the sphere of sin, death, darkness and disorder, and enters the sphere of righteousness, life, light and liberty; that he ceases to be a subject in the kingdom of Satan and becomes a subject in the Kingdom of God; that he severs his alliance with Satan's system, the world, and avows his allegiance as a member of Christ's Body the Church, to Christ Himself who is its Head.

It means, in other words, that the old creation with all that pertains to it ends at the cross and is buried in the tomb and that a new creation comes forth in the resurrection.

It means that the old relationship with sin, self and Satan is altogether annulled and a new union with God in Christ Jesus is made, and that in this new relationship Christ becomes not only the believer's Savior but his Lord and his Life.

RUTH PAXSON

May 23

Therefore, there is now no condemnation for those who are in Christ Jesus.
ROMANS 8:1

If God announces the gift of righteousness apart from works, why do you keep mourning over your bad works, your failures? Do you not see that it is because you still have hopes in these works of yours that you are depressed and discouraged by their failure? If you truly saw and believed that God is reckoning righteous the *ungodly* who believe on Him, you would fairly hate your struggles to be "better";

for you would see that your dreams of good works have not at all commended you to God, and that your bad works do not at all hinder you from believing on Him—that justifieth the *ungodly.*

Therefore, on seeing your failures, you should say, I am nothing but a failure; but God is dealing with me on another principle altogether than my works, good or bad—a principle not involving my works, but based only on the work of Christ for me. I am anxious, indeed, to be pleasing to God and to be filled with His Spirit; but I am not at all justified, or accounted righteous, by these things. God, in justifying me, acted wholly and only on Christ's blood-shedding on my behalf.

Therefore I have this double attitude: first, I know that Christ is in Heaven before God for me, and that I stand in the value before God of His finished work; that God sees me nowhere else but in this dead, buried, and Risen Christ, and that His favor is toward me in Christ, and is limitless and eternal.

Then, second, toward the work of the Holy Spirit in me, my attitude is, a desire to be guided into the truth, to be obedient thereto, and to be chastened by God my Father if disobedient; to learn to pray in the Spirit, to walk by the Spirit, and to be filled with a love for the Scriptures and for the saints and for all men.

Yet none of these things justifies me! I had justification from God *as a sinner,* not as a *saint!* My saintliness does not increase it, nor, praise God, do my failures decrease it!

WILLIAM R. NEWELL

If I allow the thought that what I am toward God will in some way or other affect what God is toward me, I shall be filled with the specter of bondage. But when I see that what God is toward me is altogether the outcome of what He is, and that He is this though knowing perfectly what I am, it puts my heart in the right direction for liberty.

C. A. COATES

Moses and Aaron, Nadab and Abihu, and the seventy elders of Israel went up and saw the God of Israel. Under his feet was something like a pavement made of sapphire, clear as the sky itself. But God did not raise his hand against these leaders of the Israelites; they saw God, and they ate and drank.

EXODUS 24:9–11

Amid the pressures of daily life, trust the Holy Spirit, who is emphatically the Divine Remembrancer, to bring all things to your remembrance, and to recall you to the consciousness of God. There is no duty in life, however trivial and commonplace, that may not be dignified by being rendered to God, as our bounden duty and service. This is indeed the secret of lifting all life to a noble and happy elevation. To do all for the Lord Jesus; to see Him standing behind every human relationship; to do the meanest and most irksome things because He takes them as service rendered to Himself, for which He will give a reward—this is Christian life, this makes the presence of God real, this dignifies the sweeping of a room . . .

Equally in our hours of recreation we may set the Lord always before us. Remember that it is said of the elders of Israel that they saw Jehovah, and there was under his feet as it were the paved work of a sapphire stone; they beheld God, and did eat and drink. How many eat and drink without beholding God! How many whose consciences were uneasy might behold God without daring to eat and drink! Happiest are they who are so at rest in Him that they do not hesitate to perform the natural functions of life with perfect ease, though all the while they recognize that He is nearer than hands or feet, nearer than breathing! The sense of God's presence would check immodesty, levity, self-indulgence, excess in eating or drinking, whilst it would give a new zest to all that was natural and innocent.

F. B. MEYER

$\mathcal{I}$t is a striking characteristic of Christianity that there is not one thing too great or too high for the Christian, so neither is anything too little or too low for God.

He concerns Himself even with a duty so simple and small as a believer's working day by day and not sponging off his brethren. Union with Christ is the key to all. If by grace I am one with His Son, no wonder that my Father should take pleasure in opening His heart and mind to me.

WILLIAM KELLY

$\mathcal{T}$o lift up the hands to God in prayer gives God glory, but a man with a dungfork in hand, a woman with a slop-pail, give Him glory too. He is so great that all things give Him glory if you mean they should. So then, my brethren, live.

GERARD MANLEY HOPKINS

May 25

Even youths grow tired and weary, and young men stumble and fall; but those who hope in the LORD will renew their strength. They will soar on wings like eagles; they will run and not grow weary, they will walk and not be faint.

ISAIAH 40:30–31

$\mathcal{T}$he spiritual life is not passive. Too often it may look that way when we speak of ceasing from ourselves and our own efforts. The point is that we need to learn to live and serve by the power God has provided, not self-effort. A true spiritual life is even more active, enlarged and vital because the limitless power of God energizes us. Normally the spiritual Christian will occupy himself with effective service for his Lord. We should be yielded and ready to do whatever

He may choose. Spirit-filled Christians are quite likely to feel physical exhaustion at the close of the day the same as other people. They are weary *in* the work, but not weary *of* the work.

LEWIS SPERRY CHAFER

*A*nywhere, provided it be forward!

DAVID LIVINGSTONE

May 26

For there is one God and one mediator between God and men, the man Christ Jesus, who gave himself as a ransom for all men . . .
1 TIMOTHY 2:5–6

*W*hat a Savior is Jesus! How fully worthy is He of our fullest praise! He stooped to us that He might put His hand upon us, degraded though we were, and He has done it tenderly and graciously, so that we are not afraid.

There is no terror for us in His hand, we do not shrink from Him. He has touched us with the touch of a man, and bound us with the cords of love. Yet was never less than God, and God has touched us in Him. He has put one hand upon us and the other is placed upon the throne of God, and He is the one mediator. With the one hand He has offered the fullest satisfaction to the righteous claims of God, and with the other He has bestowed fullness of grace upon us. He brings us to God and gives us a place in His presence without fear, and in everlasting peace, a peace established upon the infallible and immovable foundation of divine righteousness, secured for us by a divine person for the eternal glory of God.

Thus are we justified before God, and all our fear is removed, and we are free to behold the hand that has been placed upon us, and to mark the fact that it is a wounded hand: a hand that was nail-pierced for us when He identified Himself with us, as we stood subject to the judgment of God, that He might save us. We know the power of this hand too: it has smitten death for us and will not relinquish its hold upon us for ever. As He is now a man in heaven, so shall we be there; He the first-born among many brethren, we His associates identified with Him in an everlasting oneness. He will never surrender that true humanity which He has taken up, and as He is, so are they also who are His. The purpose of God is that we should be conformed to His own image. And so we shall be, and yet never shall we forget that He is "over all, God, blessed for ever more."

J. T. MAWSON

If you see any beauty in Christ, and say, "I desire to have that," God will work it in you.

GEORGE V. WIGRAM

May 27

And God raised us up with Christ and seated us with him in the heavenly realms in Christ Jesus, in order that in the coming ages he might show the incomparable riches of his grace, expressed in his kindness to us in Christ Jesus.

EPHESIANS 2:6–7

Himself has come after us! who, after all, so likely as He? Shall we measure Him by the height of His throne—and then He is far from us indeed; or by the depths of a divine nature, which has planted even in man (capable of being seen in him still, spite of his ruin) the capacity of a self-sacrificing love, which can only be the dim reflection of his Maker?

Can it be another than He—a creature—to whom He has left it to win our hearts *away from Himself* by the glory of so great a work achieved for us? No, impossible! And when we realize this work, not as provincial merely, as done for a mere corner of creation, but as under the eyes of angelic principalities and powers, "that He might show in the ages to come, the exceeding riches of His grace, in His kindness to us"—how impossible for it to be any other than Himself who should do this!—for it to be no manifestation of God at all, but of some creature merely; God, in His central glory of being, yet unknown!

"All things were created by Him and for Him" (Col. 1:6) is said of Christ; and such sayings are almost more positive affirmations of His Godhead than the most direct statements could be. How impossible to imagine a mere creature center for the universe to revolve about! or even an inferior God! Go back to the account of creation, and how naturally it reads now of Him who is God and with God, as the gospel of John declares Him, "Let Us make man in Our image, after Our likeness." Or again, look forward in thought to where we are carried in that prophecy of Isaiah with which we began, by that title of His, *not* "the everlasting Father," as the text of the common version has it, but as the Hebrew and the margin of the Revised, "the Father of eternity": the One who having made all things at the beginning shall give them at the last their final shape.

Thus we realize that at the Center of the universe there is not merely a Power that controls and holds it together—which is again true of Him "in whom all things consist" (Col. 1:17)—but a Heart: perfectly told out as the *moral* Power which is manifested now as the "Beloved" of "Love" Itself. Here in the Incarnation and Atonement it is told out to us. There could be no other. It is no satellite which has become a sun, but the diffusive Sun itself—yea, the Sun of all suns.

F. W. GRANT

I am coming to this conclusion: that the more one ministers Christ Himself the more you can count upon divine assistance. To exalt Christ is to be in communion with the mind of God. This will be our sole employment in heaven.

EDWARD DENNETT

May 28

Likewise also the cup after supper, saying, This cup is the new testament in my blood, which is shed for you.

LUKE 22:20, KJV

The personal knowledge of God is the secret of our spiritual life. It is our safeguard against error, and against sin. It is the great and the constant gift of God, the fruit of Christ's redemption.

We now see and know God and His Son; we know Jesus, because Jesus always knows His sheep, revealing Himself unto them, and giving them guidance and life. This knowledge is nothing less than walking with God, walking in the light, praying without ceasing. The secret of the Lord is with them that fear Him. In much darkness, amid many difficulties, and in constant warfare we yet walk in the light of His countenance, until at last we shall see Him as He is, and know even as we are known.

How great is the blessedness of all who are in the new, the everlasting covenant; in the covenant of grace and life, in which God Himself is revealed, and in which all things are of God. Here Christ is to us wisdom, and righteousness, and sanctification, and redemption. Our transgressions are pardoned, yea, there is no more remembrance of sin. The heart is renewed, and the Holy Ghost is given as an indwelling Spirit. God works in us both to will and to do of His good pleasure. We are in constant and filial communion with Him.

He is our God, and we are His people; He is our Father, and we are His children. And all these blessings have their root and commencement, their vitality and permanence in the redemption, accomplished on Golgotha, they are dispensed from the heavenly sanctuary by *the Mediator*, who was the Paschal Lamb on the cross. Little children and fathers, young converts and experienced Christians, *always* hear the voice of Jesus: *This cup is the New Testament IN MY BLOOD.*

ADOLPH SAPHIR

May 29

They are the messengers of the churches, and the glory of Christ.
2 CORINTHIANS 8:23, KJV

It is something to be a missionary. The morning stars sang together and all the sons of God shouted for joy when they saw the field which the first missionary was to fill. The great and loving God, before whom angels veil their faces, had an only Son, and He was sent to earth as a Missionary Physician.

It is something to be a follower, however feeble, in the wake of the great Teacher and only model missionary that ever appeared among men, and now that He is Head over all things, King of kings, and Lord of lords, what earthly commission is equal to that which the missionary holds from Him?

May I venture to young men and women, when laying down the plan of their lives to take a glance at that of missionary? For my own part, I never cease to rejoice that God has appointed me to such an honor.

DAVID LIVINGSTONE

$\mathcal{I}$ walked out to the hill just now. It is exalting, delicious. To stand embraced by the shadows of a friendly tree with the wind tugging at your coattail and the heavens hailing your heart, to gaze and glory and to give oneself again to God, what more could a [Christian] ask?

Oh, the fullness, pleasure, sheer excitement of knowing God on earth. I care not if I never raise my voice again for Him, if only I may love Him, please Him.

Perhaps, in mercy, He shall give me a host of children that I may lead through the vast star fields to explore His delicacies whose fingers' ends set them to burning. But if not, if only I may see Him, smell His garments, and smile into my Lover's eyes, ah, then, not stars, nor children, shall matter—only Himself.

JIM ELLIOT*

$\mathcal{W}$ho is conscious of possessing little in Christ, the same loveth little, and is little disposed to make Him known. Our experience of Christ is the fountain, our missionary zeal is the stream. The one measures the other.

EGBERT W. SMITH

---

*[Editor's note: Jim Elliot and four companion missionaries to the Auca Indians of South America were martyred in 1956, when Jim was just 29. The deaths of these men had repercussions around the world as their story was told in books by Elliot's widow, Elisabeth; *Through Gates of Splendor* and *Shadow of the Almighty*. Shortly after the massacre, many of the Auca Indians became Christians. Their story is one of the most dramatic of the history of the twentieth-century church.]

"My son," the father said, "you are always with me, and everything I have is yours. But we had to celebrate and be glad, because this brother of yours was dead and is alive again; he was lost and is found."

LUKE 15:31–32, KJV

There's a story about a man who dreamed that he went to a great palace, and was joyfully greeted at the door; then he went in, and at each successive room he entered, he was, each time, even more joyfully received. At last he entered into the presence of a great monarch and was there received with great acclamation. It is more than that with the believer in Christ!

The prodigal son entering the Father's house demonstrates the nature of our salvation. It is not simply for my benefit that I am there, but God has a delight in having me there. . . . Love delights to have me in its company.

If a Christian's need was the measure of Christ's work, human joys would be enough—but when divine love is the measure—the Father's house and the joys therein are the only thing that will satisfy.

It is the Father's good pleasure that His house should be filled, therefore, "We had to celebrate and be glad because this brother of yours was dead and is alive again; he was lost and is found." That is why the reception of the believer in Christ is so satisfying and completely full of joy. Every believer now has a home there. We are dwelling on the joyful gain which is ours at the finish—what we are ultimately saved *to*.

J. B. STONEY

Therefore it is of faith, that it might be by grace; to the end the promise might be sure to all the seed; not to that only which is of the law, but to that also which is of the faith of Abraham; who is the father of us all.

ROMANS 4:16, KJV

The simple truth is that the fullness of the Holy Spirit is not merely for super-saints who by their consecration and devotedness may be deemed to have qualified, but sinners and failures who have learnt to repent and who see the perfect, present cleansing available to them in the Blood of Jesus. Thank God, whereas this word is in the imperative mood, it is in the passive voice. This simply means that "it is of faith, that it might be by grace," and this in turn means that "the promise might be sure to all the seed" (Rom. 4:16), not only to saints of high attainments, but to feeble, failing people like some of us. Grace by its very nature makes the promise sure to failures who admit their failure, and they can do that *now*. Someone has said, "The Spirit's fullness is not the reward of our faithfulness, but God's gift for our defeat." He was not given to the disciples in Acts 28 as the culmination and reward of their wonderful service, but in Acts 2 when they had proved themselves cowards, meeting behind barred doors.

There is, therefore, no need to struggle for self-improvement first, for that is to seek the Holy Spirit "not by faith, but as it were by the works of the law" (Rom. 9:32). Nor is there any need to wait for Him, as some have thought—no need to wait, that is to say, any longer than it takes us to be willing to call sin "sin" and come to the Cross with it. The Holy Spirit has already been given. True, the disciples were of old told, "Tarry ye in the city of Jerusalem, until ye be endued with power from on high" (Luke 24:49); but that was because the historic moment of the giving of the Holy Spirit had not yet come. But now that He is given, all may be filled—and filled *now.*

ROY HESSION

*T*o be full of the Holy Spirit is the normal state of the believer, and if this is not so with us we should humble ourselves before God.

EDWARD DENNETT

> *The king's heart is in the hand of the LORD; he directs it like a water-course wherever he pleases.*
>
> PROVERBS 21:1

*G*od works through persons, through individual souls, instead of committees, federated bands, or great organizations. The strongest force on earth is the individual soul. God conquers some one heart, and through that heart He pours His purposes like a mighty river.

The closer we get to God, the more we prize the individual soul.

When men drift away from the Lord, the individual man counts but little, and confidence is placed in big majorities, and heavy armies. The tower of Babel was built by a national committee, who said, "let us build us a city and tower."

But God singled out one man, Abraham, and called him to be a pilgrim, and the founder of a race of those who had faith. Napoleon said, "That God was on the side of the heaviest battalions," but something happened to prevent his words proving true, and that something will in the end be found to be a Divine touch on someone's soul. The history of the world is found in the lives of a succession of individuals.

The King of Syria marshaled an army to capture the prophet Elisha, but that lone prophet prayed, and the army went blind, and He led them into Samaria. This is a sample of universal history.

Men are forever depending on armies, committees, and a show of strength; and in the most quiet, simple and unexpected way, God gently and secretly inspires some one soul who outwits the wise, and carries out God's purposes in an undreamed way.

G. D. WATSON

$\mathcal{G}$od's person, in God's place, doing God's work, in God's way [is the place for every true servant of God].

HUDSON TAYLOR

June 2

In whom also we have obtained an inheritance, being predestinated according to the purpose of him who worketh all things after the counsel of his own will.

EPHESIANS 1:11, KJV

$\mathcal{W}$e need to recover an assurance and confidence and conviction that, how ever things may seem—through all things, over all things, behind all things, God is pursuing His counsels—He is going on.

Ceaseless in action, undeviating in course, with tremendous energy, He is working all things after the counsel of His own will.

Sometimes, as we look out, we wonder if God is doing anything, and in our prayer times we try to get God to do something. What we need is to realize that God *is doing*, and we need to get into line with His doings.

Perhaps He is not doing what we want Him to do, or what we think He ought to do, and in the way in which we think He ought to do it; He is not employing the means that we think He ought to employ—*our* bit of means, *our* bit or work. He may not just be coming that way, but He is pursuing His purpose, relentlessly, persistently, undeviatingly; and the need for the people of God is to be brought right into the straight course of His goings from eternity.

For He is going, and He is going in our day; it can be seen—more or less—in the world. But, seen or not seen, the fact remains—or our Bible is not right, and Paul was mistaken! And I am glad always to recognize this: that when Paul stopped travelling about the world and had all his tremendous activities among the nations curtailed, it was then that he saw the goings of God from eternity, it was then that he wrote this letter to the Ephesians, containing the eternal counsels of God.

It is a wonderful thing, is it not? When we are taken out of our work, when we cannot run about and do all sorts of things, when we are perhaps physically unable to do anything, God is going on.

Sometimes we think that, when we stop, God has to stop, and if we do not go, well, God will not be able to go! Oh no, He is going on—He is going on! May we be helped to understand His goings, and to get into His goings.

T. Austin-Sparks

*W*e are constantly ensnared by looking at secondary causes—we do not realize God in everything. Were we more alive to the fact that there is not an event which happens to us, from morning to night, in which the voice of our Father may not be heard, His hand seen, with what a blessed atmosphere would it surround us! Man and circumstances would then be received as so many agents and instruments in our Father's hand; so many ingredients in His cup for us. Thus would our minds be solemnized, our spirits calmed, our hearts subdued.

C. A. Coates

June 3

For if you live according to the sinful nature, you will die; but if by the Spirit you put to death the misdeeds of the body, you will live.

Romans 8:13

I have never been much for "steps" in the Christian life, though they may be useful to some people. For the most part, my method has been simply to plunge in on the promises of God and let God take care of the "steps." I would, however, make a few recommendations to anyone seeking a more satisfying and more God-possessed life than he now enjoys.

First, determine to take the whole thing in dead earnest. Too many of us play at Christianity. We wear salvation as a kind of convention badge admitting us into the circle of the elect, but rarely stop to focus our whole lives seriously on God's claims on us.

Second, throw yourself out recklessly upon God. Give up everything and prepare yourself to surrender even unto death all of your ambitions, plans and possessions. And I mean this quite literally. You should not be satisfied with the mere technical aspect of surrender but press your case upon God in determined prayer until a crisis has taken place within your life and there has been an actual transfer of everything from yourself to God.

Third, take a solemn vow never to claim any honor or glory or praise for anything you are or have or do. See to it that God gets all the honor, all the time.

Fourth, determine not to defend yourself against detractors and persecutors. Put your reputation in God's hands and leave it there.

Fifth, mortify the flesh with the affections and lusts! Every believer has been judicially put to death with Christ, but this is not enough for present victory. Freedom from the power of the flesh will come only when we have by faith and self-discipline made such death an actuality. Real death to self is a painful thing and tends to reduce a man in his own eyes and humble him into the dust. Not many follow this rugged way, but those who do are the exemplary Christians.

A. W. TOZER

*I*t is one thing to be the advocate of Christianity, and another to be the disciple of it. And though it may sound strange at first, far easier is it to teach its lessons than to learn them.

J. G. BELLETT

What then shall we say, brothers? When you come together, everyone has a hymn, or a word of instruction, a revelation, a tongue or an interpretation. All of these must be done for the strengthening of the church.

1 CORINTHIANS 14:26

*A*nd so, as to church meetings—what is the true secret of power? Is it gift, eloquence, fine music, or an imposing ceremonial?

No; it is the enjoyment of a present Christ. Where He is, all is light, life, and power. Where He is not, all is darkness, death, and desolation. An assembly where Jesus is not, is a sepulchre, though there be all the fascination of oratory, all the resistless attraction of fine music, and all the influence of an impressive ritual.

All these things may exist in perfection, and yet the devoted lover of Jesus may have to cry out, "Alas! they have taken away my Lord, and I know not where they have laid Him." But, on the other hand, where the presence of Jesus is realized—where His voice is heard, and his very touch felt by the soul, there is power and blessing, though, to man's view, all may seem the most thorough weakness.

Let Christians remember these things; let them ponder them; let them see to it that they realize the Lord's presence in their public services; and if they cannot say, with full confidence, of their meetings that the Lord is there, let them humble themselves and wait upon Him, for there must be a cause. He has said, "Where two or three are gathered together in my name there am I in the midst." But let us never forget that, in order to reach the divine result, there must be the divine condition.

C. H. MACKINTOSH

A meeting ought to close when it is over. The Lord often leaves a meeting long before the people do.

EDWARD DENNETT

For we are unto God a sweet savor of Christ . . .

2 CORINTHIANS 2:15, KJV

The savor of the good ointments of Christ may flow out through the holy lives of His people. Every trait, every perfection exhibited by Himself in His walk through this world may be reproduced in those that are His.

Look, for example, at the precepts and exhortations of the epistles. Every one of them has been perfectly exemplified in Christ; and unless this is remembered, so that they may be associated with Himself as the living Word, they will become hard and legal obligations.

Christ in us, Christ our life, as set forth in Colossians, is to be followed by the display of Christ through us, in the power of the Holy Ghost. For this we need to be much in His company; for the more we are with Him and occupied with Him, the more we shall be transformed into His likeness, and the more certainly will the savor of His good ointments be spread abroad. And this will be a mighty testimony to what He is; for in this case His name will, through us, be as ointment poured forth; the sweet savor of the name of Christ will flow forth from our walk as well as from our words.

As we meditate upon it, may we not say, "What a privilege! What a mission, to be sent out into the world to make known the savor of the good ointments of Christ, that His name may, through us, be as ointment poured forth!"

EDWARD DENNETT

Jesus looked at him and loved him . . .
MARK 10:21

*N*apoleon had a number of picked soldiers whom he called "the Old Guard." He knew he could trust them through thick and thin, and in his many anxious moments Napoleon was comforted when he turned to his old guard. They stood by him, loyal to the core.

But one day it was whispered to Napoleon that there was a rebellion in the old guard. What would he do? He summoned the old guard to the Palace Court. They waited outside in the court-yard, while alone in the Throne room on a platform slightly elevated, and in the Emperor's chair, sat Napoleon. The old guard wondered what would happen. Would the great chief come out and scold and threaten them? Would they be marched off to prison and to punishment? What was the chief going to do?

A messenger came out and summoned the old guard one by one into the presence of Napoleon. The first man came in at the far door, and the door was closed, and he was alone with the Emperor.

He walked right up to the throne until he stood face to face with Napoleon, and not a word was spoken. Napoleon looked into his eyes, and the soldier looked into the eyes of his chief. Then Napoleon stretched out his hand, and they gripped hands, and the old guard passed out. And the next man came in, and never a word was spoken. He walked up to the throne, he stood, he looked, the handclasp, and he went out. The next man came, the same look, the same hand, and the next, one by one—until the entire old guard had thus passed before Napoleon. And when all had thus passed, the rebellion was over forever.

My dear friend, would you come into the Presence of your Lord? Would you look into His face, would you stretch out the hand of faith, and put it into His Hand, the Hand that was pierced for you? Would you?

I tell you, your rebellion will go, if you will come like that. Just the look, just the outstretched hand, and then the clasp from His blessed Hand, and you are His!

LINDSAY GLEGG

I looked at God and He looked at me, and we were one forever.

CHARLES SPURGEON

June 7

. . . I know whom I have believed, and am persuaded that he is able to keep that which I have committed unto him against that day.

2 TIMOTHY 1:12, KJV

I am like the good man and his wife who had kept a lighthouse for years. A visitor, who came to see the lighthouse, looking out from the window over the waste of waters, asked the good woman, "Are you not afraid at night, when the storm is out, and the big waves dash right over the lantern? Do you not fear that the lighthouse, and all that is in it, will be carried away? I am sure I would be afraid to trust myself in a slender tower in the midst of the great billows."

The woman remarked that the idea never occurred to her. She had lived there so long that she felt as safe on the lone rock as ever she did when she lived on the mainland.

As for her husband, when asked if he did not feel anxious when the wind blew a hurricane, he answered, "Yes, I feel anxious to keep the lamps well trimmed, and the light burning, lest any vessel should be wrecked."

As to anxiety about the safety of the lighthouse, or his own personal security in it, he had outlived all that. Even so it is with the full-grown believer. He can humbly say, "I know whom I have believed, and am persuaded that He is able to keep that which I have committed unto Him against that day." From henceforth let no man trouble me with doubts and questionings; I bear in my soul the proofs of the Spirit's truth and power, and I will have none of your artful reasonings. The gospel to me is truth. I am content to perish if it be not true. I risk my soul's eternal fate upon the truth of the gospel, and I know that there is no risk in it. My one concern is to keep the lights burning, that I may thereby benefit others.

CHARLES SPURGEON

Oh, Christ—He is the fountain,
The deep, sweet well of love!
The streams on earth I've tasted,
More deep I'll drink above;
There to an ocean fullness
His mercy doth expand,
And glory, glory dwelleth
In Immanuel's Land.

SAMUEL RUTHERFORD

June 8

Blessed are those whose strength is in you, who have set their hearts on pilgrimage. As they pass through the Valley of Baca, they make it a place of springs; the autumn rains also cover it with pools. They go from strength to strength till each appears before God in Zion.

PSALM 84:5–7, KJV

The Psalmist speaks of a passing through the Valley of Baca [the winepress valley]. And in truth, it is only an occasional passing through as the children of God press on in following the Lamb.

But as the divine life is increasingly imparted, and divine strength given, those who know the "place of springs" rejoice each time they are counted worthy to be given winepress joy—the joy of the Lamb, Who, as He neared the cross could say to his little company of sorrowing friends: "*My* joy I give unto you." The joy of which was set before Him for which He could endure the Cross and despise the shame. The joy which can only be known in seeing Calvary from the heart of God; from the viewpoint of heaven.

These souls who thus know the winepress valley as a place of springs, go from "strength to strength" or (Hebrew) "force to force," and "every one of them appears before God in Zion."

Yes, in New Testament language, every one of them emerge into that hidden life with Christ in God, for these are the "overcomers" who are "lifted above all" by the loss of all!

From "force to force" they go, through the winepress valleys; more and more losing the earth-life as, in distress, they are driven into resources which are to be found alone in God, more and more detached from all that earth holds dear to dwell in the heavens with the reigning Lord.

This conformity to the Son of God in His path of the Lamb, is the purpose of the Pentecostal fullness of the Spirit, rather than the "signs and wonders" which dazzle the eye of men. "Ye shall receive power to be martyrs," was the promise of the Risen Lord to His disciples, and this surely means in one aspect that just as "through the Eternal Spirit" He offered Himself to God, so all His followers would need the power of the Holy Ghost to follow Him and be conformed to His image—the image of a Lamb.

It is of the deepest importance that we co-operate with the Spirit of God in the stage of the divine life into which He has brought us.

It is possible to be turned back in our spiritual progress by seeking an experience which may *look* more advanced, but is not. The highest purpose of God in the believer is not to make him so much a powerfully-used instrument, as to bring forth in him the fullest manifestation of Christ in every aspect of His character, and this can only be done in the winepress valley of fellowship with His sufferings.

He was "crucified through *weakness,*" and there were no mighty signs and wonders wrought by Him to thrill the multitude at Calvary; but in His weakness and Lamb-silence in suffering, and His poured-out life, He did more for the world than when He healed the sick and cast out demons in Galilee.

Oh that this pure and lovely pattern may be unveiled to the eager children of God who are seeking intensely what they term "God's best"—the pattern of the Christ in His Lamb-likeness conquering the hosts of darkness, not by fighting but by death.

And this beautiful Lamb-likeness of the Lord Christ will not be wrought in us by "visions" of Calvary, nor by sudden and mystical experiences of entering into the sufferings of His Cross, but by the daily and hourly choosing of the will of God in the discipline of life. The "answering not again" when accused of many things; the hidden and silent path of sacrifice unknown to men; the doing good and suffering for it as evil-doers worthy of death.

JESSIE PENN-LEWIS

*A*s in the apostolic days, so now the desire exists for the manifestation of the Spirit in marvelous ways; but a life sober, righteous, holy, lived in the hope of the glory to come, is the more excellent way of the Spirit's manifestation and undeniable proof of His indwelling. The prayer should not be so much for this or that gift, or this or that result, as for Christ Himself to be made manifest to us and through us.

W. F. E.

*F*aith is not a power that one possesses by which he can move the arm of God and work miracles. Faith accepts quiet guidance; only unbelief demands a miracle. There is nothing in true faith that the flesh can glory in. The power is God's. It is the Father who works and does it according to His own wisdom and will. Faith is simply absolute confidence in the Father which gives the certainty that He will fulfill His Word.

A. H.

June 9

Brothers, I could not address you as spiritual but as worldly—mere infants in Christ. I gave you milk, not solid food, for you were not yet ready for it. Indeed, you are still not ready.

1 CORINTHIANS 3:1–2

There are some who pray for the Spirit because they long to have His light and joy and strength. And yet their prayers bring little increase of blessing or power. It is because they do not rightly know or desire Him as the *Holy* Spirit. His burning purity, His searching and convicting light, His making dead of the deeds of the body, of self with its will and its power, His leading into the fellowship of Jesus as He gave up His will and His life to the Father—of all this they have not thought.

The Spirit cannot work in power in them because they receive Him not as the *Holy* Spirit, in *sanctification* of the Spirit. At times, in season of revival, as among the Corinthians and Galatians, He may indeed come with His gifts and mighty workings, while His sanctifying power is but little manifest.

But unless that sanctifying power be acknowledged and accepted, His gifts will be lost. His gifts coming on us are but means to prepare the way for the sanctifying power within us. We must take the lesson to heart; we can have as much of the Spirit as we are willing to have of His Holiness.

Being full of the Spirit, must mean to us, being fully holy.

ANDREW MURRAY

*S*piritual growth is the Holy Spirit engraving the Lord Jesus on a man's heart, putting Him into his thoughts, his words, and his ways, just as the Law was engraved upon stones. It is not that there is no failure. A man who is seeking to make money does not always succeed; but everybody knows what his object is. Just so, the Lord Jesus Christ is the object of the believer's life.

JOHN DARBY

June 10

Thanks be to God for his indescribable gift.
2 CORINTHIANS 9:15

*T*here is one thing we must understand, which is that victory is a gift and not a reward. What is a gift? It is something which is freely given to you. That which you earn through work is a reward. A gift, on the other hand, asks for no effort on your part. It is that which is given gratuitously with no requirement placed upon the receiver, whereas a reward demands that someone work for it. The life that wins which we talk about does not require any effort of yours. Victory is something which God has prepared to give to us. Our victory is obtained freely, not attained through self-effort. Too often we believers have a serious misconception—imagining that while salvation comes to us freely, victory depends on ourselves. We know we cannot add any merit or work of ours to obtain salvation. We must simply come to the cross and accept the Lord Jesus as our

Savior. This is the gospel! We realize we cannot be saved by works, yet we reason that for sanctification we must do good works after we are saved. This is to say that though you cannot be saved by works, you need to depend on works for victory.

Let me tell you that just as you are not *saved* by works, so you do not *overcome* by works. God has declared that you are unable to do good. Christ has died for you on the cross, and He is now living for you within. That which is of the flesh is flesh, and God rejects all that came from it. Nevertheless, we usually surmise that while salvation is dependent upon the substitutionary death of Christ on the cross, we should think of doing good, should do good, and expect to do good for victory in our lives. Let us realize, though, that we can do *no* good. Victory is freely given us by God!

WATCHMAN NEE

If we cannot overcome where we are, we cannot overcome anywhere.

J. B. STONEY

June 11

. . . the place you are standing is holy ground.
EXODUS 3:5

I was chatting one day with a dear Christian friend who said to me, "Have you ever heard about Nat's sandpile?" When I answered in the negative he told me this story:

Nat was a beloved friend of ours. He was a building contractor. It so happened that in his native city down by the riverbank was a huge sandpile. To every one else but Nat is was merely an unsightly, worthless sandpile. But Nat had a vision about this sandpile. He saw that every truckload he sold would bring him a dollar. And when the sandpile was gone the leveled ground would make a fine site for a business block. So Nat bought the sandpile.

As word spread, many of his friends laughed at the idea of his buying a worthless sandpile. But soon Nat's vision began to come true. Week after week he sold sand and leveled off the ground. Soon the sand was all sold; the ground was leveled off; a handsome business block was built on the site. Before the year was over, a good part of the wholesale trade of the city had moved into that block, and soon after he sold out, making a lot of money on the enterprise.

Friend, your life may be obscure, untalented, and as worthless in your sight as that sandpile. But if you will treat the spot in everyday life whereon you stand as holy ground, and give that life to God in consecration, God will make of it a beautiful structure enduring for His glory through all time and eternity.

JAMES MCCONKEY

The hand of God can do the business of God, though it have but a sling and a stone, or the jaw-bone of an ass, or lamps and pitchers; and the Spirit of God can do the business of God with souls, though He use but a word, or a look, or a groan.

J. G. BELLETT

I have put my soul, as a blank, into the hands of Jesus Christ my Redeemer, and desired him to write upon it what he pleases. I know it will be his own image.

GEORGE WHITEFIELD

> *Yet to all who received him, to those who believed in his name, he gave*
> *the right to become children of God—children born not the natural*
> *descent, nor of human decision or a husband's will, but born of God.*
>
> JOHN 1:12

*G*od loves you far more than you love Him. However much you may feel you want God, God wants you a great deal more. He wants you to enter into His peace and joy far more than you can desire to do so. And when God has, so to speak, prepared your faith, He responds to the faith He Himself has prepared, and the Lord Jesus comes in.

You took, as it were, one single sip of the water of life, and you passed from death to life. You were born of the Holy Spirit; you were regenerated by water and by the Holy Spirit, and the water of life ministered to you by the Holy Spirit became in you God's own gift, and you became a living soul in the sense that you were born again by the power of God. So that your regeneration was the work of God in enabling your heart to accept Christ, and then in responding to the enabling which He Himself had given.

It is important to bear in mind, that when you received Christ you received God, for Christ is God. There is no room for a second God in the world, if we mean by God what the Bible means.

Philosophically, as well as Scripturally, the notion is impossible and ludicrous. There cannot be two Omnipotences in the world; there cannot be two Almighties. There can be, and is, but one God. When you received Christ you received God, for He is very God of very God; and when you received God you received the Holy Spirit of God, for the Holy Trinity is so indissolubly one that, whatever one of the Sacred Persons does in entering into relations with the creature, that act is shared by all Three.

To sum up, you are a Christian because you have received the Lord Jesus Christ, and in receiving Him you received the Holy Spirit. Therefore every Christian has the Holy Spirit.

J. RUSSELL HOWDEN

*A*s well might a gnat seek to drink in the ocean, as a finite creature to comprehend the Eternal God.

CHARLES SPURGEON

June 13

I consider everything a loss compared to the surpassing greatness of knowing Christ Jesus my Lord, for whose sake I have lost all things.
PHILIPPIANS 3:8

*C*hristian perfection is not the strict, wearisome, constrained thing you suppose. It requires a person to give himself to God with his whole heart, and as soon as this is accomplished, whatever he is called upon to do for God becomes easy.

Those who are wholly God's are always satisfied, for they desire only that which He wills, and are ready to do whatever He requires; they are ready to strip themselves of all things, and are certain to find a hundredfold in that nakedness.

This hundredfold happiness which the true children of God possess amid the troubles of this world consists of a peaceful conscience, freedom of spirit, a welcome resignation of all things to God, the joyful sense of His Light growing ever stronger within their hearts, and a thorough deliverance from all fears and longings after worldly things.

They make sacrifices, but for Him they love best; they suffer willingly, realizing such suffering to be better than any worldly joy.

Their body may become diseased, their mind languid and shrinking, but their will is firm and steadfast, and they can say a joyful *Amen* to every blow which it pleases God to deal them.

FRANÇOIS FÉNELON

*G*od has called you to Christ's side, and the wind is now in Christ's face in this age, and seeing you are with Him, you cannot expect the sheltered or sunny side of the hill.

SAMUEL RUTHERFORD

*A*re there sorrows that sorely test our heart? Be assured that our Father intends every one of them to be a road for us to Christ; so that we may reach Him and know Him in some character of His love and power, that otherwise our souls had not known.

C. A. COATES

June 14

Now it is God who makes both us and you stand firm in Christ. He appointed us, set his seal of ownership on us, and put his Spirit in our hearts as a deposit, guaranteeing what is to come.

1 CORINTHIANS 1:22

*S*uppose I want to buy a hundred sheep, and go to the nearest sheep-farm, and find what I want. I say to their owner, "I am prepared to give you two pounds each for your sheep." He contracts to sell me the sheep at the price, I put down the money, and thus the sheep become mine.

What do I do next with them? Drive them home? No, I do not take them home immediately, I am not in such a hurry. Before I drive them home, I take my paint pot, and I put *my mark* upon every one of my sheep.

If I fail to do this, in driving them home they might get mixed up with some other people's sheep, and I should not know which were mine.

Alas! that is the way Christians do get mixed up with the people of the world, and often you cannot know the one from the other. It will not do for me to say I think I know that sheep to be mine by a leg mark, or by the turn of his ears, or by his horns: no, I must be sure of my own, and so I put my peculiar mark on each. Similarly, in giving the Holy Ghost, God puts His mark, clearly and distinctly, upon all His own.

But let me ask you this: Did the mark I put upon the sheep make it mine? You know it did not. I put the mark on it because it was mine, but it was the money I paid for it that made it mine.

So it is the work of Christ, the blood of Christ, that redeems, and saves, and brings the soul to God, and then the Holy Ghost is given to dwell in the believer as God's seal upon him, and the earnest of the good things that belong to him, so that the believer is sure of glory; his heart is now put in possession of eternal things, and he enjoys them.

It is like the bunch of grapes from Eshcol which Israel saw in the desert, and beautiful they were; it took two men to carry one bunch. The people were not in the land when they saw those grapes, but having seen the grapes, they had a taste of the land before they got into it. Before you and I go to heaven, we have, by the Holy Ghost, a taste of heavenly things. We know that we belong to heaven, and we know the atmosphere of the place we are going to. We know the Father, we know the Savior, we have eternal life, and enjoy communion, and fellowship with the Father, and with the Son.

A Christian has thus actually begun his heaven down here on earth. People often say, "We shall be happy in eternity." Why not be happy now? Why put it off? The Lord wants you to be happy down here.

Oh, but, you say, I have seen a great many people who say they are Christians, and they are not happy. More's the pity, they ought to be happy, if they are Christians. But perhaps these may not have been real Christians, still that does not prove there are no real ones.

Young men and women think they have found a reason for remaining unbelievers, because they have found some "Christians" who are not genuine. I ask then, When you get hold of a one hundred dollar bill, do you always put it in the fire, because now and then a bad hundred dollar bill has turned up? No—you know better, for what does a bad bank-note prove? It confirms that there are plenty of good ones. So if I meet with a counterfeit saint, he only proves that there are real ones.

Now what is a Christian? He is a man clear of death and judgment, brought to God, his sins forgiven: one who has a new nature, who has received the Holy Ghost, and who has a new place before God in Christ, of whose body he is a member; one who knows he is a child of God, an heir of God, and a joint-heir with Christ; who has nothing but glory now before him, and is looking for the coming of our Lord Jesus Christ, to take him home to the rest and glory of the Father's house. It is therefore a wonderful thing to be a Christian: an unspeakably blessed thing!

W. T. P. WOLSTON

One of the great secrets of growth is the looking upon the Lord Jesus as gracious. How strengthening it is, to know that He is at this moment feeling and exercising the same love and grace toward me as when He died upon the cross for me.

JOHN DARBY

If we believe not, yet he abideth faithful: he cannot deny himself.
2 TIMOTHY 2:13, KJV

*J*esus Christ does not want to be our helper; He wants to be our life. He does not want us to work for Him. He wants us to let Him do His work through us, using us as we use a pencil to write with— better still, using us as one of the fingers on His hand.

When our life is not only Christ's but Christ, our life will be a winning life; for He cannot fail. And a winning life is a fruit-bearing life, a serving life. It is after all only a small part of life, and a wholly negative part, to overcome; we must also bear fruit in character and in service if Christ is our life. And we shall—because Christ is our life. "He cannot deny himself"; He "came not to be ministered unto, but to minister." An utterly new kind of service will be ours now, as we let Christ serve others through us, using us. And this fruit-bearing and service, habitual and constant, must all be by faith in Him; our works are the result of His Life in us; not the condition, or the secret, or the cause of that Life.

The conditions of thus receiving Christ as the fullness of our life are simply two—after, of course, our personal acceptance of Christ as our Savior—through His shed blood and death as our Substitute and Sin-Bearer—from the guilt and consequences of our sin.

1. Surrender absolutely and unconditionally to Christ as Master of all that we are and all that we have, telling God that we are now ready to have His whole will done in our entire life, at every point, no matter what it costs.

2. Believe that God has set us wholly free from the law of sin—not *will* do this, but *has* done it. Upon this second step, the quiet act of faith, all now depends. Faith must believe God in entire absence of any feeling or evidence. For God's word is safer, better, and surer than any *evidence*

of His word. We are to say, in blind, cold faith if need be, "I *know* that my Lord Jesus *is* meeting *all* my needs *now* (even my need of faith), because His grace *is* sufficient for *me*."

And remember that Christ Himself is better than any of His blessings: better than the power, or the victory, or the service that He grants. Christ creates spiritual power; but Christ is better than that power. He is God's best. We may have Christ, yielding to Him in such completeness and abandonment of self that it is no longer we that live, but Christ that liveth in us.

Will you thus take Him?

CHARLES G. TRUMBULL

*W*here has there ever been found a single blessing save in the hand of Christ? Could you wish for any, save what *He* gives?

GEORGE V. WIGRAM

June 16

For you have been born again, not of perishable seed, but of imperishable, through the living and enduring word of God.

1 PETER 1:23

*O*h, my Friend, there is an ingrafting into Christ, a being formed and newly created in Christ, a living and abiding in him, and a growing and bringing forth fruit through him unto perfection.

Oh, may you experience all these things; and, that you may so do, wait to know life, the springings of life, the separations of life inwardly from all that evil which hangs about it, and would be springing up and mixing with it, under an appearance of good; that life may come to live fully in you, and nothing else.

And so, sink very low, and become very little, and know little; know no power to believe, act, or suffer any thing for God, but as it is given you, by the springing grace, virtue, and life of the Lord Jesus.

For, grace is a spiritual inward thing, a holy Seed, sown by God, springing up in the heart. People have got a notion of grace, but know not the thing.

Don't bother about the notion, but feel the thing; and know your heart more and more ploughed up by the Lord, that his Seed's grace may grow up in you more and more, and you may daily feel you heart as a garden, more and more enclosed, watered, dressed, and delighted in by him.

ISAAC PENNINGTON

*D*o you wish to be great? Then begin by being little. Do you desire to construct a vast and lofty fabric? Think first about the foundations of humility. The higher your structure is to be, the deeper must be its foundation.

AUGUSTINE

June 17

Those who sow in tears will reap with songs of joy. He who goes out weeping, carrying seed to sow, will return with songs of joy, carrying sheaves with him.

PSALM 126:5–6

*N*one who loves the Lord does not weep. Weep with sympathy for sinners, weep with desire for the glory of God, and weep with eagerness to overcome the enemy. Of course, those who have no heart to please the Lord do not have such experience. But all whose hearts are on the Lord's work are bound to weep. Jeremiah was one of the prophets in the Old Testament greatly used by the Lord. He attained to such distinction because he shed many tears. He cared so much for the children of God that he cried day and night.

Without a doubt tears are something we must have, because this world is in great need of much tears by which to wash her. Many young believers need to be nurtured and disciplined with tears. Spiritual life needs to be maintained with tears. Numerous sinners need to have the seed of the gospel sown in their hearts with tears. Without weeping, nothing can be done. Today the Christian's consecration is not adequate. Many offer their bodies, strength, money, and time; yet they fail to offer their tears. No wonder many works are incomplete and untold numbers of believers are not nurtured.

If we shed tears for the work, what will be the outcome? Do be aware of this, that tears will not be shed forever, because there is a time for it to cease. For please note this verse: "Thus saith Jehovah: Refrain thy voice from weeping, and thine eyes from tears; for thy work shall be rewarded, saith Jehovah; and they shall come again from the land of the enemy" (Jer. 31:16). If we really shed tears for the work, God says we shall be rewarded.

WATCHMAN NEE

$\mathcal{S}$end a heavy heart up to Christ, it shall be welcome.

SAMUEL RUTHERFORD

June 18

"Therefore come out from them and be separate," says the Lord. "Touch no unclean thing, and I will receive you. I will be a Father to you, and you will be my sons and daughters," says the Lord Almighty.

2 CORINTHIANS 6:17–18

$\mathcal{I}$ do not believe that there is any doctrine more needed today in the Christian church in America than the doctrine of separation.

We have lost power because the line between the church and the world has been almost obliterated. A good many people profess Christianity, but their profession does not mean much; the result is that the world does not know what Christians really believe.

For every unconverted man that reads the Bible, a hundred read you and me; and if they see us hand-in-glove with the ungodly they are not going to have any confidence in our professions . . .

How is it with your life? Are you hand-in-glove with the world? If you are, how can you expect God to fill you with the Holy Spirit?

I believe that the cause of Christ is suffering more from this one thing than any other ten things put together. God cannot give us power because we are allied with the ungodly. The mirth that satisfies the world will not satisfy the true child of God, and yet how many of us are just looking to the world for our pleasure.

DWIGHT L. MOODY

$\mathcal{W}$orldliness in some shape or form finds an easy entrance amongst the children of God. We have need, therefore, to be always on the watch, and to remember that the love of the world absolutely excludes from the heart the love of the Father.

EDWARD DENNETT

$\mathcal{T}$his world deserveth nothing but the outer court of our soul.

SAMUEL RUTHERFORD

Anyone who chooses to be a friend of the world becomes an enemy of God.

JAMES 4:4B

My prayer is not that you take them out of the world but that you pro-tect them from the evil one. They are not of the world, even as I am not of it. Sanctify them by the truth; your word is truth. As you sent me into the world, I have sent them into the world. For them I sanctify myself, that they too may be truly sanctified.

JOHN 17:15–19

*I*n some countries today there is a great effort among the large Christian bodies to make the Church popular. Every conceivable scheme is being brought into play in order to attract people to the Church.

It is forgotten that the true church can never be attractive to the world, and was never meant to be. It is something which is completely beyond the world's understanding. People are brought into the church through the witness of the Lord's children who comprise the church. When the life of Christ is expressed through a spiritual order, believers will maintain a witness that is spiritually effective. Others will be regenerated, and they will be added to the church, not because they, as worldly people, were attracted to it, but because they have been subject to a divine change which enables them to enter into life on a higher plane.

The church's mission is not to fit in to the world, but to see men changed so that they will fit in to the church.

JOHN KENNEDY

*N*othing has so corrupted Christianity as the acceptance of worldly help for the furtherance of its goals.

EDWARD DENNETT

June 20

Behold, the bush burned with fire, and the bush was not consumed.

EXODUS 3:2, KJV

*T*he only thing which is not consumed by burning is my soul. Fire is the death of my body, but fire is the life of my soul.

When my goods are burned they perish, but when my soul takes fire, for the first time it begins to live. It is then the hunger for fire that consumes my soul. It is because I have so little enthusiasm that I have so little life. The worm of worldly care gnaws at my heart just because there is no fire in my heart to destroy it. My force is wasted by its expenditure on myself. I want something to lift me out of myself in order that I may be strong. Nothing can lift me out of myself but fire, the fire of the heart—love.

If I could only be kindled into love, the last enemy would be conquered—death. Love would consume all my cares, but it would give new strength to me. There might be a wilderness around me, but my bush would be glorious—luminous. It would be seen afar off by all the travelers in the desert. It would be a light to lighten the ages, untouched by passing clouds, undimmed by flying years.

My heart would never be consumed if only it could burn.

GEORGE MATHESON

June 21

. . . Those who are led by the Spirit of God are sons of God.

ROMANS 8:14

*D*o you know anything of being led by the Spirit? or are you led by the organizations and plans of the religious world? If so, is there any wonder that you should be a stranger, both to the enjoyed relationship of a child of God, or of suffering for Christ's sake? Can you say you are led by the Spirit in your daily life—your shop, your business—or are you led simply by the maxims of the world? If so, you grieve the Spirit, and cannot enjoy the blessed relationship of sons of God—joint-heirs with Christ. It is a wonderful *thing* to have the Comforter, the Holy Ghost, *always* abiding with us, well able to take care of us, and all our interests here below, as children of God. Oh, to be led at all times by Him.

C. STANLEY

June 22

Surely he will save you from the fowler's snare . . .
PSALM 91:3

*W*hat weapons may not men use to spoil the children of God. Surely the strongest in the faith needs constant anointing with spiritual eye-salve, in order to perceive these refined snares of the fowler.

That true believers have everlasting life, everlasting righteousness, and everlasting glory, forever secured to them in Christ risen, beyond the power of the grasp of any adversary is certain. Yet Satan seeks to rob them of the everlasting consolation and good hope, which the apprehension of this grace is calculated to produce.

In no other path can true happiness be experienced, but by walking *in* Christ Jesus the Lord; owning Him as our Master, and seeking only to do His will, as having life *in* Christ, righteousness *in* Christ, strength *in* Christ, a friend at all times *in* Christ, victory over sin, death, the grave, Satan, and the world *in* Christ. In short, as having all spiritual blessings in heavenly places in Christ (Ephesians 1:3).

"CRUMBS FOR THE LORD'S LITTLE ONES"

June 23

. . . and the peace of God, which transcends all understanding, will guard your hearts and your minds in Christ Jesus.

PHILIPPIANS 4:7

To know the indwelling of the Lord as a conscious experience, there must be inward quiet. When there are wars and fightings inwardly, His presence cannot be realized. I do not mean that when the soul is in conflict the Lord has forsaken it. A thousand times no! The Lord was with David just as truly as He was with Solomon, but it required Solomon, a man of rest, to build the house to His name and not a man, David, in the midst of wars.

What I mean is only this: His indwelling presence cannot be consciously realized when we are in the midst of internal wars. To have the conscious experience of His indwelling we must be at rest inwardly and must know what it is to keep silence from all our fears and anxieties, fussings and worryings.

HANNAH WHITALL SMITH

For a Christian to have solitude is of the deepest importance, because it is then the heart renews its acquaintance with Him who only has entrance into our most solitary retreats. When we are thoroughly alone and apart He loves to be our visitor.

J. B. STONEY

June 24

. . . Then Pharaoh's daughter went down to the Nile to bathe . . .

EXODUS 2:5A

Who would have thought that from such a little thing as Pharoah's daughter going to bathe in the river of Egypt would spring the deliverance of Israel?

The mind of Christ in us is chiefly to be seen in *little things*. To walk before God in the everyday matters of life, and to have our words and actions savored daily with the name of Jesus, this is true holiness.

In the least matters what need there is of looking upwards! I ought not to write a note without looking up to God, seeking his help; for I can write folly enough in one sentence to cause myself and others disquietude for months.

Let us turn every circumstance of the day into an occasion of communication with God. Things of small amount will then bring us great blessings.

In small points of obedience are found the best test of the soul's state.

What great grace it needs to find no excuses for our little faults!—still greater to confess them!

ROBERT C. CHAPMAN

*W*hat a delightful sensation springs up in the mind when the faculties and powers are engaged in promoting the glory of Him who is invisible.

ROBERT RAIKES

June 25

For you know that it was not with perishable things such as silver or gold that you were redeemed from the empty way of life handed down to you from your forefathers, but with the precious blood of Christ, a lamb without blemish or defect.

1 PETER 1:18–19

*I*f there is one thing more clear than another in the Levitical sacrifices, it is the substitution of the innocent for the guilty; and it is under this aspect that we must consider the death of our Redeemer.

It is in this sense that He gave Himself for us. And this is the reason why the Apostle lays such emphasis on the *preciousness* of the sacrifice. Anything less than the costliest blood would not have availed; because it must not be simply the blood of an individual sufferer but of One who could suffer for a race of sinners.

The blood of Christ was precious because of the dignity of His nature, and because of His perfect character. "Without blemish"—that is, without personal sin. "Without spot"—that is, not defiled by contact with sinners. Lamb like in meekness, gentleness, purity, and uncomplaining suffering. And thus it was adequate for the work of cleansing away the terrible aggregate of sin.

Oh, precious blood! Oh, sacred heart of Jesus, from which it flowed, holy, loving, tender, broken with grief! Oh, snowy whiteness of robes washed in that fountain, and purer than the snow!

F. B. MEYER

June 26

On the last and greatest day of the Feast, Jesus stood and said in a loud voice, "If a man is thirsty, let him come to me and drink. Whoever believes in me, as the Scripture has said, streams of living water will flow from within him." By this he meant the Spirit, whom those who believed in him were later to receive. Up to that time the Spirit had not been given, since Jesus had not yet been glorified.

JOHN 7:37–39

Nothing is more miserable than the restless efforts of a soul out of communion. We may be very busy; our *hands* may be full of work; our *feet* may run hither and thither; the *head* may be full of knowledge; but if the *heart* be not livingly occupied with the Person of Christ, it will, it must be, all barrenness and desolation so far as we are personally concerned; and there will, there can be, no "rivers of living water" flowing out for others. Impossible.

If we are to be made a blessing to others, we must feed upon Christ for ourselves. We do not "drink" for other people, we drink to satisfy our thirst; and as we drink, the rivers flow. Shew us a man whose heart is filled with Christ, and we will shew you a man whose hands are ready for work, and his feet ready to run; but unless we begin with heart communion, our running and our doing will be a miserable failure—there will be no glory to God—no rivers of living water.

We must begin in the very innermost circle of our own moral being, and there be occupied, by faith, with a living Christ, else all our service will prove utterly worthless. If we want to act on others; if we would be made a blessing in our day and generation; if we desire to bring forth any fruit to God; if we would shine as lights amid the moral gloom around; if we would be a channel of blessing in the midst of a sterile desert, then, verily, we must hearken to our Lord's words. We must drink at the fountain head. And what then? Drink still—drink ever—drink largely, and then the rivers must flow. If I say, "I must try and be a channel of blessing to others" I shall only prove my own folly and weakness. But if I bring my empty vessel to the fountain head and get it filled, then, without the smallest effort, the rivers will flow.

C. H. MACKINTOSH

May the Lord make and keep us lowly! May He also give us to see Himself in glory that all which is of this world may be ever judged in our eyes as awaiting on the hour of the harvest and of the vintage which is not yet come. Our joy is come in His glorification, meanwhile, and in the Holy Spirit given to us before that hour. Jesus we know in heavenly glory, and that He has already sent down the Holy Spirit to bring us into the present power of glory. May we be vessels of His testimony—it may be, needing to be broken that the rivers may flow out the more freely, but nevertheless channels through which the rivers of living water flow, to the praise of His own grace and glory!

WILLIAM KELLY

*Y*oung Christians are like little rivulets that make a large noise, and have shallow water; old Christians are like deep water that makes little noise, carries a good load, and gives not way.

GEORGE WHITEFIELD

June 27

Peace I leave with you; my peace I give you . . .
JOHN 14:27

*H*ow perfect is the peace which the risen Savior gives to His people! It is His own peace, which the Head gives to His members. It is a blood-bought peace. It is God's peace, ordained by Him and beloved of Him as His chosen rest—a peace which passeth all understanding, and which is secure from all the interruptions and adverse influences of the world.

Jesus has made peace between God and man (the Father Himself, the God of peace, sending Him for this purpose to His "enemies"); peace between angels and reconciled sinners, between Jew and Gentile. In Him all things which are in heaven and which are on earth shall be gathered together. He is the Peace and Bond of the whole creation. Blessed are all who dwell in Salem, who are in Christ.

ADOLPH SAPHIR

*T*hou hast touched me and I have been translated into thy peace.

AUGUSTINE

June 28

. . .We are more than conquerors through him who loved us.

ROMANS 8:37

*I*t is by the grace of God that we can be conquerors. To be a conqueror, one must allow God to live His life in and through us.

Again and again He has to break us; that is to say, He breaks the things in us that protect and maintain "self." We must surrender totally to Him, and let Him do all that is necessary.

Thus He gets more and more room in us. He does not want only a part of us, but to fill our whole heart with His power; to fill us more and more with Himself. That means a closer fellowship with Him. That is glory!

CORRIE TEN BOOM

*T*he Christian life is not merely a converted life, it is not merely a consecrated life, it is not a Christian life at all unless it is a Christ-life.

RUTH PAXSON

June 29

For the kingdom of God is not meat and drink; but righteousness, and peace, and joy in the Holy Ghost.

ROMANS 14:17, KJV

*T*here is no true joy till you can joy in God and Christ.

I know wicked men and men of pleasure will have a little laughter; but what is it, but like the crackling of a few thorns under a pot? It makes a blaze, and soon goes out. I know what it is to take pleasure in sin; but I always found the ache that followed was ten thousand times more hurtful than any gratification I could receive.

But they who joy in God have a joy that strangers intermeddle not with—it is a joy that no man can take from them; it amounts to a full assurance of faith that the soul is reconciled to God through Christ, that Jesus dwells in the heart; and when the soul reflects on itself, it magnifies the Lord, and rejoices in God its Savior.

Thus we are told that "Zaccheus received Christ joyfully," that "the eunuch went on his way rejoicing," and that "the jailer rejoiced in God with all his house."

O, my friends, what joy have they that know their sins are forgiven them! What a blessed thing is it for a man to look forward and see an endless eternity of happiness before him, knowing that every thing shall work together for his good!—it is joy unspeakable and full of glory. O may God make you all partakers of it!

Here, then, we will put the kingdom of God together. It is "righteousness," it is "peace," it is "joy in the Holy Ghost."

When this is placed in the heart, God there reigns, God there dwells and walks—the creature is a son or daughter of the Almighty.

But, my friends, how few are there who have been made partakers of this kingdom! Have you? Then you are kings, though beggars; you are happy above all men in the world—you have got heaven in your hearts; and when the crust of your bodies drops, your souls will meet with God, your souls will enter into the world of peace, and you shall be happy with God for evermore.

I hope there is none who will fear death; for shame, if you do! What! afraid to go to Jesus, to your Lord? You may cry out, "O death, where is thy sting? O grave, where is thy victory?" You may go on your way rejoicing, knowing that God is your friend, die when you will, angels will carry you safe to heaven.

George Whitefield

*Y*ou have only these two shallow brooks, sickness and death, to pass through; and you have a promise that Christ shall do more than meet you—even that He shall come Himself and go with you and bear you in His arms. O then! For the joy that is set before you, for the love of the Man (Who is also God over all, blessed for ever) who is waiting on the shore to welcome you; run your race with patience.

SAMUEL RUTHERFORD

June 30

And after the earthquake a fire; but the Lord was not in the fire: and after the fire, a still, small voice.

1 KINGS 19:12, KJV

*O*nly in the silence of all flesh can the still, small voice be heard. A large part of the difficulty experienced by Christians in hearing the voice of the Lord arises from the absence of this inward stillness.

Our own internal clamor drowns His quiet speaking. We listen for His voice in the wind and in the earthquake, expecting their thunder to sound above all our own clamoring; and because we are disappointed, we complain that He does not speak at all, when all the while the still small voice of His love is waiting for the quiet in which it can be heard.

I am convinced that there are many at this moment hungering for the voice of the Lord, who would hear it at once if they would but be silent before Him for a little while. This is the foundation thought of the silent meetings of the Quaker Friends, even though it may be that their outward stillness does not always secure the perfect inward stillness that is the vital thing.

All the saints of old have insisted upon stillness as a necessity of true communion with God and have exhorted their followers to cultivate it, and every saint of the present day knows its value.

HANNAH WHITALL SMITH

*S*peak, move, act in peace, as if you were in prayer. In truth, this is prayer.

FRANÇOIS FÉNELON

And we know that in all things God works for the good of those who love him, who have been called according to his purposes.

ROMANS 8:28

Let me ask you this question: Are you pressed beyond measure? Are you pressed above strength? Have you come to the place in your life where you say, "It's all right for other people, but somehow it won't work in my case ... What's the use of me talking about a holy life? ... What's the use of me talking about full surrender? ... What's the use of me talking about the dedicated life of the ministry of Jesus Christ? I am in a particular situation for which there is no way out; there's no way back; there's no way through. I can't find the answer!"

The answer is, to trust God just where you are:

Pressed out of measure and pressed to all length;
Pressed so intensely it seems beyond strength:
Pressed in the body, pressed in the soul,
Pressed in the mind till the dark surges roll;
Pressure by foe and pressure from friends,
Pressure on pressure till life nearly ends.

Is that it?
Then listen. If you are pressed out, you are pressed in.

Pressed into knowing no helper but God,
Pressed into loving the staff and the rod,
Pressed into liberty where nothing clings,
Pressed into faith for impossible things,
Pressed into living a life in the Lord,
Pressed into living a Christ-life outpoured.

The reason why you are in that place today is simply in order that you might trust God. Do not pull strings. Do not hold committee meetings. Do not wangle things. Do not manipulate. Do not scheme, and do not plan. Sit still and trust God, and He will deliver you from your self-despair, from the sentence of death.

Then the second thing is that we must be willing to accept the circumstances of the hour, and believe that all things work together for good to them that are called of God. We must be prepared to accept our circumstances as they are. I believe that quite a lot of people grieve the Spirit of God just at this particular place. They are not prepared to accept the circumstances of their lives, as God has given them, and allowed them to come.

I remember meeting a lady during the war, and I said, "How are you getting on?"

"Well," she said, "I am very well under the circumstances."

And I asked, "How is your husband?"

"Well," she said, "He is in the armed forces, and under the circumstances he's all right."

Next I asked, "And how's your daughter?"

"Well," she said, "She's in the [army], and what can you expect under the circumstances?"

This dear lady had the whole family "under the circumstances!" And circumstances are like a feather bed: if you are on top you are comfortable, but if you are underneath, you are smothered.

I have in my vestry some words which were written by Samuel Rutherford, which, apart from the Scriptures, mean more to me than any other words.

The words are simply these: "Expose yourself to the circumstances of His choice."

What does that mean? It means that when you and I present ourselves to God in the morning, and present the day to Him, nothing can come into that day that is not allowed by the permissive will of God. Everything has its place, and everything has its purpose. Such things may come in as cut right across our own little plans; such things as might disturb, as might change: but if we have committed our way to God, everything that comes into that day is allowed by His permissive will.

We do not rebel against it, because that only embitters the soul, and loses the very blessing that God wants to give us; but we expose ourselves to it. We say, "O God, I accept this, and I accept it cheerfully; in fact, I rejoice in it, because there is some lesson that You want to teach me. And I believe that the greatest lesson of all that You want to teach me, is just to trust You when I can't see You."

Accept the circumstances, then, as they are.

JOHN L. BIRD

July 2

"I will never leave thee nor forsake thee."
HEBREWS 13:5B, KJV

Let every believer grasp these words and store them up in his heart. Keep them ready, and have them fresh in your memory; you will want them one day.

The Philistines will be upon you, the hand of sickness will lay you low, the king of terrors will draw near, the valley of the shadow of death will open up before your eyes. Then comes the hour when you will find nothing so comforting as a text like this, nothing so cheering as a real sense of God's companionship.

Stick to that word, "never." It is worth its weight in gold. Cling to it as a drowning man clings to a rope. Grasp it firmly, as a soldier attacked on all sides grasps his sword. God has said, and He will stand to it, "I will never leave you, nor forsake you."

NEVER! Though your heart be often faint, and you are sick of self, and your many failures and infirmities overwhelm you—even then the promise will not fall.

NEVER! Though the devil whispers, "I shall have you at last; yet a little time and your faith will fail, and you will be mine." Even then the Word of God will stand.

NEVER! When the cold chill of death is creeping over you, and friends can do no more, and you are starting on that journey from which there is no return—even then Christ will not forsake you.

NEVER! When the day of judgment comes, and the books are opened, and the dead are rising from their graves, and eternity is beginning—even then the promise will bear all your weight; Christ will not leave His hold on your soul.

Oh believing reader, trust in the Lord forever, for He says, "I will never leave you."

Lean back all your weight upon Him, do not be afraid. Glory in His promise. Rejoice in the strength of your consolation. You may say boldly, "The Lord is my Helper I will not fear."

J. C. RYLE

The promises of God are the powerhouse of blessing, the eternal tools of God whereby victories are won and character is carved out of the bedrock of human experience. And remember, every promise is available. Nothing is withheld, because the Lord Jesus Christ is God's "Yes" to every question arising from the promises of His Word.

JOHN HUNTER

July 3

Be strong in the Lord and in the power of his might.
EPHESIANS 6:10, KJV

Our strength does not lie in outward armor, but in an inward attitude, in the assurance of our power in Christ. Do we enter the conflict assured of the power to win, or are we overcome with dread and fear before beginning?

"Be strong in the Lord!" The Lord is more than a match for Satan. He has already bound the strong man; He already is Victor.

Mark it so that you cannot help but see it constantly, that little word "in." "Be strong in the Lord."

That little word contains the whole secret of victory over the devil. It is where we are that determines our victory.

In Christ we are more than conquerors. "Be strong in the Lord, and in the power of His might."

Our power is in a Person.

RUTH PAXSON

My mind must rise above what I am, to what God is. It is only then that one is formed by the revelation of what God is. To this we are called.

JOHN DARBY

July 4

In his heart a man plans his course, but the LORD determines his steps.
PROVERBS 16:9

Many Christians who have given themselves up to the leading of the Holy Spirit get into a place of great bondage and are tortured because they have leadings which they fear may be from God but of which they are not sure.

If they do not obey these leadings, they are fearful they have disobeyed God and sometimes fancy that they have grieved the Holy Spirit, because they did not follow His leading. This is all unnecessary.

Let us settle it in our minds that God's guidance is clear guidance. "God is light, and in Him is no darkness at all" (1 John 1:5). And any leading that is not perfectly clear is not from Him—that is, if our wills are absolutely surrendered to Him.

Of course, the obscurity may arise from an unsurrendered will. But if our wills are absolutely surrendered to God, we have the right as God's children to be sure that any guidance is from Him before we obey it.

We have a right to go to our Father and say, "Heavenly Father, here I am. I desire above all things to do Thy will. Now make it clear to me, Thy child. If this thing that I have a leading to do is Thy will, I will do it, but make it clear as day if it be Thy will."

If it is His will, the heavenly Father will make it as clear as day. And you need not, and ought not to do that thing until He does make it clear, and you need not and ought not to condemn yourself because you did not do it.

God does not want His children to be in a state of condemnation before Him. He wishes us to be free from all care, worry, anxiety and self-condemnation. Any earthly parent would make the way clear to his child who asked to know it, and much more will our heavenly Father make it clear to us, and until He does make it clear, we need have no fears that in not doing it, we are disobeying God.

We have no right to dictate to God how He shall give His guidance—as, for example, by asking Him to shut up every way, or by asking Him to give a sign, or by guiding us in putting our finger on a Bible text, or in any other way. It is ours to seek and to expect wisdom, but it is not ours to dictate how it shall be given.

R. A. TORREY

July 5

I can do all things through Christ which strengtheneth me.

PHILIPPIANS 4:13, KJV

*I*n Christ Jesus, the believer finds strength for all things. Christ is between him and all weakness; and he can say, I can do all things in Christ who strengtheneth me.

When Paul confronted the thorn in the flesh and besought the Lord thrice that it might depart from him, he learned that great lesson that His grace was sufficient for him; His strength is made perfect in weakness—notice "made perfect"—not only made manifest.

Had God said to him, "I will reveal my strength in your infirmity," it would have been a great assurance; but, far better than this, only in the weakness of man can God display the perfection of His strength.

The weaker we are and feel ourselves to be, the stronger He can prove himself to be; so that only when we become perfectly hopeless and helpless in ourselves and absolutely abandon ourselves to Him, can He fully and perfectly glorify His own grace. Omnipotence needs impotence for its sphere of working.

ARTHUR J. PIERSON

I will not think of the infirmities of my need, except to lead me to the divine simplicity of His supply.

HENDLEY G. C. MOULE

July 6

. . . let your light shine before men, that they may see your good deeds and praise your Father in heaven.

MATTHEW 5:16

$\mathcal{W}$e must be so completely hidden away in Christ that the world will no longer see us, but the Christ who lives in us. How can we approach men with a divine message when the old man is all they can see in us?

Like the shoe salesman who always wore the same goods that he sold and always exhibited them to all to whom he tried to sell, so we must always exhibit Christ to those to whom we testify of Christ; and this we can never do until we get to the place where we are willing to acknowledge that we are nothing and He is all. He must actually be our all in our daily conscious experience, or we can never show a dying world how sufficient he is for all their need. We must be able to show the goods we advertise.

This we not only can do, but will do from the moment we so yield that Christ can really live his life in us and thus become our character in daily living, and our power in daily service.

This is the life "hid with Christ in God." This is the life in which we are literally nothing and He is all. This is the life through which the world can see Him who reveals the Father.

J. E. CONANT

$\mathcal{I}$t ennobles a Christian immensely to know and to feel that he is a channel through which the life of Christ is to flow out.

G. V. WIGRAM

The World's Bible

Christ has no hands but our hands
To do His work today,
He has no feet but our feet
To lead men in His way,
He has no tongue but our tongues
To tell men how He died,
He has no help but our help
To bring them to His side.

We are the only Bible
The careless world will read,
We are the sinner's gospel,
We are the scoffer's creed,
We are the Lord's last message,
Given in deed and word.
What if the type is crooked?
What if the print is blurred?
What if our hands are busy
With other work than His?
What if our feet are walking
Where sin's allurement is?
What if our tongues are speaking
Of things His lips would scorn?
How can we hope to help Him
And hasten His return?

ANNIE JOHNSON FLINT

July 7

Then little children were brought to Jesus for him to place his hands on them and pray for them. But the disciples rebuked those who brought them. Jesus said, "Let the little children come to me, and do not hinder them, for the kingdom of heaven belongs to such as these."

MATTHEW 19:13–14

A mother sat searching her Bible, trying to probe the secrets of life of holiness. She spent so much time seeking spiritual help that the duties of her household became irksome and were either hurried through or neglected. The "homeliness" of home was gone.

One day. as she was deep in study, her little girl toddled up to her side with a broken doll. "Mummy, please mend dolly for me." With an impatient gesture, the mother brushed the little one aside. "I've more important things to do than trouble about dolly." The little one turned sadly away, and the mother continued her search for holiness.

But the search was a fruitless one, and the mother closed her book with a sigh, and sought the little child. She was lying on the hearth rug clutching her darling doll, and with the tears still wet on her pretty face. The mother's heart was smitten. God spoke to her then and there.

Tenderly stepping over the little one she woke her with her kisses. Then taking her into her arms she breathed a prayer to God for forgiveness. She saw that holiness could not thrive on neglected duties. Her devotion to her Lord was henceforth seen in her care of the household, and shone out even in mending broken toys! Home became home again. And the very page of Scripture was lighted up with a fresh glory.

Yes, and victory shone in the mother's radiant face.

AN UNKNOWN CHRISTIAN

There are no people so hard to teach as those who imagine they are more advanced than they are.

J. B. STONEY

July 8

Examine yourselves, whether ye be in the faith; prove your own selves. Know ye not your own selves, how that Jesus Christ is in you, except ye be reprobates?

2 CORINTHIANS 13:5, KJV

What is the supreme benefit, the gift and treasure above all others which even God can give?

A little child gives you a gift. Maybe it's a homemade potholder or some little thing. It's not worth much, but it's worth a lot to you. That's all a child can give. Or suppose you get a present from a relative. That present is according to two things: the love which the person feels for you and his ability to give. We give according to our ability.

Now when the great God Almighty, who owns heaven and earth, wants to bestow upon one of His creatures that which is above all other gifts, a gift worthy of its source, a gift worthy of the One who gives it, He gives Christ to be in our nature forever.

If you are false Christians, then Christ is not in you; but "know ye not your own selves, how that Jesus Christ is in you, except ye be reprobates."

This is God's supreme and final gift. Not the pearly gates, not the golden streets, not heaven, not even the forgiveness of sin, although these are God's gifts too, such as a king might give to his queen—a dozen gifts, and then the supreme, final gift worthy of royalty.

So, not a dozen, or two dozen, or a thousand, but countless hundreds of thousands of gifts God lays before His happy people, and then bestows this supreme gift. He makes us the repository of the nature and person of the Lord Jesus.

A. W. TOZER

𝒟o we think of, and rejoice in, our blessings more than in the Person in whom we have them? As to even our doctrinal blessings, there is a wonderful charm about them when they are new to us, and they sustain the soul for a certain time; but when the first joy of them passes away, a settling-down process commences. Every new bit of blessing may seem to put a new bit of life into us, but it gradually loses its lustre and power, and we become just ordinary Christians—we make very little progress.

It is as we take the Lord Jesus by faith into the affections of our hearts that we make spiritual progress. It is as He occupies an enlarged place in our affections that we go on. The head may be filled with general theological information without producing one spark of heart-affection for the Lord Jesus, and the soul remains in a state of spiritual emaciation.

Many have been misled by thinking that by reading the Bible you become like Christ—transformed; but you will find diligent students of the Word, who may never say anything incorrect in doctrine, yet who never seem to grow in grace and walk in spiritual reality.

All blessings of this dispensation of grace are wrapped up in a Person, and, by means of the Word of God, we make spiritual progress as our hearts learn to find everything in Him—the Son of God who loves us and gave Himself for us.

C. A. COATES

July 9

" ... what is that to thee? follow thou me."
JOHN 21:22B, KJV

*W*ould it were more thus with all the Lord's servants!

Would that we all knew more distinctly and carried out more decidedly, the Master's will respecting us. Peter had his path and John had his. James had his work, and Paul had his. So it was of old—the Cershonite had his work, and the Merarite had his; and if one had interfered with the other, the work could not have been done. The Tabernacle was carried forward or set up by each man doing his own proper work.

Thus it is in this our day. God has varied workmen in His house and in His vineyard; He has quarry men, stone-squarers, masons, and decorators. Are all quarry men? Surely not; but each has his work to do, and the building is carried forward by each one doing his own appointed work. Should a quarry man despise a decorator, or a decorator look down with contempt upon a quarry man? Assuredly not. The Master wants them both, and whenever the one would interfere with the other, as, alas, we so often do, the faithful correcting word falls on the ear, "What is that to thee? Follow thou me."

C. H. MACKINTOSH

*B*lessed is the man or woman who is able to serve cheerfully in the second rank.

MARY SLESSOR

July 10

. . . and him that cometh to me I will in no wise cast out.
JOHN 6:37B, KJV

*T*he measure of our yielding is the measure of our human life. It includes everything inside—spirit, mind, heart, will, affections. It includes everything outside—home, children, possessions, occupation. It includes everything allied—friendships, time, money, pleasures, life plans.

It includes our past, present and future. No matter what the past has held of sin, sorrow or self it is all handed over to Christ in a once-and-for-all committal. But some can surrender the past who find it difficult to yield the present to Christ's control. There is the desire to reserve a bit of ground. Others can surrender the past and present because driven to it by disheartenment or desperation but they are fearful to put the future wholly into His keeping. How do they know that God can be trusted to be faithful or that they desire to live under His absolute sway for all times?

When giving a message on the yielded life at a conference I noticed the anxious, troubled face of a woman on the front seat. I said, "You are able to trust July to God but fearful to put September into His keeping." Her face lighted up with a smile which was in truth an acknowledgment of being caught in very act of worry.

After the meeting she said, "That remark about committing September to the Lord hit me. I could be very happy here, now; but I must have an operation in September and I have only half enjoyed this beautiful place because I am worrying over September!"

Yielding includes our worst and our best. Some find it very difficult to believe that God can accept or want them because there is so much "the worst" that persists in their lives. But "Him that cometh to me I will in no wise cast out" is an invitation extended to the sinning saint as truly as to the sinner.

Grace abounds from the beginning clear through to the end our lives. So no matter how often we have repeated the same sin if we come yielding ourselves unconditionally to Him He waits to receive us, and the blood of Jesus Christ is equal to any demand made upon it for cleansing.

RUTH PAXSON

I have committed myself and my all into God's hands, and He has accepted the offering. Life henceforth can never be the same.

CHARLES COWMAN

In vain you rise early, and stay up late, toiling for food to eat—for he grants sleep to those he loves.

PSALM 127:2

One morning when I awoke trying to solve a chess problem that had filled my mind as I had put my head upon my pillow the night before. I ... determined that, henceforth, I should go to sleep thinking of Christ.

As the months passed, I discovered that there was much more than a habit involved in this. Here was a proof of the presence of the Lord Jesus Christ in my heart and mind, controlling even the subconscious element of my life.

Then I learned that I must not merely go to sleep thinking about Christ, but that I must go to sleep in communion with Him.

I began memorizing verses of Scripture at night and reciting them as I fell asleep. At first these truths were merely objective. "His Name shall be called wonderful," might be my verse on a certain night. At first I would meditate on this in terms somewhat like those in which I might expound them to an audience—"His Name is full of wonders"; "His Name is the name Jesus, that of the Savior"; "He shall save His people from their sins."

Then there came a change that He brought in my procedure. Those same sentences were altered to the person, number, and tense of fellowship: "Thy Name is full of wonders"; "Thy Name is Jesus"; "Thou art my Savior"; "Thou shalt continually save me from my sins."

Soon He became more real than the inside of my eyelids. I could not see them though they were close to my eyes. Him I learned to know in everything but the touch. And closing one's eyes with Christ takes away all fear of sleepless nights.

Let others count sheep jumping over a wall; I shall talk with the Shepherd.

DONALD GREY BARNHOUSE

The friendship of Jehovah is with them that fear him; And he will show them his covenant.

PSALM 25:14, ASV

The church consists of God's covenant people. This is a way of saying that it consists of God's friends. For the covenant of grace spells friendship between God and His own.

In essence the covenant of grace was established when, immediately after the fall of man, God said to the serpent: "I will put enmity between thee and the woman, and between thy seed and her seed; it shall bruise thy head, and thou shalt bruise his heel" (Genesis 3:15). Enmity with Satan implies friendship with God.

More explicitly God established His covenant with Abraham when He said: "I will establish my covenant between me and thee and thy seed after thee in their generations for an everlasting covenant, to be a God unto thee and to thy seed after thee" (Genesis 17:7). Thus Abraham became God's friend. Repeatedly Scripture calls him by that name.

When many strong enemies came against King Jehoshaphat, he called upon God for help and pleaded: "Art not thou our God, who didst drive out the inhabitants of this land before thy people Israel and gavest it to the seed of Abraham thy friend for ever?" (2 Chronicles 20:7).

God Himself declared: "But thou, Israel, art my servant, Jacob whom I have chosen, the seed of Abraham my friend" (Isaiah 41:8). And James says: "The Scripture was fulfilled which saith, Abraham believed God, and it was imputed unto him for righteousness: and he was called the friend of God" (James 2:23).

The Psalmist equates the covenant of grace with friendship between God and His people in the words: "The friendship of Jehovah is with them that fear him; and he will show them his covenant" (Psalm 25:14, ASV).

Inasmuch as the believers of all ages are Abraham's seed (Galatians 3:7, 29), they are God's covenant people, God's friends.

R. B. KUIPER

*I*f I could hear Christ praying for me in the next room, I would not fear a million enemies. Yet distance makes no difference. He is praying for me.

ROBERT M. McCHEYNE

July 13

Father if thou be willing, remove this cup from me; nevertheless not my will, but thine be done.

LUKE 22:42, KJV

*T*here is immense danger, in the present day, of following in the wake of others, of doing certain things because others do them, or doing things as others do them.

All this has to be carefully guarded. What we really want is a broken will—the true spirit of a servant who waits on the Master to know His mind.

Service does not consist in doing this or that, or running hither and thither; it is simply doing the Master's will, whatever that may be.

It is easier to be busy than to be quiet. When Peter was young, he went whither he would; but when he was older he went whither he would not.

What a contrast between the young, restless, ardent, energetic Peter, going wither he would, and the old, matured, subdued, experienced Peter going whither he would not.

What a mercy to have the will broken to be able to say from the heart, "What thou wilt; as thou wilt; where thou wilt; when thou wilt"—and most importantly, simply "Not my will, but thine, O Lord, be done."

C. H. MACKINTOSH

July 14

Blessed is the man who does not walk in the counsel of the wicked or stand in the way of sinners or sit in the seat of mockers. But his delight is in the law of the LORD, and on His law doth he meditate day and night. He is like a tree planted by streams of water, which yields its fruit in season and whose leaf does not wither. Whatever he does prospers. Not so the wicked! They are like chaff that the wind blows away. Therefore the wicked will not stand in the judgment, nor sinners in the assembly of the righteous. For the LORD watches over the way of the righteous, but the way of the wicked will perish.

PSALM 1

God makes no mistakes in planting people where they are. He does not put any of us in a spiritual climate in which we cannot grow in beauty and strength; and wherever He plants us, He sends streams of grace to refresh us. So whatever our circumstances may be, it is possible for us to live godly lives.

The darker the night of sin about us, the clearer and steadier should be the light that streams from our life and conduct.

Anyone should be able to live well in the midst of friendly influences and favoring circumstances; but it is doubly important that we be loyal and true to Christ when surrounded by those who care not for Him.

J. R. MILLER

*H*appy is he who has learned to look beyond the actions of men to the power that controls them all, and to receive all—favor or persecution, aid or hindrance, from the Lord.

That soul has acquired the secret of perfect peace amid the confusion and turmoil of the world, as well as in the presence of Satan's power.

EDWARD DENNETT

July 15

Nevertheless, God's solid foundation stands firm, sealed with this inscription: "The Lord knows those who are his," and, "Everyone who confesses the name of the Lord must turn away from wickedness."
1 TIMOTHY 2:19

*W*hen Esther had obtained grace at the hands of King Ahasuerus and was to undo as far as possible the evil which Haman had already been authorized to inflict upon her people, she was authorized to write a letter in the king's name and seal it with the king's ring, permitting the Jews to resist to the utmost all assaults upon them.

This seal gave the full authorization of the king to her letter. It might be written in the faint, trembling hand of the woman, or in the strong hand of Mordecai, but what gave it authority and value was the seal of the king.

A gentleman of wealth desires to give a check. His bookkeeper has left the office, and he gets an office boy to fill out name and amount on the blank form. The boy brings the check, written in his cramped, unsightly style, to the master, who signs it in with his name.

Is the check any less valuable because written by the boy? Would it be worth more if written in the firm, elegant hand of the bookkeeper? Not a cent more. The name of the gentleman authenticates it and imparts to it its full value, for which all his deposit in bank is responsible.

So with the seal of the Spirit. We are, in one way, but poorly written epistles of Christ. With some of us the handwriting is cramped and blotted, and with others faint and trembling; but, blessed be God, His signature is ever the same, the Holy Christ Himself!

This authenticates us.

SAMUEL RIDOUT

$\mathscr{S}$ealing is not a question of experience. It is a precious fact to be accepted on the authority of the Word of God.

When you believed the gospel, you were sealed by the Spirit. God the Father put His stamp upon you, so to speak. He did this by giving you the Spirit to dwell in you—He who dwells in us is the seal.

H. A. IRONSIDE

July 16

I strive always to keep my conscience clear before God and man.
ACTS 24:16

$\mathscr{C}$ommunion with God is very much like breathing, it can only be maintained just one moment at a time. We must refuse to look back, or to look forward, however much the enemy may tempt us to do so. Vain regrets over the past, and vague fears for the future will harass our minds enough to break our fellowship with God.

The mind cannot be occupied with two matters at one time, so that we need to trust our Lord to keep us abiding, even unconsciously, whilst we give our attention fully to our duty in "doing the next thing" (Colossians 3:23).

But supposing we know we have made mistakes, ought we not to put them right?

"Communing" means consulting with the Lord. Do this at once! Take all the actual, and even apparent "mistakes" at once to Him. As you spread your cause before Him, ask Him to show you anything He wishes you to do, any step He would have you retrace.

If He shows you something concerning another person where you have done wrong, His Word is clear, "Confess your faults one to the other" (James 5:16, ASV).

This is necessary always for unbroken communion—a conscience void of offence toward man as well as God.

If no special light is given, leave the whole matter with your Lord; He promises that His glory (Presence) shall be your reward (Isaiah 58:8).

He can gather up and straighten all that lies behind you as well as the crooked things before you. Past and future are under His control.

JESSIE PENN-LEWIS

*R*egret for a sinful past will remain until we truly believe that for us in the Lord Jesus, that sinful past no longer exists.

The believer in Christ has only His past and that is perfect and acceptable to the Father.

ANDREW MURRAY

July 17

If I am offered upon the sacrifice and service of your faith, I joy, and rejoice.

PHILIPPIANS 2:17

*D*on't be surprised if there is an attack on your work, on you who are called to do it, on your innermost nature—the hidden person of the heart. It must be so. The great thing is not to be surprised, nor to count it strange—for that plays into the hand of the enemy.

Is it possible that anyone should set himself to exalt our beloved Lord and not instantly become a target for many arrows? The very fact that your work depends utterly on Him and can't be done for a moment without Him calls for a very close walk and a constant communion of spirit. This alone is enough to account for anything the enemy can do . . .

It costs to have a pure work. Not for nothing is our God called a consuming fire.

Don't be surprised if you suffer. It is part of the way of the cross. Mark 9:12 says, "The Son of Man must suffer much." If we follow in the way He went, we also must suffer.

You will find this truer every year as you go on. And anything is easier. Scourging is easier . . .

Have you ever gone through your New Testament, marking the places where suffering in one form or another is mentioned? It's wonderfully enlightening. The Book is full of joy, but it is also full of pain, and pain is taken for granted. "Think it not strange," "Count it all joy" (1 Peter 4:12; James 1:2).

We are meant to follow in His steps, not avoid them. What if our suffering is caused by those whom we love? Was His not caused by those whom He loved? Oh, what a Book the Bible is! If only we steep our souls in its mighty comfort we can't go far wrong; we shall never lose heart. "For hereunto were ye called: because Christ also suffered for you, leaving you an example, that ye should follow his steps" (1 Peter 2:21).

You will find that the joy of the Lord comes as you go on in the way of the cross. It was the One who had nobody all his own on earth who said, "If I am offered upon the sacrifice and service of your faith, I joy, and rejoice."

It is no small gift of His love, this opportunity to be offered upon the sacrifice and service—something you would not naturally choose, something that asks for more than you would naturally give.

So rejoice! You are giving Him what He asks you to give Him: the chance to show you what He can do.

AMY CARMICHAEL

July 18

...And the house was filled with the fragrance of the perfume.
JOHN 12:36

Service in spirit, which is the only real service, is from above. Where then does your service originate, and on what is it founded? Does it come from above? Does the spirit animating you find its source in the Sanctuary, permeating your whole being, so that you serve God restfully in the power of His life constantly renewed in you?

This service is acceptable to Him, as was Abel's sacrifice. Its origin is faith, and it is an offering which ascends to God, and is accepted by Him. Serving God in any other way is sheer delusion, and leads to waste, weariness, and loss both now and in the future.

It is true that many Christians, even though they are God's servants, serve Him in this way, without having learned the secret of true justice. The result can only be delusion and spiritual waste.

It is not that good intentions necessarily lead to failure. On the contrary! You are consecrated to your work, but unfortunately you are liable to allow yourself, through a feeling of legal obligation, to be bustled into feverish activity. Your only remedy for this is to come to Him to find rest in the midst of service.

Restless, feverish service leads to defeat on every hand. You wish to serve God, but neither the spirit in which you do it, your manner of doing it, nor the way in which you act are right ...

The first kind of service of which he spoke comes from the Sanctuary, and descends on us through the Holy Spirit, but your service claims to rise up to God, Who will never accept it.

Martha was right to serve the Lord when He arrived in Bethany with His disciples. But where she was wrong was in permitting herself to be drawn into a restless, agitated type of service.

In John 11 all this is changed and it is Martha who first goes to meet the Lord, and who is prepared to see His glory. Then in chapter 12 we see her serving Him as He should be served.

Stop and think! And learn how to serve in spirit! In the measure in which your sphere of work grows, and in which it pleases God to increase its importance, this secret will open up to you all His treasures and riches.

Then in spite of all the work that devolves on you, you will be simple and humble in your way of life. The result will be, as it was at Bethany, that the perfume of such service will fill the house.

H. E. ALEXANDER

July 19

When Christ, who is your life, appears, then you also will appear with him in glory.

COLOSSIANS 3:4

*W*e know we should have victory, so when we meet with a temptation we take great care, and we watch, and we pray. We feel it is our duty to fight against that thing, and to reject it, so we make up our minds not to do so, exerting our wills to the utmost. But that is not our victory. Christ is our victory. We do not need will-power and determination to resist the tempter. We look to Him who is our life, "Lord, this is Your affair; I count on You. The victory is Yours, and You, not I, shall have the credit." So often we gain a kind of victory, and everyone knows about it!

We achieved it ourselves; but communion is broken and there is no peace. Many of us live in constant fear of temptation. We know just how much we can stand, but alas, we have not discovered how much Christ can stand. "I can stand temptation up to a point, but beyond that point, I am done for." If two children cry, the mother can stand it, but if more than two cry together, under she goes. Yet it is not really a matter of whether two children cry, or three. It is all a question of whether I am getting the victory or Christ. If it is I, then I can stand two only. If Christ, it won't matter if twenty cry at once! To be carried through by Christ is to be left wondering afterwards how it happened!

This, too, is a matter that God delights to bring to us with a new dash of understanding. Suddenly one day we see that Christ is our life. That day everything is changed. There is a day when we see ourselves in Christ. After that, nothing can make us see ourselves outside of Him. It alters everything. Then also there is a day when we see that Christ within us is our life. That too alters our whole outlook. They may be different days with an interval between, or both may come together. But we must have both; and when we do, then we begin to know Christ's fullness, and to marvel that we have been so stupid hitherto as to remain poor in God's storehouse.

WATCHMAN NEE

The moment I consider Christ and myself as two, I am gone.

MARTIN LUTHER

July 20

I in them, and thou in me, that they may be made perfect in me.
JOHN 17:23, KJV

The Spirit becomes a personal possession—personal to each believer. This could never be true of a relationship to Jesus. He was an historical person, who was born, lived, spoke, wrought, moved about, in places definitely capable of designation.

If a person were in the place where He was, he might enjoy His presence; otherwise he was deprived of it. The Apostles were chosen to be "with Him." To respond to His call, that they might hear His teaching, see His mighty works, come to know Him, be His witnesses, they must needs leave their homes and occupation and become itinerant with Him. Only some artificial, monkish mode of life could continuously adapt itself to such conditions.

But the Spirit does not call us to be with Him; He comes to be "with us." Wherever we live our lives, there He is, adapting Himself to the circumstances surrounding His beloved. Hence there is no Mecca for the Christian faith, no sacred shrine, no foregathering to find Him whom believers worship and serve.

Though they be scattered to the ends of the earth, He is with them, dwelling in them, walking in them—the living Christ by His Spirit their intimate, personal possession.

But this indwelling Spirit, one with our spirit, is more than a presence with us. He is a molding, transforming power. To the end of Jesus' ministry, taught of Him though they were, His followers, even His intimates, remained unstable, cowardly and undependable: His was but an influence without.

When, however, the Spirit was come, these same men became at once the embodiment of fidelity, courage and conviction. True, Jesus had left them, but His Spirit within made them as new men. So does He desire to work in every believer.

All self-effort toward transformation of character is futile. The vile pictures hung upon the walls of memory by indulgence in illicit imaginations, in obscenity, in evil habits; the remorse that lingers from animosities, jealousies, ugly self-seekings—how have men sought in vain to purge their souls of these; how many suicides tell the tale of hopeless effort to be free from their relentless lashings.

No, it is only the Holy Spirit of God who, coming into the life, can impart purity of mind and holiness of heart where sin had wrought its havoc. To set sin's captive free—this He has power to do; this He delights to do.

NORMAN B. HARRISON

$\mathcal{W}$e are to understand that God loves us, and that He justifies us by the work of His Son. We have no longer conscience of sins before God, because He Himself has taken them away from before His eyes.

We know that being united to the Lord Jesus Christ, who has fully glorified God in all that concerns our sins, we have been made the righteousness of God in Him. So the heart is free to enjoy His love in the presence of the Father.

JOHN DARBY

July 21

For he shall give his angels charge over thee, to keep thee in all thy ways.

PSALM 91:11, KJV

$\mathcal{G}$od is prepared to keep us in all our ways.

Many of us expect God to bring us out at last, but we have no thought of His keeping us in blamelessness of soul. We expect to be brought to heaven, but battered, beaten and despoiled on the way. But surely our God does better for us than that! He can keep us from yielding to passionate temper, jealousy, hatred, pride and envy, as well as to the grosser forms of sin.

The promise is clear: "He shall give his angels charge over thee, to keep thee in all thy ways"—our business ways, our social ways, our ways of service into which God may lead us forth, our ways of sacrifice or suffering.

Let us simply and humbly ask for the fulfillment of the promises in this psalm. He will answer your prayers. He will be with you in trouble. He will satisfy you with many years of life, or with living much in a short time, and He will show you the wonders of His salvation.

F. B. MEYER

July 22

. . . and to whom did God swear that they would never enter his rest, if not to them who disobeyed? So we see that they were not able to enter, because of their unbelief.

HEBREWS 3:18–19

*W*hat did God mean by calling it His rest? Not they enter not into their rest, but His own. Oh, blessed distinction! I hasten to the ultimate and deepest solution of the question.

God gives us *Himself*, and in all His gifts He also gives us Himself. Here is the distinction between all religions which men invent, which have their origin in the conscience and heart of man, which spring up from earth, and the truth, the salvation, the life, revealed unto us from above, descending to us from Heaven. All religions seek and promise the same things: light, righteousness, peace, strength, and joy. But human religions think only of creature-light, creature-righteousness, of a human, limited, and imperfect peace, strength, and blessedness. They start from man upwards.

But God gives us Himself, and in Himself all gifts, and hence all His gifts are perfect and divine. Does God give us righteousness? He Himself is our righteousness, Jehovah-tsidkenu. Does God give us peace? Christ is our peace. Does God give us light? He is our light. Does God give us bread? He is the bread we eat; "as the Son liveth by the Father, so he that eateth Me shall live by Me" (John 6).

God Himself is our strength. God is ours, and in all His gifts and blessings He gives Himself. By the Holy Spirit we are one with Christ, and Christ the Son of God is our righteousness, nay, our life.

Do you want any other real presence? Are we not altogether " engodded," God dwelling and living in us, and we in Him? What more real presence, and indwelling, awful and blessed, can we have than that which the apostle described when he said: "I live; yet not I, but Christ liveth in me"? Or again, "I can do all things through Christ which strengtheneth me." Or as the Lord Himself in His last prayer before His crucifixion said to the Father, "I in them, and thou in me"?

Thus God gives us His rest as our rest.

ADOLPH SAPHIR

There are two stages in the Christian life. The one in which, after conversion, a believer seeks to work what God would have him do. The second, in which, after many a painful failure, he ceases from his works, and enters the rest of God, there to find the power for work in allowing the Father to work in him.

It is this rest from their own work which many Christians cannot understand. They think of it as a state of passive and selfish enjoyment, of still contemplation which leads to the neglect of the duties of life, and unfits for that watchfulness and warfare to which Scripture calls. What an entire misunderstanding of God's call to rest!

Truly to rest in God is to yield oneself up to the highest activity. We work, because He worketh in us both to will and to do (Phil. 2:13). Entering into the rest of God is the ceasing from self-effort, and the yielding of oneself in the full surrender of faith in God's working.

ANDREW MURRAY

When he was at the table with them, he took bread, gave thanks, broke it and began to give it to them. Then their eyes were opened and they recognized him, and he disappeared from their sight. They asked each other, "Were not our hearts burning within us while he talked with us on the road and opened the Scriptures to us?"

Luke 24:30–32

Of what value to Christ is outward service, if love be wanting? Of what value to the Bridegroom would the rigid observance of her duties be, if the bride were cold in her heart toward him? A church without heart, is a church without Christ.

Beloved, let us see well to this. Let nothing satisfy us short of the living realized presence of Christ within us. No ministry, however excellent, can supply the lack of this; neither will truth itself nourish the soul, unless the power of Him who is the Truth be present to minister it.

We need to exhort one another respecting this, for these are days when the itching ear is more common than the glowing heart, and the teacher is often more sought than the Lord. Thus Christ is, as it were, often supplanted in His own house.

It is not difficult to discern the power of the Lord's presence in our meetings; the unlettered believer is as competent to ascertain this as the most instructed.

The two disciples on their way to Emmaus were very ignorant, but their hearts were occupied with the right object. Christ was the subject of their mutual intercourse as they journeyed on together. They loved Him, they had lost Him, and were sad. Soon He joined Himself to their company, because He knew that they were occupied with Him. His presence was felt, though they knew but little; and their hearts burned within them by the way. So shall we also find it to be the case, if our hearts are occupied with Christ and

Him crucified; the presence of the Lord with us will be realized, and our souls will be filled rather with the blessedness of having been with Him, than with questions as to the ministry we may have heard.

We have also to remember, that in one sense we are always in the Church; it is not merely when we assemble together in the Lord's name, that we then form a part of the church of God; but in private, as well as public, we still belong to that body which the Lord has redeemed with His own blood, and consequently our whole life should have constant reference to our union with all the saints of God.

"CRUMBS FOR THE LORD'S LITTLE ONES"

July 24

That day the LORD saved Israel from the hands of the Egyptians and Israel saw the Egyptians lying dead on the shore. And when the Israelites saw the great power the LORD displayed against the Egyptians, the people feared the Lord and put their trust in him and in Moses his servant.

EXODUS 14:30–31

What does it mean, "the Lord saved Israel"? It means that every foe was silenced, not an enemy was left. It is the case with every one who believes on the Lord Jesus Christ—for He was delivered for our offenses, and raised again for our justification. As it is put in Colossians, "Ye are complete in him who is the head of all principality and power."

I look up into the glory of God, and, far, far above the angels that never sinned I see a Man sitting there at the right hand of the Father—a Man who is my Savior, who went into death for my sins, who died my death, who is now risen from the dead. I am risen with Him, and accepted in Him. Where are my sins? Gone in the cross of Christ. Where are my enemies? Gone also.

And where is the Savior? Risen. And where are His people? Risen too, with Christ (Col. 3:1).

Salvation is a very large word. It includes forgiveness, and deliverance, and peace, and the knowledge that I am justified. It is not only the knowledge that the Lord died for me, that He put away my sins, but that when He died, I died, and when He rose, I rose. What a blessed thing to have God's salvation and to know it!

It was after the Lord had saved Israel that they sang, "I will sing unto the Lord, for he hath triumphed gloriously: the horse and his ride hath he thrown into the sea. The Lord is my strength and son, and he is become my salvation" (Exodus 15:1–2).

It is all coupled with a person, the person of the Savior. He who possesses Christ has God's salvation.

W. T. P. WOLSTON

*I*s the living Person now in heavenly glory really the Object of our hearts? For some time after I knew the Savior I used to think of Him as One who had lived and died on earth long years ago, and I well remember the day when I knelt down with a dear brother who prayed that we might know the Lord Jesus as a living Person in heavenly glory, and it dawned on me that there was a present Object for my heart in heaven.

Our hearts will never be satisfied until that glorified Lord Jesus becomes our object, bright and fair.

C. A. COATES

*T*here are many heads lying in Christ's bosom, but here is room for yours among the rest.

SAMUEL RUTHERFORD

Now listen, you who say, "Today or tomorrow we will go to this or that city, spend a year there, carry on business and make money." Why, you do not even know what will happen tomorrow. What is your life? You are a mist that appears for a little while and then vanishes. Instead, you ought to say, "If it is the Lord's will, we will live and do this or that."

JAMES 4:13–14

Each morning remember that you may not live until evening; and in the evening, do not presume to live another day. Be ready at all times to meet the Lord, and so live that death may never find you unprepared. Many die suddenly and unexpectedly; "for at an hour that we do not know the Son of Man will come."

When your last hour strikes, you will begin to think very differently of your past life, and grieve deeply that you have been so careless and remiss.

Happy and wise is the Christian who lives his life as he wishes to be found at his death. For these things will afford us sure hope of a happy death: godly contempt of worldliness; a fervent hunger for holiness; love of discipline; repentance; ready obedience; self-denial; the bearing of every trial for the love of Christ ... do not delay the salvation of your soul to some future date, for men will forget you sooner than you think. Now is the time to make provision for eternity. ... The present time is most precious; now is the accepted time, now is the day of salvation.

It is sad that you do not employ your time better, when you may win eternal life hereafter. The time will come when you will long for one day or one hour in which to amend; and who knows whether it will be granted.

Dear soul, from what peril and fear you could free yourself, if you lived in holy fear, mindful of your death.

Apply yourself so to live now, that at the hour of death, you may be glad and unafraid. Learn now to die to the world, that you may begin to live with Christ. Learn now to despise all earthly things, that you may go freely to Christ.

THOMAS À KEMPIS

*W*hat is our death but a night's sleep? For as through sleep all weariness and weakness pass away, and the powers of the spirit are renewed, so that in the morning we rise fresh, strong and joyous, so at the Last Day we shall rise again as if we had only slept a night, and we shall indeed be fresh and strong.

MARTIN LUTHER

July 26

And thou shalt remember all the way which the LORD thy God led thee these forty years in the wilderness, to humble thee, and to prove thee, to know what was in thine heart, whether thou wouldest keep his commandments or no.

DEUTERONOMY 8:2, KJV

*D*id you ever reflect that you are responsible for what you remember and for how you remember it, and that you are bound to train and educate your memory, not merely in the sense of cultivating it as a means of carrying intellectual treasures, but for a spiritual purpose? The one thing that all parts of our nature need is God and that is as true about our power of remembrance as it is about any other part of our being. The past is then hallowed, noble, and yields its highest results and most blessed fruits for us when we link it closely with Him, and see in it not only, nor so much, the play of our own faculties, whether we blame or approve ourselves, as rather see in it the great field in which God has brought Himself near to our experience, and has been regulating and shaping all that has befallen us. The one thing which will consecrate memory, deliver it from its errors and abuses, raise it to its highest and noblest power, is that it should be in touch with God, and that the past should be regarded by each of us as it is, in deed and in truth, one long period of what God has done for us.

We can see His presence more clearly when we look back over a long connected stretch of days, and when the excitement of feeling the agony or rapture has passed, than we could whilst they were hot, and life was all hurry and bustle. The men on the deck of a ship see the beauty of the city that they have left behind, better than when they were pressing through its narrow streets. And though the view from the far-off waters of the receding houses may be an illusion, our view of the past, if we see God brooding over it all, and working in it all, is no illusion. The meannesses are hidden, the narrow places are invisible, all the pain and suffering is quieted, and we are able to behold more truly than when we were in the midst of it, the bearing, the purpose, and the blessedness alike of our sorrows and of our joys.

Many of us are old enough to have had a great many mysteries of our early days cleared up. We have seen at least the beginnings of the harvest: which the ploughshare of sorrow and the winter winds were preparing for us, and for the rest we can trust.

Brethren, remember your mercies, remember your losses; and "for all the way by which the Lord our God has led us these many years in the wilderness," let us try to be thankful, including in our praises the darkness and the storm as well as the light and the calm.

Some of us are like people who, when they get better of their sicknesses, grudge the doctor's bill. We forget the mercies as soon as they are past, because we only enjoyed the sensuous sweetness of them whilst it tickled our palate, and did not think, in the enjoyment of them, whose love it was that they spoke of to us. Sorrows and joys, bring them all in your thanksgivings, and "forget not the works of God."

ALEXANDER MACLAREN

July 27

At midnight the LORD struck down all the firstborn in Egypt, from the firstborn of Pharaoh, who sat on the throne, to the firstborn of the prisoner who was in the dungeon, and the firstborn of all the livestock as well. Pharaoh and all his officials and all the Egyptians got up during the night, and there was loud wailing in Egypt, for there was not a house without someone dead.

EXODUS 12:29–30

*W*here the blood was sprinkled, salvation was the result; and where no blood was seen, the plague fell. God passed through the land that night in judgment, and "there was not a house without someone dead." Even in the houses of Israel there was one dead— the lamb, the victim, the substitute. In the houses of Egypt there was also one dead—the first-born.

In the houses of Israel the lamb had died in place of the first-born, and that brought peace to many a household that night.

You might have gone up to a young man in one of the households of Israel, who was the first-born, and asked him, "How is it with you tonight? Have you peace?"

His reply would have been, "Perfect peace!"

We might then ask, "How do you feel?"

He would no doubt reply, "I do not rest on my feelings, but on the word of Jehovah. The blood is upon the doorpost. It was the father's work to put it there—but I assure you I took good care to see that it was done. I was much too interested in the matter not to see to it. I would lose my life this night, if the blood were not there. But the blood *is* there, and Jehovah has said, 'When I see the blood, I will pass over you.'"

So, Christian, are you at rest? Perfect rest? The blood is the basis of your peace, not what you feel.

Peace is not a feeling, not an emotion, and not an experience. Rather, it flows from the fact that the claims of God have been met by the Lamb of God, and God respects His precious blood. The blood of Jesus has reached and touched the very memory of God, for we read in Hebrews 10, "Your sins and your iniquities I will remember no more."

The blood of bulls and goats could not take away sins, but the blood of Jesus does. Its value God alone knows.

You and I do not know the value of the blood of Christ. We value it surely, but our value of it is very poor and inadequate. God knows its value perfectly, and He esteems its worth fully, and He says to you and me, "Trust that blood. Get under its shelter."

If we can answer, "Lord, I trust it," then God says, "I shall treat you according to my estimate of the value of that blood, not according to yours."

That is wherein peace lies—not on your estimate or mine of the blood of Christ, but on God's estimate. And what is God's estimate of it? He estimates it so highly, that there is nothing too great for Him to do on the ground of it. He delivers you from judgment, and brings you to glory, on the ground of the shed blood of His own dear Son. And more than that, it will give you the sweetest peace and confidence towards God.

W. T. P. WOLSTON

. . . a pure heart, a good conscience and a sincere faith.

1 TIMOTHY 1:5

It is quite possible for every one of us to have a perfectly good conscience. A happy state to be in!

Have you a good conscience? Are you under accusation, under condemnation? Are you fretting and worrying about the badness of your own heart? That means that you have not the answer of a good conscience to God.

What is the matter? You are still looking for something from nature, from the old man. You had better give it up, as that is the only way out—repudiate it.

Tell yourself and tell the accuser once and for all that in you, that is, in your flesh, dwelleth no good thing, and you never expect to find anything. The enemy knows it, and yet he is trying to get you on an impossible quest for something he knows you will never find, and that is how he worries you. Years of it!

Then why not come onto the Lord's ground and outmaneuver him? Let us settle it that we can never expect to find any good in our old nature. All our good is in another, even our Lord Jesus. It is the law of the Spirit of life in Christ Jesus.

T. AUSTIN-SPARKS

What is our link with God? It is this: the Lord Jesus Christ as the answer to God and to Satan for us. It will never be what we are in ourselves. If you are expecting a day to come when in virtue of what you are in yourself you can satisfy God, you are destined to an awful disillusionment. The day will never come when we can satisfy God in ourselves, not even more or less.

F. W. GRANT

There is no fear in love. But perfect love drives out fear, because fear has to do with punishment. The man who fears is not made perfect in love.
1 JOHN 4:17–18

*O*ne of the ways in which the blood of God come to have such sovereign virtue in the sinner's conscience is this: when our consciences toward one another are wounded, and are full of remorse and fear, nothing will heal the wound and restore peace between man and man, nothing but a great uprising of love between the alienated parties.

But if a great enough uprising and outgoing of love takes place between them, then not only is the lost peace restored, but those who were once such enemies are henceforth far better friends than ever they were before. And the same noble law of reconciling love holds even more in the world of sin and salvation. The blood of God the Son is such a manifestation of divine love toward the sinner that nothing can resist it. No guilt, no remorse, no terror, no suspicion, can stand out against the love of God in the blood of His only begotten Son.

It is not so much our Savior's payment of the uttermost farthing of our debt that heals our horrified consciences. It is not His atoning blood even that so pacifies, and so conquers, and gives such peace to the guilty conscience. It is only the love of God as seen in the atonement that can do all that. And if there are still any of the dregs of remorse, and terror, and irreconcilability, and suspicion in your conscience toward God, it is not because His blood is not of volume and virtue enough to wash away all your sins, but it is because you do not open your heart wide enough and deep enough to receive His love. For there is no fear in love. But perfect love on God's part to you, awakening on your part a corresponding love to God, such perfect love on both sides, drives out all possible fear, so much so, that he that feareth is not made perfect in love.

Fellow Christian, I recommend this great Scripture for every guilty conscience and corrupt heart. For, times and occasions without number, when every other scripture has threatened to fail myself, this scripture has been a rock and a refuge to me. The very awfulness of the word used again and again silenced the almost as awful accusation of my conscience and the almost as awful despair of my heart.

The Blood of God has an inward, and an experiential, and an all-satisfying evidence to me, and I recommend it to you with all my heart.

ALEXANDER WHYTE

July 30

Which of you fathers, if your son asks for a fish, will give him a snake instead? Or if he asks for an egg, will give him a scorpion? If you then, though you are evil, know how to give good gifts to your children, how much more will your Father in heaven give the Holy Spirit to those who ask him?

LUKE 11:11

All the discomfort and unrest of the spiritual life of so many of God's children come from this: they do not understand that God is truly their Father. They think of Him as a stern Judge or a severe Taskmaster or, at best, as an unapproachable Dignitary, seated on a far-off throne, dispensing exacting laws for a frightened and trembling world. In terror that they might fail to meet His requirements, they hardly know which way to turn. But they have no conception of a

God who is a Father, tender and loving and full of compassion; a God who, like a father, will be on their side against the whole universe.

Discomfort and unrest are impossible to the souls that come to know God is their Father. God is the kind of Father that our highest instincts tell us a good father should be. Sometimes earthly fathers are unkind, tyrannical, selfish, or even cruel. Or they are merely indifferent and neglectful. None of these can be called good fathers. But God, who is good, must be a good Father or not a Father at all.

HANNAH WHITALL SMITH

*W*hen circumstances seem impossible, when all signs of grace in you seem at their lowest ebb, when temptation is fiercest, when love and joy and hope seem well nigh extinguished in your heart, then rest, without feeling and without emotion, in the Father's faithfulness; abide in the fact that He loves you infinitely, and even now is working in you faithfully; and honor Him, and put the enemy to flight by taking to yourself the words of Job, "Though He slay me, yet will I trust in Him."

D. TRYON

July 31

Blessed by the God and Father of our Lord Jesus Christ, which according to his abundant mercy hath begotten us again unto a lively hope by the resurrection of Jesus Christ from the dead, to an inheritance incorruptible, and undefiled, and that fadeth not away, reserved in heaven for you, who are kept by the power of God through faith unto salvation, ready to be revealed in the last time.

1 PETER 1:3–5

$\mathcal{O}$h, that the saints were brought off their own dark fleshly experiences to rest more simply upon God and His work! Surely there are comparatively few who have learned to tell of all the riches of mercy which are theirs in Christ as told by these verses. Are they not a precious string of rich gems? And whose gems are they? Surely they are the property of every believer! Yet most know it not. Too many question and doubt as though nothing were theirs. And why is this?

Because instead of taking what God has done as their possession and security, they insist on looking for evidences and feelings inside themselves—which in reality, is the experience of unbelief and the carnal man. Thus they never get a firm footing in grace at all.

Blessed truth, that the resurrection of Jesus was our begetting again to a lively hope to all these blessings and glories.

May the knowledge of this as a true thing, in God eternally true, lead us into a perfect freedom and holy joy and delight.

For this will bring our darkened hearts into the place of light and peace and gladness and enable us to sing for joy, and to find strength (for the joy of the Lord is His people's strength) to go forth and do His will.

G. V. WIGRAM

$\mathcal{W}$hen a person begins to apprehend what it means to be united to the Son of God and what he has through this union, he will at once realize that his spiritual growth depends upon a clear understanding of truth rather than upon an experience. However those who really appropriate this truth cannot fail to have daily experiences with the Lord.

L. L. LETGERS

August 1

Yea, he is altogether lovely.

Song of Songs 5:16, KJV

*W*hom should we love, if not him who first loved us, and gave himself for us? If the bliss of angels and glorified souls, consists greatly in seeing, and praising the Son of God; surely, to love, to trust, and to celebrate the friend of sinners, must be a principal ingredient in the happiness of saints not yet made perfect.

Solomon, whose experience of grace was lively and triumphant when he wrote the Song of Songs, declares that he "is altogether lovely." Other objects may be overrated, and too highly esteemed; but so transcendent, so infinite, is the excellency of Christ, that he is, and will be to all eternity, more lovely than beloved.

Yet, though all the love possible for saints and angels to show, falls, and will always fall, infinitely short of the Savior's due; still it is a blessed privilege, to love him at all, though in ever so faint a manner, and in ever so low a degree.

They, that love him at all, wish to love him more: and more and more they shall love him, through the ages of endless duration, in heaven, where they shall be like him, and see him as he is.

Augustus Toplady

I think I see more of Christ than I ever saw; and yet I see but little of what may be seen.

Samuel Rutherford

August 2

I know, O Lord, that a man's life is not his own; it is not for man to direct his steps.

Jeremiah 10:23

The other day a woman called with a question on hearing God speak. She said, "How do I know when I have God's guidance and when I've heard Him speak? Not long ago, I was sure He'd spoken to me, and when I did what He told me, it didn't work out." Questioning her a little, I found that she'd told the other party emphatically that God had sent her to do thus-and-so, and the other party couldn't see that God was in it at all. What was wrong?

My own experience has taught me that I should keep God's counsel reverently in my heart before I tell someone else. Keep it, and think about it, compare it with what I know to be true of His character, and hold it there with an obedient attentive heart ready to move.

If the door of circumstances opens, I move, quietly with sensitive steps, and follow the directions God seems to have given to me. Two things can happen: the door can close in my face, and I'll know I got the directions wrong. Or the door can open wide, and I'll know I got the directions right. In either case, I'll learn a great deal. In the latter instance, I'll be ready to share what happened with the person God chooses (His choice, not necessarily mine). It is often the wisest thing to hold our sharing until God has backed up our action. After all, a true testimony is a simple recounting of what the Lord Himself is like, how He has led, what He has done for us in a given set of circumstances.

The entire matter of hearing God's voice can be greatly simplified if we remember that the Kingdom is within and the King is in His Kingdom. The Spirit of the Lord dwells within. Within the real me, within the real you dwells the Presence of God. "Not I, but Christ lives in me," wrote Paul, recognizing this inner Presence in his own being. We never have to go out looking for Him; He's never away from us, always near to us. God is never preoccupied, always attentive and aware.

If you are responding to Jesus Christ, you are a Christian. You are a fulfilled, creative Christian if your response includes the fact that His is an indwelling Presence—our Lord with us and in us in every large and small happening of our daily lives.

ROSALIND RINKER

*I*f day by day we first seek divine direction, and then follow it, we shall be ready when new circumstances arise, for the new blessings which will be offered.

Today should be preparation for tomorrow. The only proof that we shall be equal to tomorrow's test is that we are meeting today's test believingly and courageously. The only evidence that we shall be willing for God's will tomorrow is that we are subject to His will today.

W. G. S.

August 3

The blood of Jesus Christ his Son cleanseth us from all sin.
1 JOHN 1:7, KJV

*W*hat is included in the salvation which the grace of God brings? The answer is, Everything. Salvation is a precious casket containing all I want for time and eternity. It includes salvation from the future consequences of sin, and from its present power.

To be a divinely-saved person—a person saved by the grace of God, saved by the blood of Christ, as every believer is, involves entire deliverance from wrath, from hell, from Satan, from every thing that could possibly be against me. A man whom God hath saved is surely safe from all. There is nothing doubtful about God's salvation; it is all *settled*. There is no delay; it is all finished. We have neither to wait for it nor to add to it, but to receive it now, and enjoy it forever. The mighty tide of grace rolls down from the very throne of God, and bears upon its bosom a full salvation—salvation for me. I receive it as a free gift; I bow my head and worship, and go on my way rejoicing.

C. H. MACKINTOSH

*O*ur Father delights in having us with Himself. Love yearns to satisfy itself about me. It is not only that I can go in, but a much greater thing—my Father, in all His majesty and glory, can come out!

J. B. STONEY

August 4

"Pray continually."

1 THESSALONIANS 5:17

*W*e must offer all our acts to God and believe that He accepts them. Then hold firmly to that position and keep insisting that every act of every hour of the day and night be included in the transaction. Keep reminding God in our times of private prayer that we mean every act for His glory; then supplement those times by a thousand thought-prayers as we go about the job of living. Let us practice the fine art of making every work a priestly ministration. Let us believe that God is in all our simple deeds and learn to find Him there.

A. W. TOZER

*W*hile you are before the Lord, hold your heart in his presence. How? This you also do by faith. Yes, by faith you can hold your heart in the Lord's presence. Now, waiting before him, turn all your attention toward your spirit. Do not allow your mind to wander. If your mind begins to wander, just turn your attention back again to the inward parts of your being. You will be free from wandering—free from any outward distractions—and you will be brought near to God. The Lord is found only within your spirit, in the recesses of your being, in the Holy of Holies; this is where He dwells.

JEANNE GUYON

For where your treasure is, there your heart will be also.
MATTHEW 6:21

*I*n Christ Jesus we work no longer *for* life, but *from* life. Our high endeavor is not to shape our actual life in the flesh into conformity to an ideal life that is set before us in Him. It is rather to reduce our true life now hid in Christ to an actual life in ourself. And so the summons of the Gospel is not that we behold what is impossible for us in Christ, and reach forth to it; but rather that we behold what is accomplished for us in Christ, and appropriate it and live in it.

Risen with Christ, the first fruits of our spirits already carried up with Him into glory, our life hid with Him in God, how shall not our heart be where our treasure is! How shall not our love be ever kindling and burning upwards, purging itself of all earthly dress, till it is wholly intent on Him? Why hang the damps and corruptions of the grave about us still, earthliness and sinful affections, and all these clinging accompaniments of moral death, from which our Lord has ransomed us! It is ours even now to walk with Him in white, and to be ever "breathing with Him the freshness of the morning of the resurrection and of endless life."

A. J. GORDON

*B*efore my conversion I worked toward the Cross, but since then I have worked from the Cross. Then I worked to be saved, now I work because I am saved.

DWIGHT L. MOODY

Then John gave this testimony: "I saw the Spirit come down from heaven as a dove and remain on him. I would not have known him, except that the one who sent me to baptize with water told me, "The man on whom you see the Spirit come down and remain is he who will baptize with the Holy Spirit." I have seen and I testify that this is the Son of God.

JOHN 1:32–34

*Y*ou remember in the days of Noah, when the flood was upon the earth, Noah sent out a dove in order to see what was the state of matters, and in a short time the dove came back, for she found no resting-place. He sent her out seven days after, and again she came back, but this time with an olive leaf in her mouth. When she was sent forth the third time, she did not return, she had whereon to rest.

When the Holy Spirit fell upon the blessed Lord Jesus Christ in the form of a dove, what had happened? For over four thousand years the Holy Spirit had been searching in vain over this earth to find a holy, sinless, spotless man on whom to come and abide. At length here was the One upon whom He could rest. He, so to speak, like the dove, had not found any place whereon to rest. And why did not Noah's dove rest? Were there not plenty of bodies upon which it might alight?

Yes, the water was, so to speak, alive with carrion; corpses floated upon the water everywhere, but these afforded no resting-place. And the Holy Spirit had brooded over the world all these years, and had seen but moral carrion-man, a wretched, ruined, godless, sinful creature in himself. True He had come upon men like Balaam or Saul, but He left them. He had come upon men like David and Isaiah, but He left them. But here was a holy, spotless man, and He came and abode upon Him.

Because Jesus was perfect, sinless, and holy, the Holy Spirit came and dwelt in Him. He was in His moral perfection the delight of the Father, the Lamb of God, the Son of God; and, more than that, He who received the Holy Spirit would baptize with the Holy Spirit. That is, He takes your sins away and gives you the Holy Spirit. What a wonderful thing! The One who can take away the sins of men can also give them the Holy Spirit; can give them the needed power for the enjoyment of His life dwelling in their souls.

W. T. P. WOLSTON

August 7

Christ also loved the church, and gave himself for it.
EPHESIANS 5:25, KJV

*I*t never says Christ loved the world; nor does it say God loved the Church. It says, "Christ loved the Church and gave Himself for it." If we want to know what are Christ's interests to-day—where the circle of His interests are to-day, we have the answer in this beautiful passage before us: it is the Church.

The Lord thinks everything of the Church. The circle of His interests all center there in this present day. He loved it and gave Himself for it, and He is engaged in active service on high today on behalf of it; and He is going to take it to glory to be with Himself soon, and then bring it back and display it in all the brightness and splendor of His own glory with which He will adorn it, when it will shine forth as the Holy City, New Jerusalem, having the glory of God—the Bride, the Lamb's wife.

It is an immense thing, for our souls to get hold of that, and to find ourselves in the power of it.

Especially is it needful for those who are young in the ways of the Lord. It is a great thing for us all to see that the affections of the Lord's heart flow out at the present time to His Church and not to the world.

WILLIAM EASTON

August 8

But while all this was going on, I was not in Jerusalem, for in the thirty-second year of Artaxerxes king of Babylon I had returned to the king. Some time later I asked his permission and came back to Jerusalem. Here I learned about the evil thing Eliashib had done in providing Tobiah a room in the courts of the house of God. I was great-ly displeased and threw all Tobiah's household goods out of the room. I gave orders to purify the rooms, and then I put back into them the equipment of the house of God, with the grain offerings and the incense.

NEHEMIAH 13:6–9

How much room is there in your life for the Holy Spirit? Is the whole trouble that Tobiah and his furniture clutter up the place? Then they need to be thrown out, promptly and firmly. What about your bookshelves? Would the divine approval be upon all that is there? What about your clothes closet? Did you pray before you purchased all its contents? Would it be something upon which the Lord would smile? Is it designed to attract to yourself or attract to Jesus? What about your record collection? Would He be satisfied with all that is there? Or would He have to put His finger upon something that should be thrown out?

My dear fellow Christians, if you mean business for God in these desperate days, I suggest to you we need an examination of every part of our lives so that the furniture with which the enemy clutters them up might be thrown out. Oh, that we would learn to make room for God to work!

ALAN REDPATH

*I*t is not a question of whether a thing be right or wrong, but what savor have the things of Christ in it? It may be a very small thing. If we find the reading of a book makes the manifestation of Christ to become less precious to us, we have gotten away from God, and we cannot tell where the next step may take us. Satan often cheats us in this way.... If anything comes in and takes the freshness of Christ from your soul, take heed!

JOHN DARBY

August 9

And if the Spirit of him who raised Jesus from the dead is living in you, he who raised Christ from the dead will also give life to your mortal bodies through his Spirit, who lives in you.

ROMANS 8:11

*W*e are largely creatures of habit. By birth we are selfish, and by long practice we have lived to please ourselves. We have long been debtors to certain fleshly tendencies. We have settled down perchance (wicked notion) that it must be ever thus. There are certain Canaanites that "would dwell in the land." They have chariots of iron. Let us set out a few of the more common and subtle forms of the flesh which are manifest "hangovers" in many Christians.

You may always have been a murmuring, complaining Christian. You sulk and feel sorry for your "sad, sweet self." But you need not do so. "If the Spirit of him that raised up Jesus from the dead dwell in you," He will so quicken your poor mortal, murmuring frame that you will experience the power of the Cross to cancel the complaining. There is a point to be observed, however; the victory will not be automatic. It will be only: "If ye through the Spirit [note that you must co-operate] do mortify [make to die] the deeds of the body" (Rom. 8:13).

You are sensitive, "thin-skinned"? Why not call it sinful pride? The next time somebody reproves you, just say, "You don't know half the truth. If you knew me you would say much worse." This may help you into harmony with the Cross. It will at least be the truth.

The flesh reasons that if your circumstances were only different you could have victory. But circumstances only reveal what is inside. Our insistence here is this: that "the eternal substance of a thing never lies in the thing itself, but in the quality of our reaction toward it. If in hard times we are kept from resentment, held in silence and filled with inward sweetness, that is what matters. The event that distressed us will pass from memory as a wind that passes and is gone. But what we were while the wind was blowing upon us has eternal consequences" (Amy Carmichael).

You may be a zealous Christian. But have you gotten over a fleshly itch for a thrilling baptism of power? Do you demand signs and wonders before you will believe? The flesh seeks to glory in God's very presence. Those who make such imperious demands upon God keep alive the very fleshly, selfish principle which must go to the Cross. In Old Testament ceremony, the blood, representing death, always preceded the anointing with oil, representing the Spirit. Do we forget that the Spirit comes from the Crucified in Heaven? Five bleeding wounds He bears.

They still proclaim that the flesh with its passions and lusts was crucified.

L. E. MAXWELL

$\mathcal{Y}$ou are one of God's rough diamonds, and He is going to have to cut you so that you may really shine for Him. It takes a diamond to cut a diamond. You are to be ground and cut, and hurt by other diamonds, by other Christians, by spiritual Christians. But the more cutting and the more perfecting, the more you are going to shine for your Lord.

G. Marshall

August 10

Upon the first day of the week let every one of you lay by him in store, as God hath prospered him.

1 Corinthians 6:2, KJV

$\mathcal{H}$ere [a Christian's giving is said to be] providing a store, out of which can be given as the occasions arise. It is like the tithes first devoted to the Lord, but in view of being given to the Levites. Our devoted money is thus laid aside in store, and from this we can draw to give to the poor, or for the spread of the truth in books and tracts, or to give to a servant of the Lord to help on the work.

If the saints generally acted on this principle in faithfulness to God, I am sure the matter of giving would be greatly simplified, and there would be abundance in the treasuries for the various needs. A dear brother (now with the Lord) once told me he had a bag which he called "the Lord's bag," in which he placed what he habitually laid aside, and he said it was never empty. There was always something in it from which to draw in time of need.

If the saints would faithfully lay aside on the first day of the week, as the Lord prospers them, how many precious stores of money there would he to meet the many calls to give! How many poor and needy and tired ones would be made to rejoice through the bounties of God's people! How many servants of the Lord, ready to faint under pressure, would take fresh courage, and go on with thankful hearts! And would not the Lord be honored? Would not fresh blessing be the result—the windows of heaven be opened? Who can doubt it?

It is to be feared that very many feel but little or no responsibility in this matter. Why should this be so? Mark the word is, "Let every one of you lay by." It is not law but it is responsibility under grace. It is the privilege also of those who receive—even the poor—to lay by of what is ministered to them, just as in the case of the Levites. With one it may be little, with another more, according to the ability; but are any altogether exempted?

If I am poor, and devote a little to the Lord out of my "deep poverty" (2 Corinthians 8:2), shall I be the poorer for it? Will He allow me to suffer want because of my devotedness and faithfulness to Him? Such is not His way. He loves the cheerful giver, and honors those who honor Him. The wise man has also said, "Honor the Lord with thy substance, and with the first fruits of all thine increase: so shall thy barns be filled with plenty, and thy presses shall burst out with new wine" (Prov. 3:9, 10).

Let every one have a box, or bag at home, and habitually lay by a portion out of all that comes in, and do it cheerfully, and with a liberal heart, as unto the Lord, assured that it is well pleasing to the Lord, and remembering how He has said "It is more blessed to give than to receive" (Acts 20:35).

Let us not suppose, either, that because a tenth is not exacted, it does not matter whether we give that much or not. A tenth was Jacob's measure, and a tenth was the portion for the Levites, but an Israelite under the law had to give much more than that to meet its requirements. And why should not a Christian give as liberally? Grace does not exact it, but if the heart is living in the sunshine of Christ's love, will it not yield up its stores more bountifully that under law? Where the Israelite was faithful in giving, the Lord blessed him in his basket and in this store. And while the Christian's blessing is of another order, the Lord will honor such as are faithful in this responsibility.

A. H. RULE

August 11

Why are you downcast, O my soul? Why so disturbed within me? Put your hope in God,

for I will yet praise him, my savior and my God.

PSALM 42:5

*H*ow is it that Christians are often cast down? I mean not so much pressed sore because of the toils, and the sorrows, and the griefs of the way, but downcast in heart as before God in their thoughts of the Lord, and forgetful of their associations with heaven.

Why is there a cloud, a dimness, a want of the full and fresh joy of Him they belong to, and where they belong to, filling the heart?

It is precisely because they fail to look up now into heaven by the Spirit, and so fail to look down on the world as a wilderness, however much the streams of living water may flow through them. They forget what Jesus has given them; they look on earth as a desirable place.

Why should not Christ be exalted here? Why should not He and we have a name of glory here now? Not so: His hour is not yet come; nor is ours either; for we are one with Him. Here man's hour was to Him scorn, rejection, and death.

This was His lot among man. Ours, too, is to be nothing here; it is to be utterly despised now, and hated of men. Is there anything better in this world? Is there any even to compare with what Christ

Himself had? He knew it as none ever can; but at least we may by His own grace be attached and cleave to Him, and so be drawn into and appreciate it in our small measure.

WILLIAM KELLY

*T*here are some Christians who seem to be afraid of enjoying all the rays of the Son of Righteousness. They are afraid of being too happy. Perhaps some of us have not really considered that "joy" is itself a part of that fruit by which the Father is glorified.

There is nothing to be gained by despondency. Doubts are not marks of humility; unbelief is really evidence of pride. And there is no cloud that so effectively shuts out the glad sunshine of our gracious Father's face as the thick cloud of unbelief.

EVAN HOPKINS

*W*hen we once get the Lord for our beginning; we may have Him in an all-sufficient way all the way through life. The more we trust Him today the easier it will be to trust Him tomorrow. Doubts are Amalekites, against which we must wage a bitter war of extermination if we would enjoy undisputed possession of our inheritance in the land flowing with milk and honey. It is only when our faith is mixed with doubt that we can be anxious about what is to come. A blessed thing about life in Christ is, that we may not only have peace in the beginning, but all the way through.

ELIJAH P. BROWN

August 12

His lord said unto him, "Well done, thou good and faithful servant; thou hast been faithful over a few things, I will make thee ruler over many things; enter thou into the joy of thy lord."

MATTHEW 25:21, KJV

*W*hat joy it gives, and strength too, to begin each day by feeling, "On this day once again I am to live simply as a servant of Jesus Christ: His will and not my own will is to sway me every hour."

"A servant of Jesus Christ!" Then I dare not be the servant of sin; I must be holy as my Master is holy.

"A servant of—Jesus Christ!" Then I will not be the servant of men: the maxims of the will not rule me; I will not take my cue from the world; I am under orders only to my Master in heaven.

"A servant of Jesus Christ!" Then I must be the servant of men, to help them, to comfort them, and to stoop to the lowest of them in their behalf as my Master did.

"A servant of Jesus Christ!" Then, if His servant anywhere, I must be His servant everywhere; in all society with men I must never forget my servanthood to Him: I must show myself His servant openly as well as confess it secretly.

"A servant of Jesus Christ!" Then, if I want to know Him, I have simply to imitate Him, to walk as He walked, to plant my feet in His footprints. As the eyes of servants look unto the hand of their masters, to see how their work should be done, and copy what they see, so my eyes "must wait upon the Lord." If His service is sometimes difficult, I must not complain: He may use me as He wills, and at the end of all I will be more than satisfied if I only hear Him say, "Well done, good and faithful servant, enter thou into the joy of thy Lord."

G. H. KNIGHT

*C*onsecrated things under the law were first sprinkled with blood, and then anointed with oil, and thereafter were no more common. Thus under the gospel, every Christian has been a common vessel for profane purposes, but when sprinkled and anointed, he becomes separated and consecrated to God.

JOHN NEWTON

August 13

Be imitators of God, therefore as dearly beloved children and live a life of love, just as Christ loved us and gave himself up for us as a fragrant offering and sacrifice to God.

EPHESIANS 5:1–2

$\mathcal{G}$od can do such a work in us by His Spirit, that all that He commands us to do will come about naturally, and not because we feel we ought to do it. To make up your mind to praise God may be good, but it is very much better to be so filled with the Holy Spirit that you cannot help praising! What God wants out of us He will first put in. The secret of power for service is to go to Calvary and get rid of the obstacles to the outflow of the spirit of God, and then ask God for the new life that will bring forth the new fruit.

I often hear of things God's children say and do which must grieve Him—and it seems hopeless to speak to them about it. The best thing is to ask God to put a new life and a new spirit into them, so that they will not do these things.

If you have a little child and are constantly saying "You must not, you must not," you will soon crush the personality of that child. You need to show him how to have a new life within, so that he will want to do what is right. God does not expect to get out of us one thing but what He has put into us! Do let us toil, dear fellow-workers, to lead His children into a life, and then let that Life manifest itself through their personalities. God does not want us to be all of the same pattern. He will express Himself through each individual in a different way. Just as there are not two faces alike, so He has not made two of us alike in any way, and we must take care that we do not try to mould ourselves or others after the pattern of any other human being.

JESSIE PENN-LEWIS

I used to ask God to help me. Then I asked God if I might help Him. I ended up by asking Him to do His work through me.

HUDSON TAYLOR

August 14

His intent was that now, through the church, the manifold wisdom of God should be known to the rulers and authorities in heavenly realms according to his eternal purpose which he accomplished in Christ Jesus our Lord.

EPHESIANS 3:10–11

The Christian life is a great thing; one of the greatest things on earth. Made up of daily *littles*, it is yet in itself not a little thing; but insofar as it is truly lived, whether by poor or rich, by child or full-grown man, noble throughout; a part of that great whole, in which and by which is to be made known to the principalities and powers in heavenly places, the manifold wisdom of God (Eph. 3:10).

It does not need to be a *long* life; a short one may be as true and holy as a long one. A short one is not a failure. John the Baptist's was perhaps the shortest ministry in the church; yet it was no failure; it was one of the greatest successes. He was a burning and shining light. We do not need to say profanely, "Whom the gods love die young"; but we may say that it does not need the three score years and ten to unfold the beauties of holiness.

HORATIUS BONAR

If we are in a right frame of mind we don't wish to die. It is no sign of a gracious person to be weary of life. Yet it is quite true that it is "far better" to depart and be with Christ—far better than a Sunday here and then a Monday tomorrow, and the business of the week to follow.

But though this is true, we are taught to desire to remain here and serve Christ. It is only here we can pluck brands from the burning fire. Stay here and turn many to righteousness. Make it a rule not to think of death. Think of resurrection. Think of Christ's coming again.

This is what sanctifies, what strengthens, what gladdens.

ANDREW BONAR

O how quickly passes away the glory of the earth!

THOMAS À KEMPIS

August 15

But thanks be to God! He gives us the victory through our Lord Jesus Christ.

1 CORINTHIANS 5:17

*W*e must be careful of any counterfeit victory. Victory over the power of any sin in your life, which you must achieve by *working* for it, is counterfeit. Victory, which you must obtain by *trying* for it, is counterfeit. It is not the real thing, the victory God offers you.

Victory gained by a gradual conquest over evil, getting one sin after another out of our life, like pulling weeds out of our garden, is likewise counterfeit victory. No the Lord Jesus does not offer to give us any such thing as a gradual gift. It is not growth. "Thanks be unto God which giveth us the victory through our Lord Jesus Christ" (1 Corinthians 5:57).

But please do not misunderstand that in the victorious life there is no growth. That would be absolutely false to the Word of God. We only begin to grow normally, grow as God wants us to grow, *after* we have entered into victory. No, victory is not fighting your wrong desires or concealing your wrong feelings; that would mean a struggle. In real victory, He does it all.

We do not dare to help. When the Lord Jesus Christ by the Holy Spirit works in our life to give us this victory, it is a miracle every time. If it is not a miracle, it is not victory.

CHARLES G. TRUMBULL

The Christian's victory is not over others, but over himself. His sword is drawn, not to slay his fellowman, but to slay himself. He wins by losing. He triumphs by being defeated. He lives by dying. His crown is a crown of thorns. His throne is a Cross. His weapon is not strength but weakness.

F. J. HUEGEL

August 16

God is our refuge and strength, an ever present help in trouble. Therefore we will not fear, though the earth give way and the mountains fall into the heart of the sea, though its waters roar and foam and the mountains quake with their surging. There is a river whose streams make glad the city of God, the holy place where the Most High dwells. God is within her, she will not fall; God will help her at break of day. Nations are in uproar, kingdoms fall; he lifts his voice, the earth melts. The LORD Almighty is with us; the God of Jacob is our fortress. Come and see the works of the Lord, the desolations he has brought on the earth. He makes wars cease to the ends of the earth; he breaks the bow and shatters the spear, he burns the shields with fire. "Be still and know that I am God; I will be exalted among the nations, I will be exalted in the earth." The LORD Almighty is with us; the God of Jacob is our fortress.

PSALM 46

$\mathcal{L}$et nothing shake your faith. If sin overtakes you, do not let it make you doubt. Immediately upon the discovery of any sin, take 1 John 1:9 and act on it. "If we confess our sins, he is faithful and just to forgive us our sins, and to cleanse us from all unrighteousness." Then believe that God does forgive you, as He promised, and does again cleanse you from all unrighteousness.

No sin, however grievous, can separate us from God for one moment after it has been treated in this way. To allow sin to cause your faith to waver is only to add a new sin to the one already committed. Return at once and let your faith hold steadfastly to His Word.

Believe it, not because you feel it or see it, but because He says it. Believe it, even when it seems to you that you are believing a lie. Believe it actively and steadfastly, through dark and through light, through ups and downs, through times of comfort and times of despair. If you do, your wavering experience will end.

"Therefore, my beloved brethren, be ye steadfast, unmovable, always abounding in the work of the Lord, forasmuch as ye know that your labor is not in vain in the Lord" (2 Corinthians 15:58). To be unmovable in one's faith is the opposite of wavering. In the Forty-sixth Psalm we can see what it means. . . The earth may be removed, and the mountains may be carried into the midst of the sea, and our whole universe may seem to be in ruins. But while we trust in the Lord, we shall not be moved.

The man who wavers in his faith is upset by the smallest troubles: The man who is steadfast in his faith can look on calmly at the ruin of all his universe.

To be immovable in one's Christian life is a blessing to be strongly desired. It may be ours, if we will only hold the beginning of our confidence steadfast to the end.

HANNAH WHITALL SMITH

$\mathcal{F}$aith is to believe on the Word of God what we do not see, and its reward is to see and enjoy what we believe.

AUGUSTINE

August 17

. . . that you may be filled to the measure of all the fullness of God.

EPHESIANS 3:19

*H*appy is that man who never leaves his room in the morning without definitely seeking and receiving the fullness of the Spirit! We shall be a good student in God's school because of the anointing which God gives him like fresh oil. It shall abide in him and teach him all things. Above all, Christ will teach him the secret of abiding fellowship with Himself.

Whenever you are conscious of leakage or greater need, you need refilling. It may be that service has exhausted you and you have not received fresh spiritual supply. Some new avenue of ministry may have opened before you, or you discovered a fresh talent. Go again to the same source for a refilling, a recharging with spiritual power, a reanointing by the holy charisma.

F. B. MEYER

Someone once asked Dwight L. Moody, "Why do you go on and on about being filled with the Holy Spirit again and again and again?" Moody just looked him in the eye and answered, "Because I leak."

August 18

For the law of the Spirit of life in Christ Jesus made me free from the law of sin and death.

ROMANS 8:2, KJV

*W*hat was done by God the Father and accomplished by the Son becomes a reality and a personal experience only as we assent and consciously, believingly look to the Holy Spirit, who lives in us, to make it a vital experience in our lives.

The Holy Spirit can do nothing until by faith we lay hold of it (i.e., the knowledge that our old man was crucified with Christ, my old self, my self pride, in fact all that I received from Adam by my birth, all that I am apart from Christ).

When we give assent to this truth, though we cannot see the reality of it in our lives, the Holy Spirit is able to and does make this an actual experience for us.

As we stand on this truth, the Holy Spirit is able to lead us into a personal, practical experience of crucifixion with Christ. . . . Our having been crucified with Christ has to make the body of sin of none effect while we live by faith, but it can instantly become active and dominate in the life of a believer when faith becomes dormant and inactive . . .

Will you not now bow before God and thank Him that you were crucified with Christ, begin to thank Him regardless of feeling! It may take a month or a day I do not know how long, but I do know that when any child of God will believe and begin to express that faith in thanksgiving, day by day thanking Him for the fact which one may not yet have experienced, the Holy Spirit will lead that one into a glorious personal experience. Then from the heart he can say "For the law of the Spirit of life in Christ Jesus made me free from the law of sin and death."

L. L. LEGTERS

*H*ere lies the precious secret of holy living. We are dead to sin; alive to God. The reign of sin is over. What has sin to do with a dead man? Nothing. Well, then, the believer has died with Christ; he was buried with Christ; he is risen with Christ, to walk in newness of life. He lives under the precious reign of grace, and he has his fruit unto holiness. The man who draws a plea from the abundance of divine grace to live in sin, denies the very foundation of Christianity. "How shall we that have died to sin, live any longer therein?" Impossible. It would be a denial of the whole Christian standing. To imagine the Christian as one who is to go on, from day to day, week to week, month to month, and year to year, sinning and repenting, sinning and repenting, is to degrade Christianity and falsify the whole Christian position. To say that a Christian must go on sinning because he has the flesh in him is to ignore the death of Christ in one of its grand aspects, and to give the lie to the whole of the apostle's teaching in Romans 6–8.

C. H. MACKINTOSH

August 19

Then I heard the voice of the LORD saying, "Whom shall I send? and who will go for us?" And I said, "Here am I. Send me!"
ISAIAH 6:8

The recompense of the surrendered life is the use God makes of it. The history of Christian experience makes it clear that the surrendered life is the life that God uses. Robert Murray McCheyne was dominated by the desire to be useful, and he yielded his life that it might be the instrument of the redeeming purpose and power of God. Sir Wilfred Grenfell said that he was won to the Kingdom of God not merely by the promise of salvation, but by the prospect of being used by God.

The surrendered life recognizes that it is God's prerogative to choose our place, be it eminent or obscure; to select our task, be it important or insignificant—to run a hospital or scrub its floor, to be married or unmarried, to go abroad or stay at home.

Without his instruments the scientist is unable to work, and the surgeon cannot operate; without his tools the workman cannot labor. God also is looking for His tools, His instruments, His means of action. "Whom shall I send, and who will go for Me" is the cry of One in

Whose mind a message waits to be communicated, but there is no messenger; an evangel is ready, but no evangelist to make it known.

When Isaiah yielded himself to God, "Here am I, send me," the messenger had arrived, the message had found communication; the instrument had come and the energies of God were set at work. It is the human surrender that releases the divine power. "I give Him everything," said David Livingstone, "pity I have so little to give": but no gift is small if God owns it. William Booth confessed, "God always had all there was of me." Christ was the pattern and the power of their surrender.

Let Him be the same to you.

JOHN MACBEATH

If we are not our own, but the Lord's, it is clear to what purpose all our deeds must be directed. We are not our own, therefore neither our reason nor our will should guide us in our thoughts and actions. We are not our own, therefore we should not seek what is only expedient to the flesh. We are not our own, therefore let us forget ourselves and our own interests as far as possible.

We are God's own—to Him, therefore, let us live and die. We are God's own; therefore let His wisdom and will dominate all our actions. We are God's own; therefore let every part of our existence be directed towards him as our only legitimate goal.

JOHN CALVIN

August 20

And now these three remain: faith, hope and love.

1 CORINTHIANS 13:13A

The day is near in which God Himself shall be the only mystery unsolved; when faith and hope shall merge in the completeness of our knowledge, and the realization of every promise that has cheered us here; But faith and hope are now the guide and beacon of our life, and we hail this unfathomable mystery of reconciliation as placing yet another crown upon our Saviour's brow. Upon His head are many crowns, but His pierced hand now holds the only scepter, for the Father has given Him the kingdom, and all things are placed beneath His feet. The outcast of the earth now fills the throne of God.

SIR ROBERT ANDERSON

I love my God with no love of mine,
For I have none to give;
I love thee, Lord; but all the love is Thine,
For by Thy life I live.
I am as nothing, and rejoice to be
Emptied and lost, and swallowed up in Thee.

JEANNE GUYON

August 21

The stone which the builders refused is become the headstone of the corner. This is the LORD's doing; it is marvelous in our eyes.
PSALM 118:22–23

The way in which we are brought unto the Lord Jesus Christ and united with Him is not by *building* but by *believing.* The builders rejected the "headstone"; but "coming unto Christ" (1 Peter 2), simply believing, "ye also, as lively stones, are built up a spiritual house."

When we go about the works of the law we are trying to build, and as long as we *build* we are not built. When we give up working, then by faith the Holy Spirit adds us to Christ, and grafts us into the living Vine, who is also the foundation. We are rooted and grounded. The house is one, and all the children of God are united in the Spirit.

Some are strong and are pillars, others are weak and rest upon those whom God has appointed to be strong, and to support and encourage the feeble. "None liveth unto himself; and if one member suffer, all the members suffer with it." If one grows and rejoices, it is for the good of the whole.

The glory of the Lord is to show itself in the whole church, thus united by the indwelling Spirit. But not merely does God dwell in the church as a whole, it is the peculiarity; of everything spiritual that every part of it is again a whole. Not only is it true, that "wheresoever two or three are gathered together" in Christ's name, He is in the midst of them; but if a single person loves Him, the Father will love him, and will come and make His abode with him. An individual is thus also a temple, a habitation filled with the Holy Spirit. The Father and the Lord Jesus Christ dwell in him.

Israel could understand this because it was symbolized by the temple, and the reality and substance of the symbol was also promised to them in the days of the Messiah. For what was the promise of the new covenant? "I will dwell in them, and they in me." What a marvelous idea is here presented to us! A Christian is like the tabernacle; he is a sanctuary. There is the holy of holies, the holy place, and the outer court. But in all the glory of God is to be revealed; the holiness of God to be shown forth.

His body is the Lord's; the members of his body are Christ's members. His eyes, his lips, his feet, all the physical energies which God has given unto him, are a part of the house in which the Father and the Lord Jesus, through the Holy Spirit, take up their abode. His reason, memory, imagination, affections, will, conscience, all that is in him, behold, it is a house where God is to dwell. God is to walk in it, to dwell in it, to rest in it. He is to be not merely a visitor, but an indwelling guest, "abiding in him."

Sometimes God will convert this wonderful dwelling-place into His temple, and there will be heard the voice of prayer and praise. Sometimes He changes it into a banqueting-hall, and there will be heard the voice of rejoicing and the melody of thanksgiving, the assurance of that love which is better than wine. Sometimes it becomes a battlefield, and the Lord is a man-of-war, and conquers the enemies of the worm Jacob, and succors the saint who is tempted.

How manifold are the mansions in which He dwells! As there are many mansions in the Father's house above, as there are many mansions in His Church below, so also are there many rooms in the spiritual house of the individual believer; in various manifestations of grace, strength, and love, does God dwell in us.

You who believe in Jesus are His house, His own; for as the Father appointed Him to be Mediator, as the Father laid the foundation in Zion, so Jesus the Lord bought you with His own blood, and sent into your hearts His own Spirit. We are emphatically Christ's.

ADOLPH SAPHIR

I will not let you find fault with your bodies, because He made them. You may find as much fault as you like with the flesh, but that is not your bodies. Our bodies are "members of Christ." Christendom has fallen into the great mistake of making our bodies members of the church, which is quite contrary to scripture: "We are members of his body, of his flesh, and of his bones."

"FOOD FOR THE DESERT"

As you come to him, the living Stone—rejected by men but chosen by God and precious to him—you also, like living stones, are being built into a spiritual house to be a holy priesthood, offering spiritual sacrifices acceptable to God through Jesus Christ.

1 PETER 2:4–5

*W*e become living stones as soon as we come in contact with Christ, who is the Living Stone. This is the moment the blessed Lord speaks of when He says, "Verily, verily, I say unto you, The hour is coming, and now is, when the dead shall hear the voice of the Son of God; and they that hear shall live" (John 5:25).

The voice of the Son of God went down into the heart of Simon, the son of Bar-Jona, quickening him, and I think Peter became acquainted with a change within himself, though I do not judge he quite understood what was wrapped up in the Lord's enigmatical expression.

Indeed, he was like many a person whom the gospel reaches. He knows a change has come over him, but he cannot explain it. He becomes an altered man, though he cannot tell what has taken place. I think at that moment when Simon found Jesus, he responded that there was a tie between his soul and the Saviour's.

The voice of the Son of God entered into the heart of Peter, and what he heard was this, "Thou shalt be called Cephas, which is by interpretation, a stone." You and I are stones from the time we derive from Christ.

Do you know what a Christian is? He is a little bit of Christ. The Christian derives his life, his righteousness, his grace, and his sanctification from Him. He lives in the life of Christ, before God.

W. T. P. WOLSTON

And he said unto me, my grace is sufficient for thee . . .

2 CORINTHIANS 12:9A, KJV

The other evening I was riding home after a heavy day's work; I felt very weary and sore depressed, when, swiftly and suddenly as a lightning flash, the text came to me: "My grace is sufficient for thee." I said, "I should think it is, Lord," and burst out laughing. I never fully understood what the holy laugh of Abraham was till then. It seemed to make unbelief so absurd. It was as though some little fish, being very thirsty, was troubled about drinking the river dry, and the River Thames said, "Drink away, little fish, my stream is sufficient for thee." Or, it seemed like a little mouse in the granaries of Egypt, after the seven years of plenty, fearing it might die of famine; Joseph might say, "Cheer up, little mouse, my granaries are sufficient for thee."

Again, I imagine a man, way up yonder on a lofty mountain, saying to himself, "I breathe so many cubic feet of air every year; I fear I shall exhaust the oxygen in the atmosphere"; but the earth might say, "Breathe away, O man, and fill thy lungs evermore, my atmosphere is sufficient for thee." Oh, brethren, be great believers! Little faith will bring your souls to heaven, but great faith will bring heaven to your souls.

CHARLES SPURGEON

There is as much in our Lord's pantry as will satisfy all his hungry children, and as much wine in His cellar as will quench all their thirst. Hunger on then, for there it is good to hunger for Christ; go never from Him, but clamor after Him who never tires of feeding hungry souls, with a dishful of hungry desires, till he fill you.

SAMUEL RUTHERFORD

Then I said, I have labored in vain, I have spent my strength for
nought and in vain; yet surely my judgment is with the LORD and my
work with God.

ISAIAH 49:4–5, KJV

*W*hat does such a verse mean? It means that although I have not
accomplished what I had expected to, nevertheless I have my justification with Jehovah. I have labored long and seemingly without
effect, yet My justice is with God. In other words, whether I am justified in My work or not, it is nonetheless there with Jehovah. He
is not only My justice but also My recompense.

In spite of the fact that I am unable to effect anything with the
house of Jacob and the children of Israel, I am certain that I will
receive the recompense which God will give to Me. And therefore,
I am satisfied in My heart. I shall not murmur nor shall I be sorrowful. Such is the attitude of our Lord.

This, dear friends, shows us one thing: that we should not have
any direct relationship with our work, with things, or with people;
we can have direct relationship only with God. In the event we maintain a direct connection with work, things, or people, we will be hurt
and heartbroken in case we encounter any frustration or difficulty.
But if our direct relationship is only with God, we can still rejoice
when we are rejected by men, are confronted with difficulty, or suffer apparent defeat. Since we are directly related to God, neither gain
nor loss is able to touch us. One thing alone are we careful about:
whether or not we have our justice and recompense with God. If our
justice is with God, our recompense is also with Him.

WATCHMAN NEE

*W*hatever we have in our hands, our care must be to keep it out
of our hearts, lest it come between us and Christ.

MATTHEW HENRY

And when Jesus had cried out again in a loud voice, he gave up his spirit. At that moment the curtain of the temple was torn in two from top to bottom. The earth shook and the rocks split. The tombs broke open and the bodies of many holy people who had died were raised to life. They came out of the tombs, and after Jesus' resurrection they went into the holy city and appeared to many people. When the centurion and those with him who were guarding Jesus saw the earthquake and all that had happened, they were terrified, and exclaimed, "Surely he was the Son of God!"

MATTHEW 27:50–54

𝒯he most timid believer is emboldened, while gazing by faith on the wondrous cross on which the Lord of Glory died, and contemplating the sufferings He endured while hanging on the accursed tree. Similarly, the boldest believer is made timid by the neglect of that cross; as we see exemplified in Peter and Joseph of Arimathaea. Peter was so bold as to say, "Though all men should be offended because of Thee, yet will I never be offended . . . Though I should die with Thee, yet will I not deny Thee" (Matt. 26:33, 35).

Soon after, when they arrested Jesus and took Him, Peter was one of the "all who forsook Him and fled" (Mark 14:50).

Peter "followed" Jesus it is true, but it was "afar off" (Matt. 26:58). The next step was to deny his Lord with oaths and curses (Matt. 26: 72, 74).

But Joseph of Arimathæa, who was a disciple of Jesus, but secretly, for fear of the Jews, went in BOLDLY unto Pilate and CRAVED the body of Jesus. (Compare Mark 15:43 with John 19:38.) How was it that this timid disciple became so bold? Was it not from having gazed on the cross, and witnessed the sufferings of his Lord and Master?

So is it now. Do we want boldness for our Master and His service? Let us by faith seek grace to contemplate that wondrous scene. How did Peter, who was so bold as to draw his sword to defend his Master, become so fearful as to forsake Him, and so forgetful as to deny Him? Was it not because the Cross was not realized? And is it not so now?

"CRUMBS FOR THE LORD'S LITTLE ONES"

The world ... to us is nothing now but the empty tomb of Jesus.

JOHN DARBY

August 26

For you did not receive a spirit that makes you a slave again to fear, but you received the spirit of Sonship. And by him we cry, "Abba, Father." The Spirit himself testifies with our spirit that we are God's children. Now if we are children, then we are heirs—heirs of God and co-heirs with Christ, if indeed we share in his sufferings in order that we may also share in his glory.

ROMANS 8:15–17

It is indeed a wonderfully blessed thing to be a Christian, for a Christian is a man "in Christ"—he is "in the Spirit," and has the Holy Spirit dwelling in him. The Spirit is in him who believes in Jesus, and gives him an experiential sense of that which is now his, and what will be his. Nay more, the Spirit being in him, the next thing is his mouth is opened, and he cries, "Abba, Father."

But more than that, the Holy Spirit ministers to us, and shows the things of Christ to us, and brings us into the enjoyment of the Lord's love, and the Father's love, and ministers to us the comfort of the fact that we are the children of God. More still—"If children," then we are "heirs"; "heirs of God, and joint-heirs with Christ; if so be that we suffer with him, that we may be also glorified together."

Co-heirs, co-sufferers, co-glorified with Christ—that is really the word here. We are side by side with Christ. We are sons of God, even as He is the Son of God—not in His eternal Sonship, but in the place he took in grace as Man, and which He brings those into who believe in Him. As He said to Mary, "I ascend to my Father, and your Father, to my God and your God." The Holy Spirit comes down, to give us the sense, and knowledge, that we are co-heirs, co-sufferers, and that we shall be co-glorified with Him.

W. T. P. WOLSTON

August 27

After they prayed, the place where they were meeting was shaken. And they were all filled with the Holy Spirit and spoke the word of God boldly.

ACTS 4:31

We cannot have power with men if we have not power with God. The greatest mistake any of us can make is to seek to have power before men without having been in the presence of God.

EDWARD DENNETT

There can be no greater barrier to our peace and habitual enjoyment of God than our being filled with self-confidence. We must be emptied and humbled. God cannot divide the house with the creature. It is vain to expect it. Jacob had the hollow of his thigh touched in order that he might learn to lean upon God. The halting Jacob found his sure resource in Jehovah, who only empties us of nature that we may be filled with Himself. He knows that just in so far as we are filled with self-confidence, or creature-confidence, we are robbed of the deep blessedness of being filled with His fullness. Hence, in His great grace and mercy, He empties us out, that we may learn to cling in child-like confidence to Him. This is our only place of strength, of victory, and repose.

AUTHOR UNKNOWN

August 28

By faith Abraham, when called to go to a place he would later receive as his inheritance, obeyed and went, even though he did not know where he was going. By faith he made his home in the promised land like a stranger in a foreign country; he lived in tents, as did Isaac and Jacob, who were heirs with him of the same promise. For he was looking forward to the city with foundations, whose architect and builder is God.

HEBREWS 11:8–10

Faith is truly a light in the soul, but it is a light which shines only upon duties, and not upon results or events. It tells us what is now to be done, but it does not tell us what is to follow, and accordingly it guides us but a single step at a time and when we take that step under the guidance of faith, we advance directly into a land of surrounding shadows and darkness.

Like the patriarch, Abraham, we go, not knowing whither we go, but only that God is with us. In man's darkness we nevertheless walk and live in God's light. A way of living blessed and glorious, however mysterious it may be to human vision.

THOMAS C. UPHAM

The narrow path, commencing with the cross and ending with the glory of the Lord Jesus Christ, is the path on which the Lord draws near and walks with His disciples.

ADOLPH SAPHIR

Once, having been asked by the Pharisees when the kingdom of God would come, Jesus replied, "The kingdom of God does not come visibly, nor will people say, Here it is, or There it is, because the kingdom of God is within you."

LUKE 17:20–21

*G*od is especially present in the hearts of his people, by his Holy Spirit. Indeed the hearts of Christians are truly temples; and, in type and shadow, they are heaven itself. For God reigns in the hearts of his servants: there is his kingdom.

The power of grace has subdued all his enemies: there is his power. They serve him night and day, and give him thanks and praise: that is his glory.

This is the religion and worship of God in the temple. The temple itself is the heart of man; Christ is the High Priest, who from thence sends up the incense of prayers, and joins them to his own intercession, and presents all together to his Father; and the Holy Spirit, by his dwelling there, hath also consecrated it into a temple; and God dwells in our hearts by faith, and Christ by his Spirit, and the Spirit by his purities; so that we are also cabinets of the mysterious Trinity; and what is this short of heaven itself, but as infancy is short of manhood, and letters of words. The same state of life it is, but not the same age. It is heaven in a looking-glass, dark, but yet true, representing the beauties of the soul, and the graces of God, and the images of his eternal glory, by the reality of a special presence.

JEREMY TAYLOR

*I*t is worth a world to have an intimate eternity with Christ.

J. G. BELLETT

I do nothing on my own but speak just what the Father has taught me.
JOHN 8:28B

*D*o everything without excitement, simply in the spirit of grace. As soon as you perceive natural activity gliding in, recall yourself quietly into the Presence of God. Listen to what promptings of grace, and say and do nothing but what God's Holy Spirit teaches.

You will find yourself infinitely more quiet, your words will be fewer and more effectual, and though doing less—what you do will be more profitable.

It is not a question of a hopeless mental activity, but a question of acquiring a quietude and peace in which you readily consult with your Beloved as to all you have to do. Such consultation, simple and brief though it be, will be more easily held than the bustling, restless arguments we hold within ourselves when natural energy has its way.

FRANÇOIS FÉNELON

*O*ur strength is never renewed in noise and bustle. These only weaken and waste it. Try it for yourself, dear Christian. The next time you find yourself in need of renewal of strength, get still before the Lord. If possible, sit down in silence somewhere and collect your restless and wandering spiritual faculties into a silent waiting upon Him, and see if strength does flow into you from Him. This is what the old saints used to call "recollection," and it was in this way they gained the wonderful spiritual vigor for which we so envy them.

HANNAH WHITALL SMITH

So, if you think you are standing firm, be careful that you don't fall!
1 CORINTHIANS 10:12

The Christian who is wholly trusting the Lord for victory soon realizes that many Christians about him have not seen the truth of victory, and are not thus trusting Christ.

He may be in close contact with Christians who are older, much farther along in many ways, yet not living in the victory-secret that is so precious to him. And then comes the peril of pride.

Almost without realizing it the Christian who knows Christ as victory can let slip some word criticizing a fellow Christian who is not in on the secret, or a condescending comment on such a one's mistake or failure. "Holier than thou" is one of the perils of the Victorious Life.

Of course the instant one speaks thus of another, or thinks in his inmost heart thus of another, his victory is gone; he has sinned. And we must recognize this peril if we would be kept from it.

The Christian who is living in victory is in *himself* no whit better than the carnal Christian who is plainly sinning. The self-nature of the two is identical: hopelessly sinful. The only good thing about the victorious Christian is Christ; and we deserve no credit for Christ: the glory and honor and victory are all His. True victory, therefore, must keep us humble: and it will.

CHARLES G. TRUMBULL

When first we enter into the divine life, we propose to grow rich; God's plan is to make us feel poor.

JOHN NEWTON

And I will fasten him as a nail in a sure place . . .
ISAIAH 22:23A

*R*ead God's Word, and read it again; and do not despair of trying to understand the will and mind of God as revealed in His word, though you think they are fast locked up from you . . .

Pray and read, read and pray, for a little from God is better than a great deal from men. Also, what's from men is uncertain, and is lost and tumbled over by men, but what's from God is fixed as a nail in a sure place.

There's nothing that so abides with us as what we receive from God, and the reason why the Christians in this day are at such a loss as to some things is that they are contented to what comes from men's mouths, without searching and kneeling before God to know of Him the truth of eternal things.

Lessons we receive at God's hands come to us as truth from the minting house, though old in themselves, yet new to us, old truths are always new to us if they come with the shell of Heaven upon them.

JOHN BUNYAN

*T*he enemy will encourage you to do anything but carry out the systematic, Spirit-taught study of the Bible. He will give you religious experiences, feelings, and pious thoughts—all apart from God's Word. Do not be deceived. The Scriptures are our only sustenance—there are no substitutes.

J. B. STONEY

I was once teaching a Bible class of elderly men when one of them stopped a long time over a verse he was reading. I asked him at last what the matter was, if he could not understand it. "Oh, yes," he replied, "I understand it fine, and it tasted so good that I was just waiting a minute to get a good bite off of it."

HANNAH WHITALL SMITH

*The wrath of God is being revealed from heaven against all the godless-
ness and wickedness of men who suppress the truth by their wickedness,
since what may be known about God is plain to them, because God
has made it plain to them. For since the creation of the world God's
invisible qualities—his eternal power and divine nature—have been
clearly seen, being understood from what has been made, so that men
are without excuse.*

ROMANS 1:18–20

The God of Christians is not a God who is merely the author of
mathematical truths and the order of the elements—that is the
point of view of heathens and Epicureans. He is not simply a God
whose providence watches over the lives and possessions of men, so
that those who worship him will enjoy a long and prosperous
career—that is the Jewish idea.

But the God of Abraham, the God of Isaac, the God of Jacob,
the God of Christians is a God of love and consolation; He is a God
who fills the soul and heart of those whom he possesses; he is a God
who makes them inwardly conscious of their wretchedness and of
his infinite mercy; who unites himself with them in the depths of
their soul; who fills it with humility, with joy, with trust, with love;
who makes them incapable of any other end but Him.

All those who seek God outside Jesus Christ and who stop at
nature, or who do not find any form of light which satisfies them,
or who succeed in finding a means of knowing God and serving
him without a mediator, end by falling into atheism or deism, which
are two things that are almost equally abhorrent to Christianity.

Without Jesus Christ the world would not continue to exist; it
would either be destroyed, or would be a sort of hell.

If the world existed in order to instruct man in the knowledge
of God, his divinity would shine everywhere in a manner which

was undeniable; but since it only continues to exist through and for Jesus Christ, and to bring men a knowledge both of their corruption and their redemption, everything is bursting with the proofs of those two truths.

What can be seen is not a sign either of a total absence, or of the manifest presence of the divinity, but of the presence of a God who hides himself. Everything bears this character.

BLAISE PASCAL

*N*obody seriously believes the universe was made by God without being persuaded that He takes care of His works.

JOHN CALVIN

September 3

Set your mind on things above, not on earthly things.
COLOSSIANS 3:2

*T*he great need of Christians today is to be recovered for the full heavenly thought of God. They have settled down to something less. They have become involved in something less and largely other. It has always been like that. The New Testament was written almost entirely because of it. The Lord's people are always at least in peril of doing that—at least in peril. They do gravitate spiritually toward this world and lose their heavenly testimony in one way or another. The pressure is always there to bring down, and the Lord needs lives that have *seen*—for whom the center of gravity of life has been transferred from this world to heaven, within whom there is this sense— whether they can interpret it or not, whether they can put it into a system of truth, doctrine, Bible teaching, or not—there is this sense that they are in the line of some great destiny which is beyond what this world can provide, that they have been gripped by something that they can only say is the heavenly calling, which has held them. . . . The Lord needs a people like that, who just cannot be satisfied with things as they are; it is not just a matter of the mind, of the reason, at all. It is inside of them; they know that God has done something. Because God has done something, they are committed to something far greater than the poor limits of this life and this world. They have been inwardly linked with something tremendous. They may not be able to preach it, but they know it.

We shall never be useful to God beyond our vision—our true God-inwrought vision, beyond our own reach of heart. Our measure of vision will determine the measure of our usefulness. Oh, for the immeasurable measure of heaven in the heart of a people! That is the need today.

T. Austin-Sparks

September 4

When I saw him, I fell at his feet as though dead. Then he placed his right hand on me and said: "Do not be afraid. I am the First and the Last. I am the Living One; I was dead, and behold I am alive for ever and ever."

Revelation 1:17–18

*O*nce as I rode out into the woods for my health, in 1737, having alighted from my horse in a retired place, as my manner commonly has been to walk for divine contemplation and prayer, I had a view that was for me extraordinary of the glory of the Son of God as Mediator between God and man, and His wonderfully great, full, pure and sweet grace and love and meek and gentle condescension.

The grace that appeared so calm and sweet appeared also great above the heavens. The Person of Christ appeared ineffably excellent, with an excellency great enough to swallow up all thought and conception; which continued, as near as I can judge, about an hour, which kept me the greater part of the time in a flood of tears and weeping aloud. I felt an ardency of soul to be what I know not how otherwise to express, empty and annihilated, to lie in the dust and be full of Christ alone; to love Him with a holy and pure love; to trust Him, to live upon Him, to serve Him, and to be perfectly sanctified and made pure with a divine and heavenly purity.

JONATHAN EDWARDS

I had a deep peace which seemed to pervade the whole soul, and resulted from the fact that all my desires were fulfilled in God. I feared nothing—that is, considered in its ultimate results, because my strong faith placed God at the head of all perplexities and events. I desired nothing but what I now had, because I had full belief that, in my present state of mind, the results of each moment constituted the fulfillment of the Divine purposes. As a sanctified heart is always in harmony with the Divine Providences, I had no will but the Divine will, of which such providences are the true and appropriate expression.

JEANNE GUYON

September 5

Let us fix our eyes on Jesus, the author and perfecter of our faith, who for the joy set before him endured the cross, scorning its shame, and sat down at the right hand of the throne of God.

HEBREWS 12:2

*S*ome people try to have faith in their own faith, instead of faith in Jesus Christ. They keep looking for a subjective condition. They ought to be looking to an objective Christ. True faith pays no attention whatever to itself. It centers all its gaze upon Christ.

For faith is not our savior. Faith is simply an attitude of the soul through which Jesus saves. When Satan cannot beguile us in any other way, he gets us to scrutinizing our faith, instead of looking unto Christ. That Christian has the strongest heart who is the least conscious of its existence. And that faith is the strongest which pays no attention to itself.

You may weaken the heart by centering your anxious attention upon it. So nothing will quicker weaken faith than the constant endeavor to discover it. It is like the child's digging up of the seed to see if it is growing. It is a curiosity which brings disaster to the seed. It is not a man's faith, but his faith in Christ which saves him. To be looking unto Christ is faith. To be looking unto anything else, even unto faith is a trouble to the soul.

Therefore do not worry about your faith. Do not always be scanning it. Look away from it altogether—unto Jesus. For faith alone is naught. It is only faith in Jesus that counts. Take care that you are depending upon Jesus to save. And faith will take care of itself.

JAMES MCCONKEY

I looked at Jesus and the dove of peace flew into my heart. I looked at the dove of peace and she flew away.

CHARLES SPURGEON

September 6

This is how you should pray:
"Our Father in heaven,
hallowed be your name,
your kingdom come,
your will be done
*   on earth as it is in heaven.*

Give us today our daily bread.
Forgive us our debts,
  as we also have forgiven our debtors.
And lead us not into temptation,
but deliver us from the evil one."
    MATTHEW 6:9–13

$\mathscr{G}$reat faith produces great abandonment.

What is abandonment? If we can understand what it is, perhaps we can better lay hold of it.

Abandonment is casting off all your cares. Abandonment is dropping all your needs. This includes spiritual needs. Let me repeat that, for it is not easily grasped. Abandonment is laying aside, forever, all of your spiritual needs.

All Christians have spiritual needs; but the believer who has abandoned himself to the Lord no longer indulges in the luxury of being aware of spiritual needs. Rather, he gives himself over completely to the disposal of God.

Do you realize that all Christians have been exhorted to abandonment?

There must be an abandonment in your life concerning all outward, practical things. Secondly, there must also be an abandonment of all inward, spiritual things. You must come to the Lord and there engage in giving up all your concerns. All your concerns go into the hand of God. You forget yourself, and from that moment on you think only of Him.

By continuing to do this over a long period of time, your heart will remain unattached; your heart will be free and at peace!

How do you practice abandonment? You practice it daily, hourly, and by the moment. Abandonment is practiced by continually losing your own will in the will of God; by plunging your will into the depths of His will, there to be lost forever!

And how do you begin? You must begin by reusing every personal desire that comes to you just as soon as it arises—no matter how good that personal desire is, and no matter how helpful it might appear! Abandonment must reach a point where you stand in complete indifference to yourself. You can be sure that out of such a disposition a wonderful result will come.

The result of this attitude will, in fact, bring you to the most wonderful point imaginable. It is the point where your will breaks free of you completely and becomes free to be joined to the will of God! You will desire only what He desires, that is, what He has desired for all eternity.

Become abandoned by simply resigning yourself to what the Lord wants, in all things, no matter what they are, where they come from, or how they affect your life.

What is abandonment? It is forgetting your past; it is leaving the future in His hands; it is devoting the present fully and completely to your Lord. Abandonment is being satisfied with the present moment, no matter what that moment contains. You are satisfied because you *know* that whatever that moment has, it contains—in that instant—God's eternal plan for you.

You will always know that that moment is the absolute and total declaration of His will for your life.

Surrender not only what the Lord does to you, but surrender your reaction to what He does.

Do you wish to go into the depths of Jesus Christ? If you wish to enter into this deeper state of knowing the Lord, you must seek to know not only a deeper prayer but also abandonment in all realms of your life. This means branching out until your new relationship includes living 24 hours a day utterly abandoned to Him. Begin to surrender yourself to be led by God and to be dealt with by Him. Do so right now. Surrender yourself to allow Him to do with you exactly as He pleases—both in your inward life of experiencing Him and also in your outward life of accepting all circumstances as from Him.

JEANNE GUYON

*O*h the joy of having nothing and being nothing, seeing nothing but a living Christ in glory, and being careful for nothing but His interests down here.

JOHN DARBY

September 7

But whoso keepeth his word, in him verily is the love of God perfected: hereby we know that we are in him.

1 JOHN 2:5, KJV

*G*od has *commanded* us to be perfect in love; not because He was unaware that such a command far exceeded our abilities, but because He desired thereby to remind us of our weakness, and to keep before us the prize of righteousness after which we must strive.

In thus demanding from man an impossibility, it is not with the view of hurling him into sin, but of compelling him to humility, that "every mouth may be stopped," and all creation subject unto Christ; for "through the works of the law shall no flesh be justified."

When, therefore, we hear this command, and are sensible of our inability to fulfill its requirements, our only course is to cry unto Heaven; then will our gracious Father look down in mercy and supply the needed strength.

BERNARD OF CLAIRVAUX

*S*ouls are waiting for the love of Christ. We talk about it and say, "I love you!" but how cold and far from the reality such love is. We need the love that will spontaneously and unconsciously make us spend ourselves for others. The world wants it. We seem to be like alabaster boxes with the ointment inside.

The boxes need breaking.

JESSIE PENN-LEWIS

These Christians love each other, even before they are acquainted.

CELSUS

September 8

Since you died with Christ to the basic principles of this world, why, as though you still belonged to it, do you submit to its rules: "Do not handle! Do not taste! Do not touch!"? These are all destined to perish with use, because they are based on human commands and teachings. Such regulations indeed have an appearance of wisdom, with their self-imposed worship, their false humility and their harsh treatment of the body, but they lack any value in restraining sensual indulgence.

COLOSSIANS 2:20–23

Let us recognize the peril of being unhuman—not inhuman, but unhuman, because of the depth and intensity of our spiritual life. Not to be "human" is not of the Lord. We are living not only a spiritual life, but a bodily life as well: and we are living among those who also are in human bodies, in a world of rightful temporal interests as well as eternal interests.

Let us not make the mistake of so living that persons shall say of us, as some have, that we have a deep interest in others' souls, but none at all in their bodies.

Let us be human. Let us be kind. Let us deliberately make it our business to cultivate certain secular, human interests, that we may have points of contact with the many round about us who know nothing of the spiritual interests that are so precious to us.

Some of the greatest spiritual leaders, some of the most blessedly used ambassadors of Christ, have had hobbies, such as nature study, music, or something else of that sort, which God has blessed to them and to others.

Such a hobby keeps one in touch with the present-day wonderful world which God made. It gives one "bait" which he can use to catch the interest of another, and through that "bait" bring that other to Christ and to victory.

We are not to be afraid of healthy amusements of the right sort. If we go with a friend to see or play a tennis match or a baseball game, if we are watching or playing a game of checkers, let us not do it in such a way that everyone shall see that it has no real interest to us but we are just making a concession to the earthly interests of our unenlightened friends, and patiently waiting until we can give our time to the "really worthwhile things."

This is not victory. It may sound harsh to call it asceticism and even priggishness, but that is the way it will seem to others—perhaps rightly so.

God wants to deliver us all the time from the peril of narrowness in the Victorious Life. If we have any musical ability, let us praise God for it and let us ask Him prayerfully to enable us to cultivate that ability that He may use our music to His glory.

And this does not mean that we shall play or sing only hymns either. There is plenty of other music that is not of the Devil, and that God would use to keep us close to our fellows in a joyous, healthy way.

Let us be very careful, too, about social courtesies. Christian people whose life-interests are wrapped up in the deeply spiritual are often criticized for carelessness about the little courtesies and attentions of their social relationships with others. This must not be: it dishonors our Lord.

The Christian who is trusting Christ for victory should not be one whit less careful than is the man of the world or the society woman about those little niceties of life that betoken good breeding, good manners, true gentleness, and unselfish thoughtfulness for others. The King's business never requires discourtesy or lack of proper attentiveness to our fellows.

CHARLES G. TRUMBULL

*W*e still live in bodies with limitations and all of us are subject to the circumstances of life. Neither should we mistake worn nerves, physical weakness or depression for unspirituality. Often we need sleep more then prayer and physical recreation more than heart searching.

LEWIS SPERRY CHAFER

September 9

So the Twelve gathered all the disciples together and said, "It would not be right for us to neglect the ministry of the word of God in order to wait on tables. Brothers, choose seven men from among you who are known to be full of the Spirit and wisdom. We will turn this responsibility over to them and will give our attention to prayer and the ministry of the word."

This proposal pleased the whole group. They chose Stephen, a man full of faith and of the Holy Spirit; also Philip, Procorus, Nicanor, Timon, Parmenas, and Nicolas from Antioch, a convert to Judaism. They presented these men to the apostles, who prayed and laid their hands on them.

So the word of God spread. The number of disciples in Jerusalem increased rapidly, and a large number of priests became obedient to the faith.

ACTS 6:2–7

*I*t is striking to note that David, after his anointing, became "skillful in business." In Acts 6 we find seven men appointed to attend to the business of the church, and their qualification was that they were filled with the Holy Spirit.

Do you really believe that the Lord can guide you in the ordinary business of life?

He can, but you will need first to lay down your own wisdom and take His—then He will be "made unto you, wisdom." If the church relied less upon the carnal wisdom of the world it would be better. There is too much turning to businessmen to carry their natural abilities and methods into the church, and surrendering the spiritual to the natural. It is a mistake to use worldly "good business" for the church of God, when God can endue with "capability from on high" for the business side of His work.

"Look ye out seven men full of Holy spirit and wisdom to set over this business." If we did this there would be fewer blunders made. What right have we to call for carnal help? There are churches organized up to the highest degree of perfection—and with not a spark of the Life of God in them.

JESSIE PENN-LEWIS

*W*e are called Christians because we are anointed with the unction of God.

THEOPHILUS

September 10

As many as touched Him were made whole.
MARK 6:56, KJV

*D*uring our daily quiet time], may each of us touch at least the border of His garment. One knows when one has done that. It is different from just reading or even just praying. Something happens when we touch. What happens? Who can tell? We only know that something has passed from Him to us—courage to do the difficult thing we had feared to do; patience to bear with that trying one; fortitude to carry on when we felt we could not; sweetness, inward happiness, peace.

God's way is to take some word in His Book and make it spirit and life. Then, relying upon that word, it is possible for us to go on from strength to strength. There is always something new in our lives which calls for vital faith, if we are to go on with God; but there is always the word waiting in His Book which will meet us just where we are and carry us further on.

It will be fight to the end, "the good fight of faith," is His description of it—but full provision is made for victory in that fight, and whether the matter that engages us has to do with our inner life or the outer, there is nothing to fear. It is our Father's good pleasure to us the Kingdom. We need never—by His grace we shall never—be defeated.

AMY CARMICHAEL

A believer is to be known not only by his peace and joy, but by his warfare in distress. His peace is peculiar; it flows from Christ, it is heavenly, it is holy peace. His warfare is as peculiar; it is deep-seated, agonizing, and ceases not till death.

ROBERT MURRAY MCCHEYNE

September 11

The Lord is not slow in keeping his promise, as some understand slowness. He is patient with you, not wanting anyone to perish, but everyone to come to repentance.

2 PETER 3:9

$\mathcal{I}$t is vain to look into the prophetic pagan order to find the church's position, her calling, or her hope. They are not there. It is entirely out of place for the Christian to be occupied with dates and historic events, as though he were in anywise involved therein.

No doubt, all these things have their proper place and their value, and their interest, as connected with God's dealings with Israel and with the earth. But the Christian must never lose sight of the fact that he belongs to heaven, that he is inseparably linked with an earth-rejected, heaven-accepted Christ—that his life is hid with Christ in God—that it is his holy privilege to be looking out, daily and hourly, for the coming of his Lord. There is nothing to hinder the realization of that blissful hope at any moment. There is but the one thing that causes the delay—God's patience and His unwillingness for any to perish, rather, desiring all to come to repentance. These are precious words for a lost and guilty world!

The salvation is ready to be revealed; and God is ready to judge. There is nothing now to wait for but the gathering in of the last elect one, and then—oh, most blessed thought—our own dear and loving Savior will come and receive us to Himself to be with Him where He is, and to go no more out for ever.

C. H. MACKINTOSH

$\mathcal{A}$re our hearts really waiting for God's Son from heaven? I do not talk of understanding the prophecies—very blessed in their place—but the Morning Star is what belongs to us—a heavenly Christ who has given His life for us.

So then, as we are found looking to be both with Christ and like Christ forever, this encourages us as we go through this world. The virtue attached then is that of "watching." It is not understanding prophecy, but it is attachment to Christ as having received the promise that He is coming so that we are waiting for Him.

Such as have done this have found Christ all the more precious to them and they readily say, "Oh, that He would come soon!"

Are we Christians, then as those who wait for their Lord? If the Lord were to come tonight, would He be able to say of each one of us, "*There* is a blessed servant"?

Remember, He is waiting more truly than we are.

JOHN DARBY

*I*f you do not preach the coming of the Lord you only preach a half gospel.

EDWARD DENNETT

September 12

That night Jacob got up and took his two wives, his two maidservants and his eleven sons and crossed the ford of the Jabbok. After he had sent them across the stream, he sent over all his possessions. So Jacob was left alone, and a man wrestled with him till daybreak. When the man saw that he cold not overpower him, he touched the socket of Jacob's hip so that his hip was wrenched as he wrestled with the man. Then the man said, "Let me go, for it is daybreak."

But Jacob replied, "I will not let you go unless you bless me."

The man asked him, "What is your name?"

"Jacob," he answered.

Then the man said, "Your name will no longer be Jacob, but Israel, because you have struggled with God and with men and have over-come."

Jacob said, "Please tell me your name."

But he replied, "Why do you ask my name?" Then he blessed him there.

So Jacob called the place Peniel, saying, "It is because I saw God face to face, and yet my life was spared."

GENESIS 32:22–30

$\mathcal{F}$ar too many Christians live their spiritual life on the "battery system." Lest that sounds a strangely peculiar idea, let me explain at once what I mean.

I can dimly remember how, when I was a very little boy, my dear mother sometimes took me to a town where, if I remember rightly, about that time there was a change-over in the street-car system. The older type of street-car used to run on the battery system. There was an electric battery on the front or rear platform of the car, and so long as the battery was "alive" the car would run; but as soon as the battery was exhausted, the car would stop dead. It was far from satisfactory, hence the change-over.

There are Christian believers who seem to run their spiritual life and service on that system. They go to a convention on the deeper life and when they return home, they are altogether different—for three weeks! Or they read some epochal Christian biography, and as they close the book they say, "Ah, life can never be the same again" nor is it—for three weeks! Or they have an all-night of prayer. Things have been going from bad to worse with them, so they bring things to a crisis. While others sleep, they wrestle on the banks of their nocturnal brook Jabbok (Gen. 23:22), and when the sun rises they are transfigured—for three weeks, after which they lapse again to the dull average. Why! Because they are resting on a *crisis* instead of on *Christ*.

The Christian life was never meant to run on the battery system. It was meant to run on the electric circuit principle. You know what that is. Put simply, it is just this: continuous *current* through continuous *contact*. You and I have no power over the current; but we do have power over the contact; and when, by regular prayer-times, daily meditation in the written Word, consecration to Christ, and separation from unworthy ways, we maintain the "contact" then the heavenly current, the Holy Spirit, the life of Christ, is continuously communicated to us.

J. SIDLOW BAXTER

Now an angel of the Lord said to Philip, "Go south to the road—the desert road—that goes down from Jerusalem to Gaza." So he started out, and on his way he met an Ethiopian eunuch, an important official in charge of all the treasury of Candace, queen of the Ethiopians. This man had gone to Jerusalem to worship, and on his way home was sitting in his chariot reading the book of Isaiah the prophet. The Spirit told Philip, "Go to that chariot and stay near it."

ACTS 8:26–29

*E*very believer should look upon his life as Spirit-planned and Spirit-appointed. We should be as open to the Spirit's changes of program as was Philip, Paul or Peter. We should never assume that what we knew of the Spirit's assignment for yesterday will suffice for today or tomorrow. And, knowing that the Spirit must man a world-wide work, far more widely scattered than any army or navy service, we should be eagerly open to removal and relocation, wherever we may serve His purposes best.

We think of a dear, good friend in the ministry, one who had been much used of God. But he became possessed of a house. From that time forth he could hear no call beyond a limited radius of his house. What a travesty on the executive work of the Holy Spirit! Putting Him on a tether—thus far and no farther. Dictating to Him where He may, or may not, send us. Of course, all such are set aside; He does not accept such humanly imposed limitations.

NORMAN B. HARRISON

*I*f we knew the heart of our Father we would never question any of His dealings with us, nor should we ever desire His hand lifted off us till we had learnt all He would teach us.

EDWARD DENNETT

All they asked was that we should continue to remember the poor, the very thing I was eager to do.

GALATIANS 2:10

*C*hrist preferred the poor, and ever since I have been converted so have I. Let those who prefer society have it. If I ever get into it (and it has crossed my path in London) I return sick at heart.

I go to the poor; I find the same evil nature as in the rich, but I find this difference: the rich, and those who keep their comforts and their society, judge and measure how much of Christ they can take and keep without committing themselves; the poor, how much of Christ they can have to comfort them in their sorrows.

I love the poor, and have no distrust of them, living by far the most of my time amongst them, and gladly. When first I began such a life, I as to nature felt a certain satisfaction in the intercourse of educated persons: it was natural. If I find a person spiritually minded and full of Christ, from habit as well as principle I had rather have him than the most elevated or the most educated. The rest is all alike to me. The latter are apt to spare and screen themselves to get on in society: they want a fence round them. I would rather in general have a poor man's judgment of right and wrong than another's; only they are, from being thrown more together and the importance of character, apt to be a little hard on each other as to conduct, and jealous of favors conferred, but often very kind and considerate one toward another.

JOHN DARBY

. . . to this man will I look, even to him that is poor and of a contrite spirit, and trembleth at my word.

Isaiah 66:26, KJV

The essential element of our life is godly fear—a fear that trembles at God's Word, a love that fears, lest it disobey. When God singles out the Christian with whom He will dwell, it is not the Christian who has the deepest insight into His truth, not the Christian who understands all knowledge and all mysteries, not the Christian of the highest intellect, but the Christian who is of a humble and contrite spirit, and who trembles at His Word.

When pride gives place to trembling, and self-assertion to meekness and lowliness, when love trembles and godly fear seeks to obey, then, and then only, are knowledge and the fear of the Lord linked together, as they were in the full perfection in the Person and in the anointing of the Holy One of God.

These combined, form part of the holy anointing oil wherewith we are anointed; and in the measure in which we manifest these gracious gifts and operations of the Spirit of God, in that measure is the anointing abiding in us. Man can counterfeit many parts of the anointing; many of its separate features can be imitated by man in the flesh, but the combination here given never can be found but in the truly anointed of God.

Henry Groves

There is not a single operation of the Spirit of God, nor a single form of His working, but Satan does not imitate.

Author Unknown

September 16

As a man thinketh in his heart, so is he.

PROVERBS 23:7, KJV

*I*n man's nature the heart is the central power. As the heart is, so is the man. The desire and the choice, the love and the hatred of the heart prove what a man is already, and decide what he is to become. Just as we judge of a man's physical character, his size and strength and age and habits, by his outward appearance, so the heart gives the real inward man his character; and "the hidden man of the heart" is what God looks to.

God has in Christ given us access to the secret place of His dwelling, to the inner sanctuary of His presence and His heart; no wonder that the first thing He asks, a He calls us unto Him, is the heart—a true heart; our inmost being must in truth be yielded to Him, true to Him.

ANDREW MURRAY

*W*hen knowledge enters the head, it exalts me. When knowledge enters the heart, it humbles me.

EDWARD DENNETT

September 17

Praise be to the God and Father of our Lord Jesus Christ, who has blessed us in the heavenly realms with every spiritual blessing in Christ.

EPHESIANS 1:3

*T*o be "in Christ" is to be what Christ is. Christ, the Head of the body, and the Christian who is a member of that body have one life.

The blood of the human body is its life. The blood which is now in my head will soon be in my arm. It is the same blood. So the life that is in Christ in the heavenlies is the same life that is in the Christian on earth . . .

We are so enfolded by the Lord Jesus that God cannot see Christ today without seeing us. This moment as God looks at His Son He sees you and me. And what His Son is He sees you and me to be.

To be "in Christ" is to share what Christ has. All that Christ possesses, we possess. Every spiritual blessing in Him—joy, peace, victory, power, holiness—is ours *here* and *now*. If we are a child of God, then we are His heir and a joint-heir with Christ, so that all the Father has given to His Son, the Son shares with us.

RUTH PAXSON

If you can run over in your mind and find one single blessing with which God might bless us today, with which He has not already blessed us, then what He told Paul is not true at all, because He said, "God has blessed us with every spiritual blessing. . . ." It is all done. The great pity of it is that we are saying, "O God bless us— bless us in this, bless us in that! and it is all done—He has blessed us with every spiritual blessing in the heavenlies. It is our place to believe and receive.

L. L. LETGERS

September 18

. . . ye were sealed with that holy Spirit of promise, Which is the earnest of our inheritance until the redemption of the purchased posses-sion, unto the praise of his glory.

EPHESIANS 1:13B–14, KJV

The Holy Spirit of promise is the earnest of your inheritance. By that is meant the foretaste, the beginning, the indication of what is to come. We may illustrate the matter from the Old Testament. You remember when the spies went to search out the land, they returned to Moses to report, and they brought grapes from Eschol. Those grapes were the earnest of what awaited the people when the entered into the land; they were a token and a sample of what was there for them. In like manner, the Spirit of God is the earnest, the token, the foretaste of what awaits us.

However rich our experience of the Spirit of God may have been—and experience can be very rich in this regard—the richest is but a foretaste; and we are left wondering what the fullness will be if this is but a beginning. He is the "the earnest of your inheritance," the inheritance which the Apostle Peter says is "incorruptible and undefiled, and that fadeth not away, reserved in heaven for us who are preserved" on earth for it.

This is just another way of saying to the believer that the best is always to come. It is a sad thing when a person's golden day is behind, but for us who believe in Christ that is never so. However glorious may have been days that we recall with gratitude, the best is yet to come. All that the Spirit has ever been able to do in, for and through any one of us is but a beginning, an indication, a foretaste, a sample of what awaits us in that great and perfect life beyond.

W. GRAHAM SCROGGIE

Grace is but glory begun, and glory is but grace perfected.

JONATHAN EDWARDS

The LORD said unto Gideon, *"throw down the altar of Baal that thy father hath and build an altar unto the LORD thy God."*

JUDGES 6:25–26, KJV

*T*hrow down the altar; then build an altar. God is always thorough. There are things to be thrown down before He will accept the building we erect for Him. He gives His blessing to no divided allegiance, no divided service, to no heart and life that retains sin and disobedience, and that is not cleansed from iniquity.

The human tendency is always to go on with good work, so to speak, to make an offer of surrender to God, to enter into consecration, to claim all the blessings of the fullness, and to say, "We will now serve God," and all the time be failing to deal with the evil thing. And God will have none of it. There must be a breaking down before there can be an acceptable building. We have got to go thoroughly and deeply into spiritual things in our dealings with God.

It might be said that this is a true principle in all the deeper issues of life. There must be courage to sacrifice before we can attain to the heights. Death is the way to life: "Except a corn of wheat fall into the ground and die, it abideth alone; but if it die it bringeth forth much fruit."

Such is Christ's way of bringing real joy and peace and victory and fullness of life to Christians—and that is God's way of bringing revival to our land, and to the world.

How we need revival! Our land cries out for it, the Church is in desperate need of it, and the world is in dire need of new life and movement from the Spirit of God. And God has shown us the way—throw down the altar, then build the altar.

JAMES BUCHANAN DUNLOP

"But one thing is needful."
LUKE 10:42

*O*ne day on His earthly travels our Lord Jesus entered a village where a sister called Martha received Him to her house. This sister loved our Lord, so she wanted to do things for Him in order to please Him. Thus she went on to do this and that, preparing things for the Lord. Being pressed by this business, she became disturbed, grew worried and even annoyed. She was like anybody else, in that when something was wrong within her she began to blame others. She therefore came to the Lord and complained: "Lord, dost thou not care that my sister did leave me to serve alone? Bid her therefore that she help me." The Lord replied: "Martha, Martha, thou art anxious and troubled about many things: but one thing is needful: for Mary hath chosen the good part, which shall not be taken away from her." Oh, the Lord declared that only one thing was needful! Martha did many things, but the Lord said that only one thing was needful, not many. You are planning to do this thing and that thing. You are doing this and that as though there were many plans to be laid and many things to be done; but one thing alone is needful. Not so many things, only one thing!

What is the one thing needful? None other than Christ himself, whom Mary herself had chosen. How can we obtain this one needful thing? By sitting quietly at the Lord's feet; and this was exactly what Mary did. Each one of us Christians must do something. The Bible even tells us that "if any will not work, neither let him eat" (2 Thess. 3:10). We should work, and diligently so. Yet frequently while we are working we have no rest in us, as though we have forgotten the Lord. We are so busy from morning till night that we have not really prayed and studied God's word. The motive for our labors, many spiritual works, and helps rendered to this brother or that sister is undoubtedly for the Lord's sake; yet somehow these activities cause inward problems, and mental disturbances develop afterwards. The difficulty lies in the fact that many affairs tend to make us forgetful of the Lord.

Let us therefore listen to what the Lord says—"But one thing is needful"! And this thing is to rest in the Lord, which, if done, ends up in our being satisfied with the Lord.

WATCHMAN NEE

Jesus loved Martha, and her sister and Lazarus.

JOHN 11:5

*I*n this very chapter Martha does nothing save to blunder, and exhibit her blindness to the glory of the Person of her Lord and yet the chapter is prefaced by the statement that Jesus loved her. It touched me deeply as I saw a little of the significance of the statement, and it taught me that the Lord's love to us rises above all our failures, and that, therefore, we may count upon it and rest in it at all times.

EDWARD DENNETT

September 21

But we see Jesus, who for a little while was made lower than the angels, crowned with glory and honor because of the suffering of death, so that by the grace of God he might taste death for every one.

HEBREWS 2:9, RSV

*A*ll the animal blood that ever flowed in sacrifice could not erase one stain of sin, but the efficacy of His blood is so powerful and far-reaching that by virtue of it the sin of the world shall be taken away.

God's purposes in regard to the Church, the gathering and restoration of Israel, the salvation and blessing of the nations in the millennial age, and the deliverance of the groaning creation from the bondage of corruption are all founded upon His work as Lamb of God. In this connection the Apostle in Hebrews 2 speaks of Him, "by the grace of God tasting death for everyone."

On the basis of His sacrifice every trace of sin shall finally be expunged from the universe. Satan and every incorrigible foe whether man or angel shall be consigned to the lake of fire, and in the new heaven and the new earth the teeming multitudes of redeemed shall have an everlasting day of glory in which they shall feast their eyes upon Him with supreme delight, and roll forth their volumes of untiring praise to Him who by His Blood has made them meet to be partakers of the inheritance of the saints in light.

C. C. CROWSTON

Concerning the past, a Christian can say, "I was saved"—from the penalty of sin. Concerning the present, a Christian can say, "I am being saved"—from the power of sin. Concerning the future, the Christian can say, "I shall be saved"—from the presence of sin.

W. H. GRIFFITH THOMAS

September 22

For God did not appoint us to suffer wrath but to receive salvation through our Lord Jesus Christ.

1 THESSALONIANS 5:9

In the matter of peace with God, Paul makes no distinctions. This means that there is no Christian who has more peace with God than any other. Peace is not the work of man, not even of an apostle, but altogether and only of God. It all comes through Jesus Christ. He is our peace.

For this reason every one of us who truly believes in Him has the same peace with God. It cannot be greater in the future, for it is complete. Neither can it be less, for it is eternal, having Christ as its origin, its giver and its guarantor. We are no longer God's enemies. We are not under His wrath. We are His children—all equally His children—sharing the same adoption and enjoying the same peace with Him. This is completely and exclusively the work of the Lord Jesus; the gift is His and the glory is His.

PAOL MADSEN

*C*hrist is everything. He is everything to the heart of God, and He desires to be everything to the hearts of His people. That it may be so with you is the highest blessedness I can desire for you.

EDWARD DENNETT

September 23

But I trust in you, O LORD; I say, "You are my God." My times are in your hands; deliver me from my enemies and from those who pursue me.
PSALM 31:14–15

*S*caffoldings are for buildings, and the moments and days and years of our earthly lives are scaffolding. What are you building inside the scaffolding, Christian? What kind of a structure will be disclosed when the scaffolding is knocked away? What is the end for which days and years are given? That they may give us what eternity cannot take away—a character built upon the love of God in Christ, and molded into His likeness.

[We are told that] "man's chief end is to glorify God and to enjoy Him for ever." Has your life helped you do that? If it has, though you be but a child, you are full of years; if it has not, though your hair be whitened with the snows of the nineties, you are yet incomplete and immature. The great end of life is to make us like Christ, and pleasing to Christ. If life has done that for us we have got the best out of it, and our life is completed, whatever may be the number of the days. Quality, not quantity, is the thing that determines the perfectness of a life.

ALEXANDER MACLAREN

*W*hatever we do accurately must take time and collectedness of mind, and there is no accuracy in all the world like keeping company with God, and yet nothing so free from bondage or tediousness. By going slow with the Lord we accomplish more than by going with a rush, because what we do is done so much better and does not have to be undone. It is done in a better spirit, with deeper motives, and bears fruit far out in the future, when all mushroom performances have been dissipated forever.

G. B. W.

September 24

He who dwells in the shelter of the Most High will rest in the shadow of the Almighty.
PSALM 91:1

I used to think there was some mystery about abiding in Christ, but I see now that abiding only means trusting Him fully. When you understand this, it becomes the simplest matter in the world.

We sometimes say, speaking of two human beings, that they "live in each other's hearts." By this we mean that perfect love and confidence exist between them and that doubts of one another are impossible. If my trust in the fortress of the Lord is absolute, I am abiding in that fortress.

The practical thing to do since God is our Fortress and our High Tower is to surrender by faith to put ourselves and all our interests into this divine dwelling place. Then we must dismiss all care or anxiety from our minds. Since the Lord is our dwelling place, nothing can possibly come to any harm that is committed to His care.

As long as we believe this, our affairs remain in His hands. The moment we begin to doubt, we take our affairs into our own hands, and they are no longer in the divine fortress. Things cannot be in two places at once. If they are in our own care, they cannot be in God's care. And if they are in God's care, they cannot be in our own.

This is as clear as daylight, and yet, for the lack of a little common sense, people often get mixed up over it. They put their affairs into God's fortress, and at the same time put them into their own fortress as well. Then they wonder why they are not taken care of. This is all foolishness. Either trust the Lord completely or else trust yourself completely; but do not try to mix the two trusts, for they will not mix.

It often helps to put your trust into words. Say aloud, "God is my dwelling place, and I am going to abide in Him forever. It is all settled; I am in this divine habitation, and I am safe here. I am not going to move out again."

HANNAH WHITALL SMITH

The perfection of the Christian life is absolute trust in God. All roads lead to this, and the one who reaches it in any measure will never be confounded.

EDWARD DENNETT

Yet he did not waver through unbelief regarding the promise of God,
but was strengthened in his faith and gave glory to God.
ROMANS 4:20

I have read somewhere of a little street boy who was taken up out
of a cellar by [a social worker] and sent to a farmer's house in
Westchester. He had a great big room all to himself, and when he
was shown into it at night and a little candle placed on the table, it
was a perfect world of bewilderment to him and he thought he was
in heaven.

Finally he got tired and sleepy and looked at the snowy-white
bed. Why, he had never been in a bed in his life! So he slowly crept
up to it, and after a while he just laid his little cheek against the soft
pillow. He could not believe it was for him, there was some mistake.
He began to feel guilty after a while. The idea that he should lie
down on a white, snowy bed like that—it was presumption or
intrusion. But he just went far enough to let his head poke into
heaven for a moment, and then he got down on the floor under the
bed and said: "This is the place for me," and curled himself up and
was soon fast asleep.

Early in the morning the landlady came in and saw him, and
she cried, "Oh, dear me, what does the boy mean?" And she picked
him up and put him in the bed and tried to explain that the bed
was for him, but she had the hardest time to make him understand
and to induce him to get under the nice clean sheets.

How many of God's dear children are there who are sleeping
under the bed instead of resting in the bosom of His love?

We are so slow to believe all that He has for us and to take what
we are entitled to. Oh, some day when whiter than the snow and
higher than the angels, and when all the magnificence of the ages
is at our feet, how ashamed we will be to think how hard it was for

us to take a little crumb from our Father's table. God is looking for princely hearts, who, like Abraham, are willing to believe that He is the God that He says He is. We cannot quite understand it, but it is so. Get it into your heart if you do not quite get it into your intellect and be strong in faith, giving glory to God. He has let that trouble come to you, beloved, just for an opportunity to get you out of it, that it may be a stepping stone to Himself.

A. B. SIMPSON

*C*onsider the lovely and simple meaning of this truth. Wherever we find a precious Bible promise of God in the Bible, one that holds out blessing, encouragement and guidance, we can say to ourselves, "Is this true for me, really true today?" The answer comes back every time, "Yes, indeed it is true, for all God's promises find their Yes in Christ."

JOHN HUNTER

September 26

For in him we live and move and have our being.
ACTS 17:28A

*I*t is the Lord Jesus who is moving all things, carrying on by His wisdom and power the development and progress of all things, restraining and overruling, guiding and blessing, that the purpose of God may be accomplished, and that ultimately the kingdom may come.

Christ is Lord of all. The whole universe centers in Him. A star appears at the time of the Messiah's advent, the sun loses his splendor when Jesus Christ dies upon the cross. There shall be again wonders and signs in the heavens when the Son of man shall come in power.

In the material world we know that there have been many great cycles of development. And both science and revelation teach us to look forward to a new earth. It is the Lord Jesus who shall make all things new. And all developments are borne up and moved by the word of his power.

Oh, I know that the general conception which the world has of Jesus is that He is Lord of a spiritual realm, of thought and sentiment, bishop and head of ministers and pastors for edifying souls! But the world does not know that He is moving all things by the word of His power; that all politics, all statesmanship, all history, all physics, all art, all science, everything that is—all that has substance, truth, beauty, all things apart from that cancer of sin which has attached itself to it, consist by Jesus the Son of God.

Now, when the apostle has given us this idea of the wonderful glory of the Lord Jesus, the Son whom God has appointed Heir of all things, by whom He has made the worlds, who is "the brightness of His glory, and the express image of His being," who "upholdeth" and moveth "all things by the word of His power," He continues by stating something still more marvelous. Why has this wonderful and glorious being, in whom all things are summed up, and who is before all things the Father's delight and the Father's glory, this infinite majesty, come down to our poor earth? For what purpose? To shine? To show forth the splendor of His majesty? To teach heavenly wisdom? To rule by His just and holy might?

No! He came *to purge our sins*. What height of glory! What depth of abasement! Infinite is His majesty, and infinite is His self-humiliation, and the depth of His love. What a glorious Lord! And what an awful sacrifice of unspeakable love, to purge our sins by Himself!

ADOLPH SAPHIR

September 27

And ye are complete in him, which is the head of all principality and power.

COLOSSIANS 2:10, KJV

*W*hen walking in Him, every act is worship, and we do not consider whether this or that step is a right or wrong one merely, but conscious of our heavenly calling, we shall refer to a more exalted and becoming standard, and enquire rather, whether the proposed step will please God—glorify Christ—and if it be suitable for one who is complete in Him, and seated in a risen and glorified Lord.

Beloved brethren in Christ, let us not forget the depth of redeeming love, quickening us when dead in sin, nor lose sight of its glorious height as raising us up together, and making us sit together in the heavenlies in Christ Jesus.

Neither let us be unmindful, that thoughts of walking only for Christ, tend to a spirit of bondage, and consequent feelings of distance from God; while walking in Him is the legitimate province of faith, and will be accompanied with holy, humble, happy and acceptable service.

"CRUMBS FOR THE LORD'S LITTLE ONES"

September 28

So they asked him, "What miraculous sign then will you give that we may see it and believe you? What will you do? Our forefathers ate the manna in the desert; as it is written: 'He gave them bread from heaven to eat.'" Jesus said to them, "I tell you the truth, it is not Moses who has given you the bread from heaven, but it is my Father who gives you the true bread from heaven. For the bread of God is he who comes down from heaven and gives life to the world." "Sir," they said, "from

now on give us this bread." Then Jesus declared, "I am the bread of life.
He who comes to me will never go hungry, and he who believes in me
will never be thirsty.

JOHN 6:30–35

*W*e grow by what we feed on.

It is our privilege to feed on Christ day by day and grow in Him while He expands in and fills us with Himself.

We are to feed on Him by more and more appropriating Him to ourselves, appropriating Him as our perfect sacrifice and resting in the love and security of it; we are to appropriate Him as our living Head, loving us and living for us; and throwing ourselves more and more open to the penetration of His will above our will, allow Him to fill us with His own joy.

Let a Christian so appropriate the Lord Jesus Christ day by day, He will find His soul fed and filled with Christ as the living bread and living each day more and more in the consciousness that it is the living Christ that liveth in Him.

I. M. HALDEMAN

*I*f we are not living near the Lord Jesus and are not where we should be, we neither have an appetite for spiritual things, nor can we feed upon Him who is the living Bread.

When God pours into you a hunger for your Beloved and begins to reveal your privileges in Him, rejoice with great joy and gratitude toward God.

If He did not put into our hearts the longing to know Him better and to have His very best, we would be satisfied with the least we could have and be saved.

C. H. MACKINTOSH

Praise be to the God and Father of our Lord Jesus Christ, the Father of compassion and the God of all comfort, who comforts us in all our troubles ...

2 CORINTHIANS 1:3–4A

*I*t will not do for the believer to simply say, "I rest upon Scripture, and upon the Word of God." He must not be satisfied without experientially having the comfort of the Holy Spirit.

Considering the apostle Paul's words, are we to be content merely with the fact that we are forgiven, and saved, as the consequence of Christ's death and resurrection? Am I to rest in that? What would you think of the man who only knew that he was married because his wife's name was in the registrar's book? Little good, or comfort, would the relationship be to him, if he only knew that she was his wife because her name so appeared.

And is not the Holy Spirit to be, to the believer, the evidence and witness of our new place and of the actual relationship in which we stand to God our Father? Of course.

The Holy Spirit feeds the new creation, comforts him, minister to him, and unfolds the beauties and glories of Christ to him. These things are to be known, and if you do not know them, you have need to know them.

W. T. P. WOLSTON

*T*he great thing we need for progress is *restfulness of heart.* I do not believe that there is simple restfulness of heart until union with Christ is known, not merely as doctrine, but as the unalterable bond of affection.

You are not only assured of His grace in saving you, but you have found Him so necessary to you that you cannot live without Him. Then to find out that you are united to Him is absolute solace and divine restfulness.

J. B. STONEY

September 30

Thy word is true from the beginning: and every one of thy righteous judgments endureth forever.

PSALM 119:160, KJV

A subtle danger, taught by some earnest people, is to magnify the inner light and leading of the Holy Spirit to the neglect of the Word which He gave, and through which He still works on human hearts. This is a great mistake and the prolific parent of all kinds of evil. As soon as we put aside the Word of God, we lay ourselves open to the solicitation of the many voices that speak within our hearts. We no longer have a test, a criterion of truth, a standard of appeal.

How can we know the Spirit of God in some of the more intricate cases which our conscience brings into court unless our judgment is deeply imbued with the Word of God! We must not content ourselves with the Spirit without the written Word or with the Word without the Spirit. Our life must travel along these two as the train along the parallel tracks. The Word is the chosen vehicle of the Spirit. Only by our devout contact with it are we able to detect His voice. It is by the Word that the Spirit will enter our hearts, as the heat of the sun passes into our rooms with the beams of light through the open windows.

F. B. MEYER

*B*elievers today seek the blessing and power of Pentecost apart from a personal crucifixion with Christ, and the result is a counterfeit experience. Calvary is always before Pentecost, historically and experientially. The only way into the riches of the fullness of Christ is through our acceptance of our crucifixion with Him.

L. L. LETGERS

*N*owhere in Scripture is it taught that there is a sudden leap to be taken from carnality to spirituality, or from a life of comparative unconcern as to godliness to one of the intense devotion to the Lord Jesus. On the contrary, increase in piety is ever presented as a growth, which should be as normal and natural as the orderly progression in human life from infancy to full stature.

HARRY A. IRONSIDE

> *Know then in your heart that as a man disciplines his son, so the Lord your God disciplines you.*
>
> DEUTERONOMY 8:5

*G*od works by paradox. Success comes via failure; life springs out of death and so on. The only element in the believer's life that crumbles is that which has to go anyway—the new life can never be harmed or affected.

This disintegration is something the believer cannot enter into nor engineer on his own—self will never cast out self. He has to be led into it by the mercy of the Holy Spirit—into failure, abject and total.

So often the means utilized by the Spirit is an unsaved mate, or even a saved one! Or poor health; yes, and good health too! A thousand and one things are used by Him—in fact, everything (Rom. 8:28–29), to bring out the worst in us, ultimately enabling us to see that the Christian life has to be "not I, but Christ." People, circumstances, etcetera, are never the cause of failure.

Self's reaction to them is the cause and the one problem to be dealt with.

MILES STANFORD

*W*hat is true *of* us is not always true *to* us. It is true *of* every believer that he is in Christ, but in order to be true *to* him he must reach that position in his own soul experience.

EDWARD DENNETT

Thomas said to him, "My Lord and my God!"
JOHN 20:28

*I*n everything but our sins and our evil natures Jesus is one with us. He grew in stature and in grace. He labored, and wept, and prayed, and loved. He was tempted in all points as we are, without sinning.

With Thomas we confess Him Lord and God; we adore and revere Him as God—and yet there is no other who has invited us to such intimacy with Himself, none who has willingly come so close to these human hearts of ours; no one in the universe of whom we are so little afraid.

He is not one of the ancients. How wholesomely and genuinely human He is. Martha reproaches Him; John, who has seen Him raise the dead, still the tempest, and talk with Moses and Elijah in the mount, does not hesitate to make a pillow of His breast at supper. Peter will not let Him wash his feet, but afterwards wants his head and hands washed as well.

They ask Him foolish questions, and rebuke Him, and venerate and adore Him all in a breath. And Jesus calls them by their first name, and tells them to fear not, and assures them of His love. And in all this He seems to me altogether lovely. His perfection does not glitter, it glows. The saintliness of the Lord Jesus is so warm and human that it attracts and inspires.

He receives sinners and eats with them. All kinds of sinners. Nicodemus, the moral religious sinner, and Mary of Magdala, "out of whom went seven devils," the shocking kind of sinner. He comes into sinful lives as a bright, clear stream enters a stagnant pool. The stream is not afraid of contamination, but its sweet energy cleanses the pool.

"SOUL FOOD"

*T*he object of Christ's love is to take us into the enjoyment of all that He enjoys Himself.

JOHN DARBY

Blessed is he whose transgressions are forgiven, whose sins are covered.
  Blessed is the man whose sin the LORD does not count against him
and in whose spirit is no deceit.

PSALM 32:1–2

*O*ur power in drawing others after the Lord mainly rests in our joy and communion with Him ourselves.

J. G. BELLETT

*W*e are not made capable of thinking of two things at once. When we are doing something, we put all we have into it. We cannot, therefore, be thinking directly of Christ at the same time, or consciously communing with Him. We have a sub-conscious realization of His presence, like the flow of an underground stream, and we refer to Him momentarily at any time; but the great percentage of our daily lives is spent, not directly in touch with Him, but immersed in our own affairs.

Now if [our union with Him], by grace, is an automatic fact, then we do not suddenly come under condemnation when we have thought little directly of Him throughout the day; but just because He and we are one person, so what we were thinking about and doing was what He was thinking and doing. We never were apart, not for one second; such apartness is a ridiculous impossibility. Wherever we are, He is. He has joined Himself to us—by infinite grace—and that's the end of it.

So we are freed to act as normal men and women, living normal lives; yet it is not really we living, but He: that is our special secret, shared with those who know what we are talking about. We pray, we read the Scriptures, but we are not in bondage. We do not even depend on these, we are joined irrevocably to Him; and even if pressures mean that we can't get the time with Him we would like, again we don't come under condemnation or fall into the false imagination that therefore we are spiritually dry or disarmed; no, not even prayer or the Scriptures are our living water or our armor . . .

As we learn to recognize Him in us at all times, fellowship and communion with Him will spontaneously become the heart-beat of our lives.

NORMAN GRUBB

*M*any people think communion is having happy feelings. It is being in the mind of God. Communing is doing the right thing in the right moment in the right way. Once we get out of communion, we cannot do anything right.

EDWARD DENNETT

October 4

But Zacchaeus stood up and said to the Lord, "Look, Lord! Here and now I give half of my possessions to the poor, and if I have cheated anybody out of anything, I will pay back four times the amount."

Jesus said to him, "Today salvation has come to this house, because this man, too, is a son of Abraham."

LUKE 19:8–9

*R*estitution is the revealed will of God. If it is omitted, while we have it in our power to make it, guilt remains on the conscience, and spiritual progress is hindered. Even though it should involve difficulty, self-denial, and great loss, it is to be attended to.

Should the persons who have been defrauded be dead, their heirs are to be found out, if this can be done, and restitution is to be made to them. But there may be cases when this cannot be done, and then only the money should be given to the Lord for His work or His poor.

One word more. Sometimes the guilty person may not have grace enough, if the rightful owners are living, to make known to them the sin; under such circumstances, though not the best and most scriptural way, rather than have guilt remaining on the conscience, it is better to make restitution anonymously than not at all.

Nearly fifty years ago, I knew a man under concern about his soul, who had defrauded his master of two sacks of flour, and who was urged by me to confess this sin to his late employer, and to make restitution. He would not do it, however, and the result was that for twenty years he never obtained real peace of soul till the thing was done.

GEORGE MUELLER

*U*ntil the soul is at peace and in liberty, divine things cannot be communicated.

EDWARD DENNETT

October 5

So she let them down by a rope through the window, for the house she lived in was part of the city wall.

Now she had said to them, "Go to the hills so that the pursuers will not find you. Hide yourselves there three days until they return, and then go on your way."

The men said to her, "This oath you made us swear will not be binding on us unless, when we enter the land, you have tied this scarlet cord in the window through which you let us down, and unless you have brought your father and mother, your brothers and all your family into your house."

JOSHUA 2:15–18

*R*ahab's house stood on the town wall; but her window did not look into the city to allow her to witness all its sinfulness and forgetfulness of God—it looked out from it, away from it.

She let the spies down by a cord through that window. She hung "the scarlet line" by which they escaped out of that window. Out of it she saw them flee to the mountains. And from it she daily watched for their return with the army of deliverance, which was to deliver her and her friends sheltering in her house, from the certain and speedy doom awaiting the city. Her outlook was away from the doomed place, to the point where she could catch the first glimpse of her expected deliverers.

And what does Rahab's window say to us as Christian? Surely it reminds us in a forceful way that God's Son is coming from Heaven to deliver us from this doomed world. He has already saved our souls; the scarlet line hangs out of our windows; we are sheltered by the precious blood of Christ; indwelt by the Holy Spirit and are now waiting for the Lord Himself to come and take us home.

Our outlook is to be away from things seen and temporal; and to all the realities of Heaven itself which will be ours in actuality when He returns to take us there.

He is the Deliverer.

We wait for Him.

WILLIAM EASTON

*T*here are multitudes of believers whose hearts are troubled when they think of the Lord's return. To them it is not a comforting hope. They have without question accepted His words, "I will come again," but because they confuse law which demands human perfection with grace, they are very uncertain that the words "I will receive you unto myself" are for them.

It is the certainty of His coming and the certainty for every believer that he will be taken that is the comfort of grace.

J. F. STROMBECK

Therefore, since we are surrounded by such a great cloud of witnesses, let us throw off everything that hinders and the sin that so easily entangles, and let us run with perseverance the race marked out for us.

Hebrews 12:1

*D*o you as a Christian really believe in Christ? Can you trust yourself absolutely and entirely into His hand? Dare you trust Him? Dare you trust in His promises? Or is there a streak of doubt and unbelief within you which insists upon arguing, "If I give up the world what will I have left? How can I go on if I give up to world?"

Can you not believe that the Lord has something far better for you? Can you not believe He is able to deliver you from all your sin? Can you not put your trust in Him? If we truly desire to run the race we must lay aside the sin of unbelief and cast ourselves upon the Lord and trust Him.

To lay aside sin, and especially the sin of unbelief, constitutes the first requirement which must be fulfilled if we would run after God in response to His love.

But secondly, we must lay aside every weight which would heavily weigh us down. Weight may not necessarily be sin. Weight may be something legitimate, lawful, even respectable. Suppose I clothe myself with, among other things, a shirt, a tie, a coat, a heavy pair of shoes. This is respectable, this is quite legitimate, this is perfectly appropriate—if I am not running a race. But if I am running a race, then all these articles are quite unnecessary. Not only unnecessary, but they all become a burden to me! They weigh me down. They hinder me from running well. I have to strip myself to the uttermost, to the least necessaries, to the barest essentials. Then, I am free to run the race.

With some people it may be sin, with so many others it is heavy weights. Oh, the cares of this life; the ease, the comfort, the luxury of it all. The many good things in this life. All which goes to make up the so-called affluent way of life. These elements may not be bad; they may in fact be very good and very respectful.

But my dear brothers and sisters, if we desire them to such an extent that we must have them, if we desire them to such a degree that we cannot exist without them, to such a degree that they become a weight and a load upon us, then they hinder us from running fast; nay, they may hinder us from running at all! Our souls are not able to rise and ascend.

STEPHEN KAUNG

*I*f a thing is a snare to me, I must give it up entirely. Different things are snares to different people. . . . It is an individual thing with God. I cannot judge what may be a snare to you. If it *is* a snare, let it go.

JOHN DARBY

October 7

I hate vain thoughts; but thy law do I love.
PSALM 119:113, KJV

*T*he Psalmist could say, "I hate vain thoughts."

No wonder. They are truly hateful, and should be judged, condemned, and expelled. Some one, in speaking of the subject of evil thoughts, has said, "I cannot prevent birds from flying over me, but I can prevent their alighting upon me. In like manner, I cannot prevent evil thoughts being suggested to my mind, but I can refuse them a lodgement therein."

But how can we control our thoughts? No more than we could blot out our sins, or create a world. What then are we to do?

We must look to Christ. This is the true secret of self-control. He can keep us, not only from the lodgement, but also from the suggestion of the evil thoughts. In our own strength we could no more prevent the one than the other. He can prevent both. He can keep the vile intruders, not only from getting in, but even from knocking at the door. When His divine life is our source of life, when the current of spiritual thought and feeling is deep and rapid—when the heart's affections are intensely occupied with the Person of Christ, vain thoughts do not trouble us. It is only when spiritual indolence creeps over us that evil thoughts and their vile and horrible progeny come in upon us like a flood; and then our *only* resource is to look straight to Jesus.

We might as well attempt to cope with the entire marshaled hosts of hell, as with a horde of evil thoughts. Our refuge is in Christ. He is made *unto* us sanctification. We can do all things through Him. We have just to bring the name of Jesus to bear upon the flood of evil thoughts, and He will, most assuredly, give full and immediate deliverance.

However, the more excellent way is, to be preserved from the suggestions of evil, by the power of preoccupation with good. When the channel of thought is decidedly upward, when it is deep and well formed, free from all curves and indentations, then the current of imagination and feeling, as it gushes up from the deep fountains of the soul, will naturally flow onward in the bed of that channel.

This, I repeat, is unquestionably, the more excellent way. May we prove it in our own experience. "Finally, brethren, whatsoever things are true, whatsoever things are venerable, whatsoever things are just, whatsoever things are lovely, whatsoever things are of good report, if there be any virtue, and if there be any praise, think on these things. Those things which ye have both learned and received, and heard and seen in me, do; and the God of peace shall be with you" (Phil. 4:8–9). When the heart is fully engrossed with Christ, the living embodiment of all those things enumerated in the verses above, we enjoy profound peace, unruffled by evil thoughts.

This is true self-control.

C. H. MACKINTOSH

October 8

Peter replied, "Repent and be baptized, every one of you, in the name of Jesus Christ for the forgiveness of your sins. And you will receive the gift of the Holy Spirit."

ACTS 2:38

The Holy Spirit has come down to put the soul now, into the enjoyment of its heavenly relationships, with the Father, and the Son, and to lead it into abiding communion with the Father and the Son. That is Christianity.

But, alas, Christendom has forgotten that the Holy Spirit is here. That is why you so frequently hear the prayer that the Spirit of God might be poured out. If ever you hear it again, you would do the petitioner a true service, by asking him if he ever read the second of Acts. The Holy Ghost has come. The Spirit of God is here.

What would the Lord have thought, when on earth, if one day while He, and His twelve disciples were passing along, one of them had turned, and prayed to God fervently, that He would send His Son? I think one of the eleven would have turned on him, and said, "What are you talking about? He is already here."

Similarly, what inconsistency is it to pray for the Holy Ghost to be poured out! Ah! you say, "I thought He was only an influence." I know it. But I want you to see that He is a Divine Person come here, and abiding here, in the name of Christ—here to act for

Christ, and here to put the soul in the enjoyment of communion with the Father and the Son.

We should not pray, "Send power down!" There is no need. The Holy Spirit is with us already. I realize that He is here. We need not pray that He should come. In the second chapter of Acts you will find that He has already been sent. We have an accurate account that He came.

Have you any account that He went back?

EVAN ROBERTS

October 9

And it came to pass, when the LORD would take up Elijah into heaven by a whirlwind . . .

2 KINGS 2:1, KJV

The length of our life in this world is in the hands of God. We have no independent lease of life, so that we may decide of our own accord that we will remain for a year, or ten, or twenty years on earth. We have only a lease at the will of God.

Elijah went when God called him. The record does not say that when Elijah saw that his work was done, he decided that it was time for him to go to Heaven; there is nothing of the kind. It is simply written, "when the Lord would take Elijah up to Heaven."

Our lives are just as certainly at the disposal to God as was Elijah's, and we have no power that Elijah did not have to stay the hand of God when He would call us away.

CHARLES COWMAN

Happy are they who are found watching. Our hourglass is not so long as we may think. Time will have its way with us, yet we know that our heaven is in the bud, growing up to a harvest. Why should we not then eagerly follow on, seeing our life-span will surely amount to merely an inch?

Therefore I commend Christ to you as the Staff of your old age—let Him have the rest of your days, and don't worry about the storms approaching the ship that Christ also sails in. There shall be no overboard passengers, but the storm-racked ship and the sea-sick passenger shall come to shore safely.

I am in as sweet communion with Christ as a poor sinner can be, and am only pained that He has so much beauty and fairness, and I so little love; He has such great power and mercy, and I little faith; He much light, and I bleared eyes.

SAMUEL RUTHERFORD

October 10

Remember the Sabbath day by keeping it holy.
EXODUS 20:8

*G*od sanctified the Sabbath day, because in it He rested from all His work. This rest was something real. In Creation, God had, as it were, gone out of Himself to bring forth something new: in resting He now returns from His creating work into Himself, to rejoice in His love over the man He has created, and communicate Himself to him. This opens up to us the way in which God makes holy.

The connection between the resting and making holy was no arbitrary one; the making holy was no after-thought; in the very nature of things it could not be otherwise: He sanctified because He rested in it; He sanctified by resting. As He regards His finished work, more especially man, rejoices in it, and, as we have it in Exodus, "is refreshed," this time of His divine rest is the time in which He will carry on unto perfection what He has begun, and make man, created in His image, in very deed partaker of His highest glory, His Holiness.

Where God rests in complacency and love, He makes holy. The Presence of God revealing itself, entering in, and taking possession, is what constitutes true Holiness. As we go down the ages, studying the progressive unfolding of what Holiness is, this truth will continually meet us. In God indwelling in heaven, in His temple on earth, in His beloved son, in the person of the believer through the Holy Spirit, we shall everywhere find that Holiness is not something that man is or does, but that it always comes where God comes. In the deepest meaning of the words: where God enters to rest, there He sanctifies. And when we come to study the New Testament revelation of the way in which we are to be holy, we shall find in this one of our earliest and deepest lessons. It is as we enter into the rest of God that we become partakers of His Holiness.

ANDREW MURRAY

*M*an seeks rest in his surroundings—God gives rest within.

E. P. C.

O Lord God, give peace unto us—for thou hast given us all things: the peace of rest, the peace of the Sabbath, which hath no evening; yea give us rest in Thee, the Sabbath of eternal life. For Thou shalt rest in us, as now Thou workest in us; and Thy rest shall be through us, as Thy works are through us. Amen.

AUGUSTINE

October 11

. . . for my power is made perfect in weakness.

2 CORINTHIANS 12:9B

$\mathscr{B}$ear in mind that we must not expect consciousness of power. It is on this point that so many stumble. They want to *feel* power, and failing to do so they conclude that they are in the wrong condition of soul for its exercise.

No mistake could be greater. On the other hand, the Lord has to break down His servants in order to reduce them to the sense of their own utter importance, that they may learn the lesson that His strength is made perfect in weakness.

EDWARD DENNETT

$\mathscr{T}$he path of strength . . . is being made sensible of our own weakness, so that divine strength, which will never be a supplement of flesh's strength, may come in.

JOHN DARBY

[Disregard your feelings because] justification takes place in the mind of God, not in the nervous system of the believer.

C. I. SCOFIELD

October 12

Rest in the LORD and wait patiently for him . . .

PSALM 37:7, KJV

$\mathscr{H}$enry Suso, the great German mystic, once heard a knock at his door. A strange woman stood there with a babe in her arms which she thrust into his arms, saying, "Here you have the fruit of your sin."

Suso had never before seen the woman. He was as innocent as a dove. The woman hastened away leaving him with the babe. The news of what had happened went through the town like a flash. So this is the man we had revered as holy! What a hypocrite, what a fraud.

Suso was crushed. He groaned like a dying man. What was he to do? He withdrew to a desert place and called upon the Lord saying it was more that he could bear. "What shall I do, Lord?" he cried in his pain and shame. "Thou knowest that I am innocent."

The answer came to him with perfect clearness and finality. "What shall you do? Do as I did; suffer for the sins of others and say nothing." Suso saw the Cross. Peace came to his troubled soul. He returned to his home; took the child and sweetly, humbly cared for the waif and reared it as if it were his very own, never saying a word in self-defense.

Years later, the unknown woman returned to publish abroad Suso's innocence, but the work was done. Suso had been conformed to the image of God's Son. The victory was achieved. Here you have victory's essence, its deepest nature—"Christ in you, the hope of glory."

F. J. HUEGEL

*Y*ou may have gone through deep waters, and your grief may have caused many a furrow on your forehead—but as you passed through the trouble which did you find most—the trial or Christ who passed through it with you?

I judge that the great thing is to own God and be still. "I was dumb; thou didst it," said David. . . . There is rest in this—giving to God His own place.

GEORGE V. WIGRAM

*Y*our whole responsibility at the present moment is to "rest in the Lord and wait patiently for Him." And what a blessing it is that may and can rest, whatever your suffering, on the Lord's breast.

EDWARD DENNETT

October 13

"May your blessing be on your people."
PSALM 3:8

$\mathscr{B}$rethren, if only we came to recognize that in God's work every-thing hinges on His blessing, it would bring a radical change into all our service for Him. We should then cease to reckon in terms of men and money and bread, and we should be constantly expecting Him to make good every lack.

His blessing transcends all our deficiencies. Once this truth real-ly grips us we shall discard as worthless all our clever ways, and specious words, and scrupulous work. When we set store by the blessing of the Lord and keep looking for that alone, even if we are not over punctilious about the work, and even if at times we make mistakes, we shall find that the need of the hungry is being met. We definitely hope we shall be preserved from mistakes and from care-less words and acts; but we shall find that with God's blessing upon us even our serious blunders do not ultimately hinder His purpose. When He blesses the work nothing can wreck it, for the trans-forming power of His blessing turns liabilities into positive assets.

WATCHMAN NEE

$\mathscr{B}$ring Christ's Word—Christ's promise, and Christ's sacrifice—His blood with thee and not one of heaven's blessings can be denied thee.

ADAM CLARKE

October 14

You are looking only on the surface of things. If anyone is confident that he belongs to Christ, he should consider again that we belong to Christ just as much as he.
2 CORINTHIANS 10:7

$\mathcal{P}$aul [chided] the Corinthians for limiting their vision to the things immediately before their eyes.

To be spiritually shortsighted, focusing only on what is near at hand, is to become too easily satisfied and contented in the realm of things spiritual; to have a small and narrow horizon and to fail to appreciate the much more which God has in mind.

It is so easy to settle into a limited and very circumscribed area, thinking only of the spiritual things with which we are familiar and which seem so important to us, while we fail to take note of the much more which lies beyond us and to which we are being called.

There are few things more stultifying in the Christian life than an assumption that there is nothing beyond the small sphere of our experience. It is possible to get so shut-in, so near-sighted, that we go round and round in circles, never looking out to the new dimensions of spiritual experience to which God is calling us, and almost imagining that we know all there is to know about God's Word and His purposes in Christ.

The Corinthians seem to have done this, to have so focused on their own affairs, even their own spiritual gifts, that they were almost at a standstill spiritually. They were looking at themselves, full of concern for their own assembly, which was right enough, but apparently not able to appreciate the large purposes of God as represented by Paul's ministry.

Even the matters which have been clearly shown of God and blessed by Him can become a hindrance when they arrest and hold the attention as things in themselves. These are the things before our face, but we were intended always to look beyond them to the Lord, and always beyond the immediate factors to the eternal values in Christ.

T. AUSTIN-SPARKS

$\mathcal{I}$f Christians are commonplace in our day, may it not be because the gospel they believe is commonplace? Divine faith is faith in the divine. The difference in not in the faith, but in the object of it. If we have really believed the Gospel of God, we have each one of us received for himself a revelation from on high, a revelation to which flesh and blood could never reach. Let us remember this.

SIR ROBERT ANDERSON

October 15

". . . . Now ye have consecrated yourselves unto the LORD . . ."
2 CHRONICLES 29:31

*W*hat will happen if you and I really give ourselves utterly to God? The first thing that will happen is that the Lord Jesus Christ will receive you. You see, at conversion, Christ gives and you take; at consecration, you give and He takes.

That is very simple, but I would have you be in no doubt about it, that the moment you by faith really and in earnest give yourself to the Lord Jesus Christ, He takes you. Consecration is a personal thing, a transaction between two persons, the Lord Jesus Christ and you. Following that, the Holy Spirit will commence a great work in you; for the work of the Lord Jesus Christ for us needs to be followed by the work of the Holy Spirit in us.

JOHN PRITCHARD

*C*onsecration lies in Christ having full control over the bodies of His people, so that they may be organs for the expression of nothing but Himself.

EDWARD DENNETT

> Praise the LORD.
> Praise God in his sanctuary;
> *praise him in his mighty heavens.*
> Praise him for his acts of power;
> *praise him for his surpassing greatness.*
> Praise him with the sounding of the trumpet,
> *praise him with the harp and lyre,*
> *praise him with tambourine and dancing,*
> *praise him with the strings and flute,*
> *praise him with the clash of symbols,*
> *praise him with resounding symbols.*
> Let everything that has breath praise the LORD.
> Praise the LORD.
>
> PSALM 150

*W*hen I was staying in a hotel in Norway, a little girl was among the families staying as guests. She was obviously only a beginner in playing the piano. But she insisted upon practicing in the drawing room whenever she chose. She played with one finger and one note, usually discordant. Everyone bolted for open air whenever they saw her coming.

It happened that one of the finest musicians in Norway was also a guest. Instead of vanishing with the others, he took a stool and sat beside the child. For every note she struck, he struck the most exquisite chord of music, introducing a most lovely accompaniment. As the notes floated outside, the people streamed back to enjoy the music. When the child made a more terrible mistake than usual, he improvised a still finer outburst of music. After 20 minutes, he took the child by the hand and led her around the company, introducing her as "the young lady to whom you are indebted for the music this afternoon." The child knew well enough that she had not done it, but everyone paid their compliments.

The truth this story illustrates has deeply touched my heart through the years. I have been as that child at the piano of God's truth. I have tried my level best to make music with my one finger. Again and again and again I have come away feeling that I am a terrible failure and play nothing but discord. But, oh, I have also found the Holy Spirit sitting by my side. For every note of discord I have made, He has struck a nobler note. Whatever you try to do for the Lord, small or great, and feel you are only making mistakes and failures and false notes, believe that the blessed Holy Spirit is by your side turning your discords into the Hallelujah Chorus!

F. B. MEYER

You will never be transformed by continually looking at your own shortcomings, never! Nor will you ever be transformed by looking at the weakness of your fellow Christians.

You will only be conformed by continually looking upon the glory of the Lord Jesus—for they who live looking and beholding, though they know it not, are being "changed from glory to glory by the Spirit of God."

E. I.

October 17

In everything by prayer and supplication with thanksgiving, let your requests be made known unto God.

PHILIPPIANS 4:6, KJV

*A*llow me to give you a few practical words as to your prayers. Keep clear of the unprofitable habit of "saying your prayers."

Christendom is full of solemn warnings as to the tendency of our hearts to drop into a routine of religious forms. It is a very great loss to the soul to get into the habit of repeating substantially the same words in prayer every day. It is not real prayer at all.

We read, "In everything by prayer and supplication with thanksgiving, let your requests be made known unto God." How can you do that if you are using the same form of words day after day, and week after week? Today is not like yesterday, and tomorrow will not be like today. If you are really with God you will be sensitive to the fresh needs of every day.

God delights to have our confidence as to every need and care. Then let us cultivate a child's confidence, and a child's simplicity as we come to Him in prayer. Bring the trying circumstances of today, and the expected difficulties and perplexities of tomorrow to the blessed God who tells you to cast all your care upon Him, for He careth for you.

Be simple: give up the long preface; do not feel it necessary to quote a dozen scriptures; ask as a needy and confiding child would ask its parent.

C. A. COATES

*O*ne reason why we do not have more answers to our prayers is that we are not thankful enough. The divine injunction is, "Be careful for nothing, but in everything by prayer and supplication with thanksgiving let your requests be made known unto God." Someone has well said that there are three things in that verse— careful for nothing, prayerful for everything, thankful for anything.

Faith says, "Amen" to everything that God says. Faith takes God without any ifs. If God says it is, faith answers, "Amen; I believe it."

D. L. MOODY

When we put bits into the mouths of horses to make them obey us, we can turn the whole animal. Or take ships as an example. Although they are so large and are driven by strong winds, they are steered by a very small rudder wherever the pilot wants to go. Likewise the tongue is a small part of the body, but it makes great boasts. Consider what a great forest is set on fire by a small spark. The tongue also is a fire, a world of evil among the parts of the body. It corrupts the whole person, sets the whole course of his life on fire, and is itself set on fire by hell.

JAMES 3:3–6

*C*hoose a suitable time for recollection and frequently consider the loving-kindness of God. Do not read to satisfy curiosity or to pass the time, but study such things as move your heart to devotion.

If you avoid unnecessary talk and aimless visits, listening to news and gossip, you will find plenty of suitable time to spend in meditation on holy things. The greatest saints used to avoid the company of others whenever possible, preferring to serve God in solitude.

A wise man once said, "As often as I have been among men, I have returned home a lesser man." We often share this experience, when we spend too much time in conversation. It is easier to remain silent altogether than not to talk more than we should. It is easier to remain quietly at home than to keep due watch over ourselves in public. Therefore, whoever is resolved to live an inward and spiritual life must, with Jesus, withdraw from the crowd.

No Christian can live in the public eye without risk to his soul, unless he would prefer to remain obscure. No man can safely speak, unless he who would gladly remain silent. No man can safely command, unless he who has learned to obey well. No man can safely rejoice, unless he possesses the testimony of a good conscience.

THOMAS À KEMPIS

*W*here shall we find strength for practical separation to God, unless in God Himself?

John Darby

October 19

The Son does nothing on his own; he only does what he sees his Father doing.

John 5:19, KJV

*D*o we want the Holy Spirit to come on us and stay with us? Then we must be like the Lamb about every matter which He shows to us. Let us look at the Lamb on His way to Calvary. As we do so, we shall also see clearly our own hearts. It will make us humble to see how unlike Him we are. We shall see how often we have *not* taken the place of the Lamb.

Let us look at Him for a moment as the Lamb. He was the *simple* Lamb. A Lamb is one of the simplest of God's creatures. It makes no plans to help itself. It is helpless. The Lord Jesus made Himself as nothing for us. He became the simple Lamb. He had no strength or wisdom of His own. He did not make plans to get Himself out of trouble. At all times He depended on His Father. But we are not simple! We make plans to help ourselves. We try in all kinds of ways to get ourselves out of trouble. We try to live the Christian life in our own strength. We try in our own strength to work for God. We think we are something, and can do something for God. If we are not willing to be simple lambs, how can God's Spirit stay on us?

Roy Hession

*A*ll Friends be low, and keep in the life of God to keep you low.

George Fox

*I counsel thee to buy of Me gold tried in the fire; and white raiment,
that thou mayest be clothed, and that the shame of thy nakedness do
not appear; and anoint thine eyes with eye salve, that thou mayest see.*

REVELATION 3:18, KJV

The proper life for a believer is a life of faith: he lives "by the faith
of the Son of God." Our felt need keeps us "looking unto Jesus." To
suppose that we "have need of nothing" is to cease to live by faith.

Peter did not cry out, "Lord, save me!" until he was beginning
to sink—his need compelled him to seek Jesus. Self-complacency,
indolence, barrenness, and ignorance abound when the believer
does not "walk in the light, as He is in the light," in humble dependence upon the grace of God.

When circumstances, service, or anything else is sought after to
satisfy the heart, the grace of God is lost sight of, and a low and
unhealthy condition of soul is the sure result. Laodicean circumstances
were prosperous—"I am rich, and increased with goods"; but their
spiritual state was "wretched and miserable, and poor, and blind, and
naked," and *they knew it not*. Words of solemn import to us, beloved!

But there is restoring grace in Jesus as well as life-giving
grace—yea, all spiritual blessings. He counsels them to buy of Him
"gold tried in the fire," that they may be rich. Corruptible gold can
only be rightly estimated by comparing it with that which rust
doth not corrupt. Incorruptible blessings are to be had exclusively
of Him "who only hath immortality."

The common temptation presented to a declining saint is to
recover himself by redoubling his diligence in outward service, but
the counsel of the Lord is to come at once to the only source of
blessing—"Buy of Me," said He, though you are wretched, and
miserable, and poor; come, "buy of Me," without money, and without price.

Nothing is more important, when we discover that we have failed, than at once taking refuge at the throne of grace, remembering our compassionate and pitiful High Priest—our all-prevailing Advocate. No increase of effort to serve can procure the restoring grace needed; but "if we confess our sins, He is faithful and just to forgive us our sins, and to cleanse us from all unrighteousness"; or, though particular sins may not be laid on the conscience, the sense of a withered and barren state of soul should lead us to Him for refreshment, and new supplies of comfort and strength ... May we never forget the loving counsel of Jesus; and may it be ours, beloved, to respond to these gracious words, "Buy of Me gold tried in the fire, that thou mayest be rich."

He loves us to have *true* riches, but He well knows that every other refuge but Himself is deceitful, and that he who drinketh other than "living water will only thirst again."

"CRUMBS FOR THE LITTLE ONES"

*I*f a storm arise, and if Christ appear asleep, and insensible is the danger—though "he that keepeth Israel shall neither slumber nor sleep"—as disciples we are in the same boat with Him. The Lord give us to rest on that with undivided, undistracted hearts, for Christ is in the boat, as well as the water.

JOHN DARBY

October 21

Do not offer the parts of your body to sin, as instruments of wickedness, but rather offer yourselves to God, as those who have been brought from life to death; and offer the parts of your body to him as instruments of righteousness.

ROMANS 6:13

Consecration is a great word, but so much abused that it has lost much of its deepest significance. Abandonment is perhaps not an ordinary theological term, but is full of force. Whenever we make whole-hearted, absolute, unquestioning, positive, final abandonment of our life to God, filling with the Spirit results. Abandonment is twofold—abandonment to purification by the Spirit (Ephesians 4:30–31), and abandonment of the whole being to Jesus Christ so that He may offer it to God (Romans 6:13).

Abandonment may be easy to talk about, yet all men shrink from it. They would rather do anything else. But nothing can take the place of abandonment. Some people attempt to put prayer where God has put abandonment. Others profess to wait until God is willing to fill them.

Both are wrong! While they think they are waiting for God, God is waiting for them. At any moment, if they yield to the Spirit, He will sweep through every gate and avenue and into every corner of the life.

G. Campbell Morgan

The humblest believer walking in obedience to the Lord and dependence upon Him is displaying the greatest spiritual power. Power is displayed by the coming out of Christ in the daily life.

Edward Dennett

October 22

"I rejoice in the afflictions which I bear for your sake, and I fill up what yet is lacking of the sufferings of Christ . . . on behalf of the church."

Colossians 1:24, kjv

Is it not wonderful that the Christ of Calvary came and first lived the life He wants us to live? He came and lived it first, and then through His death, and our death with Him, He desires to live it all out again in us, saying of the poor dark world of men, "Through My children they will understand Me, for there is the same spirit in them as there was in Me."

We can see now why Paul was able to say, "I rejoice in the afflictions which I bear for your sake, and I fill up what yet is lacking of the sufferings of Christ. . . . on behalf of the church," and again in Philippians 2:17–18, "Though my blood be poured forth upon the ministration of your faith, I rejoice for myself, and with you all, and do ye likewise rejoice, both for yourselves and with me."

Do you "rejoice" when others are poured out for you for Christ's sake? Oh no, you say, I am willing to be spent, but I do not want anyone to be spent for me! Ah, but it takes much grace for some independent characters to allow anyone to be 'spent out' for them! But Paul said, "Though my blood is poured forth, I rejoice . . . and do ye likewise rejoice." Neither Paul, nor others, must be robbed of their fruit, when they desire to lay down their lives for others. How it pains when those in need are unwilling to have anything done for them.

Take heed lest there be "self" even in this. Christ, for the joy set before Him endured the Cross. There is a joy in sacrifice for others that is divine. "My joy I give unto you!" "Joy" on the eve of Calvary! This is the experiential path. Shall we follow it? You say, Yes? Then, let the Holy Spirit manage you, *and your circumstances,* and carry it out in His own way.

Jessie Penn-Lewis

*I*t is ever a fatal mistake when we measure the difficulties of service by what we are. The question is what God is; and the difficulties that appear as mountains, looming through the mists of our unbelief, are nothing to Him but the occasion for the display of His omnipotent power.

Edward Dennett

But whoso looketh into the perfect law of liberty and continueth there-in, he being not a forgetful hearer, but a doer of the work, this man shall be blessed in his deed.

JAMES 1:25, KJV

If a piece of iron could speak, what could it say of itself? "I am black; I am cold; I am hard." But put it in the furnace, and what a change takes place! It has not ceased to be iron; but the blackness is gone, and the coldness is gone, and the hardness is gone! It has entered into a new experience. The fire and the iron are still distinct, and yet how complete is the union—they are one.

If the iron could speak, it could not glory in itself, but in the fire that makes and keeps it a bright and glowing mass. So must it be with the believer. Do you ask him what he is in himself? He answers, "I am carnal, sold under sin." For, left to himself, this inevitably follows; he is brought into captivity to the law of sin which is in his members. But it is his privilege to enter into fellowship with Christ, and in Him to abide. And there, *in Him*, who is our life, our purity, and our power—in Him, whose Spirit can penetrate into every part of our being, the believer is no longer carnal, but spiritual; no longer overcome by sin and brought into captivity, but set free from the law of sin and death, and preserved in a condition of deliverance. This blessed experience of emancipation from sin's service and the power implies a momentary and continuous act of abiding.

The believer cannot glory in himself. He cannot glory in a state of purity attained, and having an existence apart from Christ Himself. He is like the piece of iron. The moment it is withdrawn from the furnace, the coldness and hardness and blackness begin to return. It is not by a work wrought in the iron once for all, but by the momentary and continual influence of the fire on the iron that its tendency to return to its natural condition is counteracted.

Such is the law of liberty in the spiritual life. We can thus understand how there may be a continuous experience of deliverance from the law of sin, and at the same time a deepening sense of our own natural depravity—a life of triumph over evil with a spirit of the truest humility.

EVAN HOPKINS

October 24

I am the living bread. Except ye eat the flesh of the Son of man, and drink his blood, ye have no life in you.

JOHN 6:53, KJV

*G*et hold of this clearly in your soul, my reader, that unless you have eaten the flesh of the Son of Man, and drunk His blood, *you* have no life in *you*; and do not think that this means the communion—the Lord's Supper. No—this is the substance; the Lord's Supper is the shadow. This is the reality, the communion is the figure. A man might eat the Lord's Supper a thousand times, and yet spend eternity in hell, but no man could eat the flesh of the Son of Man and not have eternal life.

When the Lord said this, He knew that He was going to die, and to rise again, and go, as man, to the right hand of God—that He was going to do a work whereby man might be brought to God, a work which enables the believer in Him in righteousness to go to the spot where He now is; and therefore here the Lord presses the necessity of knowing Himself, of eating Himself, saying, "Whoso eateth my flesh, and drinketh my blood, hath eternal life; and I will raise him up at the last day." Again, "He that eateth my flesh, and drinketh my blood, dwelleth in me, and I in him."

In plain words He says to the believer, We are one. In view of the gravity of this matter, let me ask you, my reader, Have you ever yet eaten the flesh, and drunk the blood of the Son of Man? That is a question that you must answer to God, and to Him alone.

It is a very happy thing to eat the Lord's Supper with the saints of God, but that is only the symbol; whereas what the Lord means here is, we must accept Him in His death, and feed on Him in death. Thereby only can we get life to our souls.

The result of this ministry of the Lord's was that the Jews murmur; and He then says, "Doth this offend you? What if ye shall see the Son of man ascend up where He was before?" (vv. 61, 62). He has ascended, and consequently we are immensely better off than if He were on earth. If He were on earth now—say in Jerusalem— He would not be also in Edinburgh; but being in glory the Holy Ghost has come down to dwell among us, and to abide in each believer, and He gives us the sense of the Lord's presence no matter where we are located.

W. T. P. WOLSTON

I think I can say, through grace, that God's presence or absence alone distinguishes places to me.

WILLIAM BURNS

October 25

To the angel of the church in Laodicea write:

These are the words of the Amen, the faithful and true witness, the ruler of God's creation. I know your deeds, that you are neither cold nor hot. I wish you were either one or the other! So, because you are lukewarm—neither hot nor cold—I am about to spit you out of my mouth. You say, "I am rich; I have acquired wealth and do not need a thing." But you do not realize that you are wretched, pitiful, poor, blind and naked. I counsel you to buy from me gold refined in the fire, so you can become rich; and white clothes to wear, so you can cover your shameful nakedness; and salve to put on your eyes so you can see. Those whom I love I rebuke and discipline. So be earnest, and repent . . . To him who overcomes, I will give the right to sit with me on my throne, just as I overcame and sat down with my Father on his throne.

REVELATION 3:14–21

$\mathscr{P}$erhaps the most effective weapon that Satan has ever used against a Christian is to surround him with prosperity and then let him be in as close contact as possible with a spiritually dead and indifferent world. Then, if he can, he will add to that, contact with professing Christians who are living in the world.

The Christian then falls into sin and wonders why he has no power to break away from it. The last state of the professing church just before the LORD comes is pictured in the letter to the Laodiceans. They think they are "rich, and increased with goods, and have need of nothing."

If we are now living in this Laodicean period, then we are called upon to resist, and to overcome this lukewarm state, lukewarm toward Him. What a pitiful picture Samson must have been as he stood powerless before the Philistines, and all because his hair, which was a mark of his separation unto God, had been cut off. Because he was no longer a separated one, he was powerless.

How many times have we seen Bible teachers who once gave new, fresh things from the Word when they were in close fellowship with Him, suddenly become powerless, and repeaters of their own and of other men's thoughts. Oh, let us all draw near and delight more in Him. Let His blessed Person be our chief joy. An assumed earnestness cannot make up for close fellowship with Him. Nothing can take the place of eating the Word.

LEBARON KINNEY

The fishes of the sea live in salt water, yet when we eat boiled fish there is no salt taste in the water in which they have been boiled. They have lived in an atmosphere impregnated with salt, yet they have kept free from its flavor. So do true Christians live in the world, without taking it into their hearts.

SADU SUNDAR SINGH

October 26

. . . I shall be anointed with fresh oil.
PSALM 92:10B

*S*piritual health is certain when he who is our life is given constant access to the whole being, and his access to our whole being is certain when we are in the attitude of consent to his will. It is this alone that will open the doors for Christ to possess us in his fullness, and a continuance in this attitude is the only thing that will keep the doors open.

This is why there is such a crying need for revival in the Church today. A revival is the only thing that will drive out disease and renew spiritual vigor. A revival is not a series of evangelistic meetings, but it is that opening of the whole being to God which permits the renewed inflow of his reviving life into ours. A series of meetings may bring us to see our need of a fresh yielding to God, and so bring revival, or a revival of the membership of a church may move them to hold a series of meetings to reach the lost; but the revival we need is not extra meetings, but a renewal of the life of God within us.

J. E. CONANT

October 27

Knowing this, that the trying of your faith worketh patience.
JAMES 1:3, KJV

A person whose ancestors for three or four generations have all been Christians, may inherit their virtues; but although affecting his life for good, they do not count before God as righteousness, for they are not the fruit of the directly imparted divine life. A believer may thus inherit patience, and although he may be but a babe in Christ, he is seen to be more stable than a more advanced believer, because whatever goes wrong he stands unruffled.

To empty him, the Father puts him in circumstances where his natural "patience" fails. After repeated failures of his natural virtue of patience, he realizes that it is not enough to meet all trials, and carry him triumphantly through them all. Then he turns to the Father to give him His own unfailing patience.

EVAN ROBERTS

*H*appy the person who has an empty vessel and God waiting ever ready to fill it. Unhappy they who have no empty vessel.

GEORGE V. WIGRAM

October 28

The Spirit and the bride say, "Come!" And let him who hears say, "Come!" Whoever is thirsty, let him come; and whoever wishes, let him take the free gift of the water of life.
REVELATION 22:17

*W*hen you are physically thirsty, how do you get water into yourself? You drink. God has made the provision, but you must make the decision whether you will be Spirit-filled or not. There is a boundary line, the right of every person to choose, beyond which even God cannot go. God has set a feast before you, but He cannot compel you to eat. He has opened the door into the abundant life, but He cannot compel you to enter. He places in the bank a spiritual deposit that makes you a spiritual multimillionaire, but He cannot write your checks. God has done His part, now you must do yours. The responsibility for fullness or lack of fullness is now in your hands. God is hindered by one thing only—the room that you give Him to fill. You have a clearly defined part in becoming spiritual.

RUTH PAXSON

If I am abiding in my risen Lord, it will show itself. I shall not be afraid of changes around me. I shall live not in apathy and listlessness, but in the exercise of lively affections and energies toward my Lord. Another great evidence of my abiding in Him is quietness. I have my portion in Him above, and I walk in it.

JOHN DARBY

October 29

And Abraham called the name of that place Jehovah-jireh.
GENESIS 22:14, KJV

When Abraham was about to sacrifice his son and saw no way of escape, the Lord provided a lamb for the sacrifice and delivered Isaac. Abraham made the grand discovery that it was one of the characteristics of Jehovah to see and provide for the needs of His people. Therefore, he called Him Jehovah-jireh—the Lord will see, or the Lord will provide.

A great many Christians today have never made Abraham's discovery. They do not know that the Lord is Jehovah-jireh. They are trusting Him to save their souls in the future, but they never dream He wants to carry their cares for them now.

They are like a man with a heavy load on his back who was given a lift by a friend. He thankfully climbed into the vehicle, but still kept his burden on his back, bowed down under the weight of it.

"Why do you not put your burden down on the bottom of the carriage?" asked his friend.

"Oh," replied the man, "it is a great deal to ask you to carry me, and I could not ask you to carry my burden also."

You wonder how anyone could be so silly, and yet are you not doing the same? Are you trusting the Lord to take care of you, but still carrying your burdens on your own shoulders?

Who is the silliest—that man or you?

HANNAH WHITALL SMITH

*C*an you spread out no wants before Christ, the Giver, the Healer? Believers grieve the Spirit by not *using* Christ, and then God must find means to compel them to do it.

GEORGE V. WIGRAM

October 30

He is not a man like me that I might answer him, that we might confront each other in court. If only there were someone to arbitrate between us, to lay his hand upon us both, someone to remove God's rod from me, so that his terror would frighten me no more.

JOB 9:32–34

*Y*ou cannot keep up being a Christian for a day. You cannot follow Christ for a single hour. You are not asked to. All you are asked to do is as you have received Christ Jesus the Lord so to keep on walking in Him; drawing from His fullness for all your needs, drawing upon His resources.

Your repentance is inadequate, and always will be; you cannot feel shame and sorrow for sin as you ought to do. But the Lord Jesus can, and does, on your behalf. He has condemned sin in the flesh, even though it were His own flesh. He has taken sides with God against sin on your behalf; He has taken sides with you. He is the Daysman between the two (Job 9:33).

You cannot love God as you ought to do. How many honest Christian hearts there are who are constantly bemoaning their lack of love to God! Of course you do not love God as you ought to; you never will. God does not ask for any measure of love from you to obtain salvation, but He asks you to accept His love, and having accepted His love, that love of His to you will be radiated back again from you to Him. Your love is weak and poor enough, and though you loved Him enough to die a martyr's death, your love would be inadequate to the great love wherewith He has loved you.

So I pray you not to be occupied with your own state, your own condition, your own feelings, your own anything, but with Christ.

J. RUSSELL HOWDEN

*W*e are as dependent upon God when we speak to one soul as when we preach to a thousand. I have learned this by experience; I have gone to see a sick person in great self-confidence and found I had nothing to say. And then the Lord taught me I must wait upon Him for the message for a single soul as much as when I was going to preach. May we ever remember this, that there may be no trace of self-confidence remaining in the heart.

EDWARD DENNETT

> The lamp of the Lord searches the spirit of a man; it searches out his
> inmost being.
>
> PROVERBS 20:27

*G*od, though present everywhere, has His special residence as being a pure Spirit, in our minds—"In Him we live and move and have our being." He is somewhere in the recesses of our soul, in the spring of our existence, a light in that mysterious region of our nature where the wishes, feelings, thoughts, and emotions take their earliest rise. The mind is a sanctuary, in the center of which the Lord sits enthroned, the lamp of consciousness before Him.

ADOLPH SAPHIR

*C*hrist will fill all the needs of our intellectual life. Our mental capacities will never know their full wealth of power and spiritual effectiveness until they become simply the vessels of His quickening life.

These brains of ours are to be laid at His feet simply as the censers which are to hold His holy fire.

The fullness of the Holy Spirit will be within us a perpetual source of physical and mental energy, sufficient for every function and test of human life.

A. B. SIMPSON

When he noticed how the guests picked the places of honor at the table, he told them this parable: "When someone invites you to a wedding feast, do not take the place of honor, for a person more distinguished than you may have been invited. If so, the host who invited both of you will come and say to you, 'Give this man your seat.' Then, humiliated, you will have to take the least important place.

"But when you are invited, take the lowest place, so that when your host comes, he will say to you, 'Friend, move up to a better place.' Then you will be honored in the presence of all your fellow guests. For everyone who exalts himself will be humbled, and he who humbles himself will be exalted."

LUKE 14:7–11

Someone has said, "I never was truly happy until I ceased to wish to be great." This is a fine moral truth.

When we cease to wish to be anything, when we are content to be nothing, then it is that we taste what true greatness—true elevation—true happiness—true peace, really is. The restless desire to be something or somebody is destructive of the soul's tranquility.

To the proud heart and ambitious spirit this may seem a poor, unproductive attitude—but to those of us who have entered the school of Christ and have begun to learn of him who was meek and lowly in heart—when we have drunk, in any measure, into the spirit of Him who made Himself of no reputation, we then see things quite differently.

The way to go up is to go down. This is the doctrine of Christ, the doctrine which Jesus taught and modeled for us.

Remember "Jesus called a little child unto him, and set him in the midst of them, and said, Verily, I say unto you, except ye be converted, and become as little children, ye shall not enter into the kingdom of heaven. Whosoever, therefore, shall humble himself as this little child, the same is greatest in the kingdom of heaven" (Matt. 18:2–4).

This is the doctrine of heaven—the doctrine of self-emptiness. What a contrast we Christians are called to, when we consider the worldly scene of endless self-seeking and self-exaltation!

C. H. MACKINTOSH

*W*hen we are totally emptied of ourselves, we can be full of the Holy Spirit. Then we are conquerors, and are able to accept all things from His hand. Besides this, we are being prepared to inherit all things.

CORRIE TEN BOOM

*A*s you enjoy Christ for yourself saints will find it out, and that will be your testimony to them.

JOHN DARBY

November 2

But Joseph said to them, "Don't be afraid. Am I in the place of God? You intended to harm me, but God intended it for good to accomplish what is now being done, the saving of many lives. So then, don't be afraid. I will provide for you and your children." And he reassured them and spoke kindly to them.

GENESIS 50:19–21

*I*t is said of Joseph in the dungeon that "the iron entered into his soul." And what Joseph needed for his soul was, indeed, iron. He had seen only the glitter of the gold—the rejoicing in his youthful dreams and such dreams can harden the heart.

We too need the iron to enlarge us. The gold is but a vision. The iron is an experience.

GEORGE MATHESON

A man had a beautiful estate with magnificent trees on it. But he had a bitter enemy, who said, "I will cut down one of his trees; that will hurt him."

In the dark of the night the enemy slipped over the fence and went to the most beautiful of the trees, and with saws and axes he began to work. In the first light of morning he saw in the distance two men coming over the hill on horseback, and recognized one of them as the owner of the estate.

Hurriedly he pushed the wedges out and let the tree fall; but one of the branches caught him and pinned him to the ground, injuring him so badly that he died. Before he died, he screeched out, "Well, I have cut down your beautiful tree," and the estate owner looked at him with pity and said, "This is the architect I have brought with me. We had planned to build a house, and it was necessary to cut down one tree to make room for the house; and it is the one you have been working on all night."

Do not forget that anything the devil is working at, he is but cutting down a tree God had planned to cut down; he never did anything outside the overall plan of God, for God is omnipotent and omniscient and victorious.

DONALD GREY BARNHOUSE

*I*f the external plannings of men or Satan further God's plans, they succeed. If not, they come to nothing.

JOHN DARBY

November 3

But we have this treasure in earthen vessels, that the excellency of the power may be God, and not of us.

2 CORINTHIANS 4:2

$\mathcal{I}$t is cause for great gratitude to God that no human weakness need limit the divine power. We are apt to think that where sadness exists, there joy cannot exist; that where there are tears there cannot be praise; that where weakness is present power must be absent; that where there is doubt there cannot be faith. But let me proclaim this with a clear voice, that God is seeking to bring us to the point where we recognize that all that is of man is only intended to provide an earthen vessel to contain the divine treasure. Henceforth when we are conscious of depression let us not give way to depression, but to the Lord; and the treasure will shine forth all the more gloriously because of the earthen vessel. I am not theorizing here; I know what I am talking about. Herein lies the glory of Christianity, that God's treasure can be manifest in every earthen vessel. Christianity is a paradox, and it is as we Christians live in this paradoxical life that we get to know God. The further we go on in the Christian life, the more paradoxical it becomes. The treasure becomes increasingly manifest, but the earthen vessel is the earthen vessel still.

This is very beautiful. Just look at the divine patience in a man who by nature is impatient, and compare the sight of that with a man whom nothing can ever move. See the divine humility in one who by nature is haughty, and compare that with one who is always of a retiring disposition. See the strength of God in a person of weak temperament, and compare that with a naturally strong character. The difference is tremendous.

People who are naturally weak are always apt to think they are no good because of the earthen quality of the vessel; but there is no need for dejection since the treasure within the vessel is of such a quality as to shine forth with added splendor from within such a vessel.

Brothers and Sisters, let me say once again that the whole question is one of the quality of the treasure, not of the quality of the vessel that contains it. It is folly to stress the negative aspect; our concern is with the positive. The Lord is able to manifest Himself in the life of every one of us, and when that comes to pass many will behold the treasure.

WATCHMAN NEE

*Y*ou yourself may ebb and flow, rise and fall, wax and wane, but your Lord is this day as He was yesterday; and it is your comfort that your salvation is not rolled upon wheels of your own making, neither have you to do with a Christ of your own shaping.

SAMUEL RUTHERFORD

November 4

If thine eye be single, thy whole body shall be full of light.
MATTHEW 6:22, KJV

*I*t is an immense thing for those who were once mere men on earth, severed from God and in spirit from each other by sin, only united when united for objects of human will or glory, now as His children with one purpose of heart to walk so as to please God. Yet such is Christianity practically viewed; and it is worthless if not practical.

It is true that there is in the light and truth, which Christ has revealed by the Holy Spirit, the richest material and the fullest scope for the renewed mind and heart. But there is in the mystery no breadth, no length, no height nor depth, which does not bear on the state of the affections or the character of the walk and work; and no error more dishonors God or damages man than the divorce of theory from practice.

Scripture binds them together indissolubly, warning us solemnly against those whom would part them, as evil, the sure enemies of

God and man. No truth is not merely to inform, but to sanctify, and what we received from those divinely given to communicate it is "how we ought to walk and please God."

In that path the youngest believer walks from the first, slave or free, Greek or Scythian, learned or unlearned; from that path none can slip save into sin and shame. It is not, however, a mere defined direction, as in a law or ordinance. As a life is in question, the life of Christ, there is exercise and growth by the knowledge of God.

On the state of the soul depends the discernment of God's will in His word, which is overlooked, where levity marks the inner condition, or the will is active and unjudged. Then only is there surefootedness spiritually; and a deepening sense of the word in the intelligence issues in a fuller obedience.

One knows God's mind better, and the heart is earnest in pleasing Him.

We abound more and more.

WILLIAM KELLY

November 5

Thou therefore endure hardness, as a good soldier of Jesus Christ.
2 TIMOTHY 2:3, KJV

We live in a day when the temptation to the indulgence of the flesh is very great. Luxuries are common. Piety and prosperity seldom go hand in hand, and in many a case the prosperity that piety and power have brought has been the ruin of the man to whom it has come. Not a few ministers of power have become popular and in demand. With the increasing popularity has come an increase of pay and of the comforts of life. Luxurious living has come in, and the power of the Spirit has gone out.

It would not be difficult to cite specific instances of this sad truth. If we would know the continuance of the Spirit's power, we need to be on guard to lead lives of simplicity, free from indulgence and surfeiting, ever ready to "endure hardness as a good soldier of Jesus Christ." I frankly confess I am afraid of luxury—not as afraid of it as I am of sin, but it comes next as an object of dread. It is a very subtle but a very potent enemy of power.

R. A. TORREY

*S*he Lord gets his best soldiers out of the highlands of affliction.

CHARLES SPURGEON

November 6

All things are lawful unto me, but all things are not expedient: all things are lawful for me, but I will not be brought under the power of any.

2 CORINTHIANS 6:12, KJV

*I*t is a wholly false principle that natural gifts are a reason for using them. I may have amazing strength or speed in running; I knock a man down with one, and win a prize cup with another. Music may be a more refined thing, but the principle is the same. This point I believe to be now of all importance. Christians have lost their moral influence by bringing in nature and the world as harmless. All things are lawful to me. But you cannot mix flesh and Spirit. We need all our energies under grace to walk in the latter, always bearing about in the body the dying of the Lord Jesus, that the life of Jesus may be manifested in our bodies.

Let Christ be all, and the eye is single and the whole body full of light. The converse is if our eye be evil, because it shuts out

Christ; our affections are not set on things above where Christ sits at God's right hand. That is the point for us, happy affections there, and steadfastly, not being distracted.

JOHN DARBY

*C*hurch of the living God! Be warned. Please not thyself, even as Jesus pleased not Himself. Live for Him, not for thyself, for Him not for the world. Walk worthy of thy name and calling, worthy of Him who bought thee as His bride, worthy of thine everlasting inheritance.

HORATIUS BONAR

November 7

. . . that God may be all in all . . .
1 CORINTHIANS 15:28, KJV

*W*e are assured that the power which worketh in us is all-sufficient to do exceeding abundantly above all our desire or thought. We *have* the power; we do not have to *get* it.

But let us remember ever that this power is not ours. It is never bestowed upon us, if I may so speak, in bulk. We have not a great mass of power given to us; we have no storage batteries, to use an illustration familiar to us. We have not strength in ourselves for a single moment. More than this, I am sure we are not to expect to be conscious of power.

We will be conscious of weakness, and the Spirit's power works through our weakness. We never feel as spiritual giants, ready to perform wonderful feats of strength. Ah, no! such was not Paul. His speech was not with enticing words of man's wisdom. His bodily presence was weak, and his speech contemptible; but the faith of those who heard him was established in the power of God.

God's great men are servants; God's mighty men are weak; God's noble men are base and despised—that no flesh might glory in His presence.

Such, beloved brethren, I believe to be the teaching of the word of God upon this all-important theme. It has been put briefly and meagerly, but if you are convinced that the way of power lies in just the opposite direction from that which is ordinarily supposed, I shall have hope that you will go on to learn the secret of it—"Not I, but Christ."

SAMUEL RIDOUT

The true life of holiness, the life of them are sanctified in Christ, has its root and its strength in an abiding sense of utter impotence, in the deep restfulness which trusts to the working of a Divine power and life, in the entire personal surrender to the loving Savior, in that faith which consents to be nothing, that He may be all.

It may appear impossible to discern or describe the difference between the working that is of self and the working that is of Christ through faith—if we but know that there is such a difference, if we learn to distrust ourselves, and to count on Christ working, the Holy Spirit will lead us into this secret of the Lord too.

Faith's works are Christ's works.

ANDREW MURRAY

November 8

A man is not a Jew if he is only one outwardly, nor is circumcision merely outward and physical. No, a man is a Jew if he is one inwardly; and circumcision of the heart, by the Spirit, not by the written code. Such a man's praise is not from men, but from God.

ROMANS 2:28–29

The Cross is the birthplace of a new creation for everyone who turns to Christ as his Savior, but it is also in a wider sense the birthplace of the NEW MAN consisting of Christ and His members. Each member who becomes a new creation in his own life, is but one of many units who, tempered together, form a body with Christ as Head.

All partaking of one life, made to drink of one Spirit, is "fitly framed and knit together through every joint of the supply, according to the working in due measure of each, several part, maketh the increase of the body . . . in love."

Through the Cross all the divisions of the fallen creation are done away. Distinctions of nationality or sect no longer divide, but are part of the outward order of things of earth, which are surface and temporary. For "the new man" created by God, is being renewed in the believer in a sphere in Christ, "where there cannot be Greek and Jew, circumcision and uncircumcision, Barbarian, Scythian, bondman, freeman, but Christ is all and in all . . ." and also where there "can be no male or female: for all are one man in Christ Jesus." It means, blessed be God, that no external and temporary distinction can enter that sphere in Christ where CHRIST IS ALL, and in all.

Calvary, therefore, is the center of unity for all who are in Christ a new creation. The more completely we apprehend that divisions and disunions between men who profess to follow the same Lord, belong to the old creation, and "put off the old man with his doings," the more quickly will the prayer of the Lord be answered, for His own, "that they maybe made perfect in one."

Calvary, too, is the place of reconciliation between men who, according to the flesh, may be irreconcilable through prejudice, upbringing, or religious ideals. At Calvary, "Jew and Gentile" ceased to be Jew and Gentile as they each became members of the new man—Christ—and so they were reconciled "through the Cross," Christ having "slain the enmity thereby."

Where the believer has really and experimentally apprehended his death in the death of Christ, and learned his place in the Body of Christ; that we are members one of another, as well as of Christ, the inward spirit union of life in Christ is kept unbroken. With Calvary as the center and basis of unity, no other member of Christ, can ever be looked upon as an "opponent," whilst we witness to truth which that fellow member of Christ may not yet apprehend.

When all the members of Christ can see in that death on the Tree their own death, not only to sin, but to all that pertains to the religion of the "old man," they will find a practical and real oneness with all who are one with their Risen and Ascended Head.

JESSIE PENN-LEWIS

*W*ork together in harmony, struggle together, run together, suffer together, rest together, rise together, as stewards, advisors and servants of God.

Seek to please Him whose soldiers you are and from whom you draw your sustenance; let none of you prove a deserter. Let your baptism be your arms, your faith your helmet, your love your spear, your patience your armor.

Let your good works be your deposits, so that you may draw out well-earned savings. So be patient and gentle with one another, as God is with you. May I have joy in you forever!

IGNATIUS OF ANTIOCH, MARTYR (AD 116),
WRITING TO POLYCARP OF SMYRNA (AD 156)

November 9

He who has an ear, let him hear what the Spirit says to the churches. To him who overcomes, I will give the right to eat from the tree of life, which is in the paradise of God.

REVELATION 2:7

O Friends! Feed on the tree of life; feed on the measure of life, and the pure power which God has revealed and manifested in you. Do you know where your real food comes from, do you remember the taste? Then keep to it, and do not meddle with the kind of food that seems desirable to the other eye, the one that promises to make you wise.

O abide in the simplicity that is in Christ Jesus, in the naked truth that you have felt there! It is there that you will be able to know and distinguish your food, which has several names in Scripture but is all one and the same thing: the bread, the milk, the water, the wine, the flesh, and blood of him who came down from heaven.

It is all the same food, only it is given to us in different measure—sometimes weaker, sometimes stronger—according to the capacity we have for receiving it.

ISAAC PENNINGTON

The Christian is humble . . . because he has given up seeking good in himself to adore the One in whom there is nothing else.

JOHN DARBY

November 10

"If ye continue in my word, then are ye my disciples indeed."
JOHN 8:31, KJV

The more you nourish your own soul by feeding on the Word of God, the more likely He is to use you.

JOHN DARBY

The true end of Bible study is not culture, but character; not a well-stored mind, but a well-ordered life. Consider though, the latter, is dependent on the former, and the former is the condition of the latter.

Our experiential knowledge of God is dependent upon His revelation of Himself to us, and the highest form of this revelation we find in the Bible.

I must, therefore, know the Bible if I would know Him. What do we know Christ apart from the Bible? Take from us the Bible and all the knowledge we have gathered from it, and we would be utterly ignorant that there had ever been a Christ in human history. The only way we can get back to Christ is by getting back to the Bible.

W. GRAHAM SCROGGIE

$\mathcal{W}$e do not read scripture with sufficient intimacy of heart. We read it as if we are acquainting ourselves with words and sentences. If I do not get by scripture into nearness to God in heart and conscience, I have not learned the lesson it would teach me.

J. G. BELLETT

November 11

Let the people praise thee, O God; let all the people praise thee. Then shall the earth yield her increase; and God, even our own God shall bless us.

PSALM 67:5–6, KJV

$\mathcal{T}$his matter of praising God is far more important than most Christians realize. There is a reason underlying the repeated command, "Praise ye the Lord."

God knows what praise will do for His children; therefore not once, but many, many times, He bids them utter the words of praise.

If a word of discouragement opens the door for the enemy, then a word of praise closes the door and locks it. Moreover it drives the enemy far away. Nothing is more distasteful to the powers of darkness than the praise of a trustful child of God, and nothing more truly glorifies God than the sacrifice of praise.

God has commanded His people to praise Him, and certain conditions will not be realized until all obey (Psalm 67:5–6). Viewed from the psychological and physiological standpoints, the value of praise can scarcely be estimated, as it is impossible to tabulate all the beneficial results to be realized in the spiritual, mental, and physical realms as this command is obeyed.

What would be the result if Christians should begin to praise God continually? Surely great deliverance would be realized throughout the earth, and angels would see the clearing of the heavens as the reverberations of the praises of God's people mounted upward; and God would be glorified. Yet the average Christian considers literal obedience to the oft-repeated command, "Praise ye the Lord," as foolish and fanatical, choosing instead to praise Him only when he feels like doing so.

Mary McDonough

November 12

Being justified freely by his grace through the redemption that is in Christ Jesus . . .
Romans 3:23, kjv

The worker must be justified before God, before he can work any good thing. Men judge the worker by the works; God judges the works by the worker. The first precept requires us to acknowledge and worship one God, that is, to trust Him alone, which is the true faith whereby we become the sons of God. Thou canst not be delivered from the evil of unbelief by thine own power, nor by the power of the law; wherefore all they works which thou doest to satisfy the law, can be nothing by works of the law; of far less importance than to be able to justify thee before God, who counteth them righteous only who truly believe in Him; for they that acknowledge Him the true God are His sons, and do truly fulfill the law. If thou shouldst even kill thyself by working, thy heart can not obtain this faith thereby, for thy works are even a hindrance to it, and cause thee to persecute it.

Whatsoever we do of our own power and strength, that which is not wrought in us by His grace, without doubt is a work of the law, and avails nothing toward justification; but is displeasing to God, because of the unbelief wherein it is done. He that trusts in works does nothing freely and with a willing mind; he would do no good work at all if he were not compelled by the fear of hell, or allured by the hope of present good. Whereby it is plainly seen that they strive only for gain, or are moved with fear, showing that they rather hate the law from their hearts, and had rather there were no law at all. An evil heart can do nothing that is good. This evil propensity of the heart, and unwillingness to do good, the law betrays, when it teaches that God does not esteem the works of the hand, but those of the heart.

MARTIN LUTHER

*N*ot a single cluster of living fruit was, or ever will be, culled from the tree of legality. Law can only produce "dead works," from which we need to have conscience purged just as much as from "wicked works."

C. H. MACKINTOSH

The steps of a good man are ordered by the LORD and he delighteth in his way.

PSALM 37:23, KJV

To penetrate deeper in the experience of Jesus Christ, it is required that you begin to abandon your whole existence, giving it up to God. Let us take the daily occurrences of life as an illustration. You must utterly believe that the circumstances of your life, that is, every minute of your life, as well as the whole course of your life—anything, yes, *everything* that happens—have all come to you by His will and by His permission. You must utterly believe that everything that has happened to you is from God and is exactly what you need.

Such an outlook towards your circumstances and such a look of faith towards you Lord will make you content with everything. Once you believe this, you will then begin to take everything that comes into your life as being from the hand of God, not from the hand of man.

JEANNE GUYON

Is it not a thing worth having, to have this settled conviction of your hearts, that Christ is moving through all the impulses of your life, and that nothing falls out without the intervention of His presence and the power of His will working through it? Do you not think that such belief would gird you up for difficulty, and would lift you buoyantly over trials and depressions, and would see you upon a vantage ground high above all the petty annoyances of life?

Tell me, is there any other place a Christian can plant his foot and say, "Now I am on a rock and I care not what comes!"

ALEXANDER MACLAREN

I am the LORD, the God of all mankind. Is anything too hard for me?
JEREMIAH 32:27

*T*here was a time in my Christian life when I was passing through a great deal of questioning and perplexity. I felt that no Christian had ever had such peculiar difficulties as mine. There happened to be staying near me for a few weeks, a lady who was considered to be a deeply spiritual Christian. I summoned up my courage one afternoon and went to see her. I poured out my troubles to her, expecting that she would take a deep interest in me and would do all she could to help me.

She listened patiently enough and did not interrupt me. But when I had finished my story and paused, expecting sympathy, she simply said, "Yes, all you say may be very true, but then, in spite of it all, there is God."

I waited a few minutes for something more, but nothing came. My friend and teacher had the attitude of having said all that was necessary.

"But," I continued, "surely you did not understand how very serious and perplexing my difficulties are."

"Oh yes, I did," replied my friend, "but then, as I tell you, there is God."

I could not induce her to make any other answer. It seemed to me most disappointing and unsatisfactory. I felt that my peculiar and difficult experiences could not be met by anything so simple as the statement, "Yes, but there is God." I knew God was there, of course, but I felt I needed something more than just God. I came to the conclusion that my friend, for all her great reputation as a spiritual teacher, was at any rate not able to handle my problems.

My need was so great, however, that I did not give up with my first attempt. I went to her again and again, always with the hope that she would sometime begin to understand the importance of my difficulties and would give me adequate help. It was of no use. I was never able to draw forth any other answer. Always to every-thing would come the simple reply, "Yes, I know; but there is always God."

At last, by power of her continual repetition, I became con-vinced that my friend truly believed that the mere fact of the exis-tence of God, as the Creator and Redeemer of mankind, and of me as a member of the race, was an all-sufficient answer to every pos-sible need. She said it so often and seemed so sure that I began to wonder whether God might be enough, even for my overwhelm-ing and peculiar need. From wondering I came gradually to believ-ing that, since He is my Creator and Redeemer, He must be enough. A conviction burst upon me that He truly was enough. My eyes were opened to the absolute and utter all-sufficiency of God.

My troubles disappeared, and I wondered how I could ever have been such an idiot as to be troubled by them, when all the while there was God. The Almighty and All-seeing God, the God who had created me, was on my side and eager to care for me and help me. I had found out that God was enough, and my soul was at rest.

HANNAH WHITALL SMITH

Could it be possible that God would so love an individual as to give His only Son to die for him and still love him to the extent of fol-lowing him with the pleadings and drawings of His grace until He has won that soul into His own family and created him anew by the impartation of His own divine nature, and then be careless as to what becomes of the one He has thus given His all to procure?

LEWIS SPERRY CHAFER

. . . happy is that people whose God is the LORD.
PSALM 144:15B

$\mathcal{S}$ee what easy, pleasant lives the people of God might live, if it were not for their own faults. There are those who fear God and work righteousness, and are accepted of the Lord, but go drooping and disconsolate from day to day, are full of cares, and fears, and complaints, and make themselves always uneasy; and it is because they do not live that life of delight in God, and dependence on him, that they might and should live.

God has effectually provided for their dwelling at ease, but they make not use of that provision he has laid up for them.

Oh that all who appear to be conscientious, and are afraid of sin, would appear to be cheerful, and afraid of nothing, else; that all who call God Father, and are in care to please him, and keep themselves in his love, would learn to cast all their other care upon him, and commit their way to him as a Father. He shall choose our inheritance for us, and knows what is best for us, better than we do for ourselves. "Thou shalt answer, Lord, for me." It is what I have often said, and will abide by, "That a holy, heavenly life, spent in the service of God, and in communion with him, is the most pleasant, comfortable life anybody can live in this world."

MATTHEW HENRY

$\mathcal{T}$he Christian suffers the same calamities as others, perhaps even worse; he faces difficulties and losses in the things of this life; he has to be prepared to meet death itself. In all these circumstances he is calm and trustful; he is not only sure of ultimately going to heaven, but already abides there and enjoys something of it in his own heart.

God is real to him and ever near. He knows a peace which passes all understanding, and he experiences a joy which no man can take from him. This, surely, should be our testimony in the world, but it can only be as the Lord Jesus Himself lives out this life in us.

H. F.

With God all things are possible.

MATTHEW 19:26, KJV

*W*hen walking in the narrow path, and realizing the daily difficulties of the Christian life, the grand truth that God is a God of
impossibilities, will afford a deep solace and consolation to the
tempted and harassed soul.

Whilst he contemplates this glorious character of God, he will
be led, in calmness and composure, to lay all difficulties at the foot-
stool of divine grace: he will be led to look less at the difficulties and
more at God: he will be less often disappointed, and oftener made
glad: he will be led to consider matters, and as this or that will be for
God's glory; easy though it be or difficult, he will plead with One
whom he knows is fully able to maintain his own glory and honor,
though, as to sight and reason, there may be many obstacles. The history of the children of Israel fully verifies this character of God.

Have we any difficulties, personal, family or others of graver
nature? Yea, have we not many? Let it be our business then to prove
our God, and to know Him as the God of wonders. Jeremiah pleads
thus, "Ah, Lord God! behold Thou has made the heaven and the earth
by Thy great power and stretched out arm, and there is nothing to
hard for Thee" (Jer. 32:17). Our blessed Lord said, "With God all things
are possible" (Matt. 19:26). And this He himself pleads in His hour of
sorrow, "Abba, Father, all things are possible unto Thee" (Mark 14:36).

The amount of our faith in this business is of great importance;
but these remarks are rather for those of weak faith, pointing out to
such what a God we have to do with. It is often said in such and
such a trial, "Oh! it is past hope!" the smile on the lips betrays the
unbelief of the heart, and many a child of trial succumbs under it
with the impression that there is no remedy.

Moses says, "Who is like unto Thee, O Lord, among the Gods? who
is like Thee glorious in holiness, fearful in praises, doing wonders"

(Ex.15:11). Isaiah testifies that "His name shall be called Wonderful" (Is. 9:6), and says, that "the Lord of Hosts is wonderful in counsel, and excellent in working" (Is. 28:29).

Even Job says that He does "great things, past finding out; yea, and wonders without number" (Job 9:10): and Daniel declares of Him that "He delivereth and rescueth, and He worketh signs and wonders in heaven and in earth" (Dan. 6:27).

The Scriptures, however, abound in similar testimony, and the more we read them, the more shall we learn, amid other things, of the character of God.

Let the timid, and tempted, and cast down, in this cloudy and dark day, be encouraged to trust in God, and to remember that "The things which are impossible with men are possible with God" (Luke 18:27).

Faith is a mighty principle; it grasps great things, because it is dealing with God. Oh, how near to God our souls are brought when we thus deal with Him, no matter how great the difficulties! It seems as though we had got up into one of the high mountains, from whence the men and things below look very small, and comparatively insignificant. "O give thanks to the Lord of lords; for His mercy endureth forever. To Him who ALONE doeth GREAT WONDERS: for His mercy endureth forever" (Ps. 136:3–4).

"CRUMBS FOR THE LORD'S LITTLE ONES"

The strength of the vessel can be demonstrated only by the hurricane, and the power of the Gospel can be fully shown only when the believer is subjected to some fiery trial.

If the Father would make manifest the fact that "He giveth songs in the night," He must first make it night.

W. TROTTER

When *no* circumstances lead you to have any hope, is your hope then in Him?

JOHN DARBY

November 17

When he shall come to be glorified in his saints, and to be admired in all them . . .

2 THESSALONIANS 1:10, KJV

*C*hrist vindicated in His saints—a glorious thing. We who, here and now in this world, have been despised, who have been thought little or nothing of, we who have been set aside, who have been maligned, have been persecuted, who have suffered simply because Christ is in us, simply because of our union with Christ—oh, what it has meant, what it has sometimes cost!—that Christ in us is going to be glorified in us and marveled at in us. The scene is going to change: the indwelling of Christ is not always going to be a thing which means suffering, adversity, persecution, sorrow and trial. The indwelling of Christ ultimately in the consummation is going to be a most glorious thing—glorified in His saints and marveled at. We can understand that, if we view Him objectively, we shall marvel at Him when we see Him. But here the statement is that He is going to be marveled at in all them that have believed. It is the vindication of Christ and the vindication of the saints.

T. AUSTIN-SPARKS

*N*ever fear persecution; it will make your face shine as an angel's.

JOHN DARBY

November 18

No one can come to me unless the Father who sent me draws him, and I will raise him up at the last day.

JOHN 6:44

*S*alvation is wholly of grace, not only undeserved but undesired by us until God is pleased to awaken us to a sense of our need of it.

And then we find everything prepared that our wants require or our wishes conceive; yea, that He has done exceedingly beyond what we could either ask or think.

Salvation is wholly of the Lord and bears those signatures of infinite wisdom, power, and goodness which distinguish all His works from the puny imitations of men. It is every way worthy of Himself, a great, a free, a full, a sure salvation. It is great whether we consider the objects (miserable, hell-deserving sinners), the end (the restoration of such alienated creatures to His image and favor, to immortal life and happiness) or the means (the incarnation, humiliation, sufferings and death of His beloved Son).

It is free, without exception of persons or cases, without any conditions or qualifications, but such as He, Himself, performs in them and bestows upon them.

JOHN NEWTON

*D*o we not often harbor the thought that something yet remains to be done—either by ourselves or by Him—in order for us to draw near?

Do we not often thus become occupied with the circumstancials of worship rather than with the Lord Jesus—the substance?

Are we not often false to Him in questioning our right to draw near because we find distance in our own hearts, as if it was the warmth of our affections, instead of the blood of the Lord Jesus, which brings us near?

WILLIAM KELLY

That he would grant you, according to the riches of his glory, to be strengthened with might by his Spirit in the inner man.

EPHESIANS 3:16, KJV

*W*e ought to rise higher in experience. How much of the fullness of Divine grace we know almost nothing of! How much belongs to us in Christ that we have never claimed as personally our own!

To say that it is the privilege of every Christian to enjoy to the utmost the blessings that flow to him from his union to Christ is not to say enough. It is more than his privilege. It is his duty as well. We not only may be, but ought to be, "Strengthened with all might by His spirit in the inner man," "abounding in hope," "kept in perfect peace." But do we really seek this? Do we actually attain it? Is it uncharitable to say that most Christians are only barely alive?

Their spiritual pulse is feeble; their spiritual progress is slow; their spiritual victories are few; their spiritual joys are poor. There is no vigor in their faith. If they see at all it is only dimly. The full sunshine they never know. The clouds hang always low and trail heavily across their sky. This poor and meager experience is certainly better than no experience of grace at all; just as a sick man is better than a dead man. But when Christ comes to do His saving work upon us, He does not restore us from death to sickliness; He restores from death to the fullness of happy life.

Why do we not enjoy the assured position He gives us? Why do we walk so often with drooping face and downcast eye when Christ has risen a Conqueror, to make us sharers in His triumph over sin and death and hell? Looking upon our gloom-covered faces, listening to our cheerless, half-faithless tones, who would ever dream that we were the heirs of a glorious liberty obtained for us by the Christ who dies, and rose again, and lives for evermore?

G. H. KNIGHT

*O*h do not be satisfied with ordinary Christianity, but be saying, "If nobody else is heavenly minded, why not I? If others are not full of the Holy Spirit, why not I?"

GEORGE V. WIGRAM

November 20

It hath fully been shewed me, all that thou hast done unto thy mother in law since the death of thine husband; and how thou hast left thy father and thy mother, and the land of thy nativity, and art come unto a people which thou knewest not heretofore: The Lord recompense thy work and a full reward be given thee of the Lord God, under whose wings thou art come to rest.

RUTH 2:11–12, KJV

*T*hus Boaz blessed Ruth—a blessing which he afterwards (like all blessers) shared in himself—and he also commanded his young men, saying, "Let her glean among the sheaves, and reproach her not; and let fall some of the handfuls of purpose for her, and leave them, that she may glean them, and rebuke her not." Thus we see Ruth receives more on account of her devotion to Naomi than she obtains by her honest and continual toil; and this is always the case. However great the recompense for faithful service, that of devotion immeasurably exceeds it.

Had Ruth gone to the field to glean as did the other hand-maidens, she would have obtained her due, what her labor merited, but no more. But it was far otherwise with her; devotedness to one (Naomi) was the spring of all her work, and the result was to her, as we shall find it to ourselves when animated with alike spirit— the in-gathering is exceeding abundant. And not only so, the devoted one is led on, step by step, until she attains full rest, honor and, finally, inheritance.

The sequel of her history shows us this: she ultimately becomes the wife of Boaz, the true kinsman, who redeems the inheritance; and according to the blessing pronounced on her she builds up the royal house of David, even as Rachel and Leah built up the house of Israel. The poor Moabitess is brought into close proximity to the throne of Judah, and she makes the name of her kinsman-redeemer "famous" in Bethlehem-Ephratah, the place of death and resurrection!

A wondrous result this—from so humble a beginning, but one in full keeping with God's ways in discipline.

J. B. STONEY

Faith is a divine plant that only grows out of the soil of a broken will.

EDWARD DENNETT

November 21

For we are God's workmanship, created in Christ Jesus to do good works, which God prepared in advance for us to do.
EPHESIANS 2:10

What is the secret of holiness, peacefulness, and strength, but to have no will, separate from and prior to the will of God? To run the race God sets before us, to walk in the good works foreordained by divine wisdom and love. It is one thing to ask, What good thing should *I* like to do for God? Here self is still choosing, and we please and serve after all ourselves. But to ask, like Saul, beholding the divine Master, "Lord, what wilt Thou have me to do?" is the beginning of true separation to God.

If we run the race set before us, engaging in duties God-appointed and not self-chosen, and bestowing all our energies, and that cheerfully, on the god-appointed tasks and sorrows, then may we rest in full assurance that our strength shall never fail, that our fruit shall remain, that our life shall, though apparently fragmentary, be complete, that we shall reach the end, and be counted faithful in that day.

ADOLPH SAPHIR

*T*he believer has the Holy Spirit—and where the Holy Spirit dwells, He will not suffer a Christian to be idle, but stirreth him up to all exercises of piety and godliness, and of all true religion, to the love of God, to the patient suffering of afflictions, to prayer, to thanksgiving, and to the exercise of charity to all mankind.

MARTIN LUTHER

November 22

But rejoice that you participate in the sufferings of Christ, so that you may be overjoyed when his glory is revealed. If you are insulted because of the name of Christ, you are blessed, for the Spirit of glory and of God rests on you.

1 PETER 4:13–14

*O*ne evening in my youth, the Lord Jesus lifted up my soul and showed me how this life offered an opportunity that heaven could not give, the opportunity to enter into His sufferings.

At that moment I seemed to see in the beautiful sunset all the beauty and glory and joy that Christ offers for the endless ages of eternity. He seemed to say to me, "Up there where all tears are wiped away, when there is no more sin or suffering or death, you will be able to serve me with perfect powers and sinless soul." And He also seemed to say, "Child, will you ever be able to suffer for Me again? Will you ever be able to weep for Me again, be lonely for My sake, give up something for Me, leave home and go out into the dark and enter into My sufferings?"

Then I looked into the face of Jesus and said, "O Lord, I don't mind what eternity will bring, but I want that and I want it now."

The sweetest moment of my life, when I did indeed enter into His sufferings, was during the Boxer rebellion in China in which thousands lost their lives for Christ. In a terrible riot I was beaten and stoned, and left, with my husband and others, bruised and bleeding, more dead than alive.

At that moment the thought seemed to flash on us that we had seen the face of Jesus, and had been able to suffer pain and shame and near death for His sake. *Such rapture flooded our souls that for four days we scarcely knew whether we were on earth or in heaven.*

MRS. HOWARD TAYLOR

*W*ell, it is but a little while and He will appear to answer all questions and to wipe away all tears. I would not wish, then, to be one of those who had none to wipe away. Would you?

J. H. T.

November 23

God made him who had no sin to be sin for us, so that in him we might become the righteousness of God.

2 CORINTHIANS 5:21

*T*he truth of the Gospel is this, that when the Lord Jesus was upon the cross, not only was He bearing our sins, but He was there made sin by God, and stood identified with all that the first man was, and underwent the judgement of God upon the first man; and thus, you see the end under the judgment of God of the first man.

The history of the first man, terminated before God and for faith, in the death of the second Man. Everything was condemned in the cross, and now there is no condemnation left, nothing left to condemn, as Paul puts it here, "For what the law could not do, in that it was weak through the flesh, God seeing his own Son in the likeness of sinful flesh, and of sin, condemned sin in the flesh."

God has not made light of sin. Christ has borne our *sins*, and put them away, but more, He has been made *sin*, and gone down into the depths of the judgment due to sin, and risen up from those depths. He has become my life, and the only measure of my new place before God. I am in Him, and therefore in all the impossibility of condemnation for Him. Sin in the flesh has not been forgiven. God condemned it. God never forgives *sin*. He forgives sinners, and pardons sins, blotting them out in Christ's blood, but the evil principle of sin, sin in the flesh—an intolerable and incurable principle of opposition to Himself, God can only end in judgment, either in the lake of fire for the impenitent sinner, or in the cross of the Savior, for the one, who through grace, believes in Him.

If a believer, you are *in* Christ before God, and hence there is, and can be, no condemnation, because your very place is in the One who has come out of, and left behind, in the judgment He came out of, all that pertained to your sins and you. That is the argument at the close of the chapter, "Who is he that condemneth? It is Christ that died, yea rather, that is risen again, who is even at the right hand of God, who also maketh intercession for us" (v. 34).

And is He going to condemn those for whom He died, for whom He agonized, and for whom He Himself was condemned?

Never! Blessed be His peerless name. We may well say, Hallelujah!

W. T. P. WOLSTON

*A*s there is no end to the merits of Christ incarnated and crucified; no bounds to the mercy and love of God; no hindrance to the
almighty energy and sanctifying influence of the Holy Spirit; not
limits to the improvability of the human condition; so there can be
no bounds to the saving influence which God will dispense to the
heart of every genuine believer.

We may ask and receive, and our joy shall be full! Well may we
bless and praise God, "who has called us into such a state of salvation"; a state in which we may be thus saved; and, by the grace of
that state continue in the same to the end of our lives.

ADAM CLARKE

November 24

As He is, so are we in the world.
1 JOHN 4:17

*W*e are now face to face with the inescapable implications: What
is a Christian? One in whom God lives; one through whom God
would manifest Himself in His essential nature, on the human level,
through a human personality.

We cannot escape the conclusion, and conviction, that in the
outworking of redemption and the accomplishing of its purpose to
make God known, we, the church as the Body of Christ, are taking
the place of the Man Christ Jesus.

"As He is, so are we in this world." Jesus walked this earth to
show what God is like when He lives in a man, and what man is
like when God lives in Him.

Friend, you are endowed and equipped to be that man for your
generation as Christ was for His. Are you startled? Are you measur-
ing up to your calling?

NORMAN B. HARRISON

*F*ish which live in the depths of the ocean lose some of their faculties, like the Tibetan hermits who always live in the dark. The ostrich loses his power of flying because he does not use his wings.

Therefore, do not bury the gifts and talents which have been given to you, but use them, that you may enter into the joy of your Lord.

SADU SUNDAR SINGH

I always dread my work not being solid.

JOHN DARBY

November 25

"Ho, every one that thirsteth, come ye to the waters, and he that hath no money; come ye, buy, and eat; yea, come buy wine and milk without money and without price."

ISAIAH 55:1

*I*t is God's purpose that every Christian should live a life of deep spirituality. It is not the privilege of a few but the prerogative of all and the need of all. One hundred and twenty were filled at Pentecost, and only eleven of them were apostles.

Some were women who went back home to cook, to sew, to care for a family. Others were men who returned to the field and the shop. No one is too young or too old to be filled with Spirit. It is not optional but obligatory. It is an express command for all believers to "be filled with the Spirit."

RUTH PAXSON

*I*f you feel the drawing of God within, cherish it as you would cherish a great treasure. If you are aware of a deep hunger, if you are entering into a closer walk with Him, do not look upon it carelessly, nor treat it lightly.

But if you do not feel the divine drawing and hunger for God, cry to Him that He will give it to you; and ever remember that the desire for hunger is the beginning of hunger, and that you cannot feed upon the Lord Jesus Christ until you are spiritually hungry.

H. M.

A sage of India was asked by a young man how he could find God. For some time the sage gave no answer, but one evening he asked the youth to come and bathe with him in the river. While there he gripped him suddenly and held his head under the water until he was nearly drowned. When he released him the sage asked him: "What did you want most when you were under the water?" "A breath of air," he replied. To which the sage answered, "When you want God as you wanted the breath of air, you will find Him."

G. GARDINER

November 26

Let us draw near with a true heart in full assurance of faith, having our hearts sprinkled from an evil conscience, and our bodies washed with pure water.

HEBREWS 10:22

*G*od is the incomprehensible, the hidden One. The Holy Spirit is the secret, incomprehensible working and presence of God. Do not seek to understand everything. Draw nigh—it never says with a clear head, but with a true heart. Rest upon God to do for you far more than you understand in fullness of faith.

IN FULLNESS OF FAITH, and not in fullness of feeling. When you come, and, gazing into the opened Holiest of All, hear the voice of Him that dwells between the cherubim call you to come in; and as you gaze—long, indeed—to enter and to dwell there, the word comes again, DRAW NEAR WITH A TRUE HEART!

Your answer is, Yes, Lord; with my whole heart—with that new heart Thou Thyself has given me. You make the surrender of yourself, to live only and always in His presence and for His service. The voice speaks again: Let it be Today—Now, IN FULLNESS OF FAITH. You have accepted what He offers. YOU have given what He asks. You believe that he accepts the surrender. You believe that the great Priest over the house takes possession of your inner life, and brings you before God. And yet you wonder why you feel so little changed. You feel just like the old self you were. Now is the time to listen to the voice—IN FULLNESS OF FAITH, not of feeling!

Look to God, who is able to do above what we ask or think. Trust His power. Look to Jesus on the throne, living there to bring you in. Claim the Spirit of the exalted One as His pentecostal gift.

Remember these are all divine, spiritual mysteries of grace, to be revealed in you. Apart from feeling, without feeling, in fullness of faith, in bare, naked faith that honors God, enter in. Reckon yourself to be indeed alive to God in Christ Jesus, taken in into His presence, His love, His very heart.

ANDREW MURRAY

November 27

I love the LORD because He hath heard my voice and my supplications.
PSALM 116:1

Sometimes people speak of God having answered their prayer, but what they mean is that He has answered it according to their desire and has done something about which they are glad. If he does something different they say sadly, "He has not answered." All this is a mistake.

Prayer is always heard if the one who prays comes to the Father in the Name of our Lord Jesus. "I love the Lord, because He hath heard" can be our word always, and also that other word, "This is the confidence that we have in Him, that, if we ask anything according to His will, He heareth us: and if we know that He hears us, whatsoever we ask, we know that we have the petitions that we desire of Him."

If we love Him, our real prayer is that His perfect will may be done, whatever the words are, and so it is certain that we have the petition even before we see it granted. The form the answer takes does not affect the fact.

I know that sometimes we do not see how the thing granted is all what we desire. And yet it is (I write for His lovers only).

For, after all, what the deepest in us wanted was not for our own natural will, but the will of our Father. So what is given is our hearts' desire; He hath not withholden the request of our lips. But God always answers us in the deeps, never in the shallows of our soul.

In hours of confusion, it can help to remember this.

Amy Carmichael

*Y*ou cannot expect an answer from God unless your will is gone. You shut out answers to your prayer because you have a will about the thing for which you are praying.

Edward Dennett

As for you, the anointing you received from him remains in you, and
you do not need anyone to teach you. But that anointing is real, not
counterfeit—just as it has taught you, remain in him.

1 JOHN 1:27

*G*od alone can instruct us in our duty. The teachings of men, however wise and well disposed they may be, are still ineffectual, if God
does not shed on the soul that light which opens the mind to truth.
The imperfections of our fellow-creatures cast a shade over the
truths that we learn from them. Such is our weakness that we do
not receive, with sufficient docility, the instructions of those who
are as imperfect as ourselves. A thousand suspicions, jealousies, fears,
and prejudices prevent us from profiting, as we might, but what we
hear from men; and though they announce the most serious truths,
yet what they do weakens the effect of what they say. In a word, it
is God alone who can perfectly teach us.

FRANÇOIS FÉNELON

*O*ften the work of the Lord itself may be a temptation to keep us
from that communion with Him which is so essential to the benefit of our own souls … Let none think that public prayer will
make up for closet communion.

GEORGE MUELLER

He must increase, but I must decrease.

JOHN 3:30, KJV

*O*h! For a self-emptied spirit—a heart at leisure from itself—a
mind delivered from all anxiety about one's own things! May we be

more thoroughly delivered from self, in all its detestable windings and workings! Then could the Master use us, own us, and bless us.

Hearken to His testimony to John—the one who said of himself that he was nothing but a voice. "Verily I say unto you, among them that are born of women there hath not risen a greater than John the Baptist" (Matt. 11:11). How much better to hear this from the Master than from the servant! John said, "I am a voice." Christ said he was the greatest of prophets. Simon Magus "gave out that himself was some great one." Such is the way of world—the manner of man. John the Baptist, the greatest of prophets, gave out that himself was nothing—that Christ was "above all." What a contrast!

May we be kept lowly and self-emptied, that so we may be continually filled with Christ. This is true rest—true blessedness. May the language of our hearts, and the distinct utterance of our lives ever be, "Behold the Lamb of God."

C. H. MACKINTOSH

*W*hen you are near Christ you cannot speak of your service. The more we are with Christ, self will retire, and Christ will take His rightful place.

He *has* His place in heaven. Oh, that He might have it in our hearts.

E. P. C.

A heart possessed of Christ is fortified against the most seductive allurements of the world.

EDWARD DENNETT

> *. . . being confident of this, that He who began a good work in you will carry it on to completion until the day of Christ Jesus.*
>
> PHILIPPIANS 1:6

*I*t is only the eye of the sculptor that can see beforehand the finished statue in the rough marble-block; but he does see it, and all the strokes of his tools are meant to bring out to the eyes of others what is already clear to his own. And the strokes of God's hand are only to produce the perfect beauty of the soul, and make that as visible to others as it now is to Himself. Nothing is more certain than that we will be perfectly satisfied with His work when we see it finished.

Why should we not be satisfied now when He tells us what a glorious finish He will make, and leave to Him the choosing of the tools?

G. H. KNIGHT

*M*ichelangelo lingered before a rough block of marble so long that his companion remonstrated. In reply, Michelangelo said with enthusiasm, "There's an angel in that block and I'm going to liberate him!" Oh, what unbounding love would manifest itself in us toward the most unlovable—the most vile—if only we saw what they might become, and in our enthusiasm for souls we cried out, "There's the image of Christ—marred, scarred, well-nigh obliterated—in that dear fellow, and I'm going to make that man conscious of it."

AN UNKNOWN CHRISTIAN

. . . Then Peter got down out of the boat and walked on the water to Jesus. But when he saw the wind, he was afraid and, beginning to sink, cried out, "Lord, save me!" Immediately Jesus reached out his hand and caught him. "You of little faith," he said, "why did you doubt?"

MATTHEW 14:29B–31

*H*ave we that faith which so realizes Christ's presence so as to keep us as calm and as composed in the rough sea as the smooth? It was not really a question of the rough or the smooth sea when Peter was sinking in the water, for he would have sunk *without Christ* just as much in the smooth as the rough sea. The fact was, the eye was off Jesus and on the wave, and that made him sink. If we go on with Christ, we shall get into all kinds of difficulty, many a boisterous sea; but being one with Him, His safety is ours.

JOHN DARBY

*R*emember Christian, it is not your hold of Christ that saves thee—it is Christ; it is not thy joy in Christ that saves thee—it is Christ; it is not even faith in Christ (though that is the instrument)—it is Christ's blood and merits; therefore, look not to thy hope, but to Christ, the source of they hope; look not to thy faith, but to Christ, the author and finisher of they faith. And if thou doest that, ten thousand devils cannot throw thee down.

There is one thing which all of us too much becloud in our preaching, though I believe we do it very unintentionally; namely, the great truth that it is not prayer, it is not faith, it is not our doings, it is not our feelings upon which we must rest, but upon Christ and on Christ alone!

We are apt to think that we are not in a right state, that our business is not with self, but Christ. Let me beseech thee, look only to Christ; never expect deliverance from self, from ministers, nor from any means of any kind apart from Christ; keep thine eye simply on Him; let His death, His merits, His glories, His intercession be fresh upon thy mind.

When thou wakest in the morning, look for Him; when thou liest down at night, look for Him.

CHARLES SPURGEON

*T*he work of the Savior is for the sinner; the Person of the Savior is for the saint; what He has done is for the former, what He is, is for the latter.

He had eternal life to give and He is the Son of the living God; by the former, the saint is drawn to Him; but the latter the saint is bound to Him. He not only meets all our necessities as sinners by His work, but also satisfies our affection and desires as saints by His Person.

C. H. MACKINTOSH

December 2

And he died for all, that those who live should no longer live for themselves but for him who died for them and was raised again.

2 CORINTHIANS 5:15

*I*n the place of self the believer gets the Son of God. Christ fills us, occupies us, engrosses us henceforth. He is all to us what self was before. He takes the place of self in everything from first to last, great or small. He is the substitute for self in the matter of our standing before God.

As the first thing the Holy Spirit does is to set aside self in the matter of justification and acceptance, so His next is to present to us the Son of God as the true ground of our acceptance. We no longer seek to be justified by self in any sense or on account of anything done to self, on account of amended self or improved self or mortified self, but solely on account of our Lord Jesus Christ, Who died for us and Who rose again.

And in this Son of God, Whom we take as a substitute for self, we find an object worth living for, someone we can through every part of our life and into every region of our life.

HORATIUS BONAR

*C*hrist is not valued at all unless He be valued above all.

AUGUSTINE

December 3

For all things are yours, whether Paul or Apollos, or Cephas, or the world, or life, or death, or things present, or things to come; all are yours, and ye are Christ's, and Christ is God's.

1 CORINTHIANS 3:21B–23, KJV

*L*et this be fully weighed and considered—that the justified person lives and performs every act of spiritual life by faith. This is a very important lesson, and therefore taught in Scripture as plainly as words can speak.

Everything is promised to, and received by faith. And as heirs of God and joint heirs with Christ—consider, believer, what a great estate has been bestowed on us.

Your title to it is good and you may enter into possession of it by faith. See then that you make use of such a great inheritance, and live on it daily. Do not say, when you need something, "I know not where to get it," for whatever Christ has of wisdom, righteousness, holiness, power, and glory, He has it as head of the body—for you as one of its members, for your use and benefit, and He has promised it to you in His word.

Make free with Him then. Go to Him in confidence. You cannot do Him greater honor than to receive from Him what He has to give. That is glorifying Him. It is putting the crown upon His head and confessing Him to be a perfect, all-sufficient Christ when it pleases you, as it did His Father, that in Him should all the fullness dwell and when you are content to live out of yourself upon His fullness for the supply of all your needs in time and eternity.

To thus live upon Him is His glory, and it is your privilege and your happiness to do so. In every circumstance, spiritual and temporal, and in every situation you could possibly be in, you are commanded to look up to Christ, that you may receive out of His fullness and to depend on Him to save you from every evil and to bestow upon you every good.

In your walk heavenward and in everything you meet with along the way, put your trust in Christ, and expect from Him the fulfilling of all His promises.

He has all power in heaven and earth for that very purpose. Strongly rely on Him, and cast your burdens on Him, when you are tempted; when old lusts arise, when the world and the devil assault you, when under a sense of weakness and dullness in daily duties, when in darkness and desertion, in persecution and trouble, in pain and poverty, in sickness and death. This is the Life of Faith. You will live like a Christian indeed, if being in any of these circumstances, you believe that Christ is able, because He is almighty, and willing; because He has promised to supply thy wants, and then trust Him for that supply. Depend upon it, you shall have it, and it shall be done unto you according to His word.

WILLIAM ROMAINE

. . . . .and your strength will equal your days.

DEUTERONOMY 33:25B

*I*t is a mistake to suppose that we can be *endowed*, so to speak, with spiritual power. God never gives a fund of strength to any of His servants on which they can draw from time to time until the whole is used. The power is always in Himself, and not in them, and only supplied moment by moment to those who are walking with and in dependence upon Him.

EDWARD DENNETT

*T*he Lord Jesus will make it His business to keep us alive and fruitful if we will make it our business to rely on Him. There must be no carnal straining, no natural effort; we do not have to keep ourselves alive.

Every fear to go down into daily death, every clinging to that which belongs to us, every grasp on our own personal position or ministry, will only hinder the manifestation of His life. It is to be life out of death.

Even when our trust in Him brings us into the most helpless and impossible situations, we may rest assured that all will be well, for He is indeed the God of resurrection.

H. F.

"I tell you the truth, anyone who will not receive the kingdom of God like a little child will never enter it."

MARK 10:15

Sometimes a little child leads us. A few years ago my little daughter was saying her prayers—I do not often have the privilege of hearing her. That Saturday night I was listening to her—and you know the prayers of a little child of six or seven. "God bless Mummy and Daddy, uncles, aunts, missionaries"—and so on; and I believe God hears prayers like that. But that night she closed with a postscript. She said, "Please, Lord Jesus, make me big and strong like my Daddy." I am very human, and I felt a lump in my throat. Hurriedly I tucked her in, and went to my study. I was as preparing for the next day's ministry, but I could not prepare that night. I got my Bible and I could not read it; every time I did so I heard that voice, "Make me big and strong like my Daddy." Presently I crept upstairs into her room, and there she was sound asleep. I knelt beside her and cried to God with all my heart, "O Lord Jesus, make me sweet, gentle, lovely, pure and good like my little girl."

I believe that is the secret of success. I do not know in what measure God has answered that prayer; but I believe He has answered it in a greater measure in my own life recently than He has ever done before. I pray God that may be true of you also.

ALAN REDPATH

It is a good sign when children prefer their home to any other place. How blessed if this were true of each of us with respect to our Father's house. The reason of our not doing so is that we do not sufficiently know the joy of it.

J. B. STONEY

December 6

Whether you turn to the right or to the left, your ears will hear a voice behind you saying, "This is the way; walk in it."
ISAIAH 30:21

*I*t is quite possible to get into such a strain over the question of "What is the will of God?" as quite to miss the doing of His will. In a wholly surrendered life, we can expect Him to work in us hour by hour to will His will, whilst we give ourselves up to the fulfillment of our momentary duty with our whole hearts.

Let us depend upon the withholdings of God, as well as upon His promptings. "The Spirit suffered them not"(Acts 16:7). The "voice" is only promised "when ye turn" (Isa. 30:21); if we are going straight on in the path of His will the Father gives His smile, and the heart is at rest.

The Written Word needs the illumination of the Spirit. If we go to it full of our own thoughts, we shall read our own ideas into it. Let us wait humbly upon God for His interpretation of His own Book.

Do nothing in a hurry. There is always time for all that is in the will of God. The waiting of one day may bring to light some point which will show us how near we were to a serious mistake. The walk with God appears to be a very slow one, but it is very sure in its effects, for there is no waste power in it.

To souls wholly possessed by God, the Holy Spirit gives deep rest in all things which are in accordance with His mind. It is safe never to make any decision except in perfect calm of mind and heart.

JESSIE PENN-LEWIS

*G*od's will is *delicious*. He makes no mistakes.

FRANCES HAVERGAL

> For we do not have a high priest who is unable to sympathize with our
> weaknesses, but we have one who has been tempted in every way, just
> as we are—yet was without sin.
>
> HEBREWS 4:15

I often wonder if all who have turned to Christ for pardon and
for life have every clearly realized that this Jesus has met and conquered every temptation and every failure and every difficulty that
our faith can possibly be tested with. Yes, He conquered all! "He was
in all points tempted like as we are, yet without sin." "Which of you
convinceth Me of sin?" He challenged. "Be of good cheer," He says,
"I have overcome the world." And, again, He asserts, "The prince of
this world cometh, and hath nothing in Me."

Jesus Christ, this One whom we are asked to enthrone in our
lives, was victorious over every possible sin and weakness. Where
He reigns, and where His will and His mind are accepted and yielded to, He bestows like victory. There is no more secret about it than
that. Thank God, it is an open secret, this secret of the victorious
life! It lies in the surrender of our will and mind and life to the
mind and will of Jesus Christ, as that is revealed to us by the Holy
Spirit, through the Word of God.

Satan is a defeated foe. Our Lord Jesus Christ has met and has
defeated him. Christ is the only one Who ever has. But under the
guidance and under the constraint and under the power of the
Spirit of God, Who is the Viceregent of the Lord Jesus, you and I
will be led on to a like victory. He will teach us the Jesus way; He
will show us the Jesus life; and he will enable us to walk in it and
to do it.

This, then, is the thought that is most helpful to my own soul
and life. The Holy Spirit comes to make real to us the indwelling
victorious presence of Christ. "He shall glorify Me," the Master

said, "for He shall receive of Mine, and shall show it unto you." The Jesus mind. The Jesus way. The Jesus life.

J. R. S. WILSON

If there be a growing up into the measure of the stature of Christ, there must be a conscious refusal of that which would tend to revive or invigorate the old nature.

The saint is not only a new creature to grow into the likeness of the Lord Jesus, but he has to watch and beware lest the things he has to do with should in any way minister to another will in him, which would divert him from God to himself. Self is the circle and center of man's mind in this fallen state; but when Christ is formed in the soul, God is the center and source of everything.

J. B. STONEY

December 8

For sin shall not have dominion over you, for ye are not under law, but under grace.

ROMANS 6:14, KJV

Having life in Christ, we can now look at sin, at our old sinful self, as an enemy, but an enemy that shall not have dominion. What a deliverance this is! To one who knows the utter vileness of the old nature, no words can sufficiently express the greatness of deliverance from the reign of sin.

There may be sudden temptation—even, failure—but sin shall not have dominion—it shall not reign. But why shall not sin reign? "For ye are not under the law, but under grace." The whole history of Christendom, and the history of every individual believer, proves the truth of this statement, and also its opposite. Just in proportion as the free favor of God, through Christ Jesus, is known and enjoyed, is the deliverance from the slavery of sin, and we can live a holy life. The law can give no power to those under it, but can only curse them.

The moment you make the favor of God to be conditional, whether it be concerning the law of Moses, or the precepts of the gospel, you begin at the wrong end, and will soon find nothing but misery and doubt. You will say, I do not keep the commands of God as I ought; or, I do not love Christ as I ought; am I a Christian at all? Now, is all that law, or grace? Clearly it is law. And the word says, sin shall not have dominion over you, for you are not under that principle, but under grace.

There surely can be no holiness of life, unless the heart be perfectly free, in the unbounded, free, unconditional favor of God. Has he taken me up, an ungodly sinner, who deserved hell? Has He, in pure, unmerited love, given His Son to die for our sins? Has He raised Him from the dead for our justification? Has He given us eternal redemption through His blood? Have we thus peace with God, according to all that God is? Are we identified with Christ in all the merit of his death; and more, alive in Him to God?

And all this absolute, free grace, the grace of Him who changes not? And now I am alive to God, I can reckon myself, my old man, dead. And thus I am delivered from myself, to live to God. And all unchanging grace to me, then I am not on the ground of law, or conditions for life, or salvation, or deliverance, but absolutely under grace, free and eternal.

Oh, now I am free to serve the Lord, in real separation from, and abhorrence of, evil. Oh, glorious truth! Sin shall not have dominion!

C. STANLEY

He that believeth hath the witness in himself.

1 JOHN 5:10, KJV

*I*t is absolutely essential to the enjoyment of settled peace that the heart should rest *solely* on the authority of Holy Scripture. Nothing else will stand. Inward evidences, spiritual experiences, comfortable frames, happy feelings, are all very good, very valuable, and very desirable; indeed we cannot prize them too highly in their right place. But, most assuredly, their right place is not at the foundation of the Christian position. If we look to such things as the ground of our peace, we shall very soon become clouded, uncertain, and miserable.

The reader cannot be too simple in his apprehension of this point. He must rest like a little child upon the testimony of the Holy Ghost in the Word. It is blessedly true that "He that believeth hath the witness in himself." And again, "The Spirit itself beareth witness with our spirit that we are the children of God."

All this is essential to Christianity; but it must, in no wise, be confounded with the witness of the Holy Ghost, as given to us in Holy Scripture. The Spirit of God never leads any one to build upon His work as the ground of peace, but only upon the finished work of Christ, and the unchangeable Word of God; and we may rest assured that the more simply we rest on these the more settled our peace will be, and the clearer our evidences, the brighter our frames, the happier our feelings, the richer our experiences.

In short, the more we look away from self and all its belongings, and rest in Christ, on the clear authority of Scripture, the more spiritually minded we shall be; and the inspired apostle tells us that "to be spiritually minded (or, the minding of the Spirit) is life and peace." The best evidence of a spiritual mind is child-like repose in Christ and His Word. The clearest proof of an unspiritual mind is self-occupation. It is a poor affair to be trafficking in *our* evidences, or *our* anything.

It looks like piety, but it leads away from Christ—away from Scripture—away from God; and this is not piety, or faith, or Christianity.

C. H. MACKINTOSH

*E*very year I might almost say every day that I live, I seem to see more clearly how all the rest and gladness and power of our Christian life hinges on one thing—and that is taking God at His word, believing that He really means exactly what He says, and accepting the very words in which He reveals His goodness and grace, without substituting others or altering the precise modes and tenses He has seen fit to use.

FRANCES HAVERGAL

December 10

Have I been so long with you, and yet hast thou not known me . . .
JOHN 14:9, KJV

*D*o you know Christ as a man knows his friend, or do you know Him as you know about Julius Caesar? Do you know Christ because you live with Him and He with you, or do you know about Him in that fashion in which a man in a great city knows about his neighbor across the street, that has lived beside him for twenty-five years and never spoken to him once in all that time?

Is that your knowledge of Christ? If so, it is no knowledge at all. Oh my brother and sister, the very fact that He has been so long with you is the reason why you know so little about Him.

People who are close to something, which men come from the ends of the earth to see, have often never seen it. A man may have lived all his life within sound of Niagara, and perhaps never gone to look at the rush of the waters.

Is that what you do with Jesus Christ? Are you so accustomed to hear about Him that you do not know Him? Have you so long heard of Him that you never come to see Him?

ALEXANDER MACLAREN

*S*o immensely are our lives below the mark as nominal Christians that we have next to no idea of the distance at which we walk from God, and when the soul is turned to seek Him only, we discover with amazement how many false props we have had, and how often we have been leaning on the love and approval of others and not upon the Father's love alone.

GEORGE V. WIGRAM

December 11

Whoever can be trusted with very little can also be trusted with much, and whoever is dishonest with very little will also be dishonest with much.

LUKE 16:10

*M*ost of us, when we picture God's call, think of something dramatic, revolutionary, and startling. The scene on the road to Damascus at once comes up. We see the great light in the sky; we hear the voice from heaven; we picture the revolutionizing effect of it all upon the great apostle to the Gentiles. But we forget the great number of men to whom God's call came when they stood upon the holy ground of their everyday life and service. God's call came to Samuel as he ministered in the daily round of the temple; it came to David in the sheepfold; it came to Moses after forty years in the back of the desert; it came to some of the disciples as they were mending and casting their nets. In all these cases the call came to them as they stood upon the holy ground of their daily duties.

There comes back to me an experience of my early manhood days. My health was utterly broken. All my own plans were crushed. As yet I had found none of God's. One day I was sitting at my table studying the Word of God. A great blessing came into my heart. It was glowing with joy and with the desire to give the same message to others. I leaned back in my chair and prayed, "Oh God, if you would only give me a chance to give this to others as you have given it to me." I arose from my chair and walked down stairs. My sister handed me my morning mail. The first letter I opened was from the secretary of a Young Men's Christian Association across the river from the little town in eastern Pennsylvania where I lived. It ran like this: "Dear Brother, Last night we decided to start a Bible class. We arose from our knees, after a half hour's prayer, impressed that you were the man we needed. Will you come over and teach this class for us?"

It seemed but a small thing, but it looked to me liked God's holy ground of service. That night I went and taught a Bible class of five big-hearted railroad men. God gave great blessing to my own soul, and seemed to help these dear men. I taught that Bible class as faithfully as I knew for a period of three years. Then came another class, and another.

At the end of three years I was teaching ten Bible classes, and had found my lifework. The place of daily service whereon I had been standing proved to be holy ground, and I had found the joy of God's will for my life.

Let us then heed this great truth that God's call always has come, and always will come, to Christians who are standing on the holy ground of everyday, faithful service.

JAMES McCONKEY

$\mathcal{T}$o hold ourselves at the Lord's disposal secures for us opened doors when He has work for us to do.

EDWARD DENNETT

December 12

Morning by morning, O LORD, you hear my voice; morning by morning I lay my requests before you and wait in expectation.
PSALM 5:1–3

$\mathcal{H}$ere is the great secret of success: Work with all your might; but trust not in the least in your work. Pray with all your might for the blessing of God; but work, at the same time, with all diligence, with all patience, with all perseverance. Pray then, and work. Work and pray. And still again pray, and then work. And so on all the days of your life.

The result will surely be abundant blessing. Whether you see much fruit or little fruit, such kind of service will be blessed.... Speak also for the Lord, as if everything depended on your exertions; yet trust not the least in your exertions, but in the Lord, who alone can cause your efforts to be made effectual, to the benefit of your fellow men or fellow believers.

Remember, also, that God delights to bestow blessing, but, generally, as the result of earnest, believing prayer.

GEORGE MUELLER

$\mathcal{D}$avid said, "I found it in my heart to pray this prayer unto thee O Lord." How many of us seem to begin to pray without really thinking about prayer! We rush, without preparation or thought, into the presence of God. But David did not make that mistake—he found his prayer *in his heart.*

Prayer is the product of humble heart, a believing heart, and a heart renewed by grace. I pray that the Lord will give us a heart to pray.

CHARLES SPURGEON

. . . . So that by faith we might receive the promise of the Spirit.
GALATIANS 3:14

*C*hrist's call to the soul is four-fold: Come unto Me, Learn of Me, Follow Me, Abide in Me. Come unto Me as Redeemer; Learn of Me as Teacher; Follow Me as Master; Abide in Me as Life. And all that is required of us is the one sufficient and inclusive attitude of soul which the New Testament knows as faith.

This attitude and response of trust, self-surrender, dependence, is the essential attitude and response of the soul of man to God. Every sincere man knows full well the impossibility of realizing his true life in isolation, apart from God. Faith as man's response to God for ever puts an end to the spiritual helplessness and hopelessness of the solitary man. It introduces him to a new relationship to God in Christ, and opens the door to the coming of the Holy Spirit of light and life. It is the means whereby the needed strength, satisfaction, and security come to the soul from fellowship with God.

Faith introduces the soul into a new world of blessed fellowship, uplifting motives, satisfying experiences, and spiritual powers, and from the moment the attitude of trust is taken up the Holy Spirit begins His work of revealing Jesus Christ to the soul.

He brings into the heart the assurance of forgiveness and deliverance from the burden of the past, he bestows on the soul the gift of the Divine life, and then he commences a work that is never finished in this life of assimilating our lives to that of Christ, working in us that Christlikeness which is the essential and unique element of the Gospel ethic.

In the deep and dim recesses of our personality the Holy Spirit works His blessed and marvelous way, transfiguring character, uplifting ideals, inspiring hopes, creating joys, and providing perfect satisfaction. And as we continue to maintain and deepen the attitude of faith the Holy Spirit is enabled to do His work and we are enabled to receive more of His grace. By every act of trust and self-surrender we receive ever larger measures of the life of Christ, and all the while we are being changed into the image of Christ "from glory to glory" by the Spirit of the Lord.

W. H. GRIFFITH THOMAS

December 14

. . . . for everyone born of God has overcome the world. This is the victory that has overcome the world, even our faith.

1 JOHN 5:4

The secret of complete victory is faith: simply believing that *Jesus has done and is doing it all.* Victory is entered upon by a single act of faith, as is salvation. Victory is maintained by the attitude of faith.

But suppose the believer, having experienced the miracle of victory over sin through trusting his Lord's sufficiency, comes, somehow, to doubt that sufficiency? At once his victory is broken, and he fails. This is possible at any moment. And at once, if there should be failure through unbelief, comes a real peril.

The lie of Satan is whispered in the ear, "You have sinned; and that proves that you never had the blessing you thought you had: you never had the Victorious Life." This is a lie, of course, as are most of Satan's attacks. They used to say at the Keswick conferences, "If you should fail, shout Victory!" Not with any idea of denying the reality of the failure, but in recognition of the fact that *Jesus* has not failed, and that there may be instantaneous and complete restoration through faith in His unimpaired sufficiency.

CHARLES G. TRUMBULL

$\mathcal{T}$here are seasons when many believers feel as if they can not get into the presence, or obtain the ear of God . . . Surely it would prove an antidote to Satan's temptations at such times to remember, that if we cannot pray ourselves, Christ never fails to bear us up in His prevailing intercession.

The effect of this truth should be to dispel our gloom and coldness of heart, because we would be led to look away from ourselves, expecting all from Him and His continual ministry for us before the throne of God.

EDWARD DENNETT

December 15

Wherefore he is able also to save them to the uttermost that come unto God by him, seeing he ever liveth to make intercession for them.
HEBREWS 7:25, KJV

$\mathcal{T}$he inviting voice of Christ is never silent. He calls us in the morning of life, when wondrous powers are stirring within us, when love, and hope, and ambition fill our hearts. At such a time He calls us to the realization of a life better than our brightest dreams.

And He calls us in the noontide of life, when, with developing powers and growing responsibilities, we bend to our tasks beneath the burning sun; when, also, we feel most keenly the impact of temptation on our souls. At such a time, if we will but listen, we may hear Him calling us to courage and endurance.

And also He calls us in the evening of life, when the shadows are gathering, and our powers are beginning to fail, when interests are declining, and when we have to make room for others. Christ does not leave us then but calls us to a new and rich experience of Himself as able "to save to the uttermost."

As He calls us at all times, so also He calls us in many ways. His voice may reach us by force of circumstances, as in the case of Moses, who little thought when he killed the Egyptian that God was thereby calling him to a new discipline, and to preparation for a great mission.

And Christ may call us by sudden illumination, as in the case of Saul of Tarsus. In one brief moment all the past was seen in a new light, and all the future took on a new significance. What has not happened in a millennium may happen in a moment, and what through half a lifetime may have been dark may suddenly be flooded with light.

God's call to us may come also by growing conviction, as it did to Timothy who, from his youth, was taught to listen to the divine voice. In these and other ways God calls us, men and women, young and old; and He does so because He desires to have us, delights to save us, and designs to use us.

Nothing is more certain than that he has a place and a use for each of us. It may be as minister, doctor, lawyer, artist, writer, teacher, tradesman, or something else; but what will give any and all of these their chiefest significance, and secure success in the pursuit of them, is that, in God's plan, they are not merely employments, but vocations.

W. GRAHAM SCROGGIE

December 16

In him was life, and that life was the light of men.
JOHN 1:4

*T*he secret and reality of a blissful life in God cannot be understood without receiving, living, and experiencing it. If we try to understand it only with the intellect, we will find our effort useless. A scientist had a bird in his hand. He saw that it had life, and, wanting to find out in what part of the bird's body the life was, he began dissecting the bird. The result was that the very life of which he was in search disappeared mysteriously. Those who try to understand the inner life merely intellectually will meet with a similar failure. The life for which they are looking will vanish in the analysis.

In comparison with this big world, the human heart is only a small thing. Though the world is so large, it is utterly unable to satisfy this tiny heart. Our ever growing soul and its capacities can be satisfied only in the infinite God. As water is restless until it reaches its level, so the soul has no peace until it rests in God.

SADU SUNDAR SINGH

The more believers are for *Him* the more they will in every way gain for themselves.

J. B. STONEY

December 17

My little children, these things write I unto you, that ye sin not. And if any man sin, we have an advocate with the Father, Jesus Christ the righteous.

1 JOHN 2:1, KJV

It is important to see that His advocacy is not in any sense to atone for our sins, as if they were imputed to us. He atoned for our sins once in His death on the cross, and this can never be repeated. By that one sacrifice all our sins are covered, and there can be no imputation of guilt to the believer, as it is written, "Blessed is the man to whom the Lord *will not* impute sin"; and again, "Their sins and iniquities will I remember no more."

We have been pardoned and justified, and are in Christ, according to divine righteousness, so that the advocacy of Christ can have nothing to do with satisfying God about guilt, or securing pardon for us, as if sin had been imputed to us. Even the sins we may commit after having believed were all covered by the death of Christ, and they are not imputed to us, but they hinder communion with God, and this is an immense loss to our souls.

It is God's good pleasure that we should be in communion with Himself, and that our joy should be full. But practical holiness in us is absolutely necessary for this because God is light and in Him is no darkness at all. We cannot go on in sin, and have communion with Him; and hence, if we sin, we need to be restored so as to enjoy afresh the communion we have lost. And for this Jesus our Advocate intercedes on the ground of the fact that we are in relationship with God according to divine righteousness, and according to the value of his propitiatory sacrifice.

A. H. RULE

December 18

Here I am! I stand at the door and knock. If anyone hears my voice and opens the door, I will go in and eat with him, and he with me.
REVELATION 3:20

There is no part of my being that is not laid open to the Divine Guest. There are no rooms of the house of my spirit, into which He may not go.

Let Him come with the master key in His hand into all the dim chambers of your feeble nature; and as the one life is light in the eye, and color in the cheek, and deftness in the fingers, and strength in the arm, and pulsation in the heart, so He will come with the manifold results of the one gift to you.

He will be like some subtle elixir which, taken into the lips, steals through a pallid and wasted frame, and brings back a glow to the cheek and a luster to the eye, and swiftness to the brain, and power to the whole nature. Or as some plant, drooping and flagging beneath the hot rays of the sun, when it has the scent of water given to it, will, in all its parts, stiffen and erect itself, so when the Spirit is poured out on men, their whole nature is invigorated and helped.

ALEXANDER MACLAREN

*W*e should daily diligently cultivate the enjoyment of the love of Christ that we may become molded by it, so as to express it more in our very demeanor, and be surrounded by the holy atmosphere which it creates.

EDWARD DENNETT

December 19

But of him are ye in Christ Jesus, who of God is made unto us wis-dom, and righteousness, and sanctification, and redemption . . .
1 CORINTHIANS 1:30

*G*od never acts apart from Christ. Everything that God does whether in creation or salvation He does through His son. And everything that God does in Christ for man's salvation He begins at the cross. So our sanctification begins there. At the cross the sinner becomes a saint. Every believer has been set apart for God's own possession and use by the sacrifice of His son. The believer is a saint by position. As in justification the guilty sinner is accounted righteous through the blood of the cross so in sanctification the defiled sinner is accounted holy. By the sacrifice of the Lord Jesus Christ he "hath been perfected once for all."

In this objective aspect sanctification is absolute and complete. Christ Himself and Christ alone is our sanctification.

RUTH PAXSON

*L*ook not upon a life of holiness as a strain and an effort, but as the natural outgrowth of the life of Christ within you. And let a quiet, hopeful, gladsome faith supply you with all that you need for a holy life—supplied out of the holiness of the Lord Jesus.

Thus you will understand and prove what it is to abide in Christ our Sanctification.

ANDREW MURRAY

December 20

But will God in very deed dwell with men on the earth. . . .
2 CHRONICLES 6:18, KJV

*D*id you ever think of the awful dishonor done not only to the Spirit of God, but to Christ by the denial of the permanency of His abiding in the believer?

If the Spirit could leave, after having taken up His abode in us, it would involve a denial of the work of Christ. His work would have ceased to avail before God. It would drag Christ from His throne in glory, if the Spirit could depart from a believer.

It cannot be too clearly understood that this indwelling is not because of anything in us, either at the beginning, or at any stage of the Christian life.

From first to last, the Spirit dwells with us because of the unchanging value of the work of Christ. Cease forever to dishonor the value of that work by doubting the presence of this Holy

Person. Your feelings, your faithfulness have nothing to do with this basic fact.

But what holy ground we are upon here! If Solomon could ask the wondering question: "But will God in very deed dwell with men on the earth?" when His visible glory filled the temple (2 Chron. 5:14; 6:18), what shall we say when the living God in the person of the Holy Ghost comes to abide in us? My brethren, I am persuaded we little realize what this means. If we did, what lowliness would mark us; what abhorrence of sin, what quickness in the fear of the Lord, and the detection of the most subtle forms of evil, what reverence.

Who can describe the sanctifying effect of simply a deep realization of the stupendous fact. I can but speak of it, and pray that all of us may know practically what the consciousness of this abiding would bring.

SAMUEL RIDOUT

It would make all the difference in our life and ministry if only we recognized and revered the Holy Spirit's indwelling. If only we carried about with us this solemn thought—that we form the temple of the Holy Spirit. If only we could refer everything to the Spirit of God, realizing that He indwells us, and turn to Him, no matter what the difficulty or the occasion may be, for guidance and advice and direction, just as we turn to a friend whose face we see.

Brethren, the recognition of the indwelling of the Holy Spirit makes for power in life and fruitfulness in service.

HERBERT LOCKYER

December 21

I tell you the truth, unless a kernel of wheat falls to the ground and dies, it remains only a single seed. But if it dies, it produces many seeds. The man who loves his life will lose it, while the man who hates his life in this world will keep it for eternal life. Whoever serves me must follow me; and where I am, my servant also will be. My Father will honor the one who serves me.

JOHN 12:24–26

*G*od sometimes sends us a wintry season that we may the better bring forth summer fruit.

It is the way of the Lord to work for a season, as it were, under ground: and as the seed that dies in the earth, through dying, comes to life, so God will seem to cut off the hope of fruit of our labor; yet when we have humbled ourselves under His hand, and He has secured the glory to Himself, He will put forth His power and bring to life our buried hopes.

There may be much communion with God when there is but little comfort in the soul, and much fruitfulness when there is but little joy and gladness. We bear fruit when we credit the Word of God against appearance, and when we submit our will to His.

There is no security for our bringing forth fruit in time to come, if we are not bringing forth fruit in the present hour.

How often we fail and miscarry toward the end of a trial of patience!

Do not expect to make great strides at once in believing; or that deep sanctification is to be wrought in a day.

We can never be said to have outlived our usefulness, unless we have outlived our spirituality.

We must first come to the withering of the flesh, before we can become spiritually strong and fruitful.

ROBERT C. CHAPMAN

The more we can rest in Him the more we are independent of everything outside of Him at such a time, the more vigor we really possess; and the better we get over the winter, be it ever so severe. If I am independent of the winter, it is evident that I have mastered it, and not it me; and if I have done so, through the strength of the Lord Jesus, I am relieved though in no human way. Peter is delivered from prison in a superhuman way; but first he, though enduring a very trying winter, could lay him down and sleep—take his rest, because the Lord sustained him.

J. B. STONEY

December 22

. . . but ye know him; for he dwelleth with you, and shall be in you.
JOHN 14:17B, KJV

Ye know Him!" How? "He *dwelleth* with you." That is how you get to know people. Putting it in a very rough, earthly way, that is how He is known. "He dwelleth with you; and he shall be in you!" You know Him by experience, not by theory, nor by a mental knowledge.

Anything you know in that way can soon be stripped away from you; but something that you have proved, and you know from experience, no human being in this world can take from you. This is how the martyrs lived through their sufferings.

God puts a living faith and knowledge of Himself into His people, which no martyrdom can tear out of them. Martyrdom may take away opinions from men, and views and ideas; but no martyrdom can take out of the fibre of one's being what is wrought into it through knowledge and experience.

That, I say, is what God wants to do for us. He wants the Holy Spirit to be a real Person in us to make Christ real to us in life, so that we cannot help living in the Living One. It is not what you believe or think, but it is what you are, what is wrought into you as part of you, and what is greater than all you merely see.

JESSIE PENN-LEWIS

The Christian life is not merely a converted life nor even a consecrated life, but it is the Christ-life. It is the consuming desire of the Lord Jesus to reincarnate Himself in the believer.

RUTH PAXSON

By regeneration, by the impartation of His life and nature through the operation of the Holy Spirit the risen Christ dwells in each genuine believer; each believer, each real Christian is—the reincarnation of Christ.

It is the process of reincarnating Christ in a human life that gives us the distinctive character of this age and the distinctive character of God's dealing with the word today; as it is written:

"Even the mystery (secret) which has been hid from ages and from generations, but is now made manifest to his saints: To whom God would make known what is the riches of the glory of this mystery among the Gentiles; which is—Christ in you, the hope of glory" (Colossians 1:26–27)

The believer is "joined" to the Lord as "one spirit."

1 CORINTHIANS 6:17

Christ in each believer joins each believer to every other believer, and these individual believers constitute the spiritual body of Christ n which each is a special and "particular" member.

I. M. HALDEMAN

For Zion's sake I will not keep silent, for Jerusalem's sake I will not remain quiet, till her righteousness shines out like the dawn, her salvation like a blazing torch. The nations will see your righteousness, and all kings your glory; you will be called by a new name that the mouth of the Lord will bestow. You will be a crown of splendor in the LORD's hand, a royal diadem in the hand of your God. No longer will they call you Deserted, or name your land Desolate. But you will be called Hephzibah, and your land Beulah; for the LORD will take delight in you, and your land will be married. As a young man marries a maiden, so will your sons marry you; as a bridegroom rejoices over his bride, so will your God rejoice over you.

ISAIAH 62:1–5

*I*s there any believer who has received the pardon of sin in Christ, and who yet goes doubting, mourning with a dull conscience, and with a heart that is not filled with the sweetness of God's peace?

You cannot forgive yourself; you cannot forget your past; you cannot overlook your constant sins and failures, or cease to mourn over your indwelling corruption? By a strange duality there is in your soul an elder son, who does not understand why the prodigal should be arrayed with the best robe, and that now only the voice of melody and rejoicing should be heard.

Do you not know that your frequent failures and falls do not hinder His love, that His peace is ever in you, though you are not always consciously in His peace? In Him as your representative and head the Father is pleased. God calls you no longer forsaken and desolate, but Hephzibah and Beulah.

And when you behold this eternal, never-varying love of God which is in Christ Jesus; that love which was before time; that love which gave up the Son; that love which shall keep you for ever; when you behold the love of Jesus, combining all that is shadowed further in the love of friend, of brother, of mother, of husband; that love which bore your sin on the cross, which bears you now on His High-priestly heart in heaven, which looks on you with sweet faithfulness and pity after you denied Him, then, though sin appear more loathsome and bitter, rest and rejoice in Christ, abide in the sanctuary, whither you have boldness to enter by the blood of Jesus. He is ever the same.

ADOLPH SAPHIR

December 24

Though you have not seen him, you love him; and even though you do not see him now, you believe in him and are filled with an inexpressible and glorious joy.

1 PETER 1:8

*J*oy is distinctly a Christian word and a Christian thing. It is the reverse of happiness. Happiness is the result of what happens of an agreeable sort. Joy has its springs deep down inside. And that spring never runs dry, no matter what happens. Only Jesus gives that joy. He had joy, singing its music within, even under the shadow of the cross. It is an unknown word and thing except as He has sway within.

S. D. GORDON

*T*o pursue joy is to lose it. The only way to get it is to follow steadily the path of duty without thinking of joy, and then like sheep, joy will come most surely, unsought, and we "being in the way"; the angel of God, bright-haired Joy, is sure to meet us.

ALEXANDER MACLAREN

*J*oy to the world! the Lord is come; Let earth receive her King.

ISAAC WATTS

Although I am less than the least of all God's people, this grace was given to me: to preach to the Gentiles the unsearchable riches of Christ.
EPHESIANS 3:8

*I*t is only an empty vessel that the Lord can use, that no flesh should glory in His presence.

Flesh was judged in the cross of Christ, and it was not now merely a question of promises, but of having Christ. I first find out what God is through the Son, but now I find the divine affections all centered in Christ—"the Father *loveth* the Son," then "the unsearchable riches," everything put into Christ's hands as Heir of all things, and this as man, as we get in Psalm viii. In Proverbs 8:31 I find Him delighting in man. He passes by the angels—blessed, doubtless, in their places; but He passes by them, and takes man's nature upon Him.

People keep Christmas, but the world's estimate of Christ when He came is shown by the fact that it could find no better place for Him than a manger. When Christ came, the angels sang God's good pleasure in *man*; but man would not have Him in his life, and so He must die, because if not, like a corn of wheat, He must abide alone. But His desire is to get outside of all man's rejection and to have man notwithstanding.

If man would not have Him in life, because man was dead, He must die and take man up in death, to make him partaker of a new and risen life. This was perfect, infinite love, not merely kindness (we get His goodness every day); but His *love* is coming to take a sinner's place! God's truth is brought out in this.

He has taken man clean out of the position in which he was, and the consequence is that now I see man entering into a new position altogether, in the Second Man, who has gone into sin and death and borne the judgment, and now is in the glory of God *as a man*, and *I* with Him. This is unsearchable riches, far more than promise.

JOHN DARBY

Which of you, if his son asks for bread, will give him a stone? Or if he asks for a fish, will give him a snake? If you, then, though you are evil, know how to give good gifts to your children, how much more will your Father in heaven give good gifts to those who ask him!

MATTHEW 7:9–11

*L*et us get it crystal clear in our hearts and mind that the only Person who ever lived the Christian life was Jesus Christ, and the only Person that God ever intended to live the Christian life was Jesus Christ. The only part that you and I play on earth today is to provide Him with human vehicles to that end. Hands and feet and lips; hearts to love with and eyes to see with. That is our part, and it is in the infinite, unspeakable mercy of God that even this privilege may be ours. But what a wonderful thing to consent to this fact and to know that Jesus Christ lives His life through you.

What are the limits? What are the possibilities? This is the place where you quit begging and start praising God. You need not come, cap in hand, asking God for this and asking God for that. You only have to know that at any given moment Jesus Christ has the right of way in your life and you're in the place where God wants you. You don't have to beg for blessing. You thank Him in anticipation. It is inevitable.

MAJOR IAN THOMAS

*Y*ou are grafted into Christ's present-day body, to be His Fullness, to carry out His mind and will, to rightly present and represent Him to others. To do this, you *must* be yielded.

That's understood. It's settled. (Is it, my friend?)

NORMAN HARRISON

For the Lord himself will come down from heaven, with a loud command, with the voice of the archangel and with the trumpet call of God, and the dead in Christ will rise first.

1 THESSALONIANS 4:16

*W*hat glorious fruit flows from the death and resurrection of Christ! The Holy Ghost comes down, and indwells the believer. Yes, the humblest, the feeblest believer, no matter how little the faith.

If you believe in Jesus, and in the work which He has done, not only are your sins forgiven, but you receive the Holy Ghost—the seal of your faith; and that the Holy Ghost, dwelling in your body, is the pledge on the part of God, that if you go where Jesus went—into the grave—out of that grave, like Jesus, you will rise.

W. T. P. WOLSTON

*B*uried with Christ," and raised with Him too; What is there left for me to do? Simply to cease from struggling and strife, Simply to "walk in the newness of life." Glory be to God. "Risen with Christ," my glorious Head, Holiness now the pathway I tread, Beautiful thought while walking therein: "He that is dead is freed from sin."

Glory be to God.

To restore from beyond the grave is to Him easy; to turn back the downward course is to Him a pleasure, who is the resurrection and the life.

GEORGE V. WIGRAM

*Being filled with fruits of righteousness, which are by Jesus Christ, unto
the glory and praise of God.*

PHILIPPIANS 1:11

*G*od looks for reality. He is not satisfied with mere words of high
profession. He says to us, "My little children, let us not love in word,
neither in tongue, but in *deed* and in *truth*." He, blessed be His name,
did not love us in word or in tongue, but in deed and in truth; and
he looks for a response from us—a response clear, full, and distinct;
a response coming out in a life of good works, a life yielding mel-
low clusters of the "fruits of righteousness which are by Christ
Jesus, to the glory and praise of God."

Do you not consider it to be our bounden duty to apply our
hearts to this weighty subject? Ought we not diligently to seek to
promote love and good works? And how can this be most effectually accomplished? Surely by walking in love ourselves, and faithfully treading the path of good works in our own private life.

For ourselves, we confess we are thoroughly sick of hollow profession. High truth on the lips and low practice in daily life, is one
of the crying evils of this our day. We talk of grace; but fail in common righteousness—fail in the plainest moral duties in our daily
private life. We boast of our *position* and our *standing*; but we are
deplorably lax as to our *condition* and *state*.

May the Lord, in His infinite goodness, stir up all our hearts to
more thorough earnestness, in the pursuit of good works, so that we
may more fully adorn the doctrine of God our Savior in all things!

C. H. MACKINTOSH

*W*hat we need in order to enable us to show forth Christ in our
lives is that Christ should live in us. So the Apostle travails again in
birth until Christ be formed in them.

What a Christian truly believes affects his character and his
daily walk down here. Doctrine that exalts Christ makes us holy.

Doctrine that does not exalt Christ hinders the Holy Spirit working in us, and forming us like Christ.

When the false teachers told the Galatians that they must have circumcision and the law as well as Christ in order to be saved, this was in reality an attack on Christ Himself, and meant that Christ alone was not sufficient to save them. A defective Savior is no Savior at all.

G. C. WILLIS

December 29

I will instruct thee and teach thee in the way which thou shalt go; I will guide thee with mine eye.

PSALM 32:8, KJV

*I*t is a great thing for each Christian to be ready to act on and from his own sense of responsibility before God—but never going beyond that which he sees to be his own duty, never presuming to act under the light which others have.

I would rather act under God's measure of light entrusted to me, or not to act because I had no such light, than be the one to carry out the mind of any man, without my being assured his mind was God's mind for *me*.

More and more does it become clear to me that "I will instruct *thee* and teach *thee* in the way *thou* shouldest go: I will guide *thee* with mine eye" is the only proper and safe guide for us.

GEORGE V. WIGRAM

*D*o not attempt to do too much. Let *quality*, not *quantity*, be the desire of your heart as to your service.

J. B. STONEY

A garden inclosed is my sister, my spouse, a spring shut up, a fountain sealed.

SONG OF SOLOMON 4:12, KJV

*T*o live a life in the depths, it is necessary to have direct and intimate communion with the Lord. What is spoken of here is a garden. As seen in the Bible, a garden is God's very first thought. Unlike ordinary land for general purpose planting, or a field specifically for tillage, a garden is solely for the object of beauty and visual enjoyment. In a garden there may be trees but the object is not for the wood; or fruit trees but the purpose is still not for the bearing of fruit. The importance of a garden is attached to its flowers. They are planted only for their beauty. To plant flowers is therefore for pleasantness to the eyes. To describe this garden as an "inclosed garden" is to mean that it is not a public park to which everybody may have access for seeking enjoyment but is inclosed exclusively for Christ and for His glory. The beauty within is to be seen and appreciated by Christ alone. This in-depth life is not meant to please men but Christ only.

This kind of life is "a spring shut up." A spring is for people to use; though it is so, it is still reserved for the pleasure of the Lord.

This sort of life is "a fountain sealed." A spring is brought into being by human labor but a fountain is not. A spring is of men but a fountain is of God. A fountain stands for the joy and contentment we acquire in the presence of God. Such experience is not to be deliberately disclosed to other people because it is as a sealed fountain.

In a word, a Christian should not intentionally exhibit his beauty, pursuit and spiritual experience for people to see. On the other hand, everything of his in-depth experience should be silently sealed up for the Lord. Only this kind of life in the depths will satisfy the Lord's heart.

Brothers and sisters, our life is often too shallow and too large a proportion of it is exposed on the surface. May God show us grace by permitting the Cross to do deeper work within us so that we may strike roots in order to have life in the depths to fulfill God's requirements and satisfy His heart.

WATCHMAN NEE

December 31

For we have not followed cunningly devised fables, when we made known unto you the power and coming of our Lord Jesus Christ, but were eyewitnesses of his majesty.

2 PETER 1:16

$\mathcal{S}$uch then is the Christian's faith, and such his hope: no day-dream of weak minds, no fable cunningly devised, but a hope both sure and steadfast, and a most holy faith. A vain philosophy may reason of the past, and dream about the future, but, in the calm confidence of faith, the Christian can look back to a past eternity, when, before all time, and ere there was a creature made, "IN THE BEGIN-NING" the Word was alone with God; and on through the ages of ages to "THE END," when, time having run its course, in the midst of His creation, God shall be all in all; and in adoration he exclaims, "From everlasting to everlasting Thou art God!"

SIR ROBERT ANDERSON

$\mathcal{S}$on of Man, whenever I doubt of life I think of thee. Thou never growest old to me. Last century is old. Last year is obsolete fashion, but thou art not obsolete. Thou art abreast of all the centuries, and I have never come up to thee, modern as I am.

GEORGE MATHESON

*A*nd now, Lord what wait I for? My hope is in Thee. The shadows of the evening are stretched out. The clouds are heavy on the mountains. Thou touchest the hills and they smoke. But like all the clouds of my life, these heavy clouds are edged with light; and when I look up to the highest cloud I see there no darkness at all, but light, and light beyond light shining down on the peaceful water.

And the water—for, Lord, I have said to Thee, "Bid me come unto Thee on the water," and Thou hast said, "Come"—that water is a pathway of light. I see a narrow break in the brightness because of the cloud overhead, but soon it is bright again, and then there is no more shadow. And far, far, all but lost in light, I see what I think are other hills, the hills of a better country, even an heavenly.

AMY CARMICHAEL

The grace of the Lord Jesus be with God's people.

REVELATION 22:21

Afterword ════════════════════════════════════

*A*s the year ends, and thus your trip through *His Victorious Indwelling*, it's my hope that you've come to a deeper understanding of the glorious fact that our Lord Jesus Christ dwells in you.

To encourage you further, you may want to read some of the fine books written by the authors quoted in *His Victorious Indwelling*. Though some of the titles are out of print, many are still available. If *His Victorious Indwelling* has been a blessing to you, I'd enjoy hearing from you, in care of the publisher.

Blessings to you,

Nick Harrison
c/o Zondervan Publishing House
5300 Patterson Avenue SE
Grand Rapids, MI 49530

Scripture Index

Hugh E. Alexander; (July 18) was in ministry training in Glasgow at the time of the great Welsh revival early in the twentieth century. After experiencing a genuine move of the Spirit of God in his life, he was witness to a similar revival in Switzerland, out of which grew the Geneva Bible School. He was a contributor to "The Overcomer," the deeper-life magazine started by Jessie Penn-Lewis.

Sir Robert Anderson; 1841–1918 (February 4, May 12, August 20, October 14, December 31) was a barrister specializing in political crime. He served as head of the criminal investigation department at Scotland Yard from 1888–1901. A Presbyterian layman, he spoke and wrote widely, usually on the theme of Bible prophecy.

Augustine of Hippo; 354–430 (March 10, May 18, June 16, 27, August 16, October 10, December 2) is one of the most influential Christian writers of all time. The son of a pagan father and a Christian mother, Augustine lived a rebellious life in his youth, fathering a son by his mistress of thirteen years. After searching for truth through philosophy, he found Christ and wrote such compelling reading as his *Confessions* and *City of God*, both of which are still widely read.

T. Austin-Sparks; (January 20, 27, February 21, April 3, June 2, July 28, September 3, October 14, November 17) was a twentieth-century British writer and teacher on the deeper life.

Donald Grey Barnhouse; 1895–1960 (March 4, July 11, November 2) was a Presbyterian minister and popular author. He served as pastor of the Tenth Avenue Presbyterian Church from 1927 until his death.

J. Sidlow Baxter; (March 16, September 12) is a prolific author on the Christian life. His books include *Awake My Heart* and *Explore the Book*.

Richard Baxter; 1615–1691 (March 3) was one of England's most renowned preachers. His book *The Saint's Everlasting Rest* was among the most widely read books of the seventeenth century.

J(ohn) G(ifford) Bellett; 1795–1864 (March 2, April 13, June 3, 11, August 29, September 1, October 3, November 10) was an Irish barrister and one of the early Brethren writers; a contemporary of John Darby and other Brethren pioneers.

Bernard of Clairvaux; 1090–1153 (February 11, April 22, September 7) was one of the great Christian teachers of medieval Christianity. His motto, "To know Jesus and Jesus crucified" is still quoted as the essence of Christianity. His hymns include "Jesus, the Very Thought of Thee" and "O Sacred Head Now Wounded."

John L. Bird; (July 1) was one of the many gifted teachers at the Keswick conferences in the mid-twentieth century.

Hugh Black; 1868–1953 (February 18) is best known for his classic book, *Friendship*.

Andrew Bonar; 1810–1892 (August 14) was a Scottish minister and writer who is widely remembered for his work on the *Memoirs* of his friend, Robert Murray McCheyne, and his editing of Samuel Rutherford's *Letters*. Andrew Bonar was the brother of Horatius Bonar.

Horatius Bonar; 1808–1889 (February 5, March 27, May 9, 11, August 14, November 6, December 2) was a popular Scottish minister, author, and hymnwriter. His hymns include "I Heard the Voice of Jesus Say." Horatius was the brother of Andrew Bonar.

William Booth; 1829–1912 (February 3) was an English evangelist and founder of the Salvation Army.

E(dward) M(cKendree) Bounds; 1835–1913 (May 2) was a minister in the American Methodist Episcopal Church, primarily in the Southern United States. He served as a captain in the Confederate Army. Today he's best known for his many books on prayer, notably *Power Through Prayer*.

Phillips Brooks; 1835–1893 (February 15) was an American Episcopal minister active in the abolitionist movement. He served as bishop of Massachusetts in 1891 and preached extensively throughout the state until his death in 1893. Brooks also wrote the words to the popular Christmas carol, "O Little Town of Bethlehem."

Elijah P. Brown; (August 11) was the author of several books on the Christian life, including *Lifting the Latch* and *Rounds in the Golden Ladder*.

John Bunyan; 1628–1688 (January 17, September 1), known as "the Tinker of Bedford," was an English preacher and author of more than sixty books, including the classic best-seller *Pilgrim's Progress*.

William Burns; (March 19, October 24) was a Scottish preacher and missionary to China in the nineteenth century. He influenced the young Hudson

Taylor whom he met and joined forces with for the furtherance of the work in China.

* E. P. C.; (February 2, October 10, November 29) an unidentified Brethren writer, possibly E. P. Corrin.

John Calvin; 1509–1564 (August 19, September 2) was a French Protestant Reformer, trained in law, whose teachings have had a profound impact on Christian history.

Amy Wilson Carmichael; 1867–1951 (January 5, 11, July 17, September 10, November 27, December 31) was a missionary to India and founder of Dohnavur Fellowship, a ministry devoted to saving neglected children. A prolific writer, many of Miss Carmichael's books are still widely circulated.

Celsus; (September 7) was a second century critic of Christianity who, nonetheless, admired Christian morality.

Samuel Chadwick; 1860-1932 (February 9) was a preacher and writer of the nineteenth century and served as the president of the National Council of Free Churches.

Lewis Sperry Chafer; 1871–1952 (March 6, 21, May 1, 25, September 8, November 14) was a popular preacher and writer in the early twentieth century. Chafer also was founder and president of Dallas Theological Seminary.

Robert C. Chapman; 1803–1902 (February 16, June 24, December 21) was one of the early Brethren teachers.

Adam Clarke; 1762–1832 (October 13, November 23) was a Wesleyan preacher, theologian, and commentator; the latter talent is best exemplified by his eight volume commentary on the Bible, still in use by many Bible teachers.

C(harles) A(ndrew) Coates; 1862–1945 (February 14, March 25, April 19, May 23, June 2, 13, July 8, 24, October 17) was a popular Brethren author.

Samuel Taylor Coleridge; 1772–1834 (January 2) was an influential English poet and philosopher.

J. E. Conant; (February 13, 19, July 6, October 26) was an early twentieth-century churchman best known for his classic book, *Every Member Evangelism*.

Charles E. Cowman; 1868–1924 (July 10, October 9) was a missionary to Japan and China and founder and president of the Oriental Missionary Society. His widow, Lettie, compiled the popular *Streams in the Desert* daily devotional.

C. C. Crowston; (February 29, September 21) was one of the Brethren writers of the nineteenth century.

Arthur Custance; 1910–1985 (April 5) emigrated from England to Canada in 1928. He obtained an M.A. in Languages and a Ph.D. in Education and Anthropology, becoming a research scientist in human thermoregulation with several inventions and published papers to his credit. He also published *The Doorway Papers*, 60 monographs in which a broad spectrum of the sciences is used to illuminate major biblical themes, plus six other books. His writings form a bridge between science and theology and are characterized by a rare combination of scholarly thoroughness and biblical orthodoxy.

George C. Cutting; 1843–1934 (May 19) was one of the many Brethren writers of the past century.

John Nelson Darby; 1800–1882 (January 4, 24, 25, 29; February 25; March 12, 14, 22, 23; April 9, 13; May 4, 6; June 9, 14; July 3, 20; August 8, 25; September 6, 11, 14; October 2, 6, 11, 18, 20, 28; November 1, 2, 6, 9, 10, 16, 17, 24; December 1, 25) was a prolific writer and teacher and was a leader among the Plymouth Brethren. His influence on subjects such as the deeper life and Bible prophecy have influenced millions of believers.

Edward Dennett; 1831–1914 (January 7, 13, 25; February 1, 21; March 2, 5, 13, 20, 24, 25, 28; April 7, 16, 25; May 5, 7, 27, 31; June 4, 5, 18, 19; July 14; August 27; September 11, 13, 16, 20, 22, 24; October 1, 3, 4, 11, 12, 15, 21, 22, 30; November 20, 27, 29; December 4, 11, 14, 18) was one of the many influential writers of the early days of the Brethren movement.

Norman Douty; (March 18) was a twentieth-century author.

James Buchanan Dunlop; 1840–1928 (September 19) was an active writer for the Brethren movement.

★ W. F. E.; (June 8) was an unidentified Brethren writer.

William Easton; 1850–1926 (February 7, May 4, August 7, October 5) was a popular Brethren author.

Jonathan Edwards; 1703–1758 (March 9, September 4, 18) was one of America's most influential Colonial preachers, often remembered for his sermon, "Sinners in the Hands of an Angry God" (1741).

Philip James (Jim) Elliot; 1927–1956 (May 29) was a missionary to the Auca Indians of eastern Ecuador. He and his four fellow missionaries were murdered by the Aucas—an event that gathered much attention among Christians worldwide. Subsequently many Aucas came to Christ. Jim Elliot's story has been told in books by his widow, Elisabeth, in books such as *Through Gates of Splendor* and *Shadow of the Almighty*.

★ **H. F.**; (November 15, December 4) an unidentified Brethren author, possibly Hughes Fawcett.

François de la Salignac de la Mothe Fénelon; 1651–1715 (March 21, June 13, 30, August 30, November 28) was a French churchman and author, and Archbishop of Cambrai from 1695–1715.

Annie Johnson Flint; (July 6) was a noted religious poet of the nineteenth century.

George Fox; 1624–1691 (March 28, October 19) was a controversial Christian man who urged believers to rely on the "Inner Light of the Living Christ." He founded the Society of Friends, often called Quakers—a name given when Fox urged a judge to "tremble at the word of the Lord."

★ **P. G.**; (February 26) was an unidentified Brethren writer.

G. Gardiner; (November 26) was a twentieth-century writer.

Lindsay Glegg; (June 6) was a London businessman who taught at the Keswick conferences in the twentieth century.

Rosalind Goforth; (April 11) and her husband, Jonathan, were missionaries for many years to China where they suffered many trials, including the death of five of their eleven children. The couple narrowly escaped death during the Boxer Rebellion.

A(doniram) J(udson) Gordon; 1836–1895 (March 5, August 5) was a popular Boston minister and founder of the Gordon College and Divinity School.

S(amuel) D(ickey) Gordon; 1859–1936 (January 27, March 24, May 14, December 24) was a writer and missionary lecturer whose popular books include *Quiet Talks on Power* and *Quiet Talks on Prayer*.

F(rederick) W(illiam) Grant; 1834–1902 (March 6, May 27, July 28) was one of the many Brethren writers of the nineteenth century.

Gregory of Nyssa; 330–c.395 (April 2) was a theologian, writer, and the bishop of Nyssa.

W. H. Griffith Thomas; 1861–1924 (September 21, December 13) was a noted Bible teacher, preacher, lecturer, and writer of devotional commentaries.

Henry Groves; 1818–1890 (March 20, September 15) was an active Brethren writer and editor and was the son of A.N. Groves, one of the founding fathers, along with George Mueller, of the Open Brethren.

Norman Grubb; (March 6, October 3) for many years was a popular writer and teacher on the deeper Christian life. His best known work is a biography, *Rees Howells, Intercessor*.

Madame Jeanne Marie Bouvier Guyon; 1648–1717 (March 14, May 3, August 4, 20, September 4, 6, November 13) was a controversial advocate of Christian mysticism and abandonment to God. Her views brought her both supporters and enemies, ultimately resulting in her confinement to a convent. Among her supporters was François Fénelon.

★ A. H.; (June 8) was an unidentified Brethren writer.

I. M. Haldeman; (February 12, September 28, December 22) served for nearly half a century as pastor of the First Baptist Church of New York City. He also wrote widely; his best known book was possibly *The Tabernacle Priesthood and Offerings* published in 1925.

Bishop Joseph Hall; 1574–1656 (May 17) was a highly respected English prelate of the seventeenth century.

John Harris; (May 9) is an unidentified author and teacher.

Norman B. Harrison; (January 18, March 22, May 11, July 20, September 13, November 24, December 26) was a pastor, Bible teacher, evangelist, and author of several books on the deeper life in the early twentieth century.

Frances Ridley Havergal; 1836–1879 (December 6, 9) was a popular English poet and hymnwriter, most fondly remembered for such melodies as "Take My Life and Let it Be" and "Like a River Glorious." She also authored a popular book, *Kept for the Master's Use*.

Matthew Henry; 1662–1714 (February 9, 10, March 20, August 24, November 15) was an English Presbyterian minister best remembered for his exhaustive commentary on the Bible.

Roy Hession; (February 26, May 31, October 19) is author of several books on the deeper life, including the best-selling *The Calvary Road*.

Evan Hopkins; (March 11, April 12, August 11, October 23) was a 35-year-old vicar from Richmond in Surrey, England, when he encountered Bible teacher Pearsall Smith, husband of Hannah Whitall Smith. He would forever refer to that May 1 meeting as his "May Day experience." His ministry changed as he appropriated the truths of God's grace he'd heard. Later he was to be widely used in the Keswick movement as a popular Bible teacher.

Gerard Manley Hopkins; 1844–1889 (May 24) was a poet and a priest best remembered for his magnificent "God's Grandeur" poem.

T. C. Horton; (January 9) served as editor-in-chief of "The King's Business" and was Superintendent of the Bible Institute of Los Angeles.

J. Russell Howden; (January 4, June 12, October 30) was an Anglican minister and frequent speaker at the Keswick conferences in the early twentieth century.

F. J. Huegel; (January 8, 19, August 15, October 12) served as a chaplain in World War I and a missionary in Mexico for more than twenty-five years. His writings on the deeper life include the classic *Bone of His Bone*.

John Hunter; (July 2, September 25) was a Bible teacher for many years with the Torchbearers in England, and a colleague of Major Ian Thomas.

⋆ E. I.; (October 16) was an unidentified Brethren author.

Ignatius of Antioch; died c. 107 (November 8) was one of the early church fathers. Bishop of Antioch in Syria, he was martyred circa 107.

Henry Allan Ironside; 1876–1951 (April 13, July 15, September 30) was a popular Brethren preacher and author of several Bible commentaries.

A. J. (April 27) was an unidentified author and teacher.

Julian of Norwich; c.1342–c.1413 (April 17) was an English mystic who lived a solitary life of contemplation and prayer. Her reputation rests mainly on her book *The Sixteen Revelations of Divine Love*.

Stephen Kaung; (January 10, October 6) is the author of *The Splendor of His Ways* and *Discipled to Christ*.

William Kelly; 1821–1906 (April 3, 19, May 13, 24, June 26, August 11, November 4, 18) was a writer, editor, and colleague of Brethren leader, John Darby.

John Kennedy; (June 19) was the author of *The Torch of the Testimony*.

C. Colin Kerr; (March 5, May 20) was a Keswick teacher during the mid-twentieth century.

LeBaron Kinney; (February 25, October 25) was a Brethren author.

G. H. Knight; (March 14, August 12, November 19, 30) was an English clergyman and author of *In the Secret of His Presence* and *The Master's Questions to His Disciples*.

R. B. Kuiper; (July 12) was a clergyman and author.

William Law; 1686–1761 (February 28, April 6) was an English writer whose major work *A Serious Call to a Devout and Holy Life* continues to inspire Christians worldwide.

Brother Lawrence; c.1605–1691 (February 4) served as a "lay brother" for an order of the Discalced Carmelites. His duty in the order as a cook lasted for thirty years, during which time he wrote short spiritual notes which were published after his death. Today those notes comprise his book *The Practice of the Presence of God*, which has achieved classic status down through the centuries.

L. L. Letgers; (January 16, July 31, August 18, September 17, 30) was a prolific writer on the deeper life in the early part of the twentieth century.

David Livingstone; 1813–1873 (January 11, March 15, May 25, 29) was a pioneer missionary to Africa. At his death, his native assistants were so devoted to him that they bore his body 1500 miles to the coast. His funeral was held in Westminster Abbey, and his tombstone reads, "For thirty years his life was spent in an unwearied effort to evangelize the native races, to explore the undiscovered secrets, to abolish the desolating slave trade of Central Africa."

Herbert Lockyer; (May 18, December 20) was twentieth-century author of many books on the Christian life.

Martin Luther; 1483–1546 (January 5, February 4, 6, July 19, 25, November 12, 21) was a German priest whose belief that Christians were saved by faith alone ushered in the Reformation of the sixteenth century.

★ **H. M.**; (November 25) was an unidentified Brethren writer.

★ **T. L. M.**; (May 17) was an unidentified Brethren writer.

John MacBeath; (August 19) was a teacher at Keswick in the first half of the twentieth century.

C(harles) H(enry) Mackintosh; 1820–1896 (January 7; February 3, 17, 27, 28; March 1; April 6, 28; May 8; June 4, 26; July 9, 13; August 3, 18; September 11, 28; October 7; November 1, 12, 29; December 1, 9, 28) was one of the early and most prolific Brethren writers. Still widely read today.

Alexander Maclaren; 1826–1910 (January 1, 24, March 27, May 6, July 26, September 23, November 13, December 10, 18, 24) was a British Baptist clergyman who served forty-five years as pastor of Union Chapel, Manchester.

Paol Madsen; (February 6, September 22) wrote frequently for "Toward the Mark," a deeper-life magazine of the twentieth century.

J. C. Mann; (March 26) was a teacher at the Keswick conferences in the first half of the twentieth century.

G. Marshall; (August 9) was a twentieth century writer on the Christian life.

Cotton Mather; 1663–1728 (January 26) was one of the early Puritan ministers and writers; he was also one of the founders of Yale University.

George Matheson; 1842–1906 (June 20, November 2, December 31) was a blind Scottish pastor widely beloved for his beautiful sermons. He also wrote the hymn "O Love That Wilt Not Let Me Go" during a time he described as "the most severe mental suffering." Written in only five minutes, Matheson claimed the hymn was "dictated to me by some inward voice."

R. Arthur Matthews; (February 9) was best known for this book on spiritual warfare *Born for Battle*.

J(ohn) T(homas) Mawson; ?–1943 (May 26) was a Brethren author.

L. E. Maxwell; (January 13, 20, August 9) was widely known as the editor of "The Prairie Overcomer" magazine, published by the Prairie Bible Institute, Three Hills, Alberta, Canada.

Robert Murray McCheyne; 1813–1843 (January 27, March 19, July 12, September 10) was a Scottish minister who, though he died at the age of 30, is still remembered for his "Memoirs" which were compiled by Andrew Bonar.

James McConkey; (January 6, 9, March 31, June 11, September 5, December 11) wrote widely on the deeper life in the early part of the twentieth century.

Mary McDonough; 1863–1962 (February 19, November 11) taught weekly Bible classes until shortly before her death at nearly 100 years of age. Her only book was *God's Plan of Redemption*.

F(rederick) B(rotherton) Meyer; (January 2, February 2, 5, April 10, May 24, June 25, July 21, August 17, September 30, October 16, December 3) was the author of more than seventy books and a popular London preacher who fought the forces of immorality in early twentieth century Britain.

J(ames) R(ussell) Miller; 1840–1912 (February 2, July 14) was a Presbyterian pastor (serving congregations in Illinois and Pennsylvania) and prolific writer at the turn of the nineteenth century.

Dwight Lyman Moody; 1837–1899 (January 15, May 20, June 18, August 5, 17, October 17) was one of the greatest evangelists of all time. The Moody Bible Institute in Chicago still trains students as a testament to Moody's work.

G(eorge) Campbell Morgan; 1863–1945 (January 1, 3, October 21) was a respected pastor, Bible teacher, and writer of more than sixty books.

J. Alec Motzer; (January 23) was a writer for "Toward the Mark" magazine.

Hendley Carr Glyn Moule; 1841–1920 (April 26, July 5) was a popular leader of the evangelical wing of the Church of England and a speaker at Keswick conventions.

George Mueller; 1805–1898 (January 14, March 4, 7, May 5, 10, 20, October 4, November 28, December 12) was active in the Plymouth Brethren movement, but most widely known for his work in establishing orphanages which were run totally on faith. He concluded his last worldwide mission tour at the age of 87.

Andrew Murray; 1828–1917 (January 6, 28, March 11, April 26, June 9, July 16, 22, September 16, October 10, November 7, 26, December 19) was a South African clergyman who strongly influenced the missionary movement to South Africa. Today he is largely remembered for his many devotional books, still in print and still strong sellers.

Watchman Nee; 1903–1972 (January 8, 30, February 10, March 3, April 9, May 16, June 10, 17, July 19, 24, September 20, October 13, November 3, December 30) was a prominent Christian worker in China during the first half of the twentieth century. He spent his last years in a Communist prison. Though he only authored one book, *The Spiritual Man*, his many oral messages have been transcribed into books, some of which have already obtained classic status (*The Normal Christian Life*; *Sit, Walk, Stand*).

William Newell; (March 9, April 18, May 23) was an evangelist, Bible teacher, and author of excellent commentaries of the books of Romans, Hebrews, and Revelation.

Sir Henry John Newbolt; 1862–1938 (February 5) was a British poet.

John Newton; 1725–1807 (January 1, 16, February 12, March 19, August 12, 31, November 18) was the master of a slave ship before his conversion to

Christ, after which he became an Anglican clergyman and hymnwriter, best remembered today for "Amazing Grace."

John Oxenham; 1852–1941 (April 7) was a British poet.

Blaise Pascal; 1623–1662 (January 26, February 13, March 13, 16, September 2) was a French mathematician, scientist, and Christian apologist. His best known work was published after his death as *Pensées* (Thoughts).

Ruth Paxson; (January 16, 18, 31, March 8, April 1, May 22, June 28, July 3, 10, September 17, October 28, November 25, December 19, 22) was a gifted Bible teacher and graduate of the State University of Iowa. She died October 1, 1949.

William Penn; (April 20) was a Quaker leader and the founder of Pennyslvania.

Jessie Penn-Lewis; 1861–1927 (January 17, February 8, March 23, April 8, May 10, June 8, August 13, September 7, 9, October 22, November 8, December 6, 22) was a forceful Christian worker in the early part of the twentieth century. She wrote widely and served as editor of "The Overcomer" one of the early deeper-life magazines.

Isaac Pennington; 1616–1679 (June 16, November 9) was an English Quaker author.

Arthur T(appan) Pierson; 1837–1911 (July 5) was the clergyman who succeeded Charles Haddon Spurgeon at the noted Metropolitan Baptist Church in London. He was also the biographer of George Mueller.

John Pritchard; (October 15) was a teacher at the Keswick conferences in the 1940s.

Adelaide Anne Proctor; (April 15) was a religious writer of the nineteenth century.

Robert Raikes; 1735–1811 (June 24) was a British newspaperman, noted for his philanthropy and his part in establishing the first Sunday school.

Alan Redpath; (January 15, May 8, August 8, December 5) born in England, left a position as an accountant to answer God's call to preach the gospel. He pastored several churches in England before serving as senior pastor of the Moody Memorial Church in Chicago, after which he returned to pastor the Charlotte Baptist Chapel in Edinburgh, Scotland.

Samuel Ridout; (February 22, April 14, July 15, November 7, December 20,

Rosalind Rinker; (August 2) was a prolific twentieth-century writer best known for her books on conversational prayer.

Evan Roberts; 1878–1951 (March 15, October 8, 27) was the ninth of fourteen children of a Welsh miner. At the age of twelve, he too, began work in the mines, but later received a call from God to enter the ministry. Roberts is largely remembered for his leadership in the Welsh revival of 1904–1906.

William Romaine; 1714–1795 (December 3) was a leader of the evangelical revival in London. He counted George Whitefield and John and Charles Wesley among his friends and admirers.

Christina Rossetti; 1830–1894 (March 12) was an English poet noted for her religious themes.

A(lexander) H(ume) Rule; 1843–1906 (August 10, December 17) was a popular Brethren writer and preacher.

Samuel Rutherford; 1600–1661 (January 3, 5, 13, 22, 30, April 11, 28, May 15, June 7, 13, 17, 18, 29, July 1, 24, August 1, 23, October 9, November 3) was the son of a Scottish farmer. He became an influential minister and writer.

J(ohn) C(harles) Ryle; 1816–1900 (July 2) was a minister in Liverpool and a leader of the evangelical wing of the Church of England.

★ W. G. S. (March 30, August 2) was an unidentified author of the Brethren movement. Possibly William Gibson Sloan.

Adolph Saphir; (January 28, February 24, March 26, April 23, May 28, June 27, July 22, August 21, 28, September 26, October 31, November 21, December 23)

C(yrus) I(ngerson) Scofield; 1843–1921 (May 1, October 11) was a lawyer and Confederate army officer before his 1879 conversion. He was later ordained a Congregational pastor and led churches in Dallas and East Northfield, Massachusetts. He's largely remembered for his extensive notes on the Bible which were incorporated into the Scofield Reference Bible, still used by many Christians as their primary study Bible.

Henry Scougal; 1650–1878 (April 18) was professor of Divinity at the University of Aberdeen and author of the classic book, *The Life of God in the Soul of Man*.

W. Graham Scroggie; 1877–1958 (February 23, April 29, September 18, November 10, December 15) was a Scottish clergyman, Bible expositor, and frequent teacher at Keswick conferences.

A(lbert) B(enjamin) Simpson; 1844–1919 (January 21, February 1, March 8, April 20, September 25; October 31) was a Canadian pastor and founder of what became the Christian and Missionary Alliance denomination.

Sadu Sundar Singh; 1889–1933? (February 22, March 18, April 24, May 2, 12, October 25, November 24, December 16) was an Indian mystic turned Christian missionary.

C(harles) W. Slemming; (April 16) was a preacher and author of several books.

Mary Slessor; 1848–1915 (July 9) was a Scottish missionary to West Africa.

Egbert Smith; (May 29) was a writer on the Christian life.

Hannah Whitall Smith; 1832–1911 (January 18, 31, February 15, March 10, April 21, May 15, June 23, 30, July 30, August 16, 30, September 1, 24, October 29, November 14) was raised a Quaker but was more closely associated with the Brethren and the Keswick movement, of which she was part from the beginning. Her classic book *The Christian's Secret of a Happy Life* is one of the best selling Christian books of all time.

Charles Haddon Spurgeon; 1834–1892 (January 23, March 30, April 15, May 19, June 6, 7, 12, August 23, September 5, November 5, December 1, 12) was a British Baptist preacher and a prolific writer.

Miles Stanford; 1914- (March 2, October 1) is the author of several important books on the believer's position in Christ—notably *The Green Letters*.

C(harles) Stanley; 1821–1888 (June 21, December 8) was a popular Brethren writer of the nineteenth century.

J(ames) B(utler) Stoney; 1814–1897 (January 12, 28, 29; February 16, 17, 27; March 24; April 4, 5, 20, 22; May 13, 30; June 10, 23; July 7; August 3; September 29; October 16; November 20; December 5, 7, 16, 21, 29) was a prolific and popular writer for the Brethren movement of the nineteenth century.

J. F. Strombeck; (October 5) was a preacher and writer, best known for his classic book *So Great a Salvation*.

William ("Billy") Ashley Sunday; 1862–1935 (January 26) was born in Iowa and converted as a young adult at the famed Pacific Garden Mission in

Chicago. He eventually became one of the foremost evangelists of the early twentieth century.

★ **J. H. T.**; (April 12, November 22) was an unidentified Brethren author.

Mrs. Howard (Mary G.) Taylor; (November 22) was, along with her husband, a biographer of missionary Hudson Taylor.

J(ames) Hudson Taylor; 1832–1905 (May 20, June 1, August 13) was one of the most well-known missionaries in the history of the Christian Church. Founder of the China Inland Mission, Taylor is also noted for the classic book, *Hudson Taylor's Spiritual Secret*, edited by Howard and Mary Taylor.

Jeremy Taylor; 1613–1667 (August 29) was an Anglican bishop and author whose beautiful style of writing led him to be known as the "Shakespeare of English divines."

Corrie ten Boom; 1892–1983 (May 7, June 28, November 1) was a "rescuer" of Jews in her native Holland. Arrested with her family for their illegal activities, she endured the atrocities of German prison camp and, after the war, traveled the world retelling her experiences of God's love in the midst of the horrors of war. Her book *The Hiding Place* continues in wide circulation.

Tertullian; c.160–225 (January 15) was trained to be a lawyer, but in his late thirties became a Christian and was a respected teacher in the church at Carthage.

Theophilus; (September 9) was presumably the early Christian to whom the apostle Luke addressed the book of Acts.

Thomas à Kempis; 1380–1471 (March 12, July 25, August 14, October 18) was the author of many devotional books including the classic, *The Imitation of Christ*.

Major Ian Thomas; (April 7, December 26) is the Founder and International Director of Capernwray Missionary Fellowship of Torchbearers. His best known book is *The Saving Life of Christ*.

Augustus Toplady; 1740–1778 (May 15, August 1) was a British theologian, poet, and hymnwriter, best known for "Rock of Ages."

R(euben) A(rcher) Torrey; 1856–1928 (March 29, July 4, November 5) was a Congregationalist minister and colleague of Dwight L. Moody.

A(iden) W(ilson) Tozer; 1897–1963 (February 20, June 3, July 8, August 4) was a popular Christian and Missionary Alliance pastor and writer.

Lilias Trotter; 1853–1928 (April 27) was a pioneering missionary to Algeria and a writer on the Christian life.

W(illiam) Trotter; 1818–1865 (November 16) was an early Brethren writer.

Charles G(allaudet) Trumbull; 1872–1941 (February 7, March 1, April 2, June 15, August 15, 31, September 8, December 14) was an editor, journalist (staff writer for the *Toronto Globe*), and author of several books on the Christian life.

D. Tryon; (April 12, July 30) was a writer on the Christian life.

W. M. Turnbull; (April 24) was a twentieth-century poet and writer.

Unknown Christian; (April 1, July 7, November 30) was an anonymous writer best known for *The Kneeling Christian* and other books on the Christian life.

Thomas Upham; 1799–1872 (August 28) was a New England Congregationalist pastor, prolific writer, and biographer of Madame Guyon.

J. A. Von Poseck; (February 18) was an early Brethren writer.

★ G. B. W.; (September 23) was an unidentified Brethren writer.

G. D. Watson; (June 1) was a teacher at Keswick conferences.

Isaac Watts; 1674–1748 (December 24) remains one of the church's most popular hymn writers, having written more than 500 hymns including such favorites as "When I Survey the Wondrous Cross" and "Joy to the World."

G. Christian Weiss; (April 30) was a writer associated with the Back to the Bible ministry.

Susanna Wesley; 1669–1742 (February 11) was an active prayer warrior and mother of two of the most highly regarded Christian leaders—John and Charles Wesley.

George Whitefield; 1714–1770 (March 13, June 11, 26, 29) was one of the most highly regarded evangelists of the 18th century and is the leading figure in the revival known as Great Awakening.

Alexander Whyte; 1836–1921 (April 25, July 29) was a powerful orator and Scottish minister.

George V(icesimus) Wigram; (January 4, 10, 14; February 10, 16, 29; April 22, 23; May 1, 2, 26; June 15; July 6, 31; October 12, 27, 29; November 19;

December 10, 27, 29) was one of the most popular and prolific of the Brethren writers.

Ethel Jones Wilcox; (May 3) was the author of *Power for Christian Living*.

G(eorge) C(hristopher) Willis; 1889–? (November 28) was a writer and missionary.

J. R. S. Wilson; (December 7) was a teacher at the Keswick conferences of the 1930s.

W(alter) T(homas) P(rideaux) Wolston; 1840–1917 (January 29, February 28, March 30, April 15, June 14, July 24, 27, August 6, 22, 26, September 29, October 24, November 23, December 27) was a popular and prolific Brethren writer.

Count Nicholaus Ludwig von Zinzendorf; 1700–1760 (March 31) was an Austrian noble born in Germany, who devoted his life to Christ at age six. He is best known for his part in the formation of what became the Moravian Church.

* Many of the authors chosen for inclusion in *His Victorious Indwelling* came from the Brethren movement of the nineteenth century. It was a distinction among the early leaders of that movement to prefer either total anonymity or identification by their initials only. For that reason some of these gifted writers' names may never be known. Even many of their contemporaries were uncertain of the identity of these men and women of God.

Good News Broadcasting, Inc.

Miles Stanford, *The Principle of Position*, copyright Good News Broadcasting. Used by permission.

Gospel Light

Ethel Jones Wilcox, *Power for Christian Living*, copyright Regal Books, Ventura, CA. Used with permission.

Harold Shaw

R. Arthur Matthews, *Born For Battle*, copyright 1993. Used by permission of Harold Shaw Publishers, Wheaton, IL 60189.

HarperCollins

Elisabeth Elliot, *Shadow of the Almighty* by Elisabeth Elliot. Copyright 1958. Reprinted by permission of HarperCollins.

Kingsway Publications

Watchman Nee, *Changed into His Likeness*, copyright Kingsway Publications; used by permission.

Kregel Publications

William Newell, *Romans: Verse by Verse*. Used by permission, Kregel Publications.

Living Stream Ministry

Watchman Nee, *Twelve Baskets Full* v. 2 (February 10, April 9, May 16, October 13, November 3); *Twelve Baskets Full* v. 4 (December 30); *The Collected Works of Watchman Nee* v. 38 (March 3). Used by permission, Living Stream Ministry, 1853 W. Ball Rd., Anaheim, CA 92804.

Loizeaux Brothers

LeBaron Kinney, *He is Thy Lord*, 1945. Used by permission of Loizeaux Brothers, Neptune, New Jersey.

Moody Press

L. E. Maxwell; Taken from *Born Crucified* by L. E. Maxwell. Copyright 1984, Moody Bible Institute of Chicago. Moody Press. Used by permission.

Mt. Zion Missionary Baptist Church

T. Austin-Sparks, *Union with Christ, Rivers of Living Water, In Christ*, copyright Mt. Zion Missionary Baptist Church. Used by permission.

Seed-Sowers

John Kennedy, *The Torch of the Testimony*, used by permission, The SeedSowers, Sargent, GA 30275.

Other Permissions

J. Sidlow Baxter, *Going Deeper*; Copyright by J. Sidlow Baxter. Used by permission of the author.

Arthur Custance, Reprinted by permission from *The Doorway Papers*; Evelyn White, curator.

John Hunter, *Let us Go on To Maturity*; Copyright John Hunter. Used by permission of the author.

Rosalind Rinker, *On Being a Christian*; Copyright Rosalind Rinker. Used by permission of the author.

Miles Stanford, *The Green Letters*; Copyright 1983 by Miles J. Stanford. Used by permission of the author

Major Ian Thomas, *The Mystery of Godliness*; Copyright Major Ian Thomas. Used by permission of the author.

Note: The editor of this book has made every effort to contact the copyright holders of all readings in this book not clearly in the public domain. We offer apologies to any legitimate copyright holder whom we could not trace, and we encourage anyone holding an unacknowledged copyright to any of these readings to contact the editor, in care of Zondervan Publishing House, so that proper arrangements can be made.